It Is Not Lawful For Me To Fight

Early Christian Attitudes Toward War, Violence, and the State (Revised Edition)

Jean-Michel Hornus

Translated by Alan Kreider
and Oliver Coburn

A Christian Peace Shelf Selection

HERALD PRESS
Scottdale, Pennsylvania
Kitchener, Ontario

261.873
H816x

Library of Congress Cataloging in Publication Data
Hornus, Jean Michel.
  It is not lawful for me to fight.

  Original French ed. published in 1960 under title:
Evangile et labarum.
  Bibliography: p.
  Includes index.
  1. War and religion—Early church, ca. 30-600.
  2. Sociology, Christian—Early church, ca. 30-600.
  I. Title.
  BT736.2.H613 1980   261.8'73   79-26846
  ISBN 0-8361-1911-8 pbk.

First published in 1960 as *Evangile et Labarum: Etude sur l'attitude du christianisme primitif devant les problèmes de l'Etat, de la guerre et de la violence* by Labor et Fides, nouvelle série théologique, IX, Geneva. Published in 1963 in German as *Politische Entscheidung in der alten Kirche* (transl. R. Pfisterer) by Christoph Kaiser, Beiträge zur evangelischen Theologie, XXXV, Munich.

IT IS NOT LAWFUL FOR ME TO FIGHT
Copyright © 1980 by Herald Press, Scottdale, Pa. 15683
  Published simultaneously in Canada by Herald Press,
  Kitchener, Ont. N2G 4M5
Translated from the French edition published by Labor et
  Fides, S.A., Geneva, Switzerland.
Library of Congress Catalog Card Number: 79-26846
International Standard Book Number: 0-8361-1911-8
Printed in the United States of America
Design: Alice B. Shetler

15 14 13 12 11 10 9 8 7 6 5 4 3 2

In memory of
my father
Georges Hornus
(d. June 10, 1940)
and my uncle
Charles Hornus
(d. Dec. 15, 1944)
who died as Christians
and as soldiers

Contents

Translator's Preface

Between the inception of every scholarly work and its publication there are countless pitfalls. This important study of the early Christians' attitude to warfare seems to have fallen into most of the familiar ones—and to have discovered some new ones by bitter experience! It would be tedious to recount the details of this story, but a few facts are necessary to explain its long delay in appearing. This volume, which was originally written in French, was first published in 1960. A German translation of the unrevised text appeared three years later. In 1965 Herald Press acquired rights for the publication of an English version. M. Hornus, who by that time was in the Middle East, devoted considerable time to a revision of his original text, which he completed in early 1970. By the end of that year, Oliver Coburn had finished an initial translation of the book, and the project appeared to be nearing completion.

When in the autumn of 1974 I first encountered the work, it—despite four years of negotiations and revisions—was unfortunately still not ready to be published. As I carefully read the typescript, I became convinced that as it stood the book was not in a form that would enable it to make the impact that its intrinsic scholarship merited. Its translation needed revision, and its scholarly apparatus required a com-

plete overhaul. I requested permission from Herald Press and
M. Hornus to make the necessary alterations and to see the
book through the press. These tasks have been larger than I
had expected (I had not, for example, initially thought of
substantially retranslating much of the volume); and it has
taken over five years' worth of midnight oil to complete the
job. But, in its present state, it represents a work with which
both M. Hornus and I are pleased. We trust that you will find
it to have been worth waiting for.

A few comments on method. For quotations from the
Fathers I have generally used the best English editions, which
are listed in the Systematic Tables; the few instances in which
we have preferred M. Hornus's own readings are indicated in
the end notes. Since M. Hornus has done little work on the
volume since 1970, I have attempted in the Notes [in which
my contributions are enclosed in square brackets] and Secondary Sources (Supplement) to indicate significant work which
has been done on this subject in the past decade. I would like
to thank Lesley Mabbett for help in checking patristic sources,
Eleanor Kreider and Margaret McLaughlin for assistance in
compiling the Systematic Tables, and M. Hornus for his patience.

Alan Kreider
London Mennonite Centre
December 1979

Author's Introduction

When confronted by the problem of war, most contemporary Christians, at least on the European Continent, are inclined to assume that the Church has always approved of the participation by believers in governmentally sanctioned violence. Rarely does the possibility occur to them that in the past the Church might seriously have condemned warfare. In fact, when the idea does begin to strike them that the gospel's love commandment entails the rejection of military obligations, they often fancy that they are making a new, revolutionary discovery. A nodding acquaintance with the thought of the Church Fathers will disabuse them of this innovative conceit. But it can also lead them into an opposite error about Church history. For their rudimentary knowledge of the Fathers, which is based upon a few isolated texts, may cause them to assert in good faith that all of the Fathers were "conscientious objectors" in the modern sense of the term.[1]

So it was with me during my adolescence. For the better part of a year I was in turmoil, for I had come to feel that the command to "love your enemies" had certain precise consequences. Since I was pretty sure that I was neither a lunatic nor a solitary prophet, I could not understand why no one previously seemed to have drawn such categorical conclusions.

Then I began to learn that others before me had indeed done
so. At that. time, several books which convinced me of this
were especially comforting. In the long run these have proved
to be disappointing, for they were somewhat superficial and
tended to oversimplify the issues.[2] But while my discovery of
them was still fresh, I was tempted in my enthusiasm crudely
to transplant the whole of Church history into a twentieth-
century context, and to resolve the problem of warfare by
unambiguously condemning all forms of force and violence.

I have attempted to write the following pages in a spirit
of genuine objectivity. But if the reader will allow me to inter-
ject a brief personal note, I would also like to state that the
present study bears witness to my faith. During the summer of
1940 I received the news that my father had been killed in
action; that was also the time at which I first received the call
to the ministry. Thereafter I was active for several years in the
Resistance movement in the Department of Tarn-et-Garonne.
Later on, my family suffered much at the hands of the same
movement. Since the war I have publicly stood out against the
hysteria of anticommunist crusades, and in the 1950s I vehemently opposed the repressive policies of my country in Al-
geria. Throughout these involvements I have striven painfully
to incarnate peace in the midst of a world at war. I have
allowed myself neither to compromise with the outbursts of
hatred which poison the atmosphere nor to retire into a
splendid ivory tower.

But it is now time to turn to our subject. I shall not be
dealing with the purely theological aspect of the problem.
From an evangelical perspective, this can only be solved
through a careful exegetic study of the one work which has
final authority for us—the Word of God as revealed in the Bible. Such a study has been carried out quite recently, notably
by Jean Lasserre;[3] and it would anyhow be largely outside my
competence. My limited field, which is only supplementary to
the great theological disciplines, is the history of Christian

thought. Of course we must strongly insist that the tradition of the early Church has no absolute value for us. But just because Protestantism was founded on scriptural authority, it does not follow that we should never renew our study of the Church Fathers. The first Protestants studied these men and derived great strength from them. I myself have been discovering that, if the ecumenical dialogue is to be genuinely profound, it must be carried out not only across space (between various contemporary traditions) but across time (between Christian thinkers of all epochs). And in this perspective, although the writings of Tertullian, Origen, and Lactantius are not "the gospel," they contain at least as much Christian gospel as the works of present-day theologians that we read with respect.

Moreover, in the following pages I shall attempt to limit myself to the central core of the Church's teaching. The small sects which have sprouted up periodically and the particular manifestations of individual personalities or movements will be introduced only insofar as they help to illuminate the general direction of the whole Church. Otherwise we could easily get bogged down in an endless accumulation of anecdotes. But our concern as theological historians is to debate, not about minutiae, but on a general level.

No one really disputes that some Christians, especially in the first centuries, refused to bear arms, and that there were theologians who approved of and encouraged their refusal. But in a conscious or unconsious desire to prevent these facts from undermining the very foundations of traditional Christian moral theology concerning service to the state, numerous authors have retreated behind a fourfold defense system:

1. Only a tiny minority of the early Christians adopted the position of "conscientious objection," while the great majority adopted exactly the opposite stance.

2. The position of "conscientious objection" was a late development which emerged only at the beginning of the third century, i.e., at a time at which doctrines more Platonic

than Christian had begun to obscure and contaminate the teachings of the gospel.

3. Early Christian "conscientious objection" was never more than a theoretical position held by a coterie of bloodless intellectuals. Neither in its concrete life nor in its official pronouncements did the Church accept this theory, which as a result remained the eccentricity of a few theological cranks.

4. There was only one reason why the Christians of this period refused military service: they rejected the idolatry which was intimately bound up with the life of the army. Never did they have the slightest objection to killing other men; but they stoutly refused to put themselves in a situation in which they would have to pay to the Roman emperor homage which they owed to God alone.[4]

In this book I shall attempt to refute these four assertions and to demonstrate that:

1. If there is relatively little surviving evidence of the Christians of the early centuries refusing military service, there is far less evidence of their accepting it—except at a later period.[5] Therefore it is faulty logic to argue: "Since there is so little evidence of early Christians refusing military service, these refusals can only represent the position of a minority among the Christians." On the contrary, sounder logic would suggest the opposite: "Since there is at least some evidence of Christians refusing military service and practically none of their accepting it, the majority of the believers must have been in favor of refusal." This conclusion gains even more weight if we bear in mind that silence on this matter is explicable not only by the scarcity of our documents but also by the fact that, for social and political reasons, the Christians were rarely confronted by the problem of military service.[6]

2. To allege that Christian antimilitarism must have been a late development because prior to the third century there is hardly any evidence of it is almost to lie through omission. For to do so is to ignore the fact that during the first

two centuries of the Christian era there was scarcely any patristic literature. When such literature began to appear,
however, it is evident that it from the outset dealt with the
theme of nonviolence—and it excluded the theme of military
patriotism. The great treatises by writers such as Tertullian
and Lactantius merely amplified systematically the proposi-
tions which their predecessors had already clearly enunciated.[7]

3. It is true that the actual behavior of the believers often
contradicted the attitude affirmed by Christian thinkers.[8] But
this, alas, is hardly a unique phenomenon. Repeatedly
throughout church history the same tension recurs—between
the absolute demands of Christian preaching and the compromises due to Christians' weakness and lack of faith. These
compromises are the mark of sin in the Church. But it would
be disastrous to conclude that, because certain of the faithful
have been unfaithful to the teaching which they have
received, infidelity should become the norm of Christian
conduct. If antimilitarism had only been the position of a few
eminent ethicists, and if others had considered this position to
be exaggerated, why did these others not discuss this position
and attack it? But in actual fact the Church did everything in
its power to protect itself against the temptations of compromise in this area. The disciplinary measures which it decreed showed clearly enough that, although it welcomed the
repentant sinner, it nevertheless condemned the weakness
which had led him to defy Christian teaching by accepting a
military uniform.

4. It is obvious that the early Christians stubbornly rejected idolatry. Since the writing of the Book of Daniel (if not
before then), believers have recognized that this has been the
underlying reality which has compelled them to offer
resistance to the state. Thus, from the apostles facing the San-
hedrin to the German Confessional Church confronting
Hitler, the terms of the struggle have remained exactly the

same as those which the prophet had discerned. But does the idolatry involved in military service consist only of outward ceremonies, which today have become largely outmoded? Does it not rather pervade the entire system because it is based on a false scale of values? In the place of God, the nation and the military authorities receive adoration and obedience, and like Moloch they demand the human sacrifice which God forbids. I must also emphasize that the Christians of the early centuries were motivated by another consideration which was at least as important to them as was their rejection of idolatry—their respect for life.[9] Emphasis upon the former, true though it is, becomes a distortion of historical truth when it forgets the latter and conceals its existence.

I hope, then, to prove that, from the very beginning and throughout the first three centuries of the primitive Church, its teaching—not just the fancy of a few individuals—was constantly and rigorously opposed to Christian participation in military service. I hope also to prove that this opposition was not based on a particular situation—the cult of the emperor—but on a fundamental decision: to reject violence and to respect life. Finally I shall attempt to explain how and why this position, which was so firm and clear in its principle, was abandoned during the fourth century. If my conclusions are sound, they inevitably pose two further questions. First, is it not likely that the understanding of the gospel of the Christians of the first three centuries was far closer to the authentic gospel than the understandings which have been prevalent since then? And second, did the theologians of the Constantinian era really get what they wanted from the bargain which they struck with the state, thereby justifying in their own eyes a new attitude of Christians toward the army? If not, is it not high time that we review their decision in the light of history, which demonstrates that they had been duped into a disadvantageous exchange from which nothing was gained, and in which the loss was fidelity to the gospel?

Chapter 1

The Political and
Social Setting

If we are to avoid an epidemic of anachronisms, we must begin our investigations by analyzing the ways in which the conditions in the first centuries of the Christian era differed from our own. The problem with which we are concerned is set in a framework constituted on the one hand by the Roman army, and on the other hand by the empire and the emperor. In this chapter we shall be examining this framework, primarily in light of the thinking of the early Christians about it.

In the first centuries of the Christian era military service involved a long-range commitment. Indeed, it was regarded as one of the "professions." Recruiting was generally voluntary; and despite the fact that there were occasional levies, a man could always buy himself out. Most people viewed the soldier as something akin to a mercenary; it was simply good sense—not bad citizenship—to refrain from enlisting.[1] The problem of "conscientious objection" therefore arose in acute form only for two types of men: for soldiers who were converted during their period of service; and for Christian sons of legionaries, in whose case military service might be legally obligatory.[2] Moreover the Romans strictly forbade the Jews to engage in military service,[3] except in rare instances in which they brutally imposed it upon them as a punishment.[4]

During the first century at least, despite the attempts of
some believers to shift the onus of guilt for the trial of Jesus
from the Romans to the Jews,[5] Christianity remained largely
in the shadow of the Jewish religious community and shared
its position under the law.[6] It was only when it emerged from
that shadow, and because it emerged—whether on the initiative of the Jews who denounced the Christian innovators or of
the Christians who refused to be confined within the bounds
of a Jewish Christianity—that the Church became the victim
of persecution.[7]

According to a thesis advanced by W. H. C. Frend,
however, persecution of the Christians, far from occurring
only when they became distinguished from the Jews, was at
first simply an expression of the anti-Semitism of the
Hellenistic world (as contrasted to the Roman attitude, which
was pro-Jewish).[8] Soon after the beginning of the Christian
era, Frend argued, the Greeks finally accepted the empire.
The Roman state therefore no longer needed to favor the Jews
as a counterweight to the Greeks. On the contrary, to please its
new Greek supporters it intensified its repression of all Jewish
(and Christian) efforts at proselytism. This thesis has two main
merits. First, it shows how closely the Christian idea of
martyrdom rested upon ideas which were the product of the
Jewish experience. Second, it reminds us of the importance of
proselytism as a cause of persecution. We do not need to go
along further with the thesis than this. Indeed, Frend himself
admitted that between AD 60 and 90 the Christians had to
contend more against the Jews than against the state;[9] that in
the martyrdoms of Christians the Jews regularly supplied both
the accusers and the mobs;[10] and finally that because the
Christians failed to convert Jewry, and because they also gave
up the external forms of Judaism, they did not long retain the
exemptions—which the Jews enjoyed—from military service
and from the cult of the emperor.[11]

We should also note that Christianity spread most rapidly

in regions in which there were few soldiers, and in which therefore few recruits were needed.[12] Moreover, since the morals of the soldiery were notoriously low,[13] it was all the less likely that Christians would want to join the army. Arnobius, for instance, in the course of a general diatribe against false gods, asked whether the soldiers' Venus (*Venus Militaris*) also presided over the wanton actions which were committed in military camps and the debauchery which young people found there.[14]

Even more striking was the greedy brutality of the soldiery. One of the notable texts on this point is the *Dispute between Archelaus and Manes*, which dates from the early fourth century. The story opens with the ransoming of a group of prisoners by Marcellus, a Christian, whose action touched the soldiers so deeply that "most of them were added to the numbers of believers in our Lord Jesus Christ and that they rejected the military belt."[15] Chapter 2 then recounts the misfortunes which had earlier befallen these prisoners. When setting off into the desert for an annual religious festival, they had been attacked without any reasonable motive by a band of Persian soldiers. These soldiers had hacked many of them to pieces—along with their old men, women, and children—and had dragged the survivors off into captivity amidst outrages of Hitlerite magnitude. There is no need to look for the concrete event behind the story; it is enough to see in it the view of one Christian—even after the "Church peace"—concerning the usual behavior of an army. Indeed, the author never indicated that he considered these soldiers to have been particularly cruel or that he felt that *Roman* soldiers would have behaved better than the Persian soldiers had apparently done. On the contrary, he seems simply to have taken for granted the military savagery which he described.

In any case, for centuries the Christians themselves had opportunity to experience this cruelty, for soldiers—along with kings, princes, and leaders of the people—were regularly involved in unsuccessful efforts to root out Christianity by persecution.[16] In his *Letter to the Romans,* Ignatius wrote, "All the way from Syria to Rome I am fighting with wild beasts, by land and sea, night and day, chained as I am to ten leopards (I mean a detachment of soldiers), who only get worse the better you treat them."[17] It was also soldiers and police who arrested the old bishop Polycarp to take him off to be tortured: the editor of the narrative remarked in a baleful parenthesis that "the chief of the police had a fore-ordained name. He was called Herod."[18] The account of the martyrdom of Pionius at Smyrna in 250 tells us that it was an officer who half-strangled the martyr and who tried to force him to sacrifice;[19] it also informs us that it was a soldier who nailed him to the stake.[20] The account of the martyrdom of St. Cyprian showed officers and soldiers at work at every stage of his tribulation, from his arrest to his execution. It was the same with the martyrdoms of Montanus, Lucius, and their companions, and of Marianus and James. At the beginning of his account of the marytrdom of the latter two, the narrator described the general situation: "Because of the blind madness of the pagans and the action of the military officials, the onslaughts of persecution . . . [were] surging like the waves of this world, and the fury of the ravening devil gaped with hungry jaws to weaken the faith of the just."[21] The "special fury" of these authorities resulted from the fact that "the demon is insatiable." "The madness of a blind and bloodthirsty prefect was hunting out all of God's beloved by means of bands of soldiers with a vicious and savage spirit."[22] The narrator exposed the full extent of persecutors' ferocity and violence, only to rejoice in it because it sanctified the martyrs' triumph: "And here it was not a case (as happened elsewhere) of merely one or two soldiers from the post, but an entire band of violent and unscrupulous centurions swooped on the country-house which sheltered us as though it were a notorious center of the faith. . . ." After the Christians had reached

Cirta "they were assailed by the garrison soldiery with many cruel tortures, soldiers who are murderers of the just and the good, assisted by the centurion and the magistrates of Cirta, priests indeed of the devil. . . . "[23] The narrator then described the horrific cruelty of the sufferings which the believers endured.

Eusebius's *Martyrs of Palestine* is likewise filled with accounts of refined cruelties which soldiers inflicted upon Christians.[24] One cannot excuse these barbarities by appealing to the soldiers' duty to obey the orders of their superiors. On the contrary, many of these outrages can only be described as acts of gratuitous sadism.[25] As several Egyptian brothers were returning home after having accompanied confessors to the mines of Cilicia, soldiers arrested them at the gates of Caesarea. Eusebius's description of these soldiers ("men of barbarous character")[26] could indeed have been made with equal justice of most soldiers of that era. One finds similar characterizations of soldiers in Eusebius's *History of the Church,* both on the occasion of the persecution at Lyon under Marcus Aurelius[27] and in connection with the great persecution of Diocletian.[28] At a later date, according to Eusebius, the guards of Maxentius indulged in the massacring of citizens in the heart of Rome.[29] And Lactantius dilated upon the misdeeds of Galerius's hordes in central Italy.[30]

These military brutes were grasping. Only if they were paid in gold would they allow minimal improvements in their prisoners' lot.[31] In their greed and stupidity the soldiers "wish to be decked with gold," thereby justifying the poet's ironic comment—"A man goes forth to war, wearing golden jewelry like a silly girl."[32] By the beginning of the third century, any sensible person could foresee the economic dislocation which such an unwieldy army would increasingly bring about.[33] This was particularly noticeable under the Tetrarchy, when the multiplication of armies—for which Diocletian was responsible—was considered a disaster, bringing economic ruin on the country.[34] A typical example of the army-induced waste can be found in the bounties granted by Daia, who, after his temporary reconciliation with Constantine, lavished gold and rich garments upon his bodyguard even though the country was suffering from famine and inflation.[35] If Christians were the "soldiers of Christ,"[36] and if martyrdom was their battle, then it was only logical to conclude that the soldiers of this world— who were the actual instruments of persecution—were the soldiers of the devil.[37]

But alongside the bestialities and abuses of the army, we must in fairness acknowledge that many authors also referred to soldiers who were kind and helpful to Christian martyrs. To some extent this corrects the horrifying picture given by the examples above. We might, for example, cite the apocryphal *Acts of John*,[38] or the martyrdom of Perpetua, during the course of which the tribune treated her with great humanity and the jailer Pudens showed her many favors—until he himself was finally converted.[39] A few soldiers also treated Cyprian well. While he was being transferred from one prison to another, two officers generously made room for him in their carriage; and when he was summoned to appear before the proconsul, another officer provided him with a dry garment so that he could change from his own sweat-soaked clothes.[40] When during the reign of Decius Christians were being persecuted in Alexandria, "a soldier who stood by them . . . opposed those who insulted them."[41] Later on Gregory the Wonder-Worker and his family were escorted on a long journey by a soldier who was sent to him by his future brother-in-law for that purpose; and Gregory evidently derived great pleasure from the soldier's companionship.[42]

Cases of conversion similar to that of Pudens were not uncommon. Under Trajan, for instance, Bishop Phocas, before being put to death, baptized a considerable number of soldiers. Similarly, in 306 Philoromus—"a cavalry officer in the Roman army"—was converted upon seeing the courage of the martyr Phileas. Yet another example comes from the Persian world, in which the following event took place in 341 during the great massacre of Bet Huzayeh: "A number of Christians from many different places, [namely] soldiers who had rushed up to be present at the martyrs' deaths, threw off their clothes, joined the martyrs, and said, 'We too are Christians,' and died in their turn."[43] We could also cite the case of the converts of Carchar in Mesopotamia, while noting the reservations made necessary by the text.

In addition to the brutality which was often characteristic of the soldiers of that time, there was another consideration which inspired Christians to refuse military service—the army's official idolatry. The practice of emperor-worship had evolved over several centuries. In 29 BC, at the initiative of the local inhabitants, the first temple to Augustus was built at Pergamum. From that place the new cult of Caesar spread throughout Asia and then across the whole empire.[44] Augustus himself had at first discouraged this tendency, demanding that the developing cult should always honor the name of Rome as prominently as it honored his own. But he and the other emperors were the involuntary heirs of an homage which had already been accorded to their Hellenistic predecessors.[45] Indeed, the cult originally had nothing obligatory about it, and it always kept a great suppleness and diversity of forms which allowed easy adaptation to widely differing local conditions.[46] The Jews, for instance, were given complete exemption from ceremonies which were obviously incompatible with their religious convictions.[47]

Furthermore, we must recognize that at that time this deification did not express the same qualities of monstrous pride and absurdity that it would today. Even apart from oriental polytheism, the radical division between God and man, which was peculiar to Judaism and later to Christianity, was alien to common patterns of thought of the classical era. According to these thought-patterns there was no essential difference between the human and the divine. A god was simply more than a man—perhaps even a very great man. It was therefore natural that the greatest of men should come very close to the gods and in their own lifetimes should be regarded as demi-gods.[48] To recognize the emperor's divinity was simply to acknowledge the extent and reality of his power.

The concept of divinity of the emperor was far more political in nature than it was religious.[49] Recent studies agree that nobody—neither the emperor himself nor those who competed to make the most fulsome of declarations about him—ever really believed in the imperial myths.[50] As K. M. Setton remarked,

> No man sought in an hour of peril, we may believe, despite the testimony to the contrary from the pagan panegyrists, to save his life or his soul by praying to the *numen* of the Roman emperor. He knew well enough that the god-emperor, living or dead, was not consulted about the administration of affairs in the world beyond. The votary of the emperor-cult prayed, nevertheless, as fervently and audibly as he could to the god-emperor as the savior who should deliver him from economic hardship and from social injustice.[51]

These emperor-cult ceremonies were anything but empty form. The participants were "taking communion in the tutelary power of Rome, manifested in the person of Rome's head. The imperial cult proceeded from this belief common to primitive peoples that the head of state has been invested with supernatural powers which he used for the people's benefit."[52] This cult was the only possible bond between the widely differing peoples who made up the Roman empire. It was only by such a manifestation of attachment that they could find unity.[53] As I. T. Beckwith commented, "The cult of the prince became the official bond uniting all those attracted by the fascination of Rome, and the authentic form, as it were, of Roman loyalism."[54] The Christians, however, could not accept this state religion. Its very language constantly reminded them that they must choose between two masters, between the head of the state and the Lord of the Church. The Christian theologians had invested Christ with all the titles of temporal sovereignty; but the people, in their enthusiasm and servility, had endowed the emperor with all the attributes of divinity.[55] This conflict of attitudes was felt more keenly in the army than anywhere else. As an official body intimately bound up with the emperor, it regularly repeated ceremonies of patriotic loyalty which the Christian could only regard as manifestations of idolatry.[56]

In the first work which dealt clearly with the questions of the Christian's participation in the army (*De Corona* [On the Crown]), Tertullian laid great stress on the idolatrous nature of the obligations—which a believer could not accept—which were imposed on the soldier.[57] It was also idolatry which lay behind the story of Basilides. This man, an officer in Egypt, was converted (or at least confirmed in his faith) by the virgin Potamienna and her mother Marcella, whom during the Severian persecution he was charged to bring to torture. Basilides was then himself executed, evidently because he could not take the military oath, which was an observance incompatible with his faith.[58] Similar occasions of conflicting loyalties recurred repeatedly.

Some scholars have emphasized, however, that although this incompatibility of loyalties must have been implicit from the birth of Christianity, explicit conflict on this issue does not seem to have arisen until quite late. They have explained this by observing that the transition—from the view of the emperor as "the elect of the gods," with dead emperors (or even those still alive) as vaguely "divinized," to the assertion that the emperor was quasi-biologically divine—was very gradual. In 291 the decisive step was taken: the emperors officially proclaimed themselves *diis genitus*, substantially gods and sons of gods. Diocletian claimed to be the son of Jupiter, and Maxi-

milian the son of Hercules.[59] Such claims continued to be
made into the reign of Constantine, who prior to his conversion to Christianity was styled son of Apollo. From 295
onwards, according to M. W. Seston's remarkable study,
Christian antagonism to these claims produced a significant
number of soldier martyrs, especially in Africa. But Seston's
conclusions are extreme. He asserted, "If there had not been
Jovii and *Herculii,* i.e., emperors who called themselves sons
of Jupiter and Hercules in order to install these divinities in
the very government of the empire, neither Marcellus the
centurion nor the veteran Tipasius nor Fabius the ensign-
bearer nor Julius the old officer would have faced martyrdom."[60] In Chapter 4 I shall devote considerable attention
to this question.

Between 298 and 302[61] Diocletian started a systematic
purge of Christians in his army in preparation for the great
persecution which he was about to launch.[62] "The Christian
soldiers [then] received the order either to renounce their faith
or to abandon the service."[63] The choice put before them was
simple; no research was needed. Everyone knew that a Christian could never take part in a pagan ceremony. Just as earlier
under Trajan, it was enough for the emperor if a Christian
pretended to abandon his faith. For a Christian who had been
willing to bow to idols had ceased to be a Christian.

Cerfaux and Tondriau have emphasized that the rite imposed upon the soldiers was somehow of secondary importance. After reviewing the different views of earlier
scholars who had studied the emperor cult, they have concluded that this rite was by no means the determining cause of
the persecutions. It served merely as a test to uncover Christians, who were under attack for their refusal to recognize as
supreme and unconditional values either the state or the
prince who personified it.[64] In the *Acts* of Fructuosus, before
the question of sacrificing to the emperor had arisen, a dialogue occurred which is significant in this respect. The

governor Emilian asked, "Were you aware of the emperors' orders?" Bishop Fructuosus replied, "I do not know their orders. I am a Christian." In light of such an opening Emilian's later outburst becomes quite understandable. After Fructuosus had refused the idolatrous cult, Emilian exclaimed, "Who then will be obeyed, who will be honored, if people refuse to worship the gods and pay homage to the emperors?"[65]

"No citizen had the right to refuse the honors due to the gods of the empire. The Christians, however, thought differently, and they could not compromise on this point. For it was impossible for them deliberately to take part in a religious act which they considered demon-worship."[66] This statement by M. Lods is true enough, but it must not be construed as meaning that the believers were simply rejecting the rite by itself. The rite showed that a particular power was totalitarian. Its absolute claim was the real idolatry, and it was this that the faithful were refusing.

The Christians' view of the state, then, was in part shaped by the problem of idolatry, which they faced most notably in the army. But it extended far beyond that problem. To the broader perspective—to their conception of the empire and its head—we must now turn our attention.

The believers of the early centuries had one notion which is completely foreign to modern thinking: to them the empire appeared to be a reality which was both universal and unique. Thus, at the beginning of his prayer for the governing authorities, Clement of Rome prayed, "Give us all who live on the earth harmony and peace;"[67] whereupon, by an immediate association of ideas, he proceeded to intercede for the Roman state. For Clement, in fact, concord and peace were only conceivable and realizable within its civilizing framework. Such an idea, which was already present during the days of persecution, was bound to be accentuated when the empire adopted Christianity. For this reason, it is fair to generalize that just before the empire's collapse in the fifth century, "on the intellectual as on the social level, the life of Christianity seemed bound up with the life of the Roman state and civilization."[68] In comparison to this world-view modern nationalism appears out-of-date and even reactionary. We shall be able to reinterpret the early Christians' attitude in a manner more valid for our age if we recall that the world state to which they knew that they belonged was in no respect a Christian state. One can almost detect in Clement of Rome a foretaste of the expectation of the "universal socialist republic" whose dawn was hailed in the first version of Péguy's *Jeanne d' Arc.*

Because of its extensive geographical dimensions and massive power, the Roman state confronted the early Christians—as may well be the case if Christians of tomorrow find themselves facing a United States of the World—with a dilemma: should they regard the state as an effective instrument of God's love for man? or should they view it as a power of demonic dimensions and pride? These two opposing or perhaps complementary views may respectively be called the state according to Romans 13 and the state according to Revelation 13.[69]

According to the former view, the state was the servant of God which was appointed to maintain order and peace. It was at enmity with Satan, the divider who sowed discord, trouble, and war. That was why praying for the state[70] was a duty which Christians were to carry out punctiliously in all circumstances: "The devil's art is always seeking ways to persecute, oppress and crush the saints, to prevent them from raising their holy hands towards God in prayer. For he knows very well that the prayer of the saints gives the world peace and punishes the wicked."[71]

The emperor and the empire fulfilled a very definite task which God himself assigned to them. Origen therefore objected vehemently when Celsus argued that royal authority derived from demonic powers.[72] Kings were really "higher powers ... that are ordained by God," and they had the power corresponding to that function.[73] Hence Athenagoras, in his *Legatio pro Christianis*, did not hesitate to accord to Marcus Aurelius the title of autokratōr.[74] He began by observing gratefully that "individual men, admiring your gentle and mild nature, your peaceableness and humanity toward all, enjoy equality before the law; the cities have an equal share in honor according to their merit; and the whole empire enjoys a profound peace through your wisdom." His only complaint was that this peace did not also extend to the Christians, for whom he simply requested the benefit of the blessings which were freely accorded to the empire's other inhabitants. Origen's conclusion was thus perfectly logical and sincere:

> [We] pray for your reign that the succession to the kingdom may proceed from father to son, as is most just, and that your reign may grow and increase as all men become subject to you. This is also to our advantage that we may lead a quiet and peaceable life and at the same time may willingly do all that is commanded.[75]

The Christians' respect for authority was such that Hermas could speak of an order of banishment pronounced by the emperor ("Either observe my laws or get out of my country") as an order that "the lord of this country can justly say to you."[76] Again, Justin pointed out to the emperor that the Christians were his best helpers and allies in promoting peace. Indeed, he even conceived of this collaboration as being reciprocal, since he invited the emperor to punish false Christians whose claims to be believers were belied by their failure to live according to Christ's commandments.[77] When answering those who accused God of being unjust for imposing eternal punishment, Justin went still further. If God really were unjust, he argued, "the legislators would then be unjust in punishing those who transgress their equitable laws. But these legislators

are not unjust; nor is God the Father unjust, who by his Word
teaches such punishment. Therefore, those who accept the
necessity for this punishment are not unjust either."[78] That
did not mean, however, that Justin blindly accepted all human
laws. In fact, he immediately proceeded to explain that if
there were good laws, there were also other laws which were
evil, which were inspired by the devil and were adopted by
those who resembled him. The martyr Achatius later drew the
same distinction before the prefect who was judging him:
"The public law punishes the fornicator, the adulterer, the
robber, the pederast, the person who commits abominations,
and the murderer. If I am guilty of these things, I myself
pronounce my own condemnation before you. But if I am
brought to torture because I honor him who is the true God,
then I am condemned not by the law's decision but merely by
the judge's."[79] In other words, an unjust law was merely a
human caprice—it did not deserve respect.

Tertullian devoted chapter 4 of his *Apology* to demolish-
ing the notion that law was an impersonal entity which—in
terms of justice and simple moral reasoning—stood above
analysis. On the contrary, law was not self-sanctioning; nor
was it merely based upon the good pleasure of the person who
promulgated it. It was justified only when it forbade what was
evil and, as a result, authorized what was good. In the final
analysis, what was permitted was what was good, not merely
what was legal; what really was forbidden was what was evil,
not merely what was unlawful. Indeed, for the very reason
that law did not fall from heaven but was empirically the work
of fallible man, it was always liable to make mistakes. There
could therefore be a real distinction between legal and moral
truth.[80] In light of this distinction, it was not only possible—it
was necessary—to examine and evaluate each law individual-
ly. Any law which could not stand up under such scrutiny was
inherently tyrannical.[81]

To buttress his concept of the fallibility and relativity of laws, Tertullian tirelessly piled up examples of old laws which had fallen into disuse, either because they had become inapplicable to actual situations or because the Romans had run away from the legitimate obligations the laws had imposed. In light of this legal fluidity, it was obvious to Tertullian that law was always an approximation. There was only one thing which did not change—the law of God.[82] It was to this law that one must cling; it was this law that must serve as a reference standard by which to judge all other laws. When one recognized by this divine standard that a particular human law was unjust, one was not obliged to obey it; on the contrary, one was duty-bound to break it.

Origen similarly distinguished between human laws which were of divine origin—revealed to a greater or lesser extent by the goodness of God according to a rather obscure process—and laws whose origins were merely human and which therefore were of minimal validity.[83] In the following century Basil also drew a distinction between the usurper and the legitimate power, the tyrant and the king: "The former seeks his personal advantage in every sphere; the latter looks after the welfare of his subjects."[84] These writers were agreed that the criterion of lawfulness was to be found in the common good. Power exercised solely to benefit the person holding it had lost its divine sanction.

In the same way, Theophilus argued at length that honor was due to the emperor because of God's express command. But he immediately went on to argue that there were limits beyond which that honor could not go without jeopardizing the honor of God:

> I will rather honor the king [than your pagan deities], not indeed worshipping him, but praying for him. But God, the living and true God, I worship, knowing that the king is made by him.[85] You will say then to me, "Why do you not worship the king?" Because he is not made to be worshipped, but to be reverenced with lawful honor, for he is not a god, but a man ap-

pointed by God, not to be worshipped, but to judge justly. For
in a kind of way his government is committed to him by God: as
he will not have called those kings whom he has appointed
under himself; for "king" is his title, and it is not lawful for
another to use it; so neither is it lawful for any man to be worshipped but God only.... Accordingly, honor the king, be subject
to him, and pray for him with a loyal mind; for if you do this,
you do the will of God. For the law that is of God says, "My son,
fear thou the Lord and the king, and be not disobedient to
them; for suddenly they shall take vengeance on their
enemies."[86]

Irenaeus reacted similarly. He mentioned "military and
kingly pursuits" among the human activities which people
agreed in finding useful.[87] He admired the *Pax Romana* just as
much as Athenagoras did; and apparently he, like Clement of
Rome, could conceive of no human order or empire other than
the empire whose power extended all round him at that time.
"Through their [the Romans'] instrumentality," he wrote,
"the world is at peace, and we walk on the highways without
fear, and sail where we will."[88] Irenaeus clearly saw the Lord's
hand behind the temporal powers, which for him were not the
manifestation of sin but its unavoidable consequence: "The
most righteous Retributor metes out punishment according to
their deserts, most deservedly, to the ungrateful and to those
who are insensible to his kindness; and therefore does he say,
'He sent his armies, and destroyed those murderers, and
burned up their city.' He says here, 'his armies,' because all
men are the property of God.... Wherefore also the apostle
Paul says in the Epistle to the Romans, 'For there is no power
but of God....' "[89]

Later in the same work Irenaeus resumed his detailed
exegesis of Romans 13. He stressed, as Justin had before him,
that the Christian's obedience to the law was not a passive
submission to any tyranny:

For since man, by departing from God, reached such a pitch of fury as even to look upon his brother as his enemy, and engaged without fear in every kind of restless conduct, and murder, and avarice; God imposed upon mankind the fear of man, as they did not acknowledge the fear of God, in order that, being subjected to the authority of men, and kept under restraint by their laws, they might attain to some degree of justice, and exercise mutual forbearance through dread of the sword suspended full in their view, as the apostle says: "For he beareth not the sword in vain; for he is the minister of God, the avenger for wrath upon him who does evil." And for this reason too, magistrates themselves, having laws as a clothing of righteousness whenever they act in a just and legitimate manner, shall not be called in question for their conduct, nor be liable to punishment. But whatsoever they do to the subversion of justice, iniquitously, and impiously, and illegally, and tyrannically, in these things shall they also perish; for the just judgment of God comes equally upon all, and in no case is defective. Earthly rule therefore has been appointed by God for the benefit of nations, and not by the devil, who is never at rest at all, nay, who does not love to see even nations conducting themselves after a quiet manner, so that under the fear of human rule, men may not eat each other up like fishes; but that, by means of the establishment of laws, they may keep down an excess of wickedness among the nations.... As, then, "the powers that be are ordained of God," it is clear that the devil lied when he said, "These are delivered unto me; and to whomsoever I will, I give them." For by the law of the same Being as calls men into existence are kings also appointed, adapted for those men who are at the time placed under their government. Some of these [rulers] are given for the correction and the benefit of their subjects, and for the preservation of justice; but others, for the purposes of fear and punishment and rebuke; others, as [the subjects] deserve it, are for deception, disgrace, and pride; while the just judgment of God, as I have observed already, passes equally upon all.[90]

Hippolytus of Rome gave a similar interpretation. "Those who believe in God," he wrote,

need not dissimulate, nor, unless they do evil, need they fear those who hold power. But if these powerful ones want to force them to act contrary to their faith in God, they would rather accept death than do what they are ordered. And when the apostle says one must be subject to superior powers, he is not referring to such cases. On the contrary, he demands that through respect for power we do not commit any crime, lest we be punished as malefactors. That is why he continues: "The executioner is servant of God against those who do evil. You do not want to have to fear the power? Do good and you will obtain its praises. But if you do evil, fear. For it is not in vain that he bears the sword."[91]

Commenting on Romans 13, Tertullian wrote,

Thus he [the Apostle Paul] bids you be subject to the powers, not on an opportunity occurring for his avoiding martyrdom, but when he is making an appeal in behalf of a good life, under the view also of their being as it were assistants bestowed upon righteousness, as it were handmaids of the divine court of justice, which even here pronounces sentence beforehand upon the guilty. Then he goes on also to show how he wishes you to be subject to the powers, bidding you pay "tribute to whom tribute is due, custom to whom custom," that is, the things which are Caesar's to Caesar, and the things which are God's to God; but man is the property of God alone.[92]

However, Tertullian adhered strictly to the Pauline argument in declaring that the use of the sword was no mere concession; it was a genuine religious calling for earthly justice.[93]

Tertullian also attributed to the emperors personally a rather curious sort of private natural revelation. Bad emperors as well as good had received this, but they had consciously rejected it, which made their plight even worse. Good emperors, however, recognized that this power had been given them by God, and they acknowledged that he and he alone could withdraw it from them.[94] The emperors who had really been aware of their mission had therefore always shown themselves favorable to the Christians. Tertullian introduced this pseudo-historical thesis by recounting a fanciful story, according to which Tiberius proposed that the Senate recognize Christ's divinity. Only when the senators refused to consider this did the emperor withdraw his proposal. But he nevertheless purportedly remained partial toward the Christians and declared himself to be their protector.[95] Tertullian went on to produce Marcus Aurelius, who in the period following the alleged miracle of the Thundering Legion had supposedly played, on an even grander scale, the role of the Christians' recognized protector.[96] As a final demonstration of his thesis he cited Septimius Severus, who had personally quelled a popular rising directed against the believers.[97]

Throughout the first chapter of his treatise *De Pallio* (On the Philosopher's Cloak), Tertullian appears to have been an admirer of Carthage. He was saddened to see it under Roman sway. But at the same time he recognized that Africa's peace, plenty, and prosperity, resulted from her place in the empire. Moreover, the destiny of the world depended upon God, who had declared himself in favor of the Romans. It was therefore the duty of African Christians to submit with good grace to the imperial power.

D. van Berchem, however, has given a diametrically opposite interpretation of this treatise. He argued that Tertullian's expression of admiration for the empire in *De Pallio* was tongue in cheek; and he contended that those (such as C. Guignebert) who thought it was genuine had been deluded. The treatise merely contained "a parodized echo of the propaganda themes which were being spread throughout the empire by the inscriptions on the back of coins." By making his eulogies so effusive, therefore, Tertullian was intending them to be ironical.[98] For van Berchem, the crucial thing was Tertullian's spurning—which he made as public as possible—of the toga. The toga, of course, was the identifying symbol of the Roman citizen; by rejecting it, one would be rejecting one's earthly country. (We shall be studying this attitude later.) Van Berchem's interpretation gratifyingly enables this otherwise enigmatic treatise to make sense; and, in any case, it is preferable to the idea that "the taking of the cloak" symbolized Tertullian's espousal of Montanism.[99]

I am dubious, however, that the *De Pallio* betrays as negative a view of the empire on Tertullian's part as van Berchem believed. In both his *Apology* and in the treatise *Ad Nationes*, Tertullian's assessments of Roman law and police were highly favorable. He was scandalized, however, by the fact that this judicial apparatus, which generally was so just, abruptly and inconsistently became unjust when dealing with Christians. There was, of course, a weakness in Tertullian's thinking: he found it difficult to establish a perfectly coherent synthesis between the various elements in his thought. Perhaps what appears contradictory to us would not necessarily have seemed inconsistent to him.[100]

Returning to our main line of inquiry, we come to Clement of Alexandria. From his point of view, the model statesman was Moses. Thanks to the governmental framework which he instituted, it was possible for a good "education of men" to be carried out in Hebrew society. Moses' judgments were farsighted; by a discerning use of appropriate penalties he had guided malefactors towards righteousness. At one and the same time he united in his own person all of the attributes which the philosophers require of a wise man—simultaneously he was king, lawgiver, general, judge, saint, and friend of God.[101]

This close association of religious and political qualities is also found in several other writers. The Pseudo-Melito, for example, maintained that only the knowledge and fear of God could enable a kingdom to be peacefully governed.[102] Similarly Cyprian, even though he was personally what today we would call a conscientious objector,[103] recognized the universal human need for authority embodied in a strong government.[104] He deplored the falling numbers of legionaries in the Roman army, and saw in this a sign of the calamities and degeneration affecting his age.[105] Origen also had a deep respect for government. When Celsus drew an analogy between the public realm and the world of the bees, Origen objected vigorously; for Celsus seemed thereby to be belittling the value for all men (Christians included) of cities, states, positions of authority, and wars in the country's service.[106]

This intertwining of religion and politics appears with especial clarity in the writings of Eusebius of Caesarea. Eusebius declared that laws were made for man's good: vice must be punished and virtue rewarded.[107] For this reason the sight of delinquents being tortured and executed failed to move him: he merely concluded that they had "paid the just penalty of their pernicious deception...."[108] If primitive man had been absolutely blind from the moral standpoint, it was because "at that time no laws were yet administered, nor punishment suspended over evil deeds...."[109] So Eusebius reported without the slightest surprise that Paul of Samosata, who had been under the protection of Zenobia, in 272 was "chased out of the house of the Church by the secular power (hē kosmikē archē)" at the request of a synod.[110] He was equally unsurprised that under Diocletian himself, prior to the great persecution, the Christians had been in greater favor in the imperial palaces than the other servants there. At that time princes had entrusted Christians with the government of peoples and exempted them from sacrificing "because of the great friendliness that they used to entertain for their doctrine."[111] Eusebius also pointed out that in time of persecution soldiers in the exercise of their duties had at times protected the Christians.[112] Finally, his primary criticism of Maximinus Daia was that he had "induced the army to become enervated as a result of every kind of wanton excess, encouraging governors and commanders to proceed against their subjects with rapacity and extortion, almost as if they were his fellow tyrants."[113] This line of thought led Eusebius to view Daia's defeat at the hands of Licinius as an allegory of paganism's collapse in the face of Christianity: "When he [Daia] joined battle, he found himself bereft of divine Providence, for, by the direction of him who is the one and only God of all, the victory was given to Licinius who was then ruling."[114] This, however, did not stop Eusebius later on, most notably in his ecstatic *Life of Constantine*, from hailing yet again the victory of Constantine over Licinius as the triumph of Christ over error.[115]

Eusebius's *volte-face* appears all the more remarkable in the light of recent scholarship, which has shown that Licinius's punitive measures against the Christians lasted only for a short time; they did not amount to the religious persecution which some ancient authorities afterwards saw in them.[116] By an irony of history, in fact, it seems that the famous Edict of Milan, which has traditionally been considered as the sign of Constantine's active sympathy for the Christians, did not actually exist as an edict; it was only a circular issued by none other than Licinius.[117]

I shall be returning later to Eusebius's lack of scruple when serving his own argumentative purposes.[118] At this juncture I would like, however, to mention an important piece of early Christian writing which has survived thanks to his incorporation of it in his *History of the Church*. This is the Apology which Melito addressed to Marcus Aurelius. Melito, after having described a persecution which had degenerated into shameless looting, stated to the emperor, "If this is done as you command, let it be assumed that it is well done, for no righteous king would ever have an unrighteous policy, and we gladly bear the honor of such death." He requested only that the emperor should make enquiries to be certain that his decision to persecute was just. But if the emperor were not responsible for this decision, he asked that he should put a stop to the persecution, since it would then be nothing but "brigandage by a mob." Melito then went on to argue that the Church and the empire had developed simultaneously and in parallel: "The greatest proof that our doctrine flourished for good along with the empire in its noble beginning is the fact that in the reign of Augustus it met no evil, but on the contrary [it met] everything splendid and glorious according to the wishes of all men." To enjoy the same advantages, Marcus Aurelius, like all his wise predecessors, only had to preserve and honor Christianity to the extent that he did other religions. Only Nero and Domitian had departed from this attitude, which the ancestors of the present emperor—most notably his father and grandfather—had adopted. Melito ended his Apology confidently. He was sure that Marcus Aurelius would take the same view of the Christians as his predecessors had done. Since he was filled with even more humanity and philosophy than they had been, he would therefore surely do all that the Christians were asking of him.[119]

Origen borrowed and elaborated upon this argument of Melito. To it he added the thought (which Irenaeus had also expressed)[120] that the unity and peace of the empire facilitated traveling and consequently the spread of the gospel:

For "righteousness arose in his days and abundance of peace" began with his birth [Christ's]; God was preparing the nations for his teaching, that they might be under one Roman emperor, so that the unfriendly attitude of the nations to one another, caused by the existence of a large number of kingdoms, might not make it more difficult for Jesus' apostles to do what he commanded them when he said, "Go and teach all nations." It is quite clear that Jesus was born during the reign of Augustus, the one who reduced to uniformity, so to speak, the many kingdoms on earth so that he had a single empire. It would have hindered Jesus' teaching from being spread through the whole world if there had been many kingdoms, not only for the reasons just stated, but also because men everywhere would have been compelled to do military service and to fight in defense of their own land. This used to happen before the times of Augustus and even earlier still when a war was necessary, such as that between the Peloponnesians and the Athenians, and similarly in the case of the other nations which fought one another. Accordingly, how could this teaching, which preaches peace and does not even allow men to take vengeance on their enemies, have had any success unless the international situation had everywhere been changed and a milder spirit prevailed at the advent of Jesus?[121]

Well before Origen, pseudo-Justin had contended—on the basis of the rather untheological authority of Homer—that war and other similar evils were simply the result of a superfluity of kings and emperors.[122]

Eusebius believed that the Roman empire summed up the history of the whole universe. All of his chronological tables pointed toward this one political conclusion. But Jean Sirinelli, in his recent study of Eusebius, was forced—despite his relatively pro-Eusebian prejudice—to admit candidly that this idea had little theological significance. For Eusebius was completely devoid of original theological thought; and in this as in many other matters he was merely voicing the common views of his fellow Roman citizens.[123] But his adoption of two additional ideas which his Christian predecessors had expressed was significant (more so than Sirinelli was willing to concede): that Roman domination, by unifying the world just when Christianity was beginning, had made possible extended journeys and therefore far-reaching evangelization;[124] and more specifically, that it was the police power of the state that protected the Church. It was, for instance, not mere chance but clear providential dispensation that had brought about the submission of the unruly Egyptians to the Roman state just at the time of Christ's birth.[125]

Later on John Chrysostom emphasized that since the advent of the new covenant the old atmosphere of battles and wars had been replaced by a profound peace which was disturbed only by a few frontier skirmishes.[126] He did not, however, treat that peace as a providential design favoring the spread of Christianity. He saw it rather as the consequence of that spread, which he presented as a victory of the twelve apostles, who without wealth or weapons had conquered Rome just at the time when Rome had crushed Israel. In contrast to the usual conception, he recalled the additional impediments to the preaching of the gospel which international and civil disorders had caused.[127]

Eusebius's ideas on this subject can also be found—with a slightly different emphasis which I shall discuss later—in his contemporary Lactantius. In a characteristic passage Lactantius wrote,

> They are deceived by no slight error who defame all censure, whether human or divine, thinking that he ought to be called injurious who visits the injurious with punishment. But if this is so, it follows that we have injurious laws, which enact punishment for offenders, and injurious judges, who inflict capital punishments upon those convicted of crime. But if the law is just which awards to the transgressor his due, and if the judge is called upright and good when he punishes crimes (for he guards the safety of good men who punishes the evil), it follows that God, when he opposes the evil, is not injurious; but [that person] . . . is injurious who either injures an innocent man, or spares an injurious person that he may injure many.[128]

Elsewhere Lactantius argued that "this earthly kingdom and government, unless guarded by fear, is broken down. Take away anger from a king, and he will not only cease to be obeyed, but he will even be cast down headlong from his height."[129] Moreover, God himself, just "as he is a most indulgent Father towards the godly, so is he a most upright Judge against the ungodly."[130] Lactantius therefore had nothing but scorn for Maximinus Daia, who was a bad emperor and an incompetent general.[131] But he addressed Constantine in fulsome terms:

> When the most high God raised you to the prosperous height of power, you entered upon a dominion which was salutary and desirable for all . . . restoring justice which had been overthrown.

... In return for which action God will grant you happiness, virtue, and length of days, that even when you are old you may govern the state with the same justice with which you commenced in youth. ... [132]

Among the qualities he found in Constantine was the emperor's "strict attention to all military duties (*industria militaris*) [which] ... had endeared him to the troops, and made him the choice of every individual."[133]

Lactantius's account in the *De Mortibus Persecutorum* of the respective victories of Constantine over Maxentius and Licinius over Daia[134] is suffused with the belief that the victors had conquered, thanks to the hand of God who—because they were Christian princes—was working for them in their battles.[135] Conversely, while there was an equivalence between leaders who were upright, successful, and Christian, it was only among pagans that one found "judges [who], corrupted by a bribe, either destroy the innocent or set free the guilty without punishment...."[136] In his *Moralia* St. Basil was to observe, "The leader is the promoter (ekdikos) of God's judgments." So "one must be obedient to higher powers in everything that is not contrary to God's law." And according to Basil's custom he supported these precepts by appropriate quotations from the Bible. Furthermore, he asserted that it was usually ambition and the desire to command which motivated men to hate the powerful.[137] There should therefore be no surprise that the ecclesiastical canons were severe: any priest who had insulted either emperor or magistrate should be defrocked; the layman who had done likewise should be excommunicated.[138]

In the same spirit Polycarp had responded to the proconsul who was examining him, "I should have thought you [and not the mob] worthy of such a discussion [of Christian teaching]. For we have been taught to pay respect to the authorities and powers that God has assigned us. ..."[139] Similarly, John Chrysostom, who—as we shall see elsewhere—

severely censured the moral state of the troops and public authorities, nevertheless almost simultaneously insisted that the magistrate, even if corrupt or pagan, remained *a minister of God for good.* For "if he were removed, everything would collapse." Authority in society came from God. Its perversion was a result of human corruption.[140]

But an exactly contrary line of opposition to the state—at times vociferous—was also found in the thought of the early Fathers. To the extent that the state persecuted the Christians, it showed that it refused to recognize the authority of the true God. It thereby became the figure of the Antichrist—one of the enemies to be conquered by faith. "In the case of the Christians," Origen commented, "the Roman Senate, the contemporary emperors, the army, the people, and the relatives of believers fought against the gospel. . . ." These combined forces would have defeated the gospel if it had not overcome them "*by divine power.*" Christianity had thus "conquered the whole world that was conspiring against it."[141]

Eusebius, who played the most important part theologically in the subsequent rapprochement between the Roman state and the Christian Church, found it extremely difficult to reconcile his conviction that the empire was fundamentally benevolent with the fact that it had persecuted the believers. With great penetration Sirinelli has analyzed the changing nuances of Eusebius's approach to this problem. In an initial and provisional formulation, Eusebius had simply blamed the devils for the persecution.[142] Later, in a second and more intricate analysis of the problem, Eusebius attempted to see persecution as an expression of the will of God. God had suspended his providential protection of the Christians for two reasons: to castigate an unfaithful Church; and to give opportunity for the malevolence of evil rulers to become manifest so as to justify their subsequent punishment.[143] But even though Eusebius did admit that God chastened wicked emperors, unlike Lactantius he never accorded to this idea a central place in his thought.[144] Furthermore, after Eusebius had interpreted Galerius's edict of toleration as the end of the punishment which God during Diocletian's persecution had visited upon an unfaithful Church, he must have found it difficult to cope with the other half of his analysis.[145]

Eusebius was therefore forced in the last resort to develop a third conceptualization of persecution, in which he finally and fully integrated it into the providential order. Persecution now had two functions, both of which were positive: it allowed the "athletes of faith" to demonstrate their faithfulness and inner fortitude; and it provided proof that, even though the good will of the political authorities was normal and to be expected, it was nevertheless God's power (and not that good will by itself) which explained the extraordinary efflorescence of Christianity.[146] This final stage of elaboration represented a "compromise whereby institutions—whether directly divine or human but providential—could keep their credit, while at the same time the persecutions could be accounted for."[147]

Lactantius was not yet able to go that far. Hundreds of facts obliged him to acknowledge a bit ruefully that "the state, or rather the whole world itself, is in such error, that it persecutes, tortures, condemns, and puts to death good and righteous men, as though they were wicked and impious."[148] From this initial shock of persecution, Lactantius developed a wide-ranging critique of the imperial power which in the end thoroughly shattered its pretensions.[149] While the public law punished those who were obviously guilty, hidden crimes—as well as crimes which people had been able to cover up by petitions, gifts, favors, and influence—all too often remained unpunished.[150]

Half a century earlier Cyprian had been just as severe in his judgment upon the administration of justice: "The crime is committed by the guilty, and the guiltless who can avenge it is not found. There is no fear from accuser or judge; the wicked obtain impunity, while modest men are silent; witnesses are afraid; and those who are to judge are for sale."[151] To the pagan accusation that wars and famines occurred because of the presence of the Christians, Cyprian answered forthrightly, "These things happen not . . . because your gods are not worshipped by us, but because God is not worshipped by you."[152] And one of his anonymous contemporaries (who covered himself with Cyprian's name), far from seeing God's hand in the establishment of each sovereign, viewed this simply as the workings of chance.[153]

Origen was similarly severe. He argued that even if it were God's plan to use wicked men to administer the world, this would not make them any less liable to judgment.[154] Pseudo-Melito, addressing Caracalla, likewise denounced the scandalous attitude of a king who did evil himself and yet who claimed to judge and condemn offenders.[155] And Irenaeus, who was anything but a fanatic, significantly deciphered in the mysterious number (666) of the Book of Revelation the letters of the word *Lateinos*, indicating that the empire itself was the Antichrist.[156]

A contemporary text of slight theological value, the *Ascension of Isaiah*, referred to Belial (i.e., Satan) as the great prince, the king of this world; and it clearly identified him with the Roman emperors, above all with Nero, whose imminent return was anticipated by a popular superstition.[157] The *Acts of John*, too, portrayed the apostle as telling the Ephesians that military conquerors, like kings and princes, tyrants and the proud, would one day suffer eternal punishment.[158] Such language might give a bad impression to those in power; it might even plant dangerous ideas in the minds of the Christians.[159] It is therefore hardly surprising that in 303 in Syria, when certain people "had attempted to take possession of the empire, an imperial command went forth that the presidents of the churches everywhere should be thrown into prison and bonds" and that "bishops and presbyters and deacons" had joined "murderers and grave-robbers" in the jails.[160]

Tertullian enjoyed inveighing against Rome. When doing so, he did not confine himself to rehearsing the unsavory tales of the city's past ("Their fond father Aeneas ... was never glorious, and was felled with a stone—a vulgar weapon, to pelt a dog withal ... Romulus slew his brother ... and tricksily ravished some foreign virgins.").[161] He also decried the state of the city's present, using language which harked back to the Book of Revelation. Rome was "the impure, the new Babylon, the enemy of God's saints."[162] The empire itself he occasionally called the Antichrist because it was the persecutor of Christians.[163] By the time that he wrote the *De Idololatria,* Tertullian had come completely to identify the realm of Satan with that of the public authorities. In doing so, he employed a generalization which bordered on sophism and which he often abused, particularly, it seems, during his Montanist period. Jesus, he argued, refused civil dignities for himself; and what he thus rejected, he condemned completely and for ever. The powers and dignities of the world were not, in his view, merely strangers to God; they were positively his enemies. It was persecution which actually made this obvious. But Tertullian cautioned against believing the state to be evil simply because it was a persecutor. The persecution merely made visible the invisible conflict between human powers and God's power. In reality this conflict belonged to the metaphysical realm.[164] Thus Tertullian, in a significant enumeration, was able to juxtapose "the pomp of the devil and his angels, offices of the world, honors, festivals, popularity huntings, false vows, exhibitions of human servility, empty praises, base glories...."[165]

It was Hippolytus of Rome who most closely and systematically connected the empire with the Antichrist. In doing this he made less use of Revelation 13 than he did of the Book of Daniel, to which he devoted an entire volume of commentary. In his introduction to this work, G. Bardy wrote, "It is surprising ... to see the place accorded by our exegete

[Hippolytus] to the Roman empire. He doubtless knew the order given by the apostles to obey the appointed authorities. ... But whereas many of his brethren appeared profoundly loyalist and showed a sincere attachment to the Roman cause, he had nothing but contempt for it."[166] Thus Hippolytus was able to explain that the tree in Nebuchadnezzar's vision was the king himself, while the savage beasts who lived under its shade were "the warriors and armies which adhere to the king and do his bidding, ready to make war and destroy and tear asunder like wild beasts."[167] Further on, Hippolytus was still more direct in identifying the fourth beast of Daniel's vision with the empire:

> The beast which now has the power is not one nation; from all tongues and every race of man, it gathers to itself and prepares an army for the marshalling of war: they are all called Romans, though they are not all from one country. So the prophet, frightened by the prospect of the future, was quite right not to define the species to which that beast belonged.[168]

In the following chapter, in an item-by-item parallel which was an exact counterpart both to Melito's text (which Eusebius had quoted) and to the Origen text, Hippolytus explained why the incarnation had taken place when the Roman empire was at its height: "The currently reigning empire has attempted to imitate us, in accordance with Satan's activity."[169] It is very interesting to see, conversely, how Eusebius modified Hippolytus's interpretation of the last of the seventy weeks of Daniel,[170] even while agreeing with Hippolytus in separating it radically from the preceding weeks.[171] Eusebius understood it to apply in its entirety to the *earthly* life of Christ. By so doing "he closed once and for all the door to apocalyptic interpretations of Daniel's prophecy, which was indeed one of the masterpieces of the eschatological panoply."[172] Thus it was Eusebius who marked the departure of Christian thought—in its conception of the state as well as in numerous

other areas—from the dialectical approach which until then
had been its strength.

The fundamental ambiguity of judgment as to the nature
of the empire was found also in St. Paul's concept of the
katechon, katechōn (restrainer).[173] Tertullian had already
identified this quite unambiguously with the empire:

> We know that the great force which threatens the whole world,
> the end of the age itself with its menace of hideous suffering, is
> delayed by the respite which the Roman empire means for us.
> We do not wish to experience all that; and when we pray for its
> postponement [we] are helping forward the continuance of
> Rome.[174]

It is clear that for Tertullian "whatever delayed the final
catastrophe was a good thing that should be maintained as
long as possible...."[175]

Far from being the Antichrist, the empire by maintaining order and peace was the reality which stopped the Antichrist from manifesting himself; the Antichrist, in contrast,
seemed to be a false god or a prince of Semitic origin who
would establish himself by means of anarchy and would pro-
fane the most sacred mysteries.[176] The empire also played its
role of "restrainer" in a second fashion which was absolutely
essential for the Christians: it allowed them, through the order
which it preserved, to propagate their faith and above all to be
spared the constant exposure to arbitrary massacres by an ex-
citable and cruel mob.

Of course, the Antichrist was already at work. Citing
Matthew 24:14, and mentioning the apocalyptic catastrophes,
Hippolytus observed, "All this has happened and will happen
again."[177] In one sense the persecutors within the empire's of-
ficialdom could be considered as opponents of the empire's
positive vocation, and thus as workers for the Antichrist. Hippolytus preferred, however, to distinguish clearly between the
beast, which was the empire, and the Antichrist, to which the

empire—even though demonized—was still opposed.

But since the Antichrist was the necessary predecessor to the coming of the kingdom, Hippolytus could equally assert that by opposing the Antichrist the empire was effectively, though no doubt indirectly, delaying the reign of Christ: "Since the abomination of desolation has not yet been realized and since the fourth beast possesses the power for itself alone, how could the Lord's coming be brought about?"[178] Then, after quoting 2 Thessalonians 2:1-9, he wrote: "So who could be the one who restrains until now (ho katechōn arti heōs) except the fourth beast who, after having been overthrown and ejected, will be succeeded by the Deceiver."[179] Then, in chapters 23 and 24, by complex allegorical calculations, Hippolytus showed that the end of the empire and the end of the world—which for him were one and the same—would occur in the year 500. As Bardy commented, "The empire, although the fourth beast, was also the obstacle opposing the coming of the Antichrist.... No one could desire the disappearance of that obstacle, so great would be the evils which would descend upon the world on the arrival of the Man of Sin. But it is easy to see that the disappearance of the empire itself would not have caused any sorrow to the Roman priest [Hippolytus]."[180]

The Fathers of the Church thus believed that the empire in which they lived would last as long as the universe; indeed, the empire ensured its preservation. This idea was naive enough in itself. But it was dear to all the Romans of that age, as similar ideas have no doubt been to patriots of other eras. Together with this patriotic illusion went an elaborate state conservatism: the empire was the instrument—necessary and willed by God—of an order and justice which though imperfect were real. It did not occur to the Christians to use revolutionary force to replace the empire by a new this-worldly order which would be somewhat less imperfect than its predecessor.[181] But at the same time the Christians were living in expectation of a new and marvelous reality which would succeed the existing system and was already germinating mysteriously within it. For this reason they could not identify themselves completely with this world's order; in fact, they always judged it from a viewpoint which transcended it.[182] At the convergence of these two lines of thinking—provisional acceptance of the empire and ultimate rejection of it—was Tertullian, who penned the mysterious phrase which has disconcerted many interpreters: "But Caesars too would have believed in Christ, if either Caesars had not been necessary for the world, or if Christians, too, could have been Caesars."[183]

In the final analysis, we must view every judgment of political and social conditions in light of a fundamental tension—between a realistic appreciation of the present situation and a confident expectation of the advent of a different reality. The true Christian character of such a judgment will only be preserved if the "delay in the coming" does not lead us to forget the eschatological dimension of Christianity.[184] By emphasizing this eschatological criterion A. Molnár has illuminated the fundamental difference between two authors—Eusebius of Caesarea and Lactantius—who were otherwise so similar; he has also made a significant contribution toward getting this criterion recognized in more general studies.[185]

Eusebius had completely lost the apocalyptic perspective: for him there remained only Romans 13 and a near deification—at least by proxy—of the power which, because it existed, had necessarily been appointed by God.[186] As a result, "empire and state were in fact the ultimate realities. The theology of history had become useless and had been completely transformed into a political theology. It had once and for all become static."[187] For Eusebius, eschatology had been reduced to the Alexandrian or Origenist view of an immediate entry into Paradise by the soul of the departed believer; he had lost the older and more scriptural view of a resurrection on the Last Day.[188] Eusebius's determined opposition to millenarianism was also rooted in that Alexandrian tradition, and was, after all, little more than a particular consequence of this general attitude.[189] Lactantius, on the other hand, was on the side of the millenarians. Although he often was as blindly deferential toward the Constantinian state as Eusebius, he was redeemed by the fact that he never forgot the gospel's eschatological dimension. This enabled him to stand out as a prophet, judging present scandals without compromise in the light of the eternal demands of God, whose reign, though as yet hidden, would be revealed brilliantly at the end of history. I have just mentioned Eusebius's Origenism as a source of his secularized view of history; but it is only fair to recall that Origen himself did not share in what was to be the Eusebian view of "the *Pax Romana* as identified with the *Pax Messianica*" which became the undergirding ideology first of the Byzantine empire and then of the Holy Roman Empire. For Origen "the unity of the world would be fully accomplished only in eschatology. Up to that point this unity belonged only to the sphere of the Church, where all differences were already abolished."[190]

John C. Bennett has admirably remarked, "Eschatology . . . is nothing more than a coherent view of the future which gives meaning to the present moment in which we stand. Our eschatology is our ultimate hope or perhaps our ultimate fear."[191] And the central thesis of Oscar Cullmann's *The State in the New Testament* is that the primitive Christians could never either completely reject or wholeheartedly accept the state, but could only consider it as a "provisional" reality—[192] precisely because of their eschatology, which was at once Schweitzer's (everything is still to come) and Dodd's (everything is already realized).[193] Thus the two attitudes of the Epistle to the Romans and of Revelation, although both written with the same Neronian state in mind, are only superficially in conflict. In reality they are complementary and mutually correcting.[194]

Chapter 2

The Theological and Religious Setting

Let us now turn from the social context in which primitive Christianity developed to the biblical framework for the early Christian attitude toward war. The battles described in the Bible, the martial language which it employed to portray the life of the Christian believer, its prophecies concerning the Prince of Peace, and its explicit injunction to pray for the authorities—all these contributed powerfully if somewhat indirectly to the direction taken by the thinking of the Church Fathers.

The Fathers, who knew their Old Testament well, could not forget that it was full of narratives of battles.[1] In accepting this fact and integrating it into their thought, they employed two complementary methods, both of which are often found in the works of the same author. First, they emphasized the difference between the old covenant and the new. What had been permissible and necessary under the law had become unthinkable under grace. Thereby they relegated the Old Testament to the past. The Fathers firmly refused, however, to adopt any attitude which would have made them into Marcionites. While the Christians agreed with the supporters of Marcion that war was a punishment sent by God the Creator, the Christians also affirmed that Christ was somehow involved in this punishment, and that the grace which he brought could not be known apart from the sword which accompanied it.[2] There were examples of love in the Old Testament, just as there were examples of violence and punishment in the New.

In the *Dialogus de recta in Deum Fide*, Adamantius was discussing this divergence of Old and New Testament ethics on the treatment of sinners with a Marcionite or Manichean. At one point the unknown author caused Adamantius to advance an interesting argument:

"Let us use an illustration to make more comprehensible what we are saying. Does not a woman, after she has borne a son, first nourish him on milk, and only later, after he has grown up, give him more solid foods? But no one charges this woman with acting inconsistently." Then after having quoted St. Paul's use of the same simile (1 Cor. 3:2), the author continued,

In the same way, God has given laws to men according to the stage of their intellectual development. To Adam he gave a law which was suited to a little child. He gave a different law to Noah, another to Abraham, and still another through Moses to the people of Israel. In similar manner, the law which he has given in the gospel is different from the others, and is in accord with the new development of the world. How therefore can we accuse God of inconsistency? For we can see that the same process, through which a person develops from infancy to old age, is also at work in the world. It began like a newborn baby, then developed into middle years, and finally has attained the maturity and perfection of old age. For each of these stages of development God has assigned laws which are appropriate to them and through which he might lead his children. But lest you should think I affirm this without evidence, consider how in Scripture itself it is one and the same God who commands these different things. God ordered Abraham to sacrifice his own son; afterwards, through Moses he forbade that anyone should be put to death, but prescribed punishment for any person who should commit such a deed. Because, therefore, he at one time ordered a son to be slain, but at another time ordered the slayer to be punished, are we to conclude that there are two Gods contrary to one another?

At that point Eutropius, the pagan referee of the discussion, interrupted, "Does he himself order a man to be killed and yet say, 'Thou shalt not kill?'" To which Adamantius replied, "Certainly. And this contradiction is found not only in this matter, but in many others as well. For sometimes he orders sacrifices to be offered to himself, and at other times he forbids them."[3]

This historical development did not, however, mean that the Christian authors thought that the Old Testament was now worthless. Its continuing value for them lay in its spiritual sense, which was complementary to its historical sense and which could be extracted through a study of its symbolism. For example, Clement of Rome, who gave a detailed account of the story of Rahab and the Israelite spies, concluded by observing that the spies "gave her a sign that she should hang a piece of scarlet from her house. By this they made it clear that it was by the blood of the Lord that redemption was going to come to all who believe in God and hope on him."[4]

The first part of the Letter of Barnabas is devoted to showing precisely how the Christians were the true heirs to the symbolic sense of the Old Testament. Particularly striking in this respect is chapter 12, in which Moses' holding out his hands to ensure the Israelites' victory[5] was "a fresh allusion to the cross and to him who was to be crucified.... The Spirit said to the heart of Moses, that he should make a symbol of the cross and of him who was to suffer, because, he says, unless they hope in him, they will be warred against forever."[6] Military battle was the symbol of spiritual battle. National salvation was the symbol of eternal salvation in Christ. Barnabas, like St. John (John 3:14), interpreted the bronze serpent[7] which Moses raised up in the desert as "a symbol of Jesus, showing that he must suffer and he whom they will think they have destroyed will himself give life. . . ."[8] Similarly, Moses bestowed a name on Joshua (Jesus), son of Nun, as on a prophet,[9] "solely in order that all the people might hear that the Father was revealing everything about his Son Jesus."[10] In the prophecy concerning the destruction of the house of Amalek,[11] Barnabas detected an anticipation of "Jesus, not as son of man, but Son of God, and symbolically revealed in the flesh."[12]

Clement of Alexandria devoted an entire section (I, 24) of his *Stromata* to a description of Moses as the symbol of the perfect leader of his people.[13] From the outset it is clear that this story concerned the Christians directly. Indeed Clement did not hesitate to use the possessive, "*our* Moses." Prominent among Moses' qualities of leadership were those of the "tactician" and the "strategist."[14] These qualities contained a divine aspect, according to which the king conformed to God and his holy Son, who gives us the goods of the earth; this had to do with external relations and complete happiness.[15] There follows a detailed paragraph on the art of tactics[16] and another one on the art of strategy.[17] Clement illustrated the latter of these by a meticulous study of the Israelites' journey into the desert following their exodus from Egypt. In this it is notable that Clement commented upon each episode to demonstrate both its implications for military strategy and its underlying spiritual significance.

In his *Adversus Haereses* Irenaeus quoted a Christian priest who explained that "Solomon . . . announced the peace about to come upon the nations, and prefigured the kingdom of Christ."[18] Origen explicitly stated that through their special insight the Christians could interpret the Old Testament's militant passages in the correct, spiritual fashion: "In a wonderful manner, too, an account of wars is presented [in the Old Testament], and the different fortunes now of the conquerors, now of the conquered are described, and by this means, to those who know how to examine writings of this kind, certain unspeakable mysteries are revealed."[19] "Indeed, if these wars in the flesh had not contained the image of spiritual wars, I do not think the apostles would ever have transmitted, for reading in the churches, the historical books of the Hebrews to the disciples of Christ who came to bring peace."[20] At a later date Philoxenus of Mabbug, following a well-established tradition,[21] wrote these words: "[We] have in the beginning of our discourse interpreted Egypt as the model of the world, and our departure from the world as the departure of the Israelites from Egypt...."[22]

Occasionally the Fathers went so far as to make a sharp distinction between the historical sense of a text and its spiritual sense. They did this not because the former had a past significance and the latter a present meaning, but because the former stood in contradiction to the sole real meaning which was revealed to the true Christian. Thus Origen warned the believers against making literal and materialist interpretations of God's wrath and of the punishment which he would inflict on those who offended him.[23] Even earlier, Aristides had attributed the numerous wars (especially those waged by the Greeks) to men's erroneous ideas about their gods, whom they imagined to be waging wars:

> For if those who are called their gods have done all those things that are written above, how much more shall men do them who believe in those who have done these things! And from the wickedness of this error, lo! there have happened to men frequent wars and mighty famines, and bitter captivity and deprivation of all things....[24]

In a later passage he specifically mentioned that Ares and Herakles had been discredited by their warlike character.[25]

In a similar vein, Arnobius employed an apologetic argument which, although it may appear questionable from our contemporary point of view, is significant:

Actually, regarding the wars which you say were begun on account of hatred for our religion, it would not be difficult to prove that after Christ was heard on earth, not only did they not increase but in great measure were reduced as a result of the repression of fierce passions. For when we, so large a number as we are, have learned from his teachings and his laws that "evil should not be repaid with evil"; that it is better to suffer wrong than be its cause, to pour forth one's own blood rather than to stain our hands and conscience with the blood of another: the world, ungrateful as it is, has long had this benefit from Christ by whom the rage of madness has been softened and has begun to withhold hostile hands from the blood of fellow beings. And if all without exception who understand that [they] are men, not through the form of their bodies but through the power of reason, would for a little while be willing to lend an ear to his wholesome and peaceful commandments, and would believe not in their own arrogance and swollen conceit but rather in his admonitions, the whole world, long since having diverted the use of iron to more gentle pursuits, would be passing its days in the most placid tranquillity and would come together in wholesome harmony, having kept the terms of treaties unbroken.[26]

If God were thus completely pacific, the Israelites had on this point seriously misunderstood the divine revelation. However, now that the Messiah had come in lowliness and gentleness, and now that Jerusalem had been destroyed, Christians could no longer make this mistake. For paradoxically—and this points ahead to a second line of development which we shall examine in a moment—the divinely ordained destruction of the earthly Jerusalem, which destruction symbolized the disappearance of the illusion that God was the God of military victories, had manifested in violence the triumph of the God of peace and love:

When our Lord and Savior came . . . he taught the things of salvation, destroyed the things which were useless, and abolished the things which do not save. He did these things not only by his teaching but also by using the Romans. It is he who caused the temple to fall, superseded the altar, and annulled the sacrifices along with the other obligations of the ceremonial law.[27]

This radical transposition is also to be found in the Letter of Barnabas. After contending that the temple in Jerusalem had been destroyed because the Jews had gone to war,[28] Barnabas proceeded to argue that the real temple, in which the promises of its reconstruction were being fulfilled, was spiritual in nature and consisted of the regenerate souls of redeemed sinners.[29] Origen, for his part, gave the following consolation to the Israelite who came to Jerusalem and found it in ruins:

> Do not go on weeping as though you had the uncomprehending mind of children. Do not lament, but, rather than the earthly city, seek out the heavenly city. Look up towards heaven and there you will see the celestial Jerusalem which is the mother of all. . . . It is by God's loving-kindness that your earthly heritage has been taken from you so that you may seek the heavenly heritage.[30]

It was presumably in this frame of mind that the Christians left Jerusalem during the war of AD 70. "Why should they have taken part in the war? . . . Had not the teaching of Jesus and his cross underlined his rejection of a Jewish national kingdom? The Christians of Jerusalem, probably almost all of them Jews, withdrew from the city. This was a clear expression of the fact that the Jews and the Christians understood zeal for Zion in markedly divergent ways." These lines were written by F. Lovsky, who like Goguel believed that it was this which precipitated the Jews' systematic and permanent hostility toward the Christians, whom they from that time onwards viewed as traitors.[31]

In addition to this transposition of the meaning of historical events into the spiritual realm, the Fathers employed a second interpretive device: they ascribed to events, which themselves remained completely historical, a variety of celestial causes. Sometimes these causes—especially in apocryphal works of a more or less gnostic coloration—consisted of conflicts, which were only dimly reflected on earth, between demonic angels. An excellent example of this is found in the *Ascension of Isaiah,* in which the prophet described a spectacle which had unfolded before him as he ascended into heaven:

> I saw Sammael and his hosts, and there was great fighting therein [in the firmament] and the angels of Satan were envying one another. And as above so on earth also; for the likeness of that which is in the firmament is here on the earth. And I said to the angel (who was with me): "(What is this war and) what is this envying?" And he said to me: "So it was since this world was made until now, and this war (will continue) till he, whom thou shalt see will come and destroy him [Satan]."[32]

But at the end of time, as in the vision of the Book of Revelation, God would carry out his judgment in a warlike fashion:

> The white horse and his rider are the figure of the Lord coming to reign with a heavenly army. At his coming all the nations will be gathered together and almost all of them will be annihilated. Only the most noble of the nations will be preserved to serve the saints. But these nations too will finally be slaughtered when the reign of the saints comes to an end, i.e., at the time prior to the last judgment when Satan is once again sent into the world.[33]

From then on eschatological wars would begin to break out, which would prove that the kingdom of God was near.[34] However, God's judgment was also revealed in history, and the Jews had been his right arm. As long as they had worshiped God unarmed, "they overwhelmed armed troops, by the command of God and the support of his elements."[35] The *Dialogus de recta in Deum Fide* thus opened by according complete approval to the Jews' plundering of the Egyptians and to Moses' punishing of the rebels:

> It is completely just that those who unjustly started war should be despoiled like enemies according to the laws of war. ... It was just that those who rebelled should be slaughtered like enemies and conspirators. ... We have shown that those who precipitate a war unjustly must as a matter of course receive what is the result of the law of war. Thus Christ himself has ordered that the enemies should be hurled into outer darkness where there shall be weeping and gnashing of teeth.[36]

Irenaeus was convinced that God had chosen Gideon for the specific vocation of using arms to save his people, Israel, from foreign domination.[37] Hippolytus, in his commentary upon Daniel's visions, practically identified with Jesus Christ the angel who announced to Daniel, "I intend to wage war on the king of the Persians ... for it came into his mind not to let the people go. But I have set myself against him so that what you requested may quickly come to pass."[38] Basil also, even though as we shall see he expressly condemned all forms of homicide, was quite ready to write, "Whether you wish to examine ancient evidence—the blessings of the patriarchs ... the valorous feats (ta andragathēmata) in war, the signs wrought through just men—or on the other hand the things done in the dispensation of the coming of our Lord in the flesh—all is through the Spirit."[39]

But God's arm could also turn against Israel. Tertullian recalled that God had punished those who offended him, often by slaughter. "And thus, throughout almost all the annals of the judges and of the kings who succeeded them, while the strength of the surrounding nations was preserved, he meted out wrath to Israel by war and captivity and a foreign yoke, as often as they turned aside from him, especially to idolatry."[40] Theophilus made the same point:

> And when the people transgressed the law which had been

given to them by God, God being good and pitiful, unwilling to destroy them, in addition to his giving them the law, afterwards sent forth also prophets to them from among their brethren, to teach and remind them of the contents of the law, and to turn them to repentance, that they might sin no more. But if they persisted in their wicked deeds, he forewarned them that they should be delivered into subjection to all the kingdoms of the earth; and that this has already happened, is manifest.[41]

That the Jews had been overwhelmed by countless calamities was punishment for their sins, especially since they had rejected Jesus.[42]

Tertullian explained to the Romans that Palestine had fallen under their domination only because Israel, in crucifying Christ, had committed the most grievous sin in history.[43] In his polemic against Marcion, he cited numerous prophecies to show that the destruction of Israel had been the consequence of its spurning of Jesus.[44] Pionius at the time of his martyrdom at Smyrna in 250 was apparently pondering the crimes which the Old Testament had recorded. Palestine, he reflected, was a land "which bears witness even to this day of the divine anger that has afflicted it by reason of the sins committed by its inhabitants, who killed foreigners, drove them out, or did violence."[45] As signs of the land's condemnation he pointed to the barrenness of its desert and to the Dead Sea, which refused even to accept swimmers into its waters. In sum, as Hippolytus observed, "Since the Lord had come to the Jews but had not been acknowledged by them, they were scattered throughout the whole world, having been cast out of their own land. And having been defeated by their enemies, they were thrust out of the city of Jerusalem and so became a source of vindictive glee for all nations."[46] Elsewhere he contended that Isaiah's prophecies concerning the destruction of Jerusalem had now been fulfilled.[47]

The early Christian writers therefore considered the destruction of Jerusalem in AD 70 to have been a kind of in-

verted messianic war. Far from showing forth God's judgment
on the nations through the Jews, it revealed his judgment on
the Jews through the nations. The first writer to develop this
idea—which was deeply rooted in the Bible—was Justin, in
his *First Apology*.[48] In his *Dialogue with Trypho* (the Jew) he
went even further: "Now if you were cast out by being conquered in war, with justice have you endured such suffering,
as all the Scriptures bear witness."[49] And again, "It is clear
that the sons of Japhet, in accordance with the judgment of
God, themselves came upon you, and took away your land and
held it in possession."[50]

Time and again in primitive Christian writing, above all
in Origen, there recurred the idea that the destruction of
Jerusalem had been a just punishment for the crucifixion of
Christ:

> If after treating Jesus in the way in which they dared to act
> against him, the Jews were destroyed from the youth upwards
> and their city burnt down with fire, the cause of their suffering
> these things was simply the wrath which they treasured up for
> themselves; there came to pass God's judgment against them
> which had been fixed by God's appointment, this judgment be-
> ing called "wrath" by traditional Hebrew usage.[51]

Since the Jews had shed the blood of Jesus and assumed
responsibility for it, God could no longer allow them to go on
living an independent life in the land of Palestine.[52] In
another passage, Origen asserted that

> one of the facts which show that Jesus was some divine and
> sacred person is just that on his account such great and fearful
> calamities have now for a long time befallen the Jews. We will
> go so far as to say that they will not be restored again. For they
> committed the most impious crime of all, when they conspired
> against the Savior of mankind, in the city where they performed
> to God the customary rites which were symbols of profound
> mysteries. Therefore that city where Jesus suffered these in-
> dignities had to be utterly destroyed. The Jewish nation had to

be overthrown, and God's invitation to blessedness transferred to others. . . . [53]

Similarly, in Minucius Felix's *Octavius*, the protagonist replied to his pagan interrogator, "You will realize that they [the Jews] deserted before they were deserted, that they were not, as you blasphemously put it, taken captive along with their God, but that they were delivered up by their God as deserters from his law."[54] The same attitude is evident in the dialogue *De Recta Fide*,[55] in Pseudo-Cyprian,[56] Eusebius of Caesarea,[57] the Christian interpolator of the *Sibylline Oracles*,[58] and St. Augustine.[59] These texts, some of which could have applied equally to the siege of AD 130, seem generally to have referred to the siege of AD 70, after which the Temple of Jerusalem "with the city itself was again destroyed (*exterminatum*) in the reign of Vespasian by our Lord himself because of the Jews' disbelief."[60] In a similar vein, Lactantius reported that when Peter and Paul were in Rome they had foretold, both orally and in writing, that God would soon send a king to destroy the Jews. "And so, after their [the apostles'] decease, when Nero had put them to death, Vespasian destroyed the name and nation of the Jews, and did all things which they had foretold as about to come to pass."[61]

These passages sound so much like a systematic theological interpretation that Jules Isaac was able to demonstrate that the final dispersal of the Israelites after the destructions of 70 and 135 belongs more to the realm of myth than to that of historical fact.[62] But Lovsky, who quoted him on this point,[63] later recalled "that myths of a theological type arise from temporal or spiritual situations and not from any dogmatic teaching or a theological dictum."[64] To support this contention, he noted that Hegesippus,[65] followed in three passages by Origen,[66] attributed the real cause of these catastrophes to the murder—not of Christ—but of St. James. It is essential to bear in mind this last point if we are to restore what Lovsky has called "the Christian anti-semitism of differentiation" to its proper perspective.

The early Christian writers, however, did not see God's hand solely in the violence of the past or in the turbulent history of the Israelites. They also saw it in contemporary events. Theophilus quoted a Sibylline Oracle to the effect that it was invariably God who caused wrath, war, the plague, and other calamities against the wicked.[67] Tertullian pointed out to the pagans the manifold catastrophes which surrounded them: "Wars without and wars within lacerate the peoples ... kingdoms clash with kingdoms." All of these baleful events, he assured them, were the fulfillment of what had been foretold in the Scriptures.[68] And in his reply to Marcion, Tertullian argued that Christ was intimately connected with the stern and just Creator. For Christ had predicted that eschatological wars were going to break out and had not made the slightest attempt to prevent them, as he must have done if they had been contrary to his own purposes.[69] Various writers incorporated this idea into specific warnings about future events. For example, Clement of Rome, brandishing Isaiah 1:20 and breathing threats of the military destruction with which the Lord would punish unbelievers, exclaimed, "If you are unwilling and do not heed me, the sword shall devour you."[70] Commodian made the same point. After having described—in typically barbarous language—the abduction of defenseless children by the enemy, he concluded,

> And yet I do not pity them. Their fathers' iniquities certainly earned them this punishment. For this reason God gave them up.[71]

In 396, at the time of the first great invasions, St. Jerome wrote in a more humane fashion than Commodian but with equal urgency:

> For a long time now we have felt that God is offended with us, but we do not try to appease him. It is by reason of our sins

that the barbarians are strong, it is our vices that bring defeat to the armies of Rome.... Unhappy are we, who have so displeased God that his anger vents its fury on us by the barbarians' mad attacks.[72]

Earlier, Eusebius, after having drawn a close parallel between the persecution of the Church and Israel's national misfortunes, like Jerome had concluded that all these events were simply the punishment of God.[73] Nevertheless, amidst the unleashing of all this violence the Christian remained a passive agent. He was a witness, not a warrior. He accepted the wrath of God upon himself; he discerned it in the history of others. He warned and admonished. He did not himself administer the punishment.

Tertullian, however, revealed that certain Christians were themselves eager to resort to arms. To justify their attitude, they appealed to the Old Testament and to John the Baptist.[74] And Irenaeus, in his commentary on the verse (Matthew 22:7) "and he sent his troops and destroyed those murderers and burned their city" from the parable of the wedding feast, noted that Jesus had used the possessive "his" because all men belonged to God. Irenaeus went on to base his thinking on the text dealing with the magistrate in Romans 13:1-6,[75] which at least suggested that the Christians might themselves be the agents of God's wrath.

In Eusebius and Lactantius the same tendency was present in a more disturbing form.[76] The former rejoiced, in a thoroughly unpleasant way, in the calamities which befell the adversaries of Christianity. Under Decius many people were violently attacking the Christians at Alexandria, which "state of things continued at its height for a long time. But strife and civil war came upon the wretched men [the persecutors], and turned on themselves the fury of which we had been the object...."[77] In chapter 9, Book IX of the *History of the Church* Eusebius gave a detailed account of the grim end of the "tyrants" (i.e., Constantine's enemies); Constantine, on

the other hand, he presented as having been "stirred up by
the King of kings, God of the universe and Savior." "God,"
Eusebius asserted, "proved his [Constantine's] ally in the most
wonderful manner."[78] God's help, which had assisted Moses
in delivering the Hebrew people from Egypt, thus had a
recent counterpart—in the circumstances which enabled
Constantine to seize the city of Rome. Throughout this
chapter Eusebius repeatedly identified Constantine's triumph
with the work of God; conversely he also attributed to God's
activity the defeat and death of the emperor's adversaries. The
ensuing chapters continue in the same vein. In chapter 10, for
instance, Eusebius regretted, in a manner quite astonishing
for a Christian writer, that Daia while dying had suffered "less
. . . than it behooved him to suffer." Eusebius explained this
clemency on God's part, which he deplored, by the fact that
Daia at the end of his reign had called a halt to the violent
persecution of the Christians and had even issued an edict in
their favor. Nevertheless, in punishment for his previous
cruelty, Daia was "smitten by a stroke of God over his whole
body." In the end his terrible suffering had forced him to acknowledge "that he suffered thus justly because of his violence against Christ."[79] In this manner "the whole race of
God's enemies had been removed . . . and in a moment blot-
ted out of men's sight."[80]

    The other Christian historian of this era, Lactantius, even
though he was less contaminated by Caesaro-papism than
Eusebius, saw things in the same light. In his *De Mortibus
Persecutorum* he, like Eusebius, discerned God's hand in the
victories of Constantine and Licinius over Maxentius and Daia
respectively.[81] He also described with almost sadistic joy
Daia's sufferings, his prolonged death-throes, and the vision in
which God appeared to him as judge.[82] Lactantius's convictions on the significance of these events were, "Thus did God
subdue all those who persecuted his name, so that neither root
nor branch of them remained...."[83] Finally, in the last

chapter of his work, Lactantius provided insight into the philosophy of history by which he interpreted such events. The emperors had been criminals against God both in arrogating to themselves divine titles and in persecuting the Church. For these reasons God had condemned them.

> The Lord has blotted them out and erased them from the earth. Let us therefore with exultation celebrate the triumphs of God, and oftentimes with praises make mention of his victory; let us in our prayers, by night and by day, beseech him to confirm for ever that peace which, after a warfare of ten years, he has bestowed on his own. . . .[84]

The potential dangers of such an attitude are obvious. The first of these was an undignified flattery of power. Once one admitted that Constantine was God's elect, one was compelled to falsify historical truth where necessary to make his personality correspond to expectations. I shall later deal with the reciprocal fraudulence which seems to me to be at the root of this flattery.[85] But this basic dishonesty led inevitably to others. Thus, while Constantine and Licinius were still fighting as allies against Maxentius and Daia, the first editions of Eusebius and Lactantius depicted both men—Licinius as well as Constantine—as acting in God's name and with his help. But later, after Constantine had quarreled with Licinius and then disposed of him, the two Christian writers had to make hurried and clumsy emendations in their work. Now they vilified Licinius and attempted to demonstrate retrospectively that in reality the light of God's grace had all along been shining on Constantine alone.[86] The most egregious Soviet historians of the Stalinist period could scarcely have done better—or worse. A second danger, which was derived from the first, was to discern in temporal power and victory the sure sign of God's grace, and to detect in defeat and misery the sign of his rejection. This surely is precisely the opposite of the gospel message.

Once one had accepted that the punishment of the end times would assume a military form and that the military events of the present were the beginning of this last judgment, a third danger arose—the temptation to try to hasten God's judgment by actively cooperating with it. St. Cyprian, for example, wrote, "I know, beloved brethren, that very many, either because of the weight of their pressing injuries or because of resentment toward those who attack them and rage against them, wish to be revenged quickly without waiting for the day of judgment. . . ."[87] Lactantius also, in his chapter on patience, commented that if anyone attacked the Christian and did him wrong, the believer "must bear it with calmness and moderation, and not take upon himself his vengeance, but reserve it for the judgment of God."[88] It seems in fact that the early Christians, outraged by the sufferings which the state was inflicting upon them in the persecutions, were genuinely tempted to take violent and revolutionary action against it. Strong evidence has recently been adduced to show that this temptation persisted into the fourth and fifth centuries. The exhortations of the Church Fathers to remain submissive and obedient are thus to be explained precisely by their need to check such inclinations.[89]

There was another element in early Christian thought— the use of military language to describe the Christian's life— which, although closely related to the element we have just been examining, should have helped to avoid the dangers that we have mentioned. In the Old Testament, the image which the biblical writers habitually used to express the mutual fidelity between God and his people was a marital image, an image of conjugal love. To this St. Paul added another image, a martial image, an image of the soldier in battle; and in his epistles he employed this image frequently and elaborated upon it extensively.[90] In a recent paper E. Nielsen has stressed that this transposition—from the *militia sacra* to a *pietas militaris*—had already been found among the Essenes, who

spoke of religion and the religious life as a war, a military campaign.[91] While explaining the psychological motivation behind such a transposition, Nielsen has suggested that this was
the origin of the subsequent Christian change in the same direction. Be that as it may, this new tradition, which also had
antecedents in Greek and Latin philosophy,[92] was widely
followed, especially in Latin Christianity. Harnack, in fact,
rightly observed that the word "image" is probably too weak
to indicate the full weight of meaning of the military metaphors for the early Christians: "They felt themselves truly and
literally to be soldiers of Christ. They had sworn fidelity to
Christ and had enlisted as his soldiers. This was the reason
why they used military terms."[93]

There is no space here for an exhaustive discussion of this
subject.[94] The detailed study which Miss Mohrmann has made
of the single word *statio*, in which she followed the evolution
of its various shades of meaning in Christian and secular Latin
usage, gives us some idea of what such research would entail.
She concluded, "The image of the *militia dei*, which became
extremely popular in some Christian circles during the third
century, inspired word-plays with the military meaning of
statio; these word-plays were also found for a short time in
monastic circles of the fifth century, notably in Cassian."[95]
Thus, Christian usage transformed even a word which did not
have a military origin into a martial expression, so habitual
had this type of metaphor become for the Church.

The evolution of the word *sacrament* is similar, if the
other way round. Its original meaning was the "identity
plate," the tessera or tattoo which was assigned to each soldier
when he entered military service. From this the word was then
transferred into the vocabulary of the Church. "Since the life
of the Christian is in a very real sense a *militia spiritualis*, it
was proper that it too should have its *sacramentum militiae*, as
did the secular military service. It was from this source that
first of all baptism and then the other sacraments gradually

came to be known by the name of sacraments."[96]

In addition to these philological transpositions, I shall quickly describe a few adaptations that the Christians made of military concepts. Clement of Rome, for example, spoke of God as "he who fights for us and takes our defense (huperma-chos kai huperaspistēs)."[97] When he wished to give an example¦ of the disciplined and hierarchical order which should exist in the Christian Church, he could find no better comparison than the organization of the Roman army, for which he obviously had great admiration. "Who are [our] enemies?" he asked.

> The wicked and those who oppose God's will. Let us campaign, O men, my brethren, as strenuously as we can under his irreproachable orders. Let us consider the soldiers who serve our governors. What discipline! What obedience! What submission in carrying out orders! All are not prefects or tribunes, centurions or captains of fifty and so on; but each in his own rank carries out what is ordered by the emperor and the governors. The great cannot be under the lower, nor can the lower exist without the great.[98]

Since God is our captain, "it is right . . . that we should not be deserters, disobeying his will."[99]

The homily called the *Second Epistle of Clement* likewise devoted a chapter to an extended exhortation to Christian combat, which closely intertwined allusions to military and sporting pursuits.[100] There was similar imagery in Ignatius of Antioch's *Epistle to Polycarp*. "Give satisfaction to him in whose ranks you serve and from whom you get your pay," Ignatius admonished. "Let none of you prove a deserter. Let your baptism be your arms; your faith, your helmet; your love, your spear; your endurance, your armor."[101] In his *Epistle to the Smyrnaeans* he wrote, "By his [Jesus Christ's] resurrection, he raised a standard to rally his saints and faithful forever. . . ."[102]

In the writings of many early Christian authors, Christian warfare took on the aspect of martyrdom. This gave the devil opportunity to launch an attack in the hope of overcoming Christ in the person of the believer. But those who remained constant under persecution were victorious soldiers.[103] Quite frequently, in fact, either in summary fashion[104] or in considerable detail, the Church Fathers identified the Christian who had fought for his faith with the victorious soldier.[105] Among those who elaborated upon this comparison was Minucius Felix, who developed Christian applications for numerous military expressions.[106] This tendency was taken to such an extent that the term *paganus*, which originally and up to AD 300 had meant civilian as opposed to soldier, came eventually to mean non-Christian as opposed to believer. By approximately 420 the evolution of the word was complete.[107] Indeed, the Christian had come to be "the soldier *par excellence.*"[108]

On a broader plane, the apocryphal text of St. Paul's *Martyrdom* proclaimed that Christ was going to make war on the world by fire.[109] It further referred to Christians—always in the same manner—as soldiers in God's service.[110] Justin was certain that it was "the demons and army of the devil" against which the believers must fight.[111] Marcel Simon rightly observed that the early Christians identified this "army of the devil" not only with the pagan masses but also with local authorities that tried slowly to stifle the infant Church or brutally to uproot it.[112] Justin, however, also believed that he could discern Christ's cross in the *vexilla* and *signa* which were carried before the imperial representatives as marks of their authority and power.[113] In the *First Apology* he fully developed the contrast between the two forms of service—imperial and Christian. "It would be ridiculous," he wrote, "when the soldiers whom you have recruited and enrolled stick to their loyalty to you before their own life and parents and native land and all their families, though you have nothing incorruptible to offer them, for us, who desire incorruption, not to endure all things in order to receive what we long for from him who is able to give it."[114]

Pseudo-Justin used military terminology to refer to God, to his Word, and to his faithful, while explaining that each of them actually brought peace instead of war and slaughter.[115] Irenaeus, who frequently alluded to the Old Testament wars,[116] used numerous military metaphors.[117] Clement of Alexandria, for whom it was "a glorious venture to desert to God's side,"[118] envisaged Jesus Christ as a captain of soldiers, mustering his people for action. Clement exclaimed,

> When the shrilling trumpet blows, it assembles the soldiers and proclaims war; and shall not Christ, think you, having breathed to the ends of the earth a song of peace, assemble the soldiers of peace that are his? Yes, and he did assemble, O man, by blood and by word his bloodless army, and to them he entrusted the kingdom of heaven. The trumpet of Christ is his gospel. He sounded it, and we heard. Let us gird ourselves with the armor of peace, "putting on the breastplate of righteousness," and taking up the shield of faith, and placing on our head the helmet of salvation; and let us sharpen "the sword of the spirit, which is the word of God."
>
> Thus does the apostle marshal us in the ranks of peace. These are our invulnerable arms; equipped with these let us stand in array against the evil one. Let us quench the fiery darts of the evil one with the moistened spear-points, those that have been dipped in water by the Word. . . . [119]

In the *Stromata* Clement also wrote,

> It is the business, in my opinion, of the maleficent powers to endeavor to produce somewhat of their own constitution in everything, so as to overcome and make their own those who have renounced them. And it follows, as might be expected, that some are worsted; but in the case of those who engaged in the contest with more athletic energy, the powers mentioned above, after carrying on the conflict in all forms, and advancing even as far as the crown wading in gore, decline the battle, and admire the victors.[120]

Or again, "Our struggle, according to Gorgias Leontinus, requires two virtues—boldness and wisdom . . . you have been trained to meet attacks."[121] "For peace and freedom are not otherwise won, than by ceaseless and unyielding struggles[122] with our lusts . . . [which are] stout and Olympic antagonists."[123]

We must use the *Extracts from Theodotus* more cautiously, for it is hard to distinguish between the ideas of the heretic philosopher and those of his orthodox editor. But the *Extracts* contain powerful expressions which are characteristic of Clement's thought and style. One such is the following description of the heavenly battle which was the lot of both spiritual leaders and simple believers, but from which a special grace would release the gnostic. "From this situation and the battle of the powers the Lord rescues us and supplies peace from the array of powers and angels, in which some are arrayed for us and others against us. For some are like soldiers fighting on our side as servants of God, but others are like brigands. For the evil one girded himself, not taking the sword by the side of the king, but in madly plundering for himself."[124] The gnostic[125] must, however, "put on the Lord's armor and keep body and soul invulnerable—armor that is 'able to quench the darts of the devil,' as the apostle says."[126]

Tertullian, who felt a special repugnance for all military service (although he was the son of a proconsular centurion),[127] nevertheless was among those who used military metaphors most frequently.[128] For example, he was prepared to heap scorn upon the cowardice of Pythagoras "who shrank from the military exploits of which Greece was then so full. . . ."[129] Jesus Christ he saluted as the true *Imperator*.[130] But he also, time and again, took care to stop and explain to his reader that the military metaphors, especially when they applied to Christ, *were* metaphors; they were to be understood figuratively and spiritually, not literally. War in the strict sense of the term produced a proliferation of the evils which were the diametrical opposites of the good things which Jesus Christ had come to bring.[131]

Origen, as we have seen, interpreted the Old Testament wars in light of their underlying spiritual meaning. Thus he continually spoke of the religious life as a combat, of which military battles were but a pale reflection. This form of interpretation was especially characteristic of his homilies on Exodus, Numbers, Joshua, and Judges, from whose military narratives he felt called to extract suitable material for the preaching of his own day.[132] Origen, in fact, was one of the writers who created the expression *Miles Christi*.[133]

Similarly, Cyprian wrote, "It is a good soldier's duty to defend the camp of his general against rebels and enemies. It is the duty of an illustrious leader to keep the standards entrusted to him."[134] In another passage, he described the plight of the believers who were being harassed by the devil's onslaughts. These believers, "standing daily in the front of the battle, are wearied by our combats with an old and well-tried enemy;... [they are enduring] the various and constant attacks of temptations and the struggle of persecution...."[135] If it was glorious for the soldiers of this world to return to their country in triumph after having defeated their enemy, how much better and greater was the glory of those who returned in triumph to Paradise after having vanquished the devil?[136] Cyprian's imitator used military analogies in much the same way.[137]

Commodian's *Instructions* contains a series of pieces which resound with the clash of arms. One of these, a sixteen-verse piece entitled "To the Soldiers of Christ,"[138] was entirely constructed upon the military metaphor. Another piece, "The Daily War," began as follows:

> Fool, you desire to fight, as if wars had ceased.
> From the first created day to the last, battle has been raging.
> Appetite is falling upon you; that is the war; fight against it!
> Lust flatters you, but heed it not; you have won your battle.[139]

Also martial was a comment in the *Didascalia* upon the Book of Ezekiel: "The sword is the judgment; the trumpet is the gospel; and the sentinel is the bishop placed at the head of the Church."[140] Lactantius concluded the epilogue to the *Divine Institutions* with these words, "Let every one train himself to justice, mould himself to self-restraint, prepare himself for the contest, equip himself for virtue, that if by any chance an adversary shall wage war, he may be driven from that which is upright and good by no force, no terror, and no tortures...."[141]

Eusebius of Caesarea, fully in the same tradition, spoke of the martyrs of Lyons as "combatants among the Christians."[142] Elsewhere he quoted approvingly from Denys of Alexandria, who had called the martyr Besas "that brave warrior of God" who had distinguished himself "in the great war of piety...."[143] Eusebius entitled chapter 3 of Book VIII of his *History of the Church* "The Conduct of Those Who Fought in the Persecution"; and in the *Martyrs of Palestine* he again called those who suffered for their faith "true soldiers of Christ."[144] In the same period Athanasius spoke of "these weapons which are the virtues"; thanks to them, enemies would not be able to overrun the positions which the Christians had taken.[145] Finally, Basil used the vocabulary of "combat"—half athletic, half military—to refer not only to the struggle against persecution but, more broadly, to the fight "against the invisible enemies."[146]

The use of this analogy was thus continuous throughout the history of early Christianity. St. John Chrysostom, for instance, spoke of Christian widows as "those who are stripped for the contest" of the ascetic life.[147] He also referred to the devil as "he who makes war" on the faithful.[148] St. John began one of his letters to Olympias with the following words:

How could you have imagined ... that you would lead a life without troubles and without wars? Indeed, if those who fight against others receive a thousand wounds in battles and wars, how could you hope for a tranquil and carefree life—you, who have engaged in combat against the principalities and powers, against the masters of this century of darkness? No, you must not be surprised if you are surrounded by countless wars, conflicts, and troubles of all sorts. Quite the contrary! You should be surprised only if none of this were taking place.[149]

This theme of "combat" took on a very special importance through the development of eremitism, whose discipline and heroism naturally brought to mind military parallels. Aphrahat the Syrian had already commented that "it is the solitaries who are fitted for battle."[150] Pachomius, who founded Coptic cenobitism and who (as we shall see later) had been converted to Christianity through the witness of Christian "draft-refusers," in similar vein exhorted his followers, "Be patient, so that you may be admitted into the legion of the saints."[151] E. Malone has demonstrated that the Christians not only conceived of their sufferings as a continuation of Israel's tribulations; they also viewed monachism as a real self-inflicted martyrdom.[152] These three themes—the Jews' battles, martyrdom, and monachism—were thus organically interrelated, and it is hardly surprising that the common image of combat was used for them all.[153] For example, St. Sabas, when sent to accompany one of his associates on the trip to Alexandria, met his parents there. They urged him to enter the "military chaplaincy" by becoming the priest of the body of troops which his father commanded. Sabas answered bluntly, "I am a soldier (*estratheuthen*) in God's forces and cannot abandon his army. Those who incite me to desertion— I can no longer call them my parents."[154] Another example comes from the life of St. Euthymius. When this saint's first three disciples came to him—they were three brothers from Cappadocia—he began by rejecting one of them who was eunuchoid. Then, in response to the brothers' protest, he relented. But he told the eldest of them, Cosmas, "See that your young brother does not leave his cell. Indeed, it is not right that there be a feminine face[155] in the monastery because of the war waged by the enemy."[156] Similarly, Theodosius was hailed as the one who "for fifty years in the desert fought [and] acted like an athlete. [He] presented himself as crowned victor, and transformed an innumerable crowd into fighters and victors."[157] R. Génier summed up all of these illustrations with the comment, "The afflictive practices of asceticism constituted what the monks called combat." He continued by pointing out rightly in this perspective that asceticism was not at first (as it became later) a matter of "appeasing divine justice by voluntary suffering." For the early monks the objective was rather "to release the soul from the slavery of the body, to break down all the barriers which could stop or even delay its flight toward God."[158]

In the Cappadocian tradition the same theme appears. The Basilian *Preliminary Sketch of the Ascetic Life* was constructed on the concept of the monk as the good soldier of the divine army. The author exclaimed, "Set before thyself a life without house, city, or possessions. Be free, released from all worldly cares. Let not the love of woman enchain thee, nor solicitude for child. For in the divine warfare this cannot be."[159] The English translator, after remarking that the idea of the religious devotee as soldier was common in pre-Christian times as well as throughout the entire period of primitive Christianity, added, "As conditions of life in the world became easier for Christians it was natural to look upon monks as the true soldiers of Christ."[160] St. John Chrysostom also drew an extensive parallel between the monk and the soldier.[161] Centuries later in the West, St. Bernard of Clairvaux devoted an entire treatise to the same subject—*In Praise of the New Militia of the Soldiers of the Temple.*[162]

In Chapter 4 I shall have occasion to show that the life of St. Martin of Tours was an illustration of this transposed "service." Here I shall only mention that the analogy of the

military life applied as well to the believers whom he had
under his supervision. A hermit who had formerly been a
soldier came to St. Martin to ask permission to reclaim his
wife, who at the time was living in a convent. The hermit
argued that he was a soldier of Christ, and that his wife had
also sworn allegiance to the same commander; therefore the
bishop should allow them to serve side by side as soldiers. St.
Martin responded by appealing to the man's military
experience: "When you were in the war in the line of battle,
you certainly never saw a woman standing there and fighting." This "true and rational analogy relating to the life of a
soldier" was enough to convince the monk.[163]

Writing to Paulinus of Nola to congratulate him on a fine
oration, St. Jerome exclaimed, "Bravo for your courage! If
your first exploits [on the battlefield of Christian oratory] are
like this, what will you not do when you are a trained
soldier!"[164]

At the end of the sixth century St. Gregory the Great, in
his *Morals on Job*, transposed the description of the spiritual
struggle to the plane of warfare and combat.[165] This fact is all
the more interesting because in the Book of Job there was no
material which would suggest military imagery. Similarly, the
funeral inscription of the Italian bishop Ticianus (of 476)
began with two lines of striking parallelism:

> Ticianus, priest of Christ, trained in doctrine,
> Praiseworthy soldier of Christ, while he longs
>   for the cross. . . .[166]

Marshaled against the faithful, who thus formed God's
army, were the devil's own battalions which comprised his
triumphal retinue—the *pompa Diaboli*.[167] Even if this last
expression should not be interpreted as strictly as I am doing
here, the severest critic of such an interpretation was still compelled to acknowledge that the evidence indicates that the
primitive Church saw in the unfolding of events a constant

struggle between the army of Christ and that of the devil.[168]

A superficial observer might suppose that the repeated use of martial allegories inevitably implied an exaltation of patriotic and militaristic values.[169] But in reality we usually find a phrase-by-phrase juxtaposition, in which the writers present the *militia mundi* and the *militia Christi* as being mutually exclusive. As James Moffatt commented, "This rich and varied use of military metaphors . . . throws no light upon the opinions cherished by the early Christians about war in itself."[170] Thus Lactantius was able to recount in detail the battles of the Christians—battles which were willed by God and which placed demands upon human courage and endurance comparable to those of carnal warfare.[171] But he began by declaring that the Christian's weapon, with which he would overcome all these difficulties and all opposition, was patience.[172] As we shall see in Chapter 7, in the theological language of that era the connotations of the term patience were similar to those of the term nonviolence in contemporary parlance. In any event, Lactantius's conclusion left no room for ambiguity: "It is not lawful for a just man to serve as a soldier, for justice itself is his military service."[173] It has furthermore been possible to describe St. Gregory the Great as the patron saint of theologians who wish "to maintain the primacy of peace," precisely because he, by using military language allegorically, took all the actual historical content out of the Old Testament's bellicose passages.[174] St. John Chrysostom, in fact, contrasted the battle of the world with the Church's battle, in which "the victim receives the crown, and he who is slaughtered wins the victory." The Church was the only "army which becomes glorious in proportion to the number of its people who are destroyed by their adversaries."[175]

But although most of the early Fathers drew a sharp distinction between these two sorts of service, a few of them seem not to have been so sensitive to this issue. In the letter which he wrote concerning Valerian's persecution,[176] for example, Dionysius of Rome continued the tradition which spoke of courage under persecution in the vocabulary of military conflict. As I have just pointed out, persecution—which made martyrdom the Christian's true conflict—tended as a matter of course to exclude the Christian from participation in other fields of human conflict. Yet Dionysius, without apparently realizing what he was doing,[177] included mention of soldiers in his enumeration of those who were fighting for the Lord. Similarly, Basil, who a century later was still interpreting military service spiritually,[178] nevertheless began by listing soldiers along with athletes and farmers among the many professions which were commonly carried on "in the great house of God which is the Church."[179] With Basil there was thus no longer the slightest indication that spiritual and temporal service might be mutually exclusive.

The arm of spiritual conflict *par excellence* is prayer. And in accordance with the specific injunctions of the New Testament, Christians have never ceased to practice it on behalf of the state. In time of persecution this could take on the form of scathing irony. As Tertullian observed, since God had asked the believers to pray for their enemies, it was certain that they would pray for the state, since it was their greatest enemy.[180]

Generally, however, the accent was different from this. As we have noted in Chapter I, Christians living within the Roman empire knew that the state was responsible for maintaining temporal peace and order. The empire was identical with the civilized world, which they could legitimately hope would be extended to the ends of the earth. So they felt that it would be calamitous if the number of imperial soldiers declined or if their morale plummeted. The best-known document which is symptomatic of this state of mind is Clement of Rome's *Letter*. Only when we recall that it was written in Rome at a time when memories of Nero's persecution were still fresh can we appreciate its full impact. In the

Letter's great prayer just before the final doxology, comes this extended intercession—within the framework of the general providence of God—for the authorities:

Grant that we may be obedient
To your almighty and glorious name,
And to our rulers and governors on earth.

You, Master, gave them imperial power
Through your majestic and indescribable might,
So that we, recognizing it was you who gave them the glory and
honor,
Might submit to them,
And in no way oppose your will.
Grant them, Lord, health, peace, harmony, and stability,
So that they may give no offense in administering the
government you have given them.

For it is you, Master, the heavenly King of eternity,
Who give the sons of men
Glory and honor and authority over the earth's people.
Direct their plans, O Lord,
In accord with "what is good and pleasing to you,"
So that they may administer the authority you have given them,
With peace, considerateness, and reverence,
And so win your mercy.
We praise you, who alone are able to do this
And still better things for us,
Through the High Priest and Guardian of our souls,
Jesus Christ.[181]

Commenting on this text, H. Hemmer wrote,

The Christian authors did not always profess affection for Rome—the Babylon of the Apocalypse—or for the Roman empire, which they sometimes considered to be an instrument of the devil. But the Christians in their assemblies loyally prayed for the princes and governors of civil society. For to do so was in accord with the prevalent doctrines of the Church concerning the respect and obedience which were due to civil authority.[182]

From the earliest days of the Church, continual practice of intercession for the authorities is well attested. It was already clearly affirmed by the martyr Apollonius.[183] Arnobius expressed surprise that the authorities so brutally dispersed the gatherings of the Christians, for in them the believers prayed to the supreme God and besought peace and forgiveness[184] for all: "magistrates, armies, rulers, friends, enemies. ..."[185] An identical conjoining of authorities and enemies is found in Polycarp's injunction to prayer in his *Letter to the Philippians:* "Pray also for emperors and authorities and rulers, and for those who persecute you and hate you and for the enemies of the cross. ..."[186] Justin affirmed, "We worship God only, but in other matters we gladly serve you, recognizing you as emperors and rulers of men, and praying that along with your imperial power you may also be found to have a sound mind."[187]

Tertullian himself pointed out the eminently positive content of this prayer for the state: "We are ever making intercession for all the emperors. We pray for them long life, a secure rule, a safe home, brave armies, a faithful senate, an honest people, a quiet world—and everything for which a man and a Caesar can pray."[188] He even believed that the effects of the prayer were already being revealed: "If we compare ancient disasters, the troubles nowadays are lighter, since the world received the Christians from God. Since that day innocence has tempered the sins of the world, and there have begun to be intercessors with God."[189] The martyr Achatius showed a similar concern for the well-being of the empire. When the emperor's legate said to him, "You live under Roman law, therefore you love our princes," he replied, "Who then is more eager to do so than we are? No one loves the emperor as we do; we unceasingly address urgent prayers to God that he be accorded a long life, that he may govern the peoples with equity, and that his reign may pass in peace. We pray also for the safety of the empire and of the world."[190] And Cyprian wrote, "We always ask for the repulse of enemies and for obtaining showers, and either for the removal or the moderating of adversity; and we pour forth our prayers and, propitiating and addressing God, we entrust constantly and urgently, day and night, for your peace and salvation."[191]

At Caesarea, according to Basil, Christians prayed publicly for their brethren in the armies on the same basis as they interceded for their brethren who were traveling.[192] Eusebius, referring to Licinius's reversion to paganism after 315, reported, "He drove away every Christian from his palace; thus by his own act depriving himself, wretched man, of the prayers to God on his behalf, which after the custom of their fathers they are taught to make for all men."[193] The *Apostolic Constitutions* enjoined the Christians to pray "for the king and all in authority," as well as "for the whole army," so that the Christian community might have peace and tranquillity and be able to glorify the Lord.[194]

The most symptomatic text of all is in Origen's *Contra Celsum*. "If everyone were to do the same as you," Celsus taunted the believers of his day, "there would be nothing to prevent him [the emperor] from being abandoned, alone, and deserted, while earthly things would come into the power of the most lawless and savage barbarians." "If the Romans were to become convinced by the doctrine of the Christians," Origen retorted,

> ... if they pray with complete agreement they will be able to subdue many more pursuing enemies than those that were destroyed by the prayer of Moses when he cried to God and by the prayer of his companions. . . . If all the Romans were convinced and prayed, they would be superior to their enemies, or would not even fight wars at all, since they would be protected by divine power. . . .[195]

Celsus was also distressed that the Christians were neglecting their military obligations, and he exhorted them to change their attitude.[196] Origen responded,

> At appropriate times we render to the emperors divine help, if I may so say, by taking up the whole armor of God. And this we do in obedience to the apostolic utterance which says: "I exhort you, therefore, first to make prayers, supplications, intercessions, and thanksgivings for all men, for emperors, and all that are in authority." Indeed, the more pious a man is, the more effective he is in helping the emperors—more so than the soldiers who go out into the lines and kill all the enemy troops that they can. We would also say this to those who are alien to our faith and ask us to fight for the community and to kill men: that it is also your opinion that the priests of certain images and wardens of the temples of the gods, as you think them to be, should keep their right hand undefiled for the sake of the sacrifices, that they may offer the customary sacrifices to those who you say are gods with hands unstained by blood and pure from murders. And in fact when war comes you do not enlist the priests. If, then, this is reasonable, how much more reasonable is it that, while others fight, Christians also should be fighting as priests and worshippers of God, keeping their right hands pure and by their prayers to God striving for those who fight in a righteous cause[197] and for the emperor who reigns righteously, in order that everything which is opposed and hostile to those who act rightly may be destroyed? Moreover, we who by our prayers destroy all demons which stir up wars, violate oaths, and disturb the peace, are of more help to the emperors than those who seem to be doing the fighting. We who offer prayers with righteousness, together with ascetic practices and exercises which teach us to despise pleasures and not to be led by them, are cooperating in the tasks of the community. Even more do we fight on behalf of the emperor. And though we do not become fellow-soldiers with him, even if he presses for this, yet we are fighting for him and composing a special army of piety through our intercessions to God.[198]

Origen continued by contrasting the human military command which won outward vainglory with that other authority, inward and secret, by which the Christians through prayer acted as priests in behalf of their fellow citizens. Christians thus "do more good to their countries than the rest of mankind, since they educate the citizens and teach them to be devoted to God, the guardian of their city."[199]

Indeed, whatever the nature of the state, the Christian himself was unequivocally a person of peace. This was an expression of his certainty that through the coming of Jesus Christ and the common life of his followers the identical prophecies of Isaiah 2:4 and Micah 4:3 had been fulfilled.[200] The first writer thoroughly to exploit this theme was Justin, who was followed by many others. Commenting on Micah 4:2 ("For the law will go forth from Zion, and the word of the Lord from Jerusalem") Justin wrote,

> We can show you that this has really happened. For a band of twelve men went forth from Jerusalem. They were common men, not trained in speaking. But by the power of God they testified to every race of mankind that they were sent by Christ to teach to all the word of God; and [now] we who once killed each other not only do not make war on each other, but in order not to lie or deceive our inquisitors we gladly die for the confession of Christ.[201]

That was the reason, contrary to what the Jews believed, that the prophecy of verse 4 had also been fulfilled. It had been fulfilled in the Christians, who

> were filled full of war, and slaughter one of another, and every kind of evil, [and] have from out of the whole earth each changed our weapons of war, our swords into ploughshares and our pikes into farming tools, and we farm piety, righteousness, the love of man, faith, and hope which comes from the Father himself through him who was crucified. . . .[202]

Theophilus, a bishop and thus the first representative of what strictly speaking was ecclesiastical authority, enunciated the same theme in more general terms:

It is not only to those of our own tribe (as some think) that we are well-disposed. The prophet Isaiah[203] declared: "Say to those that hate and detest you, you are our brothers, that the name of the Lord may be glorified and that it may be seen in their gladness." And the gospel[204] decreed: "Love your enemies, and pray for those who seek to harm you. For if you love only those that love you, what reward have you? Even the robbers and the tax-collectors do as much."[205]

Irenaeus used the text of Isaiah 11:6-9,[206] but he also returned to the double passage of Isaiah and Micah, giving an exegesis of it which he seems to have modeled upon Justin's *First Apology*. Like Justin, Irenaeus began with Isaiah 4:2, recalling that the apostles had broadcast the good news in all directions beginning from the center—Jerusalem. Then he continued,

If therefore another law and word, going forth from Jerusalem, brought in such a [reign of] peace among the Gentiles which received it [the word], and convinced, through them, many a nation of its folly, then [only] it appears that the prophets spake of some other person [than Christ]. But if the law of liberty, that is, the word of God, preached by the apostles (who went forth from Jerusalem) throughout all the earth, caused such a change in the state of things, that these [nations] did form the swords and war-lances into ploughshares, and changed them into pruning-hooks for reaping the corn, [that is] into instruments used for peaceful purposes, and that they are now unaccustomed to fighting, but when smitten, offer also the other cheek, then the prophets have not spoken these things of any other person, but of him who effected them. This person is our Lord. . . .[207]

Once again a passage from Origen is illuminating:

To those who would ask us where we have come from or who is our author, we reply that we came in accordance with the commands of Jesus to beat the spiritual swords that fight and insult us into ploughshares, and to transform the spears that formerly fought against us into pruning-hooks. No longer do we take the sword against any nation, nor do we learn war any more, since we have become sons of peace through Jesus who is our author instead of following the traditional customs, by which we were "strangers to the covenants." [208]

In the *Dialogus de recta in Deum Fide,* which is possibly also by Origen, the author explicitly stated that the text of Isaiah 2:3 applied to the new order which Christ had already established, and that his faithful must therefore obey it. [209] So also commented Pseudo-Cyprian. [210] A clear echo of this theme can be heard in Cyprian himself: "God has willed that iron be used for tilling the earth; therefore he has forbidden its use for killing one's neighbor." [211]

Tertullian, after quoting the same text, asked rhetorically,

Who else, therefore, are understood but *we,* who, fully taught by the new law, observe these practices—the old law being obliterated, the coming of whose abolition the action itself [of beating swords into ploughs, etc.] demonstrates? For the custom of the old law was to avenge itself by the vengeance of the sword, and to pluck out "eye for eye," and to inflict retaliatory revenge for injury. But the new law's custom is to point to clemency, and to convert to tranquillity the pristine ferocity of "swords" and "lances," and to remodel the pristine execution of "war" upon the rivals and foes of the law into the pacific actions of "ploughing" and "tilling" the land. [212]

In his treatise against Marcion, Tertullian once again cited this prophecy:

"And they shall break down their swords into ploughshares, and their spears into pruning-hooks," that is, all the devices of injurious minds and hostile tongues and of all malice and blasphemy, they shall convert into the interests of moderation and peace. And "nation shall not take up sword against nation," that is, follow up hostilities: so that here too you may learn that the Christ who was promised was not one powerful in war, but a bringer of peace. [213]

Eusebius, in his *Praeparatio Evangelica,* referred to these same passages. He commented,

> That which the prophecies foretold has been fulfilled precisely. The various independent governments were destroyed by the Romans; and Augustus became the sole master of the entire universe at the very moment when our Savior came down to earth. Since that time no nation has waged war on another nation, and life is no longer squandered in the former confusion.

In his polemic against Porphyrus, who was to him what Celsus had been to Origen,[214] Eusebius recalled that in other eras the world had been torn by civil as well as foreign wars. But "our Savior's perfectly pious and peaceful teaching has brought about two things at once—the destruction of polytheistic error, and the immediate cessation of the ancestral evil which is conflict between peoples." In a later chapter he returned to these affirmations: "Our Savior's teaching has freed all men from the evils of former times. . . . Since his coming there is no longer a multiplicity of sovereigns reigning over the world's peoples."[215]

Athanasius claimed that in the time of their idolatry the Greeks and barbarians had been rent by international and civil wars; but by becoming Christians they had become peaceful.[216] He then asked rhetorically, "Who . . . is he who has done these things and has united in peace those who hated each other, save the beloved Son of the Father, the common Savior of all, Jesus Christ, who by his own love underwent all things for our salvation? Even from the beginning, moreover, this peace that he was to administer was foretold [by the text of Isaiah 2:4]. . . . "[217] The proof of this, Athanasius argued, was the state—idolatrous, savage, and warlike—of those who were still barbarians:

> But when they hear the teaching of Christ, forthwith they turn from fighting to farming, and instead of arming themselves with

swords extend their hands in prayer. In a word, instead of fighting each other, they take up arms against the devil and the demons, and overcome them by their self-command and integrity of soul. These facts are proof of the Godhead of the Savior, for he has taught men what they could never learn among the idols. It is also no small exposure of the weakness and nothingness of demons and idols, for it was because they knew their own weakness that the demons were always setting men to fight each other, fearing lest, if they ceased from mutual strife, they would turn to attack the demons themselves. For in truth the disciples of Christ, instead of fighting each other, stand arrayed against demons by their habits and virtuous actions, and chase them away and mock at their captain the devil.[218]

Among Christian authors there was undeniably a tendency, most notably in these last texts, to broaden the applicability of this prophecy. But this does not weaken the "antimilitarist" argument. It rather reinforces it, for it further demonstrates the idea's important place in Christian thinking. All of these writers knew that the Christians were already participating in the kingdom of peace which the prophets had foretold and which Christ had come to found. The whole world would not recognize this sovereignty until the last day; but the believers for their part had no reason or excuse to disobey its laws.

On this theme St. John Chrysostom made a somewhat idiosyncratic comment. From his vantage point it was scandalous that in former times "the law had called everyone without exception to military service." But he noted that in the age in which he was writing it was only volunteers who were soldiers. Even though the believers might still hear about far-off wars, they were therefore no longer required to take part in them. The prophecy of Isaiah 2 had thereby been fulfilled. For it did not say that "there shall be no more wars," but simply that "nation shall not take up sword against nation."[219] This was a curious defense of the mercenary. No doubt it extended the implicit position of the writers of the previous period—that there must be soldiers, but that the Christians must not be among them. But Chrysostom's position was equivocal, for by his time all of the inhabitants of the empire were deemed to be Christians.

The theme of the Christian's peaceableness, both with and without explicit allusion to the prophecies of Isaiah and Micah, thus recurred again and again in the writings of the Fathers. Here I shall quote one final example—from Clement of Alexandria, who claimed in his *Paedagogus*, "We Christians are a peaceful race . . . bred not for war but for peace." He proceeded to develop this idea according to a dual analogy borrowed from the world of music. Man was an instrument designed to play an irenic tune; and of all the musical instruments, warlike or lustful, which humanity could play, the Christian used but one: "The one instrument of peace, the Word alone by which we honor God, is what we employ."[220] Of course we dare not forget the warlike prophecies which I have cited earlier, such as, "If you are unwilling and do not heed me, the sword shall devour you."[221] But we should remember that as a rule the early Church well understood that it was not the Christians' duty to constitute themselves into a secular arm for God. As we have seen, the consequences for their self-understanding when they happened to forget this were disastrous.

At the end of the previous chapter I argued that eschatological certainty freed Christian thought from the complete domination of political power. Let me close this chapter by noting that the Christians, by interpreting the whole Bible in light of the law of love which had been most clearly revealed in the gospel, could use the military narratives and bellicose expressions while at the same time disarming them of their brutal character. They knew that their battle was a real one. But it took place on a different plane, and with quite different weapons, from the battles of the world.

Chapter 3

The Christian Attitude

In the first two chapters I have established the framework within which early Christians reflected concerning matters of war and military service. We must now turn to their actual behavior. I shall deal in turn with service of the state, the Christians' feelings about their earthly country, and their respect for life. In the previous chapters I have already discussed the first two matters extensively, but primarily on a theoretical basis and within a theological perspective. Let us now look at them more concretely—as they related to the believers' daily life.

The early Christians could recognize no absolute master but God. In general it was right and proper for them to obey God through his representatives on earth—the temporal authorities; but they could never submit themselves blindly to an obedience which would make them slaves of man rather than slaves of God. They knew that the political and military powers, as soon as they were regarded as autonomous, became demonic realities. It was then that the systematic opposition which we have already examined—between the *militia mundi* and the *militia Christi*—became necessary. Throughout the world the devil, "the Prince of this world," was at work. Christians could discern his activity outside the Church in the persecution which he inspired, within the Church in the lives of heretics and backsliders, in the believers themselves through the temptations of the outer world, and in the "old Adam" who still slumbered in their hearts.

Ignatius devoted chapter 7 of his *Letter to the Romans* to this point. "The prince of this world," he wrote, "wants to kidnap me [away from God]." He showed that battle was not only thrust on the Church from outside; on the contrary, he encountered the enemy within the Church, in the guise of believers who through compassion were trying to save him from martyrdom. On a deeper level, he even faced the devil in himself, in the form of dread and discouragement. The immediacy of the devil's role is also evident in the beginning of chapter 3 of the *Martyrdom of Polycarp*. Referring to the attempt by torture to make Polycarp and his companions deny Christ, the account of their martyrdom concluded, "Many were the stratagems the devil used again them."

Eusebius in typical fashion attributed the wars which had ravaged the world before the establishment of Christianity to the demons which reigned as masters over the nations that worshiped them.[1] In contrast to the kingdom of God, Tertullian regarded the whole world as the camp over which the devil's standard flew.[2] The devil and his fallen angels had penetrated everywhere.[3] Tertullian even declared that the world was "the church of the devil."[4] The *Ascension of Isaiah* promised that the princes, angels, and false gods of this world would all be subject to the same judgment, for all had rejected God and had asserted, "We alone are and there is none beside us."[5] Ignatius stressed that the prince of this world had not known about the miraculous events of Christ's virgin birth and redemptive death. Yet it was by these events that the devil's ancient hegemony had been destroyed, since God had manifested himself in human form to realize the new order, which was eternal life.[6]

Christ's kingship was very different from the Roman

Empire. For had Christ ever done as the emperor was doing? "Did he ever," Arnobius asked, "as he claimed royal power for himself, infest the whole world with fiercest legions, and of nations at peace from the beginning did he destroy and exterminate some and force others with necks bent under the yoke to be obedient to him?"[7] For this reason Tatian did not hesitate to place royalty and military power in the same category as riches and fornication—as things which he as a Christian rejected. He declared, "I do not wish to be a king ... I decline military command...."[8]

Although these two dominions were in parallel, they were also in opposition to each other. Tertullian, for example, "often compared baptism, the *sacramentum fidei*, with *sacramentum militiae*, or military oath";[9] but he always did so to show their opposition to each other. Ignatius exclaimed, "Not the wide bounds of earth nor the kingdoms of this world will avail me anything. 'I would rather die' and get to Jesus Christ, than reign over the ends of the earth."[10]

The most acute statement of this contradiction is to be found in Hippolytus's *Commentary on Daniel*:

> The Lord was born in the forty-second year of Caesar Augustus, during whose reign the Roman Empire began to reach its zenith. It was also this period in which the Lord through his apostles summoned all nations and all tongues to make them into a nation of faithful Christians, who bear in their hearts the new and sovereign name. That is why the currently reigning empire has attempted to imitate us, in accordance with Satan's activity. This empire likewise collects the most nobly born men from all nations, arming them for war and calling them Romans. That is why the first census took place under Augustus, at the very moment of the Lord's birth in Bethlehem; so that the men of this world, who are brought together by an earthly king, should assume the name of Romans, while on the other hand, those who believe in the heavenly King should take the name of Christians, bearing on their forehead the sign at which death turns and flees.[11]

One of the most striking practical applications of this attitude is given us by St. Martin. In the next chapter I shall recount the narrative of this in detail. Here I shall only point out that at the very moment of receiving a *donativum* Martin decided that he had no right to accept this gift of money, for thereafter he did not expect to go on in the imperial service. So he told the emperor, "Hitherto I have served you as a soldier; allow me now to become a soldier to God. Let the man who is to serve you receive your donative. I am the soldier of Christ; it is not lawful for me to fight."[12] Several centuries earlier a similar dialogue had occurred between Polemon, verger of the pagan temple, and the martyr Pionius. " 'Surely you are aware,' said the verger Polemon, 'of the emperor's edict commanding us to sacrifice to the gods.' 'We are aware,' said Pionius, 'of the commandments of God ordering us to worship him alone.' Polemon said, 'Come then to the marketplace; there you will change your minds.' Sabina and Asclepiades said, 'We obey the living God.' "[13]

When Christ's reign would finally and visibly be realized, earthly empires would disappear. In fact, it would be the Lord Jesus himself—as Irenaeus remarked in a matter-of-fact fashion, as if stating something quite obvious—who would be the stone who would shatter the feet of clay of the last empire.[14] But this necessary differentiation did not imply a Manichean separation, for the Christians knew that even the wicked were under God's rule, and he made use of them.

Origen even went so far as to question whether the Word had not assigned tasks to the evil demons "like public executioners in cities and officers appointed for unpleasant but necessary work in states...."[15] He had been careful, however, to warn his readers beforehand that such an argument should not make them think that

the nature of evils is not entirely pernicious because something which is thought to be evil for a particular individual may possibly be of advantage to the universe. However lest anyone should misunderstand my opinion and find in it an excuse for crime on the ground that his sin is, or at any rate could be, beneficial to the world as a whole, I will say that while God preserves the free will of each man, he makes use of the evil of bad men for the ordering of the whole, making them useful to the universe; yet such a man is none the less guilty, and as such he has been appointed to perform a function which is repulsive to the individual but beneficial to the whole. It is, to take an illustration from cities, as though one said that a man, who had committed certain crimes and on that account was sentenced to do certain public services of benefit to the community, was doing something of benefit to the whole city, although he himself was engaged in a repulsive task and in a position in which no one of even slight intelligence would want to be.[16]

St. Gregory of Nazianzus reported the following dialogue between the prefect Modestus—who had been successively a Christian under Constantius, an apostate under Julian, and a fanatical Arian under Valens—and St. Basil. Modestus reproached Basil for not joining the popular movement to Arianism, since it was the religion of the sovereign. Basil replied, "My King to whom I am subject does not wish it. I cannot agree to worship a fellow-creature when I myself am a creature of God and am invited to be a god."[17] Later Modestus asked whether Basil would be happy to have him in his congregation. To this Basil responded affirmatively, but with the following explanation: "In fact you also are the work of God, just like the other believers for whom I am responsible. For the mark of the Christian is not his external rank but his faith."[18]

Since the emperor was thus subject to God, he came to occupy a place which was highly respectable—subordinate but essential. Already in the late second century Tertullian was quite firm on this point.[19] Later writers, especially Eusebius, developed the argument further, although with some exaggeration, as we have seen. Eusebius in fact devoted the

entire first book of his *Life of Constantine* to demonstrating
that God honors pious princes but destroys tyrants.
Constantine, the only Roman power-holder who was a friend
of God, was a shining example of the godlike life. In chapter
16 of the same book Eusebius recounted a significant anecdote
which showed that good Christians also made reliable officials. Emperor Constantius, according to this account, having called numerous Christians to serve him as advisers, began
by ordering them to a sacrifice to idols under pain of being expelled from court. In this way he ascertained which advisers
were genuinely faithful to their God and kept these, saying,
"Those who had been false to their God must be unworthy of
the confidence of their prince."[20]

Even Basil, whose proud retort to the misuse of authority
I have quoted above, was eager to cooperate with political
power whenever possible.[21] And he required that others follow
his example. Thus he vigorously urged a Christian, who had
long been an official, not to reject appointment as a *censitor*
(census taker). "Since the Lord did not wish the country of
Ibora to be in the power of knavish men, nor the taking of the
census to be like a slave market, but he wished each one to be
registered as is right, accept the office, as is right, but still securing for you approval from God."[22]

Well before Basil, even Tertullian had allowed the faithful a considerable margin of liberty to enable them to maintain contact with society. Tertullian saw no reason why Christian women should not go to visit their pagan friends and relatives.[23] He authorized believers to take part in the pagan rites
which were part of the normal round of family ceremonies. To
be sure, believers were not to do this in a light-hearted manner. "But since the Evil One has surrounded the world with
idolatry, we may legitimately be present on some occasions
when we are at the service of a man, not an idol."[24]
Tertullian's position had other applications as well: "So we
Christians may, if necessary, allow the bordered *toga*

praetexta to the boys and the stole to the girls: as a mark of birth, not authority; of family, not office; of class, not religion."[25]

Tertullian applied the same principle, more generally, to participation in the state. The Christians claimed for themselves the title of Roman, the same designation as that of the empire's other citizens.[26] If since the rise of Christianity the Roman state had suffered, it had been solely the fault of the pagans, who had not been willing to acknowledge the true God[27] and who had bled the world through their persecutions of the Christians.[28] The believers should be ready to serve the magistrates and the civil power. They should even be ready to assume these positions in person if necessary. The only thing they must refuse to do is to take part in idolatry.[29] The emperor was a mere man, of course, but God had placed him in the highest station on earth. By virtue of this, he was entitled to the respect, loyalty, and obedience of his subjects.[30]

Obviously, the problem lay in finding out where real idolatry began, since that was the borderline which the Christians dared not cross. Tertullian, it is true, defended the positive qualities of the world—at times vehemently—against Marcion;[31] but he also remarked, referring in this case to the spectacles, "For the world is God's; what is worldly is the devil's."[32]

The Fathers thus attempted to preserve a clear hierarchy of values. On occasion they even cited the Jewish Sabbath as an example and symbol of the Christian's freedom in temporal matters as a result of his submission and responsibility to God. The day of prescribed rest signified "that the soul should not become weary in earthly affairs nor submit to a servitude incompatible with the service of God."[33] All the goods and governments of this world must be made secondary "to true piety and faith in our Saviour and Lord Jesus Christ."[34] In his *Homily on St. Lucian,* St. John Chrysostom observed that the martyrs had responded to all of the magistrate's questions

with the identical phrase, "I am a Christian." He then commented, "He who answers thus has declared everything at
once—his country, profession, family; the believer belongs to
no city on earth but to the heavenly Jerusalem. The Apostle
has said it."[35]

Here, summed up in a few words, are all the elements of
a *de facto* divorce between patriotism and the Christian faith,
a divorce which has its roots in the tradition of the martyrs.
For instance, immediately after St. Sabina's companions had
proclaimed, "We are Christians," a pagan asked her while on
the way to prison, "Why could you not have died in your own
native city?" Sabina replied, "What is my native city? I am
the sister of Pionius."[36] In the same vein, St. Augustine's
mother, Monica, who was dying far from her home, proudly
declared that her location was a matter of complete insignifi-
cance to her, since her earthly country was no longer what
counted in her eyes.[37]

Similarly, Eusebius related that as Pamphilus and his
companions in martyrdom were being interrogated, they all
exchanged their names for those of Old Testament prophets,
"thus manifesting . . . the Jew which is one inwardly and the
genuine and pure Israel of God. When Firmilian [the judge]
had heard, then, some such name from the martyr's lips, not
understanding the force of what was said, he next asked him
what his city was. But the martyr let fall a second expression in
harmony with the former one, saying that Jerusalem was his
city—meaning, to be sure, that one of which it was said by
Paul, 'But the Jerusalem that is above is free, which is our
mother,' and 'Ye are come into mount Zion, and unto the city
of the living God, the heavenly Jerusalem.' This was the one
he meant. But the other had his thoughts fixed on this world
here below, and enquired closely and carefully as to what city
it was, and in what part of the world it was situated."[38] In fact,
it was in the Old Testament covenant that Eusebius sought to
root the differentiation between the Jews, a this-worldly

people similar in the last resort to any other individual nation, and the Hebrews, the spiritual people who were therefore the legitimate ancestors of the Christian community. The Christians—like the Hebrews—were thus freed from national particularisms[39] and they constituted a "third race" (of which more later).

We should also note the clear implication of the form of greeting which Christians habitually used in their letters. Clement of Rome himself began his *Letter to the Corinthians* with the words "the Church of God (hē paroikousa Rhōmēn) to the Church of God (tē(i) paroikousē(i) Korinthon)."[40] In a footnote on the first page of his critical edition of the *Letter*, H. Hemmer stressed that the sense of paroikousa is "one who lives as a foreigner," in contrast to katoikousa, which means "a resident citizen." He then briefly traced the history of this Christian idea, which originated here and has led to our modern "parishes." Translating the same paroikōn, F. Sagnard suggested "one who sojourns on earth."[41] In a footnote he commented, referring to an article by Labriolle,[42] that the word "applies primarily to the foreigner domiciled in a country: hence the sense of temporary residence. For the Christian the word meant life here below as opposed to the life of the heavenly fatherland (katoikia, in Gregory of Nazianzus, *Or. fratr. Caesarii*, VII)."

Cyril of Scythopolis, the biographer of the hermit saints of the Palestinian desert, regularly introduced each of them as "citizens of Heaven" (ho ouranopolitēs)[43], and Chrysostom gave the same appellation to the whole community of monks.[44]

Thus the Christians, who relied heavily on the true present community (the Church), and who were living in expectation of the future community (the kingdom), tended to withdraw from the world which was rejecting them. Hermas, at the beginning of the second century, developed this idea as follows:

You know that you slaves of God live in a foreign country, for your city is far from this city. So if you know your city in which you are going to live, why do you prepare lands and expensive establishments and buildings and useless rooms here? So the man who prepares these things for this city cannot return to his own city. Foolish, doubtful, wretched man, don't you understand that all these things belong to someone else, and are in the power of someone else? For the lord of this city will say, "I do not want you to live in my city, but get out of this city, for you do not observe my laws." So if you have lands and dwellings and many other possessions, what will you do with your land and house and all the other things you have prepared for yourself, when you are put out by him? For the lord of this country can justly say to you, "Either observe my laws or get out of my country." So what are you going to do, when you have a law in your own city? For the sake of your lands and your other property, are you going to repudiate your law altogether and live by the law of this city? Take care that it does not prove disadvantageous to repudiate your law. For if you make up your mind to return to your city, you will not be received, because you have repudiated the law of your city, and you will be shut out of it. So take care; as one who is living in a foreign land, provide for yourself no more than an adequate competence, and be ready, so that when the master of this city wants to put you out of it for disobeying his law, you can leave his city and go to your city and joyfully observe your own law, uninjured.[45]

Chapters 5 to 8 of the homily called the *Second Epistle of Clement* developed the same argument—that since the truth was not of this world one could live there only as an alien: "Ceasing to tarry in this world, let us do the will of him who called us and let us not be afraid to leave this world."[46] There followed a fragment which he quoted from an unknown gospel. "You will be like lambs among wolves," Jesus warned Peter. "What if the wolves tear the lambs to pieces?" Peter asked. Jesus replied, "After their death the lambs should not fear the wolves."[47] The homily continued by admonishing believers to regard this world's goods as foreign things and not to desire them, for those who coveted them were straying from the path of righteousness.[48] It was fruitless simultaneously to attempt to serve God and Mammon.[49] The present age and the age to come were at enmity with each other.[50] Finally, in chapter 8 the author declared the earth to be a place of penitence, and one's sojourn on earth to be a time during which the earthenware vessel could still be molded; afterwards, on the other hand, sin would be incurable, as a fired vessel could no longer alter its shape.

For this reason Tertullian admonished the Christian, "You are only a pilgrim in this world, you are a citizen of the Heavenly City, the Jerusalem on high."[51] Whenever he discussed the verse "Render unto Caesar . . ." he interpreted it as narrowly as possible. Whereas the believer owed Caesar the pieces of silver on which his effigy was printed, he owed God his whole being, which was fashioned in God's image.[52] Tertullian used pointed words to emphasize and sharpen this dichotomy. Boldly he explained that the Christian was obliged to pray for the emperor precisely because the emperor was his greatest enemy. The Christian indeed was always to intercede for and seek the good of the one who was persecuting him.[53] As a declaration of loyalty this was quite original! And in light of the clarity with which the final proclamation of the *Apology* sounded the death knell of governmental absolutism, it is hard to imagine how anyone could view Tertullian as a forerunner of caesaropapism: "You [judges and magistrates] condemn us. God absolves us." This appeal from earthly justice to divine justice was unanswerable; in the face of so radical a challenge, no earthly justice could henceforth claim to be absolute.

Tertullian, far from being content with the knowledge that he had justified himself by this appeal, then proceeded to counterattack. He gloated over the wreckage of a world which he knew was already doomed to eternal vengeance. What a sight it will be, and sooner than men think, when the Lord will appear upon the clouds in the sky in triumph! For some it will be a day of joy and glory; for others it will be a day of retribution. The pagans, the princes of this world, the unworthy magistrates who have condemned Christians, even the philosophers and the poets—the whole lot will roast in eternal fire.[54] It is true that, in accordance with Tertullian's general dialectical approach, only the thought that vengeance remained in God's hands enabled him to write at the same time pages of considerable ruthlessness and sentences of authentic Christianity.[55]

Tertullian repeatedly pointed out the desperate plight of the Christians' persecutors—as well as of other non-Christians.[56] He was intensely concerned to save as many of these as possible from the "eternal flames." But his argument, which was in any case not peculiarly his own, provided the Christians' adversaries with more than one pretext to accuse them of being enemies of the human race. Tertullian responded to that charge in the second paragraph of the *Apology:* "Truth asks no favors in her cause, since she has no surprise at her present position. Truth knows that she is a stranger on earth and easily finds enemies among men of another allegiance, but she knows that her race, home, hope, recompense, honor are in heaven."[57] We can appreciate the full significance of this passage only when we remember that the *Apology's* purpose was to prove to the pagans that the Christians, far from being a danger to the empire, were in fact its best upholders and guardians.[58]

St. Cyprian similarly declared, "We have renounced the world and as strangers and foreigners sojourn here for a time. . . . We account Paradise our country; we have already begun to look upon the patriarchs as our parents. Why do we not hasten and run, so that we can see our country, so that we can greet our parents?"[59] In the same vein, Clement of Alexandria wrote, "Let the Athenian, then, follow the laws of Solon, the Argive those of Phoroneus, and the Spartan those of Lycurgus. But if you record yourself among God's people, then heaven is your fatherland and God your lawgiver."[60]

These assertions were in harmony with the attitude, already evident in the *Preaching of Peter*,[61] which considered the Christians to be a race apart, a third race alongside of the two old races which had until then divided the world among themselves.[62] This idea was contagious. Soon the adversaries of Christianity were reproaching the believers for having formed a *latebrosa* and *lucifugax natio*,[63] "a new race of men without country or tradition, in league against the religious and civil institutions."[64]

This was one of the topics in Origen's great debate with Celsus:

> Celsus exhorts us also to accept public office in our country if it is necessary to do this for the sake of the preservation of the laws and of piety. But we know of the existence in each city of another sort of country created by the Logos of God. And we call upon those who are competent to take office, who are sound in doctrine and life, to rule over the churches. We do not accept those who love power. But we put pressure on those who on account of their great humility are reluctant to take upon themselves the common responsibility of the Church of God . . . If Christians do avoid these responsibilities, it is not with the motive of shirking the public services of life. But they keep themselves for a more divine and necessary service in the Church of God for the sake of the salvation of men.[65]

For a long time after the Constantinian reconciliation between Church and state, Christian preaching continued to contrast the two kingdoms and to call for a choice between the two "nationalities," the earthly and the heavenly:

> As long as you do not strip yourself of fleshly morals, you are of a different race and an alien, and you can have neither participation nor communion in the Holy One, in the Christ who comes from heaven; for one must be heavenly to approach what is heavenly, and nobody can become heavenly without first rejecting what is earthly.[66]

S. Giet has made a thorough study of this problem in the case of St. Basil. This scholar, while completely rejecting Victor Duruy's accusation that Basil was indifferent to the welfare of the empire, has nevertheless conceded: "Basil never had the attachment to the empire that a Roman had to his city nor the devotion of an Athenian who was ready to sacrifice his life for his country's independence. If any one is surprised at this, let him be! Basil was a Cappadocian, not a Roman."[67] If Basil had a deep love for his country, his patris, it was for the whole of Cappadocia,[68] or even, on one occasion, for the village where he was born, but never for the political and national reality taken altogether.[69] His indifference to his country in the wider sense is less attributable, however, to outmoded regionalist considerations than to his Christian faith, which impelled him "to detach himself increasingly from the empire because of a presentiment that a new order was going to replace the old one."[70]

It was also a result of his understanding that "the time had come when God would apportion the whole world to his people."[71] In this connection it is interesting to note the shift in usage wherby the word oikoumenē, which had commonly denoted the whole Roman world, for Basil came to encompass the totality of the inhabited world without consideration of political boundaries, because Christian churches were springing up everywhere.[72]

Also noteworthy is St. Gregory Nazianzus's discourse in memory of Basil, in the course of which Gregory recounted a remarkable dialogue between Basil and the prefect Modestus.[73] Basil told the prefect, "I know no exile, since nowhere is there a boundary for me. The earth I live on at the moment does not belong to me; but the land to which I might be banished is mine, or rather, it belongs to God, whose itinerant lodger I am."[74] A little later Basil replied as follows to the threat of physical tortures: "How long could these have any effect on one who is detached from his body? Unless, that is, you are speaking of the death blow, which is the only thing which you really control. But death will be a kindness for me, for it will send me more swiftly to God for whom I live and for whom I fulfill my earthly functions. It is for him that I have died already as far as I can, and I have long been in haste to arrive at his side." When Modestus expressed astonishment at this, Basil explained that it was this attitude which made bishops so dauntless when it came to defending the faith. In all other matters they, in accordance with divine law, were accommodating and humbler than anyone else, not only toward the authorities, but equally toward everyone.[75]

But the most systematic statement of the Christian's paradoxical situation in the world occurs in the famous chapters 5 and 6 which form the central core of the *Epistle to Diognetus*. The Christians

> live in Greek and barbarian cities alike, as each man's lot has been cast, and follow the customs of the country in clothing and food and other matters of daily living, at the same time they give proof of the remarkable and admittedly extraordinary constitution of their own commonwealth. They live in their own countries, but only as aliens. They have a share in everything as citizens, and endure everything as foreigners. Every land is their fatherland, and yet for them every fatherland is a foreign land.[76] . . . It is true that they are "in the flesh" but they do not live "according to the flesh." They busy themselves on earth, but their citizenship is in heaven.[77] . . . To put it simply: What the soul is in the body, that Christians are in the world. The soul is dispersed through all the members of the body, and Christians are scattered through all the cities of the world. The soul dwells in the body, but does not belong to the body, and Christians dwell in the world, but do not belong to the world.[78] . . . The soul is shut up in the body, and yet itself holds the body together; while Christians are restrained in the world as in a prison, and yet themselves hold the world together. The soul, which is immortal, is housed in a mortal dwelling; while Christians are settled among corruptible things, to wait for the incorruptibility that will be theirs in heaven.[79]

As Lietzmann commented, "Thus the Church is the origin and goal of all earthly phenomena; but this does not mean that she consists in this world, and still less, by this world. . . . The idea of an antithesis between the divine and earthly state, to which Augustine's most important work gave classical expression, belongs to the original essence of Christian self-consciousness within the Church."[80] This idea was expressed, for example, in a passage in the *Life of Cyprian*. "To the Christian, the whole of this world is one home. While honestly serving God, he is a stranger even in his own city. Among the parents themselves of his earthly life, he is a stranger."[81]

To understand this conception properly, we should note that it operated on two levels, which one can view as complementary, but which were also in a sense contradictory. First of all, the Christians considered every nation, every empire, as incomplete. Because they enlarged the concept of service and love of the commonwealth to world-encompassing dimensions, they refused to let themselves be enclosed within the limits of a narrow nationalism. This expansion of brotherhood to all men whoever they may be can be summed up in Tertullian's famous formula: "One state we know, of which all are citizens—the universe."[82] I shall be discussing this in a moment. But at the very time that the Christians claimed that they were putting the world before their particular country, they were simultaneously accusing the entire world of its guilt. And what was true for the world obviously reflected *a fortiori* upon the empire which was a part of it: the Christians' real country was heaven. The present system was fallen and sinful, and was therefore completely uninteresting. One could only let this mad planet go its own way and desire personally to leave it as soon as possible.

Such an attitude is obviously rooted in the New Testament.[83] But unless one is careful it may rapidly lead to an attitude justifying Marx's accusation that "religion is the opium of the people."[84] Some early Christian texts are disquieting for precisely this reason. In chapter 5 of his *Letter to the Romans,* for example, Ignatius told of his ardent desire for martyrdom. If the wild beasts—to which he was about to be thrown— turned away from him, he would if necessary compel them. For, as he continued in the following chapter, what men called life was really death, and what they called death is eternal life. To those who were trying to persuade him to avoid martyrdom, he therefore wrote, "Sympathize with me, my brothers! Do not stand in the way of my coming to life— do not wish death on me. Do not give back to the world one who wants to be God's. Do not trick him with material things. Let me get into the clear light and manhood will be mine. Let me imitate the passion of my God."[85]

It is equally impressive that as late as the end of the sixth century a man like Gregory the Great could insist that the Christian's only true country was heaven: "The good [persons] that are married,[86] . . . while they give up everything that is of the world, do as it were advance to their heavenly country by the paths of earth." There were pagans of good will who practiced good works, because they wanted to hasten toward the "land of life eternal," "the eternal country." But the foolish had other preoccupations. "They never bend the keenness of desire to the contemplation of their eternal country, but forsaking themselves amidst those things in which they are cast away, instead of their country they love the exile which is their lot." The genuine Christians, on the other hand, aspired

> to have a place among the citizens above; and each one of them, while yet in the body an inhabitant of the world, in mind already soars beyond the world, bewails the weariness of the exile which he endures, and with the ceaseless incitements of love urges himself on to the country on high. When he sees grieving how that which he lost is eternal, he finds the salutary counsel, to look down upon this temporal scene which he is passing through. . . .[87]

Commodian expressed this self-distancing of the Christians from the earthly city. In his *Carmen Apologeticum* he did so by employing against the state a verbal imagery of astonishing violence.[88]

The Christians also translated this "alienation" into action. Already in AD 70, at the siege of Jerusalem, the Christians abandoned the city before the battle began. It is not clear whether this was because they were convinced that the Mosaic faith was already doomed and finished, because they knew that their Master had forbidden them to take the sword, or merely because they wanted to save their lives. In any case, Eusebius, who reported the fact, was ready to attribute it to a direct revelation from God.[89] Cardinal Daniélou, without mentioning this flight in particular, attached great significance to the choice which the Christians made at about that time. In fact, he considered that by far the greatest danger for a Christianity born within a Jewish environment was that it might sink into nationalism, with the threefold risk that the Christian community might be physically destroyed by repression, that the believers by becoming completely absorbed in politics might turn away from the faith, and finally that Christian universalism might be compromised. Daniélou argued that both Christ and St. Paul saw this danger clearly and reacted against it. It is thus to their teaching, when properly understood, that one must attribute "the incontrovertible fact of the refusal [by the Christians of the early centuries] of military service."[90]

Two centuries later, at the siege of Alexandria, Eusebius of Laodicea, who was among the besiegers, managed to communicate with Anatolius, the bishop of the invested city. Together they made arrangements for the escape of the women and children, but especially of all members of the church.[91] The text is rather confused. But in any case, it emerges that the two bishops with all their power encouraged and fostered desertion. Neither they nor their historian (Eusebius of Caesarea) apparently saw anything reprehensible in this. Most of the early historians were anxious to interpret such cases of military disobedience, which I shall be discussing in the next chapter, along identical lines—as a betrayal of human solidarity which was at least objective. In the reply which the martyr Pionius made to his fellow citizens, however, there was no scorn and mistrust for the world; on the contrary, there was a fertile tension between it and ultimate values. When pressed to save himself from torture by recanting, Pionius responded, "Life is good, but the life that we long for is better; so too is light, but we long for the one true light. All these things are indeed good, and we do not run from them as though we are eager to die or because we hate God's works. Rather, we despise these things which ensnare us because of the superiority of those other great goods."[92]

A final element which is essential to the Christian attitude to war is all too often passed over in silence. This is the affirmation that human life is sacred,[93] and that in this regard each individual represents a value which is rigorously identical. As Athenagoras put it in a lapidary sentence, "We [Christians] cannot endure to see a man being put to death, even justly."[94] The context of this passage had to do with circus games, which Athenagoras condemned and forbade the Christian to attend. But the judgment which he pronounced here was so manifestly a general one that it is hard to see how some scholars can refuse to see its natural implications for the Christian attitude in time of war.[95]

St. Athanasius commented persuasively, "How does it come about that each one of us has turned away from his brother and has transgressed against the covenant of life, despising the peace which we had been given? Yet your brother, your neighbor, is not only a man, but is God himself. And if your brother is God, he is also a son of God, one whom God has redeemed by the blood of his only Son."[96] St. Basil similarly expressed the Christian's universal good-will: all

honest men were *a priori* his friends, even if they lived in a
distant country and if he had never met them.[97] By the same
token, Basil maintained that murder could never be justified.
Even when committed in a situation of legitimate self-
defense, it remained a crime and as such deserved punishment.[98]

To be sure, in the middle of the fifth century, by which
time the just war theory had taken on its classical contours, Isidore of Pelusium declared, "Private murders are impure and
guilty. But there is no guilt in killing in a just war." Yet at the
same time Isidore recalled that according to Mosaic law those
who returned from battle must isolate and purify themselves.
In fact, he wrote, despite the legitimacy of the soldiers' cause
and the enthusiasm earned by their victory, "if we examine
thoroughly the indisputable blood relationship which exists
between all mankind, they are not without sin, either."[99]

Clement of Alexandria pointed out that the Lord had
commanded one "to love strangers, not only as friends and
relatives, but as oneself, in respect of both body and soul." He
continued with an exegesis on the verse, "Thou shalt not have
disgust for the Egyptian, because thou wast a stranger
received in Egypt." The word *Egyptian*, he argued, should
not be understood in a limited sense, but rather in a general
sense encompassing every inhabitant of the world who is
humanly a stranger to us. In consequence, "enemies, although
drawn up before the walls attempting to take the city, are not
to be regarded as enemies." Instead one should always try to
negotiate with them to maintain peace and avoid bloodshed.[100] Arnobius likewise expressed indignation at the notion,
which was common among the pagans, that a divine being
could have anything at all to do with warfare. Of the god Mars
he wrote,

> If he is a calmer of martial insanity, why is it that every day wars
> continue? If, on the other hand, he is their instigator, we should

say that at the inclination of his own pleasure the god sets the
whole world at variance; sows the seeds of discord and strife
among far-separated nations of the earth; brings together from
different places so many thousands of mortals and, before you
can say a single word, piles the fields with corpses; causes
bloody torrents to flow; destroys the most firmly established
empires; levels cities to the ground; takes away freedom from
the free-born and places on them the condition of slavery; rejoices in civil strife, in the fratricidal slaughter of brothers dying
together, and, finally, in the horror of murderous conflict
between sons and father.[101]

Tertullian had a more highly developed sense of humanity
than has generally been recognized. Although on occasion he
affirmed it explicitly, it was still more striking in certain
passages where he was arguing some other point and where he
affirmed the primacy of man as it were involuntarily—with
parenthetical spontaneity. For Tertullian it was man who was
in fact the unique center of creation. Everything had been
created in his image, and everything was subject to him.[102] All
animals were under his domination, and it was impossible that
any of them should ever attain his level.[103] A man's life was
therefore the most precious thing in the world. The humblest
living man was worth more than the greatest dead man.[104]
Tertullian, as a consequence, revolted passionately against the
bloody games which the Romans held in Jupiter's honor. To
those who said that only the blood of criminals was shed there,
Tertullian retorted that this made it all the more shameful for
Jupiter. In any case, homicide was always homicide.[105] The
Christians, Tertullian claimed, were all brothers, and not only
brothers among themselves but brothers of all men, for they
saw all men as sons of the same human race. It was when the
pagans failed to act in a brotherly way toward other men that
they were in danger of forfeiting this quality of true humanity.[106]

There was a certain naiveté, which was not without value,
in one of the arguments with which Tertullian countered the

bloody, anti-Christian defamations which some pagans were spreading abroad. They insinuated that there was a motive behind the "crimes" of the Christians—in return they had all been promised eternal life. But, Tertullian asked, was it worth attaining eternal life if one's conscience were burdened with such crimes? Bluntly he declared that it was not, and that the purported outrages would be far too exorbitant a price to pay for immortality. In any event, even if someone wanted to commit the misdeeds of which the Christians had been accused, he wouldn't have enough courage. Were not the Christians as human as anyone else? How could they have not only the will but the strength to carry out such horrors?[107]

Tertullian's argument is not very convincing: we sadly know all too well what men are capable of doing—for a goal far less exalted than eternal life. But the argument showed his remarkable estimation of human worth in its assertion, without the slightest qualification, that there were boundaries of horror which no man would cross, regardless of how low he had fallen. It also demonstrated Tertullian's preference of a minimum demand of human dignity and honor to eternal life. In any case, this confidence did not prevent him from basing human brotherhood on his faith. With the death of Christ the reign of privileged peoples had ended. Christian preaching was reaching even those who lived outside the confines of the Roman Empire.[108] In fact, one of the reasons why the Christians refused to fight was that they might kill a brother in the faith among the barbarians whom the Romans were fighting.

This must not be taken to mean, of course, that only the lives of Christians were of value. On the contrary, the universalism of the Church, which Christians accepted on faith even before observing it empirically, opened the way to an all-encompassing universalism. This can be seen in Tertullian's words: "Is the laurel of triumph made of leaves or of corpses? Is it adorned with ribbons or with tombs? Is it bedewed with ointments, or with tears of wives and mothers?—it may be of some Christians, too, for Christ is also among the barbarians."[109] As he reminded his readers elsewhere, the Christians knew that Christ had died for all men, without exception.[110]

When one man killed another, it was therefore always a crime against God and an act of the devil.[111] This conviction was already evident in the Christians' absolute rejection of any kind of abortion.[112] It was also evident in their prohibition of judges from imposing capital punishment on anyone. For a man, even though a criminal, still remained a man. How inconsistent it would be, Tertullian observed, religiously to respect the life of a fetus or a murderer and yet thoughtlessly to sacrifice the life of a man whom circumstances had placed in the ranks of an enemy army.[113] Nor, as regards the Christian's attitude to his own suffering, did Tertullian defend pain as a kind of asceticism or self-mortification. Instead, to those who reproached and mocked Christians for their lamentations under persecution—"Why do you grumble, for you desire to suffer"—he retorted gravely, with a slight bitterness through which a confidence in final victory was glimmering: Yes, we wish to suffer, as a soldier accepts the blows of war. No one likes these blows, but victory makes one forget the sufferings of battle; the victor has no right to complain. "Our battle," Tertullian asserted, "consists in being challenged to face the tribunals, that there, in peril of life, we may fight it out for truth." Our victory thus has a double significance: "It means the glory of pleasing God, and the spoils are eternal life."[114] In none of this was there any masochism or morbid neurasthenia. Tertullian loved life on this earth as much as anyone, and he knew the price of suffering. But he also knew what fidelity to God meant, and that it was worth staking everything upon it.

At a later date St. John Chrysostom too was an eloquent interpreter of the horror which death inspired. "The nature of death is altogether horrifying," he wrote. "That is why, as it swoops down daily on our race, it strikes us down and makes us shudder at the sight of each corpse, as if we were seeing it for the first time."[115] He continued by writing a whole paragraph on the gruesome details of physical death and bodily decay. In his *Homilies on the Gospel of John* he characterized the battle of Christ as well as that of the Christian as being a battle against death.[116] He maintained, moreover, that mankind was the center and purpose of all creation.[117]

More distinct and formidable than the witness of any other Christian writer was the voice of Lactantius, especially in his *Divine Institutions*. Although a Roman to the core of his being, he did not hesitate to write the following stinging words:

> For they [the Romans] despise valor in an athlete, because it produces no injury, but in the case of a king, because it occasions widely-spread disasters, they so admire it as to imagine that brave and warlike generals are admitted to the assembly of the gods and that there is no other way to immortality than to lead armies, to lay waste the territory of others, to destroy cities, to overthrow towns, to put to death or enslave free peoples. Truly the greater number of men they have cast down, plundered and slain, so much more noble and distinguished do they think themselves; and ensnared by the show of empty glory, they give to their crimes the name of virtue. I would rather that they should make to themselves gods from the slaughter of wild beasts,[118] than approve of an immortality so stained with blood. If anyone has slain a single man, he is regarded as contaminated and wicked, nor do they think it lawful for him to be admitted to this earthly abode of the gods.[119] But he who slaughtered countless thousands of men, has inundated plains with blood, and infected rivers, is not only admitted into the temple, but even into heaven.[120]

Virtue could not consist of pursuing the good of one's own country as if it were the only thing which mattered:

> For what are the interests of our country, but the inconveniences of another state or nation?—that is, to extend the boundaries which are evidently taken from others, to increase

the power of the state, to improve the revenues—all which things are not virtues, but the overthrowing of virtues; for in the first place, the union of human society is taken away, innocence is taken away, the abstaining from the property of another is taken away; lastly, justice itself is taken away, which is unable to bear the tearing asunder of the human race, and wherever arms have glittered, must be banished and exterminated from thence. For how can a man be just who injures, who hates, who despoils, who puts to death? And they who strive to be serviceable to their country do all these things.[121]

If war was thus the negation of all virtue, it was because the supreme value was man, who could not be destroyed without incurring God's explicit condemnation. Man was not simply a part of the world; he was God's direct creation.[122] "The Sacred Writings," Lactantius wrote, "teach that man was the last work of God, and that he was brought into this world as into a house prepared and made ready, for all things were made on his account."[123] "But he [God] made man—reason being granted to him and the power of perceiving and speaking being given to him—destitute of those things which are given to other animals, because wisdom was able to supply those things which the condition of nature had denied to him. He made him naked and defenceless, because he could be armed by his talent and clothed by his reason."[124]

Lactantius also spoke of a mysterious golden age in the past in which man had been better acquainted with God's will. In those days the severest punishment had been exile, "for as yet it seemed unlawful to inflict capital punishment on any, however guilty, inasmuch as they were men."[125] Thereupon justice had disappeared and men began to persecute those who were good. But even

if they should put to death the wicked only, they would deserve to be unvisited by justice, who had no other reason for leaving the earth than the shedding of human blood. . . .[126] Therefore humanity is to be preserved if we wish to be called men. But what else is this preservation of humanity than the loving of a man because he is a man, and the same as ourselves? Therefore discord and dissension are not in accord with the nature of man; and that expression of Cicero is true, which says that man, while he is obedient to nature, cannot injure man.[127]

To be carried away by anger, the generator of murder, "deprives him not only of the title of a good man, but even of a man; since to injure another . . . is not in accordance with the nature of man."[128]

Lactantius, like several other Fathers, indicated that a spectator's approval was enough to bring condemnation.

For he who reckons it a pleasure that a man, though justly condemned, should be slain in his sight, pollutes his conscience as much as if he should become a spectator and a sharer of a homicide which is secretly committed. . . . For when God forbids us to kill, he not only prohibits us from open violence, which is not even allowed by the public laws, but he warns us against the commission of those things which are esteemed lawful among men. Thus it will be neither lawful for a just man to engage in warfare, since his warfare is justice itself, nor to accuse anyone of a capital charge, because it makes no difference, whether you put a man to death by word, or rather by sword, since it is the act of putting to death itself which is prohibited. Therefore, with regard to this precept of God, there ought to be no exception at all, but that it is always unlawful to put to death a man, whom God willed to be a sacred animal.[129]

Lactantius, of course, was not the first Christian writer to show that beneath and sometimes in opposition to men's written law there was God's eternal law.[130] Nevertheless these texts assume a special importance when we realize that, even though they were written during a period of persecution, they also were written only a few years prior to the securing of "the alliance of the broadsword and the holy-water sprinkler" in the Roman Empire. What is more, Lactantius was no mere provincial fanatic; he was to become one of the court's official intellectuals and the instructor of Constantine's son, Caesar Crispus.[131]

The Christian attitude, then, with its weakness and ambiguities, but also with its amazing steadfastness, was not a flight from the world, but was rather a vocation to live within the world according to the law of love which the world had rejected. It was not a spurning of what was positive in one's own community, but was rather a refusal to forget that this community was limited in space and time and was infinitely surpassed by the values which it embodied only partially.[132] It was not a refusal to defend one's neighbor, but was rather a confession that there was no one anywhere who was not one's neighbor. In our final chapters we shall see the concrete consequences which resulted from this attitude, both in the lives of the Christians and in the legislation of the Church.

Chapter 4

Christian Soldiers and
Soldier Saints

Nobody would contest the fact that there were Christians in the Roman army. But it is important first of all to determine the dates at which the earliest documents referring to Christian soldiers appeared. Having done this, we must then ascertain what the state of mind of these soldiers actually was.

An initial category of sources indicating the presence of Christians in the legions is that of the funereal inscriptions. In the past Edmond Le Blant, who was able to find only twenty-seven soldiers among the 4,734 Christian inscriptions given in the Séguier Index,[1] and whose systematic studies enabled him to add only eighteen other soldiers, concluded that this tiny percentage was an evidence of the extreme repulsion that Christians felt for the military profession.[2]

Dom Leclercq, who quoted this opinion, claimed that he could show its worthlessness by noting a far larger number of inscriptions.[3] But he did so in a rather haphazard way. First he listed fifty-four funereal inscriptions, then ten funerary representations.[4] Next he mentioned an additional funereal inscription, that of Flavius Memorius, about whose career he was delighted to provide details.[5] Leclercq concluded by enumerating 150 other funereal inscriptions, most of which he simply listed without comment, and only a few of which he deigned to evaluate carefully.[6] In column 1178 he stated that he could not, in a mere dictionary article, undertake to provide a complete corpus of inscriptions relating to Christian soldiers and officers. But he implied that such a corpus would simply add weight to the conclusions which he claimed to have based on the inscriptions which he had been able to list. For over fifty years many scholars, relying upon this evidence and upon Leclercq's authority, have felt justified in asserting that the lapidary inscriptions supplied massive and irrefutable proof of a general acceptance by Christians of the soldier's trade well before the Constantinian period.

If one looks at this evidence more closely, however, its ostensibly massive quantities begin to shrink. Leclercq himself presented his list as follows: "We have collected inscriptions, of which *a certain number* belong certainly *or probably* to the period before the Church Peace."[7] When we examine seriously the relevant inscriptions—those relating to people who, before the empire became "Christian," were soldiers and Christians either at the same time or even successively— their number shrivels drastically: to a grand total of seven!

The first of these is the tomb of the veteran P(ablius) Marcellus, which was found in the Christian cemetery of Priscilla at Rome.[8] The second is a fragment of a sarcophagus found at Rome in 1937; its inscription, which is thought to date from the years 246-249, mentions the praetorian centurion Aelius Martinus.[9] A third is the inscription concerning a certain Aurelius Poseidonius, a former soldier (palaistratiōtēs), who was buried in the tomb of a Christian family at Philippoupolis in Thrace.[10] Two other inscriptions come from Phrygia, where they were brought to light by W. M. Ramsay.[11] One of these, found at Hodjalar, concerns two brothers (Aurelius Caius and Aurelius Menophilus), both soldiers, and dates from before 250.[12] The other is the epitaph of the standard-bearer Aurelius Manos, who came from Edessa and—in the last years of the third century or the earliest years of the fourth century—was buried at Eumenia, capital of Phrygia, where he was then serving.[13] Another inscription is that which the freedman Ampelius, who was returning from war *(regrediens in Urbem ab expeditionibus)*, appended in 217 to his master's epitaph in Rome.[14]

Finally, there is a seventh inscription which stands out by virtue of its importance and clarity, and which is the only one that directly and indisputably conflicts with my general interpretation in this book. This is the inscription of Marcus Julius Eugenius, bishop of Laodicea Combusta, in East Phrygia (where it was discovered in the eighteenth century and then found again in 1908). At about 340 this bishop composed the inscription and ordered it to be placed on his own sarcophagus. The inscription, which ends with these charming words—

> I caused the above to be engraved
> For the distinction of the Church
> and of my family—

has something of the character of an autobiography written in the third person singular. It indicates that during the previous twenty-five years Eugenius had been bishop of that see, and that he had supervised the lavish restoration of its cathedral church. But it also states that Eugenius, who came from a senatorial family, earlier in life had been a career military officer who had served with distinction (met' epiteimias strateusamenon) in the troops of the governor of Pisidia. The inscription then goes on:

> When a command had meanwhile come from Maximinus
> That Christians should offer sacrifice and not quit the army,
> [He, Eugenius,] having endured many tortures[15]
> Under Diogenes governor [of Pisidia], and having contrived
>   to quit
> The army, maintaining the faith of the Christian. . . .[16]

This man thus was a Christian who at about the year 310 was not only a soldier but an officer, and a good officer at that. Only the obligation to sacrifice forced him to leave the army, and after the establishment of the Church Peace he became a bishop. His military past was not an obstacle to such a promotion, nor did he express regret at it or attempt to cloak it in the silence of oblivion.[17] It is true that W. M. Calder, who rediscovered this inscription and analyzed it most carefully, was definite in his conclusion that Eugenius was bishop not of the main Church but of the sect of the Saccophores.[18] But this does not weaken the contradiction; quite the contrary. For these Saccophores are thought to have been Encratites— descendants of the Montanists—who were unlikely to have countenanced a reduction in the strictness of Christian discipline.

There are other inscriptions which are almost as important for our enquiry as the seven which I have already cited. These are the inscriptions that soldiers consecrated to deceased Christian members of their families. For one may concede that if these soldiers had not been in some sympathy with the new faith, they would not have accepted Christian burial for their kin. Four such cases are known. The first is a sarcophagus in Besançon, which the centurion Marius Vitalis and his son, the quaestor Marius Nigidianus, ordered to be crafted for the remains of their wife and mother.[19] Then there are two late third-century inscriptions which were found in the Christian cemetery at Salona, in Dalmatia. One of these, which is no longer extant, was a fragment of the memorial in which Ulpius Asclepius honored the memory of Octavia Cara, wife of the veteran Sabinianus.[20] The other is the epitaph of Quintilia, who was both daughter and wife of officers.[21] Finally, there was another epitaph, which has also been lost, which Licineus, a soldier of the Sixth Praetorian Cohort, had engraved for his wife.[22]

All other testimonies—those which Leclercq quoted as

well as those which others have produced subsequently—are
either obviously irrelevant or at least extremely doubtful.
Thus the following inscriptions certainly come from the period
after the empire became Christian: Nos. 2 (dated 484 by Leclercq himself), 7 (dated 386), 9[23], 15[24], 16[25], 17 (dated 346),
26[26], 27 (dated 450), 28[27], and 41[28]. The following also
probably come from a later period: Nos. 3[29], 6[30], 13[31], and
20[32]. According to Lopuszanski, who has made the most
thorough study of the whole collection of these inscriptions,
No. 19[33] is certainly not Christian, and Nos. 25[34], 33[35], 45[36],
and 48[37] are probably not Christian either.

Eleven inscriptions—scattered over a period of two
centuries—referring directly or indirectly to soldiers is not a
very impressive total. However, as Bainton rightly commented, their relevance is certainly greater than their number,
for their presence in Christian burial grounds implies at least
an implicit consent on the part of the believing community.[38]
We must also admit that since during this period Christianity
was prohibited, it was not likely to be mentioned, even by
allusion, on inscriptions which also listed official titles.
Nevertheless, even after we have taken these allowances into
account, the evidence compels us in the main to uphold the
conclusion reached by Le Blant and to reject Leclercq's
claimed refutation of it.

In the literary sources subsequent to the New Testament—the New Testament texts[39] can be variously interpreted and in any event are outside the range of this
study—the question of Christian soldiers, in one sense or
another, does not arise again until the end of the second
century. This fact, tallying with the negative evidence of the
inscriptions, indicates that the "subject of military service obviously was not at that time controverted," probably because
everybody took for granted the incompatiblity between the
Christian faith and military service.[40] In any case, the *written*
sources (including the tombstones) contain nothing which

would lead us to attribute this silence to the Christians' unquestioning acceptance of military service. Such an interpretation might conceivably explain the silence of the literary texts; but the silence of the tombstones makes the opposite explanation unavoidable.[41]

The first author who treated the question other than by incidental allusions was Tertullian, who protested vigorously against the presence of Christian soldiers in the army. In his testimony we can see clearly the contradiction which also existed, more or less covertly, for the other authors: when the Christian thinker, whether theologian or moralist, asked himself whether military service was legitimate for the believer, he always answered that it was not. However, there was by this time a fair number of Christians in the army, and Tertullian was quite ready to acknowledge this fact and even on occasion to make argumentative use of it. This fact was largely explicable, no doubt, by the persecutions in which the authorities used compulsory enrollment to bring the refractory to heel. It was also a result of Roman recruiting methods, whereby a certain category of persons would be impressed all over the empire at a time when Christianity, as an unrecognized religion, could not provide grounds for exemption.[42]

But we can say confidently that the Christians then in the army had not enlisted voluntarily after they had become Christians. Their presence in it, which initially was a result of the persecution, soon ran the risk of eliciting further persecution, as uncompromising Christians began to bring out, for all to see, the latent opposition between their faith and the empire. The more cautious believers were therefore enraged and terrified to hear of the soldier's daring exploit in Tertullian's *De Corona*. This relation between the presence of Christians in the army and their persecution is also shown by the story of Diocletian's diviners, who accused the Christians of preventing the success of the emperor's sacrifice by making signs of the cross which put the demons to flight.[43]

We must now turn to the texts themselves. Let us begin by considering the *De Corona* treatise, which concerns a soldier who suddenly refused to wear a laurel wreath which was being given to him, in accordance with custom, at the time of a *donativum*. Many Christians were critical of this refusal; but Tertullian defended it by moving progressively from a discussion of the nature and significance of garlands to a clear and categorical denunciation of military service.[44]

Two things are especially noteworthy here: until his sudden gesture this Christian had been a soldier; and Tertullian informs us that there were other Christian soldiers who did not have the courage to follow his example.[45] These themes are also evident in two famous passages in Tertullian's *Apology*: "We are but of yesterday, and we have filled everything you have. . . . Forts, yes! and camps. All we have left to you is the temples!"; and "we go to the wars . . . with you."[46] Christian thinkers of that period were more inclined to emphasize the universality of places where Christians could be found than to concentrate upon the unique importance of each situation. For instance, Clement of Alexandria's *Protrepticus* includes a similar enumeration:

> Till the ground, we say, if you are a husbandman; but recognize God in your husbandry. Sail the sea, you who love seafaring; but ever call upon the heavenly pilot. Were you a soldier on campaign when the knowledge of God laid hold on you? Then listen to the commander who signals righteousness.[47]

I have quoted this text in full because of the discussion which it has provoked. Twice in his article on "Militarisme," Leclercq appealed to it to demonstrate that the early Christians were authorized to do military service. In fact, on the second occasion, he presented the text as being in express contradiction to the antimilitarist tradition which he acknowledges to have existed in the Church.[48] J. Zeiller was clearly aware of the problem raised by the passage and he therefore discussed it at some length. Finally, however, he decided that one could not detect in it antimilitaristic overtones.[49] Such, it must be pointed out, was also the opinion of Cadoux, who quoted a footnote in which Harnack argued that this text "does not, of course, mean that one must give up the army."[50] Elsewhere Cadoux declared himself against the view that Clement was one of the Fathers who had absolutely forbidden the Christian to be a soldier or to bear arms.[51] It is my conviction, however, for the reasons which I provide in notes 48 and 49 to this chapter, that this text is not to be interpreted as an approbation of military service; rather it must almost certainly be understood as an invitation to leave the army.

It is true that Clement elsewhere stated that the phrase with which John the Baptist enjoined the soldiers to be content with their pay had an authority emanating from "the divine *Pedagogue*" himself.[52] It is also true that in another place, although on quite a different subject, he mentioned military service as a neutral reality which formed a part of daily life. He also spoke of "the hope entertained by the soldiers" as one of the various elements which constituted his present reality.[53] But it is apparent that in the context Clement was referring to *de facto*, however unfortunate, situations whose reality was not sufficient to separate us from "the love of God which was manifested in Jesus Christ."[54] We must also bear in mind the following passage in which Clement commented upon the legal regulations promulgated by Moses: if someone has not yet enjoyed what he has bought or built (house, vineyard, wife), "such a person the human law orders to be relieved from military service; for military reasons, in the first place, lest ... they turn out sluggish in war."[55] From these various passages we may conclude that military service was a reality which Clement observed in the world; but it was not a course of action which he endorsed for the Christian.

In the same way we must give close study to the text in

which Cyprian had told of Celerinus, who in 250 had suffered martyrdom under Decius. Cyprian added, "Moreover his [Celerinus's] paternal and maternal uncles, Laurentius and Ignatius, who themselves also were once warring in the camps of the world, but were true and spiritual soldiers of God, casting down the devil by the confession of Christ, merited palms and crowns from the Lord by their illustrious passion."[56] For Leclercq this passage proved simply and unequivocally that Christians, who were so devoted that they were ready to face martyrdom for their faith, had no objection to remaining soldiers.[57] But it is just as likely to have meant the opposite. So long as Celerinus and his companions were "warring in the camps of this world," they were serving the devil; it was only by refusing to remain under arms that they overthrew him and brought about their martyrdom.

The fact that there were numerous Christians in the army is even clearer in the writings of St. Basil. But Basil was highly reserved in passing judgment on this situation. Two of his *Homilies* refer directly to soldiers who were Christians and martyrs. The first of these concerned Gordius, a centurion who had withdrawn to the desert during the persecution but returned to share martyrdom in order to be a comfort and help to his friends. According to Basil, Gordius assured them that "it is by publicly confessing our faith that we shall be saved. Would there be any hope of being saved for the soldier? Has any centurion ever been able to prove faithful?" After having cited the example of the three centurions of Matthew 8 and 27 and Acts 10, he concluded, "I would be their disciple."[58]

In his second *Homily* Basil dealt with the forty soldiers who were martyred in Sebastus.[59] To be sure, he praised them unreservedly for their faith and courage. But it is striking that their fate inspired him to consider at length whether they had been "without a country" or whether they had been "citizens of the world."[60] Giet, who studied this text in detail, was obliged to conclude that neither in Basil nor in his supposed heroes was there the least trace of patriotic sentiment.[61]

In a letter to Firminius, the son of one of his friends and a Christian who joined the army, Basil wrote, "You have yourself been silent, ashamed, I suppose, of your intentions, and therefore I must implore you not to entertain any project which can be associated with shame. Bid a long farewell to soldiering."[62] It is not fully clear whether Basil was reproaching the young man for having chosen the military profession or for having run away from home. In another letter, to an unknown soldier whom he had met on a journey, on the other hand, he expressed his joy and surprise to discover a soldier who was at the same time a true Christian. "We have come to know a man," he wrote, "who proves that even in military life one may preserve the perfection of love for God."[63] And Basil admonished him to continue on this way.

Finally, in one of his *Homilies on the Psalms,* Basil took the fact that "for the most part the soldiers grow to be like their commanders" as an example of the way in which "the dignities of this world by themselves make the life of those who are thereby distinguished into something special."[64] Basil here clearly indicated that the army was a part of the world's vanities, but he does not appear to have implied a specific condemnation of it.

Moving from the literary sources in general into the more restricted domain of hagiography, we are immediately struck by the existence of an astonishing swarm of soldier saints. H. Delehaye devoted a whole book to them and to the problems which they raise. He showed first of all how these legends could be used to buttress the conclusions of a particular Christian system of morality. The large number of soldiers among the martyrs had impressed a group of historians, who had "sought to appreciate the success of Christian propaganda in the camps. So there was no incompatibility, the repeated assertions of some scholars to the contrary, between the profession of arms and the religion of Christ; and the Church did not bring to bear upon the soldier's calling the severe judgments of some rigid moralists."[65] These historians therefore had set out energetically to investigate the reasons for the diffusion of Christianity in the army and to study the army's role in spreading Christianity throughout the world. But, at the end of his meticulous study, Delehaye was able to demonstrate the futility of these historians' efforts: in reality "many . . . saints who according to legend were soldiers . . . joined the army only in the hagiographer's imagination."[66]

Of the five cases which he studied, which he selected simply because they were among the most celebrated of all accounts of warrior saints, he concluded that "at least two, St. Procopius and St. Demetrius, had nothing to do with the army;" it was exceedingly probable that the same was true as well of the other three, St. Theodore, St. George, and St. Mercury.[67] The case of Dasius, who was said to have been a soldier in Moesia and to have refused to play the part of king in Saturnalia, was similar. This legend, as Delehaye demonstrated, was completely without foundation.[68]

The purported interrogation of Dasius, however, may be an authentic fragment which was inserted into this fictional framework. In any case it is illuminating. When the legate asked him what his name was, he replied, "Of my name, I shall tell you that I have the excellent one of Christian. But the name given me by my parents is Dasius." Later he declared, "I am a Christian, and I do not fight for any earthly king but for the King of heaven." When commanded to bow to the image of the emperor, he responded, "I am a Christian and I obey no one else but the one undefiled and eternal God." Finally the legate, in a last attempt to persuade him, exclaimed, "You forget, Dasius, that every man is subject to the imperial decree and to the sacred laws." Thereupon Dasius became almost coarse and termed the emperors godless men and criminals. In forthright terms he concluded, "As for your emperors and their honor, I spit upon it and despise it."[69]

One of the most obvious and rather amusing sources of error which contributed to the "militarization" of the saints had to do with the distance from one place of pilgrimage to another. In the Hieronymian Martyrology, and in other Latin martyrologies as well, the indication *milario*, followed by the appropriate figure, has been shortened to *MIL*. These three capital letters in turn were interpreted as an abbreviation of *milites*, thereby signifying that the saint in question had been martyred with a specified number of other soldiers. In actual fact, the number simply referred to the number of kilometers from the previous sanctuary.[70]

In explaining this process of "militarization" Delehaye has rejected (too completely, from my point of view) the influence of the symbolism of *militia Christi*. Instead he has attributed the phenomenon to popular curiosity. Unable to be content with what history actually offered—a name and sometimes a date—the hagiographers dressed up the evidence by using a model which was fashionable at the time and which was always much the same.[71]

I shall now refer briefly to several other accounts which are either apocryphal or of doubtful authenticity. The first is the story of the "Thundering Legion," which in a mission of 172 into Bohemia had been saved from catastrophic defeat by an unexpected downpour.[72] From the vantage point of the Christians, this rain had clearly been the result of the prayers of the 12th Legion, the *Legio Fulminata*, which was said to have been comprised entirely of believers. The legendary character of this last point appears obvious to us today.[73] It is interesting to note, however, that the imaginary existence of this Christian legion under Marcus Aurelius was embarrassing neither to the historian Eusebius nor to the apologist Tertullian.[74]

A second account is the martyrdom of the *quattuor coronati*—four soldiers who were said to have been executed at Rome for refusing to sacrifice.[75] Other purported soldier-

martyrs who are worthy of mention were Getulius and
Amantius, of whom we know only their names;[76] Hieron and
his forty companions, the tale of whose martyrdom is historically worthless, since it is an obvious plagiarism of the account of the forty martyrs of Sebaste;[77] and Menas, the most
celebrated saint of the East, who may have been only a hum-
ble camel-driver. The cloak in which Menas was depicted was
later assumed to be a military uniform. An anonymous hagiographer thereupon eulogized Menas by repeating almost verbatim St. Basil's panegyric of Gordius, simply replac-
ing Gordius's name by that of Menas (although allowing
Menas to keep his Egyptian origin).[78] Then there were Sergius
and Bacchus, leaders of the *Schola gentilium*, that era's
equivalent of the Foreign Legion; these men were arrested
after being denounced by jealous colleagues.[79] Finally, there
is the intriguing case of Hippolytus of Rome, who, as we shall
see in the next chapter, was in the "antimilitarist" tradition.
But this did not prevent later hagiographers from splitting his
personality by fabricating the biography of a soldier saint
bearing his name.[80] In general, the oriental tradition
continued to luxuriate in stereotyped clichés; Latin hagiography, on the other hand, increasingly tried to be faithful
to the historical data.

In addition to these spurious or improbable "soldier
saints" there was a certain number of Christians who actually
followed a military career or who suffered as a result of their
obstinate refusal to allow it. To these we must now devote our
attention.

Bishop Dionysius's account of the Decian persecution at
Alexandria, as reported by Eusebius, indicated that in the
Christian community there were illustrious people and officials.[81] A little later Dionysius told the story of a squad of
four Christian soldiers who during the trial of one of their coreligionists were standing guard before the tribunal. When the
accused showed a tendency to apostasy, they urged him to

remain firm, and spontaneously mounted the platform to testify to their faith. They were then sentenced themselves.[82] It was probably also under Decius that the double martyrdom took place of St. Ferreolus, who was military tribune at Vienne in Gaul, and St. Julian, who may have been under his orders.[83] In 262, under Gallianus, there was the case of Marinus, who evidently saw no problem in being both a soldier and a Christian.[84] Without difficulty Marinus could have risen in the ranks of the army, had not a rival, who hoped to be appointed centurion in his stead, denounced him in these terms: "In accordance with the ancient laws Marinus cannot share in the rank that belonged to Romans, since he is a Christian and does not sacrifice to the emperors." It was only then, when Marinus would have had to renounce his faith to continue serving in the army, that the bishop intervened and required him to choose between the sword and the gospel. Marinus thereupon accepted death for his faith.

The great persecution of Diocletian, after a period in which the emperors had been favorable to the Christians, began with measures specifically designed to purge the army of all believers within it. Eusebius of Caesarea, who was an exact contemporary of these events, briefly noted that "the persecution commenced with the brethren in the army."[85] He then gave a lengthy description of the persecution in terms which show with absolute clarity that the Christian soldiers, who were the primary targets of the special proceedings, must have been quite numerous in the army.[86]

At the very end of the third century and in the early years of the fourth, there was a sudden increase in the surviving records of soldier martyrs.[87] I have already referred to Seston's explanation of this fact. Lods agreed:

The decisive step [in the deification of the emperors] was taken by Diocletian and his colleague Maximian, who proclaimed themselves, probably in 291, as *diis geniti* ["born of gods"], i.e., to have been divine beings by their very birth. This is a fact of the highest interest which has had its repercussions on the history of the Church. Some Christians at that time saw an organic identity between the empire and the kingdom of demons, between obedience to the emperor and idolatrous worship. And, among the Christians, those who recognized most clearly the new situation created by the imperial decisions were the soldiers who were required in the daily exercise of their profession to obey the prince's orders.[88]

"Up to that point," Seston observed, "the emperor cult in the army had required only manifestations of loyalty, to which a Christian could in a pinch accommodate himself, for all that was asked of him was to look at the standards bedecked with statues or images, *which however were in no way those of a god*.[89] So the emperor cult—insofar as it remained only the traditional mark of enthusiasm or fidelty—was lawful for a Christian. But if the emperor became a god, all religious acts carried out before his image were tainted with idolatry."[90] Such a view of the problem led Seston and Lods to discern a radical break between the "soldier saints" and the "Christian antimilitarists" who had preceded them. From the point of view of the "soldier saints," only the specifically religious acts which were demanded of them were "fraught with a meaning which was intolerable to their faith. Before Diocletian it had never been like this. Tertullian's antimilitarism, of which one cannot help thinking, had had a very different basis."[91]

Personally, I cannot make such a clear differentiation between the two attitudes. On the contrary, the pages which I devoted earlier to the emperor cult demonstrate that, although it had undeniably developed gradually,[92] to the pagans divinity never meant very much; to the Christians, on the other hand, it was from the outset absolutely unacceptable. The believers had not waited until "the epiphany of the emperors" of July 291 to denounce as intolerable—as manifestations of idolatry—the ceremonies and divine honors which were being accorded to the emperors. And conversely, the martyrdom of Maximilian, which was the first account to which Seston applied his explanation, in fact contained practically no allusion to the problem of idolatry; it rather restated many of the themes that Tertullian had previously enunciated.[93]

According to this narrative, Maximilian was brought to enlist by his father, Fabius Victor, who like some other Christians did not yet recognize clearly the contradiction between the faith and military service, but who afterwards came to acknowledge the genuineness of his son's Christian martyrdom.[94] At the outset, Maximilian declared, "I am not allowed to be a soldier, for I am a Christian."[95] And throughout the discussion it was the very fact of being a soldier, of *militare*, that he refused. It is astonishing that Seston seems deliberately to have shut his eyes to this evidence. Thus he could assert that it was only the *signaculum*, which bore the emperor's name or image, that Maximilian rejected with horror, because following the recent "epiphany of the Augustuses and the Caesars" the *signaculum* had taken on a very new meaning. Seston could thus write, "Maximilian allowed himself to be measured, but when they tried to put the recruit's lead locket around his neck he put up an obstinate resistance."[96] The text, however, says, "*While he was being measured*, Maximilian said, 'I cannot be a soldier, I cannot do evil. I am a Christian.'"[97] In these words it is hard to detect even a qualified acceptance of the formalities of enlistment.

It was the same a little later when the young conscript refused the imperial badge. "I do not accept your mark," he said, "for I already have the sign of Christ, my God. . . . I do not accept the mark of this age, and if you impose it on me, I shall break it, for it is worth nothing. I am a Christian, and it is not lawful for me to carry a medal on my neck after having received the sign of salvation of my Lord Jesus Christ." Far

from reflecting a new attitude, this statement contains the unmistakable accents of the entire early Christian tradition
which I have described in Chapter 2.

Lods, although a resolute supporter of Seston's thesis,
when dealing with Tertullian's attitude commented,

> The soldier on being enlisted received a locket of lead which was
> attached to his neck and which bore the name and the emblem
> of the emperor; this was the *signum*. Now *signum* is the word
> which the Church used to designate the baptism which gave the
> novice the mark, the seal *(signum)* of Christ. . . . One could not
> have on oneself two contradictory signs. The soldier . . . was re-
> quired to swear an oath of obedience to the prince. This was the
> *sacramentum,* which signified consecration. This word was also
> a Christian expression. It likewise denoted baptism, in the sense
> of the commitment which the baptized person made in response
> to the *signum* of God. One could not honor two oaths at the
> same time.[98]

In light of this position which had already been so
throughly defined, it is hard to imagine how Seston and Lods
thought that Maximilian was innovating. A little earlier, when
the consul had told him, "You must serve or die," he replied,
"I am not a soldier. . . . I am not a soldier of the world but of
God."[99] He then declared, "It is he [Christ] whom we serve,
all of us who are Christians. It is he whom we follow as the
guide of our life and the author of salvation." Once again he
reiterated, "My service is by the side of my God. I cannot
serve the world. I have already said it; I am a Christian."[100]

Maximilian did not deny, however, that there were Christians who were willing to be soldiers.[101]

> Proconsul: "In the guard of honor of our lords Diocletian and
> Maximian, Constantius and Galerius, there are Christian
> soldiers and they serve *(militant)*." Maximilian: "They them-
> selves know what is proper *(expediat)* for them. But as for me, I
> am a Christian and I cannot do evil." Proconsul: "Those who

serve, what evil do they do?" Maximilian: "You know very well what they do."

That these last two sentences are missing in certain manuscripts is hardly surprising. For they contain a ringing declaration, by a martyr whose memory the Church honors, of a position which its official moral teaching later came to reject.[102]

My critics have charged that I have been excessively vigorous in the preceding discussion of W. Seston's thesis. It would have been more seemly, they have implied, for me to dissent from it by subtle shades of interpretation.[103] True, I recognize that Seston has established that in 291 something changed in the nature of imperial worship, and that by doing so he has made an important contribution to our understanding.[104] But depending on the interpretation which we give to this crucial point, all the remaining history takes shape according to one perspective or the other, more or less like the figure and ground configurations used in Gestalt psychology. In these, one shape or another asserts itself, in a momentarily total and absolutely compelling way, depending on the meaning given to a particular detail which is unimportant in itself but which establishes the general orientation of the whole.

It was as a historian of the empire that Seston interpreted the 291 conflict. In the imperial cult he discerned a new phenomenon which, he was convinced, was the primary reason for that conflict.[105] I, on the other hand, interpret the same events as a historian of the Church. From that perspective, I cannot but be struck by the complete identity between the conception which the Christians revealed in the years following 291, the motives which they professed during that period, and the similar conceptions and motives which recur elsewhere in our study. My interpretation of these events, in fact, is a cornerstone of my entire argument. The whole structure holds together because all of the other elements concur with it; and it, in turn, guarantees the coherence between all of *them*. The preceding pages, I believe, have demonstrated that Seston was forced to take liberties with the text of the *Passio* to squeeze it into his general explanation. On the other hand, it fits without difficulty into my interpretive framework. That which may be a mere "shade" of interpretation to someone who is chiefly interested in the emperor cult becomes paramountly important to someone whose main objective is to understand the Christians' motivation. Hence the "vivacity" of my attack in order to occupy this strategic point; hence also—if the whole of my interpetation has carried conviction—the need for Seston to abandon it to me.

The other soldier martyrs were in a situation nearer that of Marinus, since they had at one time agreed to be soldiers. But they parted company from him in that after a certain time they took the initiative to break with the army. This they did either by leaving it and then refusing to rejoin it, or by declaring while they were still in it that they could no longer remain soldiers. It is not always easy to see whether these martyrs were converted to Christianity during their time of military service, in which case conversion would have been the reason for their change of view, or whether they had been Christians for some time who gradually reached the conclusion that their faith required them to leave the forces. In any case we shall see that, according to the actual accounts of the various martyrdoms, the explanation which Seston gave appears, to put it mildly, seriously inadequate.

Let us begin with Tipasius. According to Monceaux the texts of the minutes of the two court hearings which constitute the main part of the account are authentic in content.[106] But they actually refer to a single trial in which Tipasius refused military service, thereby leading to his execution (probably on January 11, 298). The amplification of the account, with the interpolation of visions and the attribution of frequent appearances in court, was the work of a clerk from Mauretania at the end of the fourth century or the beginning of the fifth century.

According to the present text of the account, Tipasius, who was again called to the colors under Maximian, thereupon refused the *donativum*: "The blessed martyr would not receive the gold which Maximian's hand extended to him and declared himself to be a soldier of Christ." But although like St. Martin after him[107] Tipasius refused to fight, he prophesied victory. Apparently he felt no repugnance at the idea that others were going to do combat. When after several years he was mustered a second time "to serve in the army and sacrifice to the gods," he answered, "Now I serve Christ. Before I served the world." To the reiterated command that he take his place in the ranks, once again he responded, "No one after victory returns to the battle. As far as I am concerned, I have conquered the world; I have enrolled among the servants of Christ. I am a soldier of Christ, I serve Christ; and if you want to rage against me, it is for Christ that I shall suffer." Vigorously refusing to be considered a deserter, he maintained his resistance to the end; for anyone who was a soldier of Christ could no longer serve under the orders of anyone else. According to the version that we possess, following this refusal, Tipasius once again was spared. Only later, after a revolt by soldiers who were indignant at the clemency which had been shown to him, was he put to death. At that time, and at that time alone, was rejection of idolatry given as his sole motivation.

There is also the case of the centurion Marcellus, who suffered martyrdom in 298 at Tangier. He clearly asserted that his repudiation of idolatry had in large measure determined his decision, but just as clearly he enunciated the themes of the *militia Christi* and of "no man can serve two masters." "After throwing down his soldier's belt in front of the legionary standards which were there at the time, he bore witness in a loud voice: 'I am a soldier of Jesus Christ, the eternal

king. From now I cease to serve your emperors and I despise
the worship of your gods of wood and stone, for they are deaf
and dumb images!' "[108] Marcellus was then brought before
the tribunal, where he revealed that this was the second occasion on which he had made his convictions known. "Already
on the 12th of the calends of August,[109] before the standards of
this legion, while you were celebrating your emperor's birth-
day, I declared publicly in a loud voice that I was a Christian
and that I could not serve under this standard[110] but only
under the orders of Jesus Christ, the son of God the Father
Almighty." The governor Fortunatus, who was interrogating
him, could not ignore his new public disobedience. In view of
the gravity of the case, he sent the accused to his superior,
Aurelius Agricolanus, at Tangier. Agricolanus asked
Marcellus, "You served in the army as a common centurion?"
Marcellus: "I was a soldier." Agricolanus: "What madness has
driven you to reject the military oaths (*sacramenta*) and to
speak as you have done?"[111] Marcellus: "There is no madness
in those who fear God." Agricolanus: "You have thrown away
your weapons?" Marcellus: "I have thrown them away. For it
is not fitting that a Christian, who fights for Christ his Lord,
should be a soldier according to the brutalities of this
world."[112] And the martyrologist concluded, "Thus it was fitting that Marcellus should depart a glorious martyr from this
world."

Similar characteristics are evident in the long passion of
the color-bearer Fabius and in that of Cassian, who was supposed to have been the scribe at the trial of Marcellus. But, as
to the latter account, Delehaye has shown that it, like many
others, was in fact completely unhistorical. St. Cassian of
Tangier was only a name. He had been given a history which
had been inspired by St. Cassian of Imola and St. Marcellus of
Tangier.[113]

Dom Leclercq—at the end of the columns in which he reproduced these five accounts almost entirely and quite

uncritically—emphasized that the characteristics which they manifested were strictly localized in time and space.[114] He, like Seston, then used this as an argument to minimize their significance for the general position of the Church. But he did not attempt to explain the martyrs' attitude by a purported change in the religious content of the army's attitude toward the emperors. Instead, he pointed to the special influence of the African theologians (of whom he mentioned Tertullian; and we clearly can add Cyprian as well).

The case of Julius the veteran in 302 is somewhat more in keeping with Seston's theory. Although Julius had served faithfully for twenty-seven years and had fought as well as anybody,[115] he seems all the while to have been a Christian[116] and to have remained proud of his past service record. No less significant, however, is the way in which he introduced his account of his military past ("when it appears that I made a mistake in serving in that worthless army [*uana militia*]").[117] It is also noteworthy that in his testimony there was the usual contrast between the empire's provisional law and God's eternal law.

Several similar cases can be adduced from the same period: Isichius, a Christian soldier who like Julius was arrested and who (as the end of Julius's *Acts* informs us) intended to follow Julius into martyrdom; Seleucus, who had not only served in the army but who had acquired a brilliant reputation within it;[118] Nicander and Marcianus, who were soldiers who in about 297 suffered martyrdom in Moesia; and Tarachus, who had obtained permission to leave the army when Diocletian had begun to purge it of Christians, but who was not tried and executed at Tarsus until about 303. At that time Tarachus declared that as a Christian he had been compelled to become a civilian.[119]

The *Acts of the Coptic Martyrs* also show us that under Diocletian and Maximian the Christian soldiers were the first victims of the persecution; both in Upper[120] and Lower

Egypt[121] they supplied a large proportion of the martyrs. The historicity of all of these cases is doubtful, and the primitive minds of their narrators and editors may have distorted considerably the facts which they record. Even so, from these *Acts* we can glean certain general conclusions about the prevailing mentality at the time. They contain numerous cases in which believers voluntarily sought martyrdom, without anyone apparently finding anything to criticize in this.[122] The theme of the incompatibility between the service of Christ and the service of Caesar also emerges vividly in them, as can be seen in the case of the soldier Abadious. When commanded to appear at a parade at which his commander—in preparation for the emperor's visit—was to read an official letter ordering all to sacrifice, Abadious showed up without wearing his sword-belt. When the officer indignantly rebuked him for his behavior, he answered, "I am not afraid of your threats, for a soldier cannot serve two kings; well, I am a soldier in the service of the Lord, the Messiah, the King of kings."[123] Later, having managed to escape from prison just as Maximian arrived, "he got up onto the roof of the flag storehouse, took his sword-belt and flung it down in front of the king, crying, 'I am a soldier of Jesus the Messiah, the King of kings.' "[124]

One can detect very little Christian gentleness in these records. Abadious himself prophesied first the death of one of the officers who was examining him, then the death of the other officer's wife. This, of course, was not personal revenge, for vengeance belonged to the provider of divine justice—to Providence. But there was better (or worse) to come. At the sight of the wonders which accompanied the martyrdom of certain believers, "three of the main executioners took off their sword-belts and threw them in the governor's face, saying, 'Henceforth we are no longer your soldiers but those of Jesus the Christ.' When the governor attempted to intimidate them by threatening them with the death penalty, the three soldiers responded, 'By the life of our Lord Jesus the Christ, if you do not pronounce our sentence, it is we who will behead you!' The soldiers had their swords, and out of fear the governor hastened to satisfy them."[125]

In connection with Diocletian's persecution a question of chronological sequence arises. Eusebius located the persecution of the Christians in the second half of the reign, from 303 onwards. But several of the above *Acts* date from the first part of the reign. In two cases at least—those of Maximilian and Marcellus—this dating seems beyond dispute. We may indeed wonder how such incidents could still have been possible after the bloodless purge of the years 298-303.[126] Must we conclude, then, that the persecution began in 285? Moreau has contended that in these cases we cannot speak of persecution in the strict sense, i.e., a hostile initiative which the state undertook against the Christians as such.[127] On the contrary, it was the Christian soldiers who took the initiative of refusal and thus of conflict. Although Moreau felt that Seston's theory provided sufficient explanation for their attitude, his argument concerning chronology is interesting. For it proves that neither the state of international war, nor the Church Peace, nor the numerical disproportion of the forces facing each other could make the martyrs hesitate to display their opposition openly.

Egypt offers us a text which is particularly striking because of its date, but which does not seem to have attracted much attention. When St. Pachomius, the creator-to-be of Egyptian cenobitism, was still a young pagan of twenty, "the great Constantine became emperor, the first Christian among the Roman emperors." Since Constantine at the beginning of his reign was forced to struggle against "tyrants,"[128] he gave orders for mobilization. At that time Pachomius was embarked with other young men who were already Christians. When all of them were put in chains and imprisoned at Thebes, they were generously maintained by the members of the local church.[129] "While they were still detained in the prison at

Antinoae, through divine help the pious Constantine triumphed over those who were making war on him. At once he
issued a decree throughout the entire world that the recruits
be released. As soon as they were released, everyone went
home in great joy."[130] These Christian recruits were thus put in
chains during the whole time of their service, and their Church
seemed to find this situation normal. So, later on, did the editor
and readers of the life of Pachomius, although these events had
occurred under the reign of an emperor whom the account
presented in the most favorable light. The only possible explanation is that given unhesitatingly by E. Misset: "These [impris-
oned Christian recruits] were simply catechumens or baptized
Christians who were subject to the Church's disciplinary regulations of the time."[131] After we (in Chapter 5) have seen what
these regulations were, we will be certain that Misset's answer
was correct. Finally, let us notice that it was precisely this
company of rebels who converted Pachomius. Immediately
upon his liberation, Pachomius requested baptism and dedicated himself to a life of asceticism.

Scholars have systematically ignored these special conditions of Pachomius's time in the army.[132] Some, such as Mrs.
Chadwick, in order to explain the genuine sense of discipline
which the founder of cenobitic monasticism displayed, have
gone so far as to suggest that he was the son of a family of
Roman soldiers, and was himself a former soldier.[133] But
Fr. Vogüé, a specialist in monastic history, has issued a strong
warning against this wholly illegitimate exploitation of the
military experience of Pachomius.[134] Fr. Camelot, for his part, was
even more severe. Dealing specifically with Mrs. Chadwick's
statement, he commented with asperity, "Pachomius was never
anything but a drafted man, who was enrolled against his will,
and who soon became a deserter. One could as well speak of the
military experience of the Curé d'Ars."[135]

Let us now turn to another and later group of famous
saints, whom the Catholic Church has canonized, and who

refused military service. The best known of these was St. Martin of Tours, who was the son of a military tribune and who from adolescence had himself been a soldier. Martin had not accepted service, however, of his own free will. His father, in obedience to the edict requiring the enlistment of veterans' sons,[136] had handed him over by force. Martin was thus in fetters and chains when he was brought to take his military oath. Thereafter he was a model of kindness and consideration toward his fellow soldiers.[137] At eighteen he was baptized.[138] It is hard to be certain whether he then remained in the army for only *two* additional years, as the wording of Sulpicius Severus—who as his contemporary and quasi-official biographer[139] is our primary source—would at first glance seem to indicate; or whether he continued in the legions for *twenty* more years, as the same text seems to imply when scrutinized carefully, and as Gregory, who was archbishop of Tours two centuries later, actually stated.[140] The crux of the matter is this. On the one hand, the *Vita* reports that Martin was a soldier from the age of fifteen onwards, and that he served under both the Emperor Constantius and the Caesar Julian, "against his will since, from his very youth ... he preferred seeking after God's service." On the other hand, the *Vita* states that Martin, after having been baptized at eighteen, stayed only about two more years in the army—and this "in a purely nominal fashion only."[141] There is substantial agreement among scholars for dating Martin's birth in 316/ 317, his baptism in 334, and his election to the bishopric of Tours in 370. But if we date his leaving of the army at around 336, this cannot have been under Julian. And if, conversely, we keep the general historical framework which includes both Constantius and Julian, then Martin's leaving of the army must have taken place a good twenty years later—at the end of his regular term of service.

At first, in the French and German editions of the present study, on the basis of the then prevailing opinion[142] I had adopted the shorter periodization. But more recent scholarship has by and large returned to the longer periodization, which Ernest Babut, the first scholar to examine this question from a scientifically historical point of view, advocated as early as 1910.[143] Even though the arguments which current scholars are employing are not all of equal value,[144] I am now willing to accept the new consensus as the most likely hypothesis. This would mean that Martin did not actually leave the army until the end of 356. But even at that date Julian was still a young man; and his rejection of Christianity as his own faith and as the official religion of the empire was yet to come.[145] Therefore, even if we accept the latter and longer periodization, the explanation which would dismiss St. Martin's behavior as a mere refusal to take part in a ceremony with idolatrous overtones cannot possibly be correct. Once again, the texts are clear beyond all doubt, if we will simply let them speak instead of "interpreting" them. Listen to Martin's declaration to his sovereign:

> Hitherto I have served you as a soldier. Allow me now to become a soldier to God. Let the man who is to serve you receive your donative. I am the soldier of Christ. It is not lawful for me to fight.[146]

Moreover, the rest of the story clarified two things—both that it was the shedding of blood which Martin considered an intolerable evil, and that he nevertheless considered it highly desirable that the empire should be in a position of dominance over its enemies. Indeed Martin, in order to silence those who had accused him of cowardice, demanded that on the following day he might be positioned, without arms, in front of the line of battle. "I will take my stand unarmed before the line of battle tomorrow, and in the name of the Lord Jesus, protected by the sign of the cross and not by shield or helmet, I will safely penetrate the ranks of the enemy." But on the following day the barbarians surrendered without battle. Martin's biographer, a contemporary, saw God's hand in this unexpected *dénouement*. God could of course have protected his soldier amidst the enemy forces. "Yet that his blessed eyes might not be pained by witnessing the death of others, he removed all necessity for fighting. For Christ did not require to secure any other victory in behalf of his own soldier, than that, the enemy being subdued without bloodshed, no one should suffer death."[147]

In order to explain St. Martin's behavior, scholars and historians have resorted to many subtleties. According to Ménard, the most recent of the saint's historians, Martin was approaching the end of his regular term of service, and having a legitimate desire not to reenlist, he refused to participate in the *donativum* ceremony which would have symbolized his entry into a new term of service.[148] This explanation is so imaginative that Ménard did not even attempt to justify it by reference to the sources! Other writers have simply pretended not to understand the text.[149] Still others have contended that the saint acted as he did because he already considered himself to be a monk and no longer to be an ordinary Christian.[150] Finally, there have been scholars who have attempted to discredit this most embarrassing witness by making him out to be an uneducated simpleton. Martin, alas, had indeed acted as a conscientious objector, but only because he had been incapable of appreciating the spiritual and symbolic meaning of the teaching he had received.[151]

Abbé Misset was the *enfant terrible* of French Catholicism in the last years of the nineteenth century. In a series of potent pamphlets he replied to Lecoy de la Marche and his followers, proving—once for all, one would have thought— that St. Martin had left the army, not because of some priestly or monastic privilege, but solely as a result of his baptism, since he was convinced that a Christian could not be a soldier. Martin was, of course, to become the first monk of the West. But as one of the best historians of that period has written,

"From the little that we know about the origin of monasticism in Gaul, I should be very ready to believe that everything started with the arrival of Martin at Ligugé, towards the end of 360 or the beginning of 361."[152] It is therefore hard to see how Martin, when he repudiated military service, could have availed himself of a tradition that did not yet exist. Moreover, not until the twelfth century were monks accorded clerical immunity from armed service.[153] And St. Martin had left the army fourteen years before being ordained priest. Misset, who had shown what St. Martin's attitude was not, was therefore in a position to prove what his primary motivation actually was— the strict application of the law of the Church, which we shall be studying in the next chapter.[154] Moreover, the revulsion from military service was widely shared in the saint's religious *entourage.* Brictio, one of the monks who later rebelled against him, during an altercation once threw in his face an ultimate insult: "You spent your youth amidst the vices of the army."[155]

J. Fontaine, the most recent editor of the text, has advanced another objection.[156] He has expressed skepticism about the historicity of the *"Pugnare mihi non licet,"* which he has characterized incredulously as "an aggressive proclamation of conscientious objection, forty-two years after the Council of Arles, forty-three years after the peace of the Church, forty-four years after the victory of Milvian Bridge, when the chrismatory was stamped on the imperial flag and when the safety of the Christian empire tended to become identical with that of the Church." In the light of this timing, Fontaine reasoned, Martin's purported proclamation was hard to credit, especially when one considered that it would have been made by "an old legionary who was perhaps even an officer, and who had reached the time of his honorable discharge."[157]

It was incidents such as the altercation involving Brictio which to Fontaine best explained why Sulpicius Severus should have felt compelled deliberately to distort the text by fabricating Martin's antimilitaristic outburst.[158] Martin's actual views could thus have been far from the antimilitarism with which he has been credited. However, the fact that he had been a soldier, and on this hypothesis one who had not revolted against his position, was shocking both for good society in Gaul, which knew only too well the exactions of the army, and for the juridical circles of the pontifical court.[159] It was also objectionable to the ascetic groups, of which Jerome and Paulinus were the chief figures.[160] Therefore, in order expressly to ensure that St. Martin might be accepted as bishop of Tours, his biographer felt compelled drastically to contract the period of time during which his hero had done military service and to imagine that at the end of his service he had displayed an attitude of radical condemnation of the army.[161] So (as Fontaine expressed it in the title of one of his papers) Sulpicius "dressed Martin up" as a military objector by artificially forcing the real facts of his life into the hagiographic framework provided by the passions of Maximilian, Marcellus, and Tipasius.[162]

I cannot personally follow Fontaine this far. Even after having taken account of the fact that the methodology of ancient hagiographers is not that of modern historians, I am unable to believe that Martin's actual behavior and assertions—on this vitally important matter at the turning point in his life—could have been so drastically different from what his closest friends and disciples believed that he had done and said. People do change, of course; and fundamental change is central to conversion. Therefore there may be some truth in the contention that Martin's attitudes in 361 were not the same as they had been in 356. But this change—if one indeed occurred—was not necessarily a gradual one which smoothed out all differences between the two stages. It may have been a drastic one, emphasizing the distinctiveness of each stage. Furthermore, even if Fontaine's argument were convincing in its entirety, it would not weaken my own general interpretation; on the contrary it would make it all the more compelling. For Fontaine has conceded that the elite of the fourth-century Christians did not regard the rebellious pre-314 soldiers as embarrassing precedents; they rather viewed them as models which faithful Christians who after 314 were engaged in military life should still have emulated. Fontaine defined the ideal which they personified, which the fourth-century believers thus recognized as a fundamental Christian demand, as a "thirst for the absolute in a conversion from the army of Caesar to the army of Christ, [and] the will to be faithful to the evangelical principles, without compromise of any kind with the world."[163]

St. Victricius, who from 380 to 407 was bishop of Rouen,[164] and St. Paulinus, who was born at Bordeaux in 353 and from 409 to 431 was bishop of Nola in Italy,[165] belonged to this same circle. The essence of our knowledge of their attitude derives from three letters of St. Paulinus. The first of these, which was addressed to Victricius, dates from just a year after Sulpicius's completion of the *Vita Martini*.[166] Having first asked his correspondent the rhetorical question—"By what paths did he [God] lead you to the way of his truth?"—Paulinus then answered it himself by recalling the tribulations that his friend had suffered. Paulinus wrote his second letter to an unnamed friend who had been brought to his attention by a certain Victor, who formerly had been his tent companion.[167] In the third letter Paulinus used numerous military metaphors, attributing to them a purely spiritual meaning, and thereby placing himself in the mainstream of the tradition which we have been studying.[168]

To Victricius Paulinus wrote,

> Training you through carnal tasks for spiritual duties, God first made you a soldier, you whom he afterwards chose as priest. He suffered you to be Caesar's soldier so that you might learn to be God's soldier. His aim was that by exercising your body in the

work of the camps you should fortify yourself for spiritual battles, fortifying your spirit for confession, and hardening your body to suffering. Divine Providence's immense plan for you has been revealed through your leaving military service and entering into the faith.

Then Paulinus described the military assembly in which Victricius, still wearing all the military equipment which he had already "vomited out in spirit," "overturned the military oaths before the feet of the sacrilegious tribune." As Paulinus reminded his correspondent, "You have thrown away the arms of blood, and, as it were, put on the arms of peace. You have scorned to be armed with the sword because you were armed with Christ." On the tribune's order Victricius had been beaten unmercifully, and had then been shut up in a dungeon paved with fragments of pottery, whose sharp edges had opened up his sores and made all rest impossible. Thereupon he had been taken before the governor's court and condemned to death for desertion. While he was marching to his execution, the executioner, laughing sadistically, had shown him the spot where it was to take place. At once this wicked man had been struck blind. Victricius had then asked that his chains, which were hurting him cruelly, might be loosened. On the escort's refusal, they had fallen off of their own accord. This double marvel had saved the life of Victricius. In fact, when the governor heard of it, he "praised as holy men and released those whom he had previously savagely condemned as guilty. He who was eager to punish the holy witness to the faith, himself bore witness to the truth."

Even if it is possible to believe that Martin had actually completed the whole of his military career and that it was his friends and disciples who were forced to camouflage what they unanimously considered to be a blot on the saint's life, such an explanation cannot work for Victricius. For him we do not have precise chronological data, and the specification given by the Roman martyrologist—"under Julian the

Apostate"—is worthless.[169] But a whole group of converging elements allows us to guess confidently that he could not have been much more than twenty years old when he refused to continue serving in the army. We may, of course, omit the purely demiurgic details. But it is impossible to doubt the dramatic atmosphere of Victricius's leaving the army, since this was recorded in a text which was addressed to the hero of the drama himself.[170]

Many scholars have emphasized that, although the mid-fourth-century army certainly contained a large proportion of Christians, St. Martin never attempted to call them to follow his example. His firm position, they have argued, seems to have been more of a personal testimony to which his conscience impelled him than of a customary, generally applicable rule. However, it is also clear that Victricius came from the same background as Martin,[171] and that his attitude was that of a conscious imitator.[172] And Victricius, the letter from Paulinus records, was not alone. A number of his fellow soldiers followed his example, although Paulinus's failure to provide precise figures may indicate that there were fewer of these than he would have wished. Nevertheless, it is abundantly clear that Martin, far from being an isolated case, had his emulators.

Moreover, St. Martin's antimilitaristic gesture was an essential part of the inner logic of his Christian life. It may be relevant in this connection to recall that after he became a bishop, he was one of the few persons in the Priscillian affair who had the courage openly to oppose the emperor Maximus and the accusing bishops.[173] In order to plead for mercy for the eminent personages who had supported the cause of Gratianus—the legitimate emperor—against Maximus, Martin traveled to Trier. When Maximus invited him to a luncheon, Martin at first declined. "He could not," he said, "take a place at the table of one who, out of two emperors, had deprived one of his kingdom, and the other of his life."[174] In the end, however, he accepted. But he made no gesture of flattery toward the emperor. Priscillian's accusers were in the city. Martin obstinately refused to communicate with those ecclesiastics who were demanding the use of violence against heresy. He even took the same attitude toward the local clergy who had not broken ties with them. But he did approach the emperor, on the one hand begging him to grant a reprieve to Priscillian and his associates, and on the other hand imploring him not to send troops into Spain to subdue their supporters. Martin then proposed a farsighted compromise, which his antagonists (although they later broke their part of it)[175] accepted. Thereupon, having refused to flinch in the face of appeals and threats, Martin suddenly decided—in exchange for assurances that the heretics would not be executed and that the forces of repression would not be sent into Spain—to communicate with the sanguinary ecclesiastics. This action of St. Martin has led some to accuse him—along with his friends—of upholding the doctrines of the heretics whom they were defending.[176] This charge was never very convincing, and scholars have now unanimously rejected it. Even though Priscillian's views were not as noxious as his unedifying adversaries alleged, Martin, Paulinus, and Sulpicius Severus were certainly not in agreement with them.[177] Martin's intervention over Priscillian was therefore a result of his rejection of the use of secular power against heresy.[178]

There were other occasions on which Martin and his friends gave practical expression to this principle. A good example of this is Martin's pleading for the pardon of the guilty persons whom the provincial governor Avitianus had condemned.[179] We should also remember that it was the nonviolent Victricius who later pacified western Belgium.[180] Paulinus described the fruits of his friend's apostolate in the following terms: "Where once barbarian strangers or native brigands dwelt in deserted, equally hazardous areas of forest and shore, now cities, towns, islands with churches and

monasteries, crowded with people and harmonious in peace,
are thronged by revered, angelic choruses of saintly men."[181]

At about the same time Pope Damasus composed an
inscription to the memory of Nereus and Achilleus, two
soldiers who—no doubt under Diocletian—were said to have
been martyred for refusing obedience. The historicity of these
martyrs is dubious. But there can be no doubt about the state
of mind which, in the last years of the fourth century, was ani-
mating the bishop of Rome. The epitaph reads as follows:

> They had signed up for service, and undertook cruel
> Duties. Together [or, at the same level] they were attentive
>   to their tyrant's commands,[182]
> Ready to obey his orders at the spur of fear.
> Astonishing events, yet credible: suddenly they laid aside
>   their anger,
> They turned and fled, they abandoned the general's
>   impious camps,
> They threw down their shields, their decorations and blood-
>   smeared weapons.
> Having confessed [the faith], they rejoiced to bear
>   Christ's trophies.
> Through Damasus believe what the glory of Christ can do.[183]

This document is especially significant. For just as some
writers have attempted to minimize the testimony of the African martyrs as a purely local episode inspired by Montanist
heresy, so also have other writers tried to dismiss the ecumenical significance of the actions of St. Martin and St. Victricius—as well as the approval which St. Paulinus and Sulpicius
Severus accorded to these actions—as the lamentable repercussions upon a localized coterie of Gauls of the ascetic rigors
of the Priscillian heresy. We have already seen that neither of
those judgments was fair. The inscription of Damasus confirms this refutation. It demonstrates that the antimilitarist attitude was not peculiar to the Gallic saints. In the next chapter
we shall see that Damasus' immediate successors—and even,

according to Babut, Damasus himself—had determined that former soldiers should not be ordained, and had renewed this decision whenever it had proved necessary. Thereby they indicated how little esteem they had for the military profession. Victricius, as bishop of Rouen, received a letter to the same effect from Pope Innocent I. In it there was no mention of Victricius's earlier misadventures. But unless Innocent had given his complete approval to these Gallic deserters, he would surely not have missed the opportunity to comment on the subject when sending these disciplinary canons.

Ambrose's poem, composed for the anniversary of the martyrdom of Victor, Nabor, and Felix—three Moorish soldiers who had been executed in Milan—has a similar ring:

> The faith of the maternal Church
> Filled them with Holy Spirit
> And was crowned thrice
> By the holy blood of martyrs.
> Having torn them away from the impious camps,
> She consecrated them as Christ's soldiers....
> They do not request iron arms
> Nor weapons, these soldiers of Christ....
> For ... [the true] man, faith is a shield
> And death a victory.[184]

A hymn of Prudentius is also interesting. Written to honor Emeterius and Chelidonius, two soldiers who had been beheaded in Calahorra, the hymn clearly attributes their martydom to their rejection of pagan religious ceremonies. But at the same time it underscores the choice which they made between the standards of Caesar and the sign of the cross; and it praises their refusal "to stain with bloody carnage the hands that wield unholy swords."[185] A little later in the hymn the martyrs, supposedly expressing their own convictions, ask:

Shall we stoop to sway of Mammon who have been reborn in
   Christ?
Formed to God's eternal image, shall we serve the fleeting
   world?

They then speak of their "former existence, enslaved by their
enlistment."[186]

Another martyrdom, that of St. Ferrutius of Mainz, is of
doubtful historicity. We do not know whether it occurred at
all, or if it did occur, whether it was before or after the Church
Peace. Nevertheless, the metrical epitaph composed by Re-
culf, archbishop of Mainz at the beginning of the ninth
century, is eloquent:

Here lies Ferrutius, remarkable for his merits.
He abandoned the soldier's sword-belt for the altar of Christ.
For this reason the martyr was cruelly tortured,
Imprisoned and enchained for long months,
Until his spirit rose[187] towards the heavenly abode.[188]

Once again, a methodological caveat: it is irresponsible to
generalize about "the Church's attitude" on the basis of in-
dications that there were some Christians in the army, and
then to dismiss the teachings of the Fathers on the subject as
symptoms of personal perversity or sectarian deviation.

One final text on soldier saints remains for us to examine.
The text, which differs markedly from the earlier ones,
demonstrates the position which the Church finally adopted,
in glaring contrast to the attitudes we have previously encountered. This last position has subsequently functioned as a
distorting mirror, by means of which later writers have arrived
at a tendentious view of the earlier attitudes. The text in question—the *Passion of the Martyrs of Agaunum*—relates the
story of the martyrdom of St. Maurice and the Theban Legion. The events it chronicles purport to go back to the
persecution of Diocletian. But the text which we possess was
written only in the fifth century by Bishop St. Eucher of Lyon,

on the basis of relics which Bishop Theodore discovered at the end of the fourth century. Monceaux himself was forced to admit, "In this account, which is swarming with errors, reality has been smothered by the legend."[189] D. van Berchem, in his fine study of the subject, has been even more severe, and his conclusions have been widely accepted.[190]

Since the publication of the first edition of the present book, however, L. Dupraz has devoted a large volume to a refutation of van Berchem.[191] According to Dupraz, the collective martyrdom actually took place—at the end of 285 or the beginning of 286.[192] If this thesis were right, it would mean that in the second half of the third century there were already Christians in the Roman army—in great numbers and in fact comprising entire fighting units. This would obviously contradict my entire interpretation of the early Church's attitude toward military service. And, of all the objections to my arguments which have been advanced to date, it would be the only one which I would consider to be of genuine importance. I have elsewhere explained in detail why I have concluded that Dupraz's thesis—despite its genuine scholarly value—cannot be maintained or even be seriously considered.[193] I therefore continue to believe that the only (although real) interest of the text consists in its revelation of "the sentiments . . . of a Roman Christian of the fifth century."[194]

The broad outline of the narrative, with the statements which are relevant to our subject, are as follows. A legion of Christian soldiers which had been brought from the East refused to take part in anti-Christian persecutions. In the hope of breaking their resistance, Maximian twice had them decimated, but in vain. He then ordered that the surviving troops be put to death, and without resistance they allowed themselves to be slaughtered.

"They were men," the Passion reports, "practiced in matters of war, noble in their courage but even nobler in their faith. They rendered their valor to the emperor and their worship to Christ. Even in the army they did not forget the gospel precept. They rendered to God what is God's and to Caesar what is Caesar's."[195] After the second decimation they wrote to the emperor:

> We are your soldiers, O emperor, but also, we confess it freely, the servants of God. To you we owe military service, to him not to do evil.... We cannot follow the emperor to the point of denying God the Creator, our Creator and also, whether you like it or not, the God who is your Creator. If we are not forced into acts which are wicked enough to offend him, we shall serve you as we have done hitherto. Otherwise we shall serve him rather than you. We bring our hands against any enemy[196] whoever he may be, but we consider that it would be blameworthy to plunge them in innocent blood. These hands can fight against the godless and enemies;[197] to destroy believers and fellow-citizens is something they cannot do. We remember that we have taken up arms for our fellow-citizens and not against them. We have always fought for justice, for the faith, for the protection of the innocent. Hitherto these have been our rewards for facing dangers. We have fought to keep our promises.[198] How could we keep them toward you if we did not respect them toward our God? We enlisted first of all under the divine standards, then under those of the king.[199] You cannot have any confidence in us for the latter obligations if we break the first.... For ourselves, the need to defend our lives does not drive us to rebellion. Even that which is most powerful in time of peril, despair, will not cause us to raise our arms against you, O emperor. Look! We have our arms in our hands and we do not resist, for we would rather die than kill and we choose innocently to be slaughtered rather than to live in guilt.[200]

And according to the text, when the executioners were sent to them a last time, "they did not sink to defending the cause of justice with the sword."[201]

For St. Eucher, thus, the soldier could have two parallel loyalties, one toward God, the other toward the emperor. The latter automatically implied fighting and exterminating outward enemies and ideological adversaries. But St. Eucher justified this necessity because it simultaneously protected the true religion and the citizens of the state. As soon as earthly power misused its resources by diverting them from their legitimate functions, however, the Christian was bound to refuse obedience to it. Here, in a curious manner, these old soldiers on two points returned to the themes of conscientious objection. First of all, they refused blind obedience to their superiors. They were convinced that they remained personally responsible for their deeds, and that they must therefore make their own judgments upon the morality of actions which their commanders ordered them to perform. Second, these men— who had accepted violence in the service of the state—became thoroughly nonviolent when opposing the state.

Obviously we have here an attitude which is personally heroic[202] but illogical. For how can one "fight for justice" at the emperor's command, and yet refuse to "defend the cause of justice by the sword" when it is the emperor who imperils justice? How can one justify battles against the enemy by invoking the "protection of the innocent," and yet refuse to fight against the emperor who likewise orders the slaughter of the innocent? Either violence is a legitimate means, which must be used whenever it seems necessary; or it is illegitimate and must therefore never be used. Either the authority of the earthly power is absolute, entailing an obedience which is invariable and blind; or it is not absolute, in which case those who accept violence must also accept the possibility of revolution.

Chapter 5

Antimilitarism—The Church's First Official Position—and Its Withering Away

At the very moment when World War I was breaking out, Henri Secrétan published an original but little known article which attempted to reconcile the seemingly contradictory facts which I have assembled in the present book. His explanation was based on the distinction between two Latin verbs— *bellare* and *militare*. The early Church, he argued, had permitted a believer—when compelled by a worldly pressure of sufficient potency—to submit to the command that he become a member of the military community (*militare*). But in the eyes of the Church it had never been lawful for a believer to make an attempt on another man's life, and therefore to fight (*bellare*). Thus, in the final analysis, all early Christians were agreed upon the rejection of military violence. But whereas Tertullian and other Christian ethicists were not afraid of martyrdom and rejected all compromise, those who were more directly responsible for the entire body of the faithful sought to maintain the essentials of their faith at the least possible cost. Although they refused to betray their ideal, they were ready to compromise to the farthest possible limits.

This explanation, I am convinced, is the only one which fits the texts. From the earliest period onward, such a refusal appears to have been a spontaneous reaction by the Christians, a virtual state of mind, rather than a dogma or a Church law.[1] And from the beginning it was clear: if the civil law contradicted God's will, one must obey the latter. For it was better to be accounted a rebel by humans than by God. All Christians would therefore have agreed with Tatian's terse statement, "All [human] law is relative."[2]

Arnobius could not see that the world profited in any way from "generals, masters of military science, experts in the taking of cities; soldiers unyielding and utterly invincible in cavalry battles or in infantry combat."[3] Tertullian's treatise *De Corona* was likewise definite and unequivocal. In a later writing, in response to critics who had attempted to confound him with arguments based upon the Bible, he asserted, "Even if soldiers came to John and were given instructions to keep, even if the centurion believed, the Lord afterwards unbelted every soldier when he disarmed Peter."[4] In the *De Pallio*, in which Tertullian imagined his philosopher's cloak to be speaking, the cloak declared roundly that the Christian was "no judge, no soldier."[5]

In a similar vein, Clement of Alexandria threw discredit on all sorts of preparation which were necessary for war— which he contrasted to peace and love. He went so far as to attack the kind of music of those "who are expert in war and despisers of the fear of God."[6] Elsewhere he remarked that the Christians "do not train women like Amazons to manliness in war, since we wish even the men to be peaceable."[7] Moreover, the complete Christian "never harbors a grudge nor grows angry with anyone, even though it were someone deserving hatred because of his actions. For the Christian honors the Creator and loves anyone living, having pity on him and praying that his ignorance be removed."[8] Those who had prayed that their adversaries might be divinely punished were better than those who wished to avenge themselves by the application of the law. However, even the former were not yet perfect and were not applying the Lord's precepts. The true Christian, on the other hand, "considers it right not only for the good man to leave to others the judgment on those who have done him evil, but even wishes him to ask the judges to forgive those who have acted evilly against him."[9]

St. Cyprian's armory of insults for heretics contained only one word more stinging than *pestes: gladii.*[10] Normally he considered homicide to be a mortal sin, but the development which he later gave to this idea showed that for him the word "homicide" must be understood in its broadest etymological compass. "The hand that has held the Eucharist," he admonished, "must not be sullied by the blood-stained sword."[11] Moreover, not only was human justice terribly cruel; it often condemned the innocent without disturbing the guilty. Cyprian also denounced the

> wars scattered all over the earth with the bloody horror of camps. The whole world is wet with mutual blood; and murder, which in the case of an individual is admitted to be a crime, is called a virtue when it is committed wholesale. Impunity is claimed for wicked deeds, not on the plea that they are guiltless, but because the cruelty is perpetrated on a grand scale.[12]

The body of Maximilian, who (as I have noted earlier) had been executed for explicit conscientious objection, was brought back to Carthage to be buried at the foot of Cyprian's tomb. This provides additional confirmation of the fact that the bishop of Carthage completely shared the pacifist position of Tertullian. It also indicates yet again how misleading it is to attribute the latter's pacifism to the Montanism which he eventually espoused. As for Origen, he—when responding to the pagan Celsus' accusation that the Christians were bad citizens because they rejected military service ("If everyone were to do the same as you, the . . . earthly things would come into the power of the most lawless and savage barbarians")— strikingly made no attempt to deny the fact of their refusal. "We defend the empire better in another way,"[13] he stated, conceding by implication that the Christians did not defend it by arms. Thus, at the end of the second century,[14] a pagan who had made a thorough investigation of Christianity had found only Christians who refused military service. Origen, who was replying some years later in a more or less official capacity, and who was speaking not as a private individual but in the name of the Church, did not dream of disputing the facts; but he completely rejected the interpretation which his antagonist had given to them. C. M. Kaufmann, who was writing at a time (1917) when such an observation was courageous, recalled this accusation which pagans had flung at the Christians. Acknowledging that it had a solid historical basis, he pointed out that it was rooted in the believers' rejection of blind obedience to any human superior. "Instinctively the Christians realized the particular dangers to their faith which were caused by military service, in which oaths were required which committed them to gods and men."[15]

There is, moreover, one text—the *Apostolic Tradition* of Hippolytus—which proves that the Church expressed itself officially on this subject, and that it clearly condemned in the army the homicidal violence which is its fundamental characteristic. There have been countless attempts to minimize the significance of this document. The exuberant proliferation of writings which have grown up around it, and the resultant difficulty of dating and placing the original, have often served as pretexts.[16] Today, however, scholars have managed to bring some order out of this confusion.[17] One of them, Dom Botte, has not hesitated to claim that the *Apostolic Tradition* was "the source of the primitive canonico-religious literature."[18] This recognition—that this basic text proceeded to give birth to almost all of the canonical Christian collections in many parts of the world[19]—does not reduce the importance of the *Apostolic Tradition* in itself; on the contrary, it enhances it, for it is evidence of a kind of early Church consensus. Finally— and this is significant for the subject with which we are dealing—scholars no longer unanimously date the composition of the *Tradition* after Hippolytus's break with Callistus in 217. Dom Connolly has dated it two years prior to this; C. C. Richardson has even located it as much as nineteen years earlier than this. In either case, no one could responsibly characterize the text as the product of individual extremism. Instead, it represents the moderation of strict Roman doctrine, which was confronted with the Montanist tendencies with which Pope Zephyrinus was charged.[20]

I shall not dwell here on P. Nautin's revolutionary hypothesis concerning Hippolytus.[21] In the first place, this is because, although this hypothesis has found some support,[22] most experts have treated it with extreme reserve.[23] Second, this is because Nautin only discussed the problem of the *Tradition*'s author quite incidentally; it is almost as if he had deliberately passed over it. Above all, it is because his conclusions, even if we were to adopt them, would shed no new light upon our present question but would only complicate things a little further.[24]

The basic text which really deserves the title of Hippolytus's *Apostolic Tradition* has been preserved under the name of the *Constitution of the Egyptian Church*.[25] This text is to be found in a Coptic version in Bohairic[26] (which is not of great interest, for—except in one point—it is only a translation from the Sahidic version), a Coptic version in Sahidic,[27] an Arabic version[28] and an Ethiopic version.[29]The original Greek text, which has completely disappeared except for the title of *Apostolic Tradition* (Apostolikē paradotis) which has been preserved solely on the base of St. Hippolytus's statue, has to be reconstructed, therefore, from these four sources and from a Latin text.[30] This last would be by far the best source,[31] because it is a translation which is excessively literal (and therefore includes linguistic barbarities).[32] But, alas, it is woefully incomplete.[33]

From these materials Dom Botte reconstructed a Latin

text which probably restores for us the teaching of the church at Rome at the very beginning of the third century—and possibly even at the end of the second century. After several clauses which exclude from the catechumenate brothel-keepers, participants in gladiatorial combat, and idol-worshipers, the document states:

Miles qui est in potestate (exousia) non occident hominem. Si iubetur, non exequetur rem, neque faciet iuramentum. Si autem non vult, reiciatur. Qui habet potestatem (exousia) gladii, vel magistratus (archōn) civitatis (polis) qui induitur purpura, vel cesset vel reiciatur. Catechumenus vel fidelis qui volunt fieri milites reiciantur, quia contempserunt (kataphronein) deum.[34]

The soldier who is of inferior rank shall not kill anyone. If ordered to, he shall not carry out the order, nor shall he take the oath. If he does not accept this, let him be dismissed. Anyone who has the power of the sword or the magistrate of a city who wears the purple, let him give it up or be dismissed. The catechumen or believer who wish to become soldiers shall be dismissed, because they have despised God.

Since the Latin version is deficient for this section, the above reconstruction rests essentially on the substantial agreement between the Sahidic,[35] Arabic,[36] and Ethiopic[37] versions. The last of these, however, represents a slightly more rigid tendency, since it reads as follows:

A *soldier of the prince they shall not receive,*[38] and [if indeed they did receive him] if he was ordered to kill men, he shall not do it. *If he will not submit his resignation,* let him be rejected.[39] Anyone among the believers and catechumens who is a *soldier* or an astrologer or sorcerer or anything else of that kind, or a magistrate with a sword or a magistrate of a city who wears the purple, either let him desist or let him be rejected. The catechumen or believer who wish to become soldiers will be dismissed because this is far from God.

We should note, on the other hand, that this Ethiopian

version, like the Arabic version, does not retain the prohibition
on taking the military oath; this, as we shall see in a moment,
is found only in the Sahidic version, as well as in the so-called
Canons of Hippolytus. Dom Botte maintained that this
omission resulted from the fact that such a prohibition would
have seemed unthinkable in an age when the empire had become Christian.[40] But it is all the more striking that the versions which fail to proscribe the military oath are especially
categorical in their prohibition of military service.

By the time of the *Apostolic Constitutions*, the essential
characteristics of these dispositions had disappeared.[41] In their
place is only John the Baptist's exhortation to soldiers,[42] although elsewhere a new section was appended (which I shall
discuss later) which must be understood as forbidding a
bishop to become a soldier.[43] Here too, however, the omission
which I have just pointed out in the text which modern critical
scholarship has reconstructed rests solely on the agreement
between the Sahidic and Arabic versions. Once more the
Ethiopic text[44] is sterner and reintroduces the demand
(which the other sources ignore) to leave the military service.
It states:

> If a soldier desires to be received and instructed and wishes
> to submit to our law, let him give up his looting and violence, let
> him give up his slander, disobedience and folly, let him be
> content with his pay. Then, *if he has given up this trade*, let him
> be received; if not, let him be dismissed.

We know, of course, thanks to the researches of Dom
Connolly, that the Ethiopic text is only a version of the
Arabic text, which itself had been translated from the
Coptic.[45] But Dom Dix had already recognized that the Arabic
text from which this Ethiopic translation had been made was
certainly older than the Arabic version which we currently
possess.[46] Furthermore, Father Salles—on the basis of a
systematic study of the variants and their meaning—has con-

cluded that the Ethiopic version, as a whole, represents a very ancient source which takes us back to the original Judeo-Christian tradition.[47] We dare not forget, to be sure, that Ethiopia was first evangelized from Arabia Felix and not from Egypt. But Salles' thesis appears too vulnerable to criticism to be accepted without serious question.[48]

It is more likely that the severe elements in the Ethiopic translation of the *Tradition* have their source in the lack of skill of the translator who rendered it out of Arabic. A present-day parallel is that of Haneberg, who, when translating the *Canons*, printed "[the soldier] shall not be received," even though his manuscripts read "[the soldier] shall not kill." Botte, who has pointed out this error in his critical notes, has explained it in a perfectly satisfactory way "*ex confusione graphica inter qtl et qbl in lingua arabica.*"[49] Such an explanation doubtless applies as well to the Ethiopic version of the *Tradition*, as is evidenced by the need to append a clause to the end of the sentence in order to make the whole sentence fully intelligible. The Ethiopic text's transition, from a prescription of excommunication for refusing obedience to the Church's law to a prescription of excommunication for actually obeying the state's law, is also explicable by an evident mistake—in a sentence of highly elliptical construction—over the meaning of the words. Similarly, the reappearance of the word "soldier" at the beginning of the next canon, in a list in which authorities both civilian and military have been intermixed with "authorities" of pagan superstition, seems to have been a case of mechanical association of ideas. For the preceding canon and the end of this one make redundant the repeated reference to "soldier."

Nevertheless, we should not allow the lateness and unclarity of the Ethiopic manuscripts to delude us into considering them to be unimportant. They are, in fact, a good example of the phenomenon of "fossilization"—the process whereby old rules were recopied and preserved, even though in other respects the text itself was evolving together with Church law. We may indeed assert without paradox that for our subject the criterion of greater age is less applicable than it is, for example, when evaluating evidence about liturgy or when studying the work of an individual theologian. Indeed, the *less* ancient a document may be, the greater will be its significance for our study if in a legislative text it prescribes strict demands which are incompatible with the agreement which previously had been concluded between Church and state. The survival of a rule which conflicts with the behavior and thought of the time—even the introduction of such a rule by a simple mistake in reading—can only be explained by the existence of a very stable and therefore very primitive traditional basis. This is all the more striking because the corrections (or, if one prefers, "the mistakes") in the Ethiopic translation invariably go in the same direction: greater severity. It would be too facile merely to explain these as a series of coincidences.

As a matter of fact, the *Testament of Our Lord*, which slightly postdates the *Constitutions* and which like them probably came from Syria, is once again categorical:

> If anyone be a soldier or in authority, let him be taught not to oppress or to kill or to rob, or to be angry or to rage and afflict anyone. But let those rations suffice him which are given to him. But if they wish to be baptized in the Lord, let them cease from military service or from the [post of] authority. And if not let them not be received.
>
> Let a catechumen or a believer of the people, if he desire to be a soldier, either cease from his intention, or if not let him be rejected. For he hath despised God by his thought and, leaving the things of the Spirit, he hath perfected himself in the flesh, and hath treated the faith with contempt.[50]

Consider also the *Canons of Hippolytus,* which originated in Alexandria and date from the middle of the fourth century:[51]

Canon 13: Of the magistrate and the soldier: *let them not kill anyone,*[52] even if they receive the order to do so; let them not put crowns on. Anyone who has an authority and does not do the justice of the gospel, let him be cut off and not pray with the bishop.[53]

Anyone who has received the power to kill, or else a soldier, *let them not kill in any case, even if they received the order to kill.*[54] Let them not utter an evil word.[55] Let those who have received a distinction[56] not put a crown on their head.

Anyone who is raised to a prefect's authority or to the magistracy and who does not put on the justice of the gospel, let him be cut off from the flock and let the bishop not pray with him.

Canon 14: Let a Christian not become a soldier: a Christian must not become a soldier, *unless he is constrained by a chief who has a sword.*[57] Let him not take on himself the sin of blood.[58] But if he has shed blood, let him not take part in the mysteries, unless he had been purified by a punishment, by tears and groans. Let him not exercise his command with duplicity but with the fear of God.[59]

The reader may feel rather exhausted by the recitation of texts that I have presented in these last pages; but he will perhaps excuse it in light of its decisive importance for our investigation. For this accumulation of legislative texts forms together the basic disciplinary law of the primitive Church which was in force from the first years of the third century until well into the fifth century, in Rome as well as in Syria and Egypt. In these laws, the following stipulations are beyond dispute:

(1) Anyone who is either a Christian or a catechumen is absolutely forbidden to join the army.

(2) Anyone who had been a soldier at the time of his conversion and who is an ordinary ranker may if necessary remain one, but only on condition that he neither becomes involved in warfare nor becomes guilty of homicide.

(3) For anyone who occupies a position of responsibility, such tolerance cannot be maintained. Such a person must give

up his position if he wishes to become a Christian.

However, I have quoted the different texts because—in addition to the local relaxation in the middle of the fourth century which is perhaps evidenced by the silence of the *Constitutions*—they contain varying shades of meaning. The original text of Hippolytus, as one may conjecture confidently on the basis of the Arabic and Sahidic translations, probably did not use the sentences in Luke 3:14; instead it included passages which concentrated their severity on the officers and on those who had enlisted voluntarily. By substituting for these passages the words of John the Baptist, the *Constitutions* reduced Christian strictness merely to a level which any moral code might reasonably expect of the soldier. The *Testament* more or less retained this biblical reference, while ignoring the difference, which had been fundamental in Hippolytus, between the ordinary soldiers and those with responsibility. But then it introduced a new element. Having admonished all soldiers to obey the exhortation of John the Baptist, it immediately qualified this admonition by stating that this—although no doubt enough for a benevolent and just pagan— could not be sufficient for a Christian. In order to qualify for baptism, one must definitely leave the forces. A *fortiori*, anyone who, while receiving or after having received Christian instruction, accepted a position in which he had the power of the sword must be dismissed at once. For thereby he had proved that he had understood nothing of the gospel.

This insertion of exhortations addressed to non-Christians into the middle of a rule which was concerned with the receiving of baptism is curious. If an unbeliever were willing to listen to the Church, it could not merely encourage him in his natural goodness; on the contrary, it was compelled to invite him to be converted and thus to begin to act like a Christian. The text of the *Testament*, it seems to me, can therefore only be explained by an ambivalent attitude which must have existed in the Church. For various reasons there were Christians in the army. The Church did not want to close its eyes to this reality, but it had not resigned itself to abandoning them completely to their evil instincts. Therefore, on the one hand, it held out before all the minimum demands of morality; but on the other hand it was unwilling to lower its own ideal to the level of its members' unfaithfulness. That is why the Church continued to maintain the great principle—in all its intransigence—that there should be no Christians in the army.

A gradual change of the same kind can be found in the *Canons*. First of all, the *Canons* maintain a basic distinction concerning the use of violence. A Christian, the *Canons* conceded, might be in the army, if he had been forcibly impressed into service; but he must remain there passively, and must not commit any act of violence. But the door which admitted the initial concession—that a man might submit to being compelled to do something which he normally ought not to have done—also admitted a second and far more serious concession. In stark contradiction to the beginning of Canon 13, Canon 14 ended by conceding that the soldier who against his will had been constrained to shed blood could still be reconciled with the Church, provided that he did strict and public penance for a deed which remained a terrible dereliction. Neither the pretext of patriotic duty nor the theory of obedience to a superior could absolve him of responsibility. In this canon we note once again the same ambivalence that we have noted before. In the army there should not have been any Christians, but there were; they were not to kill, but sometimes they did. Let them at least be quite clear that the Church condemned such conduct, and that they could be readmitted to the ranks of the faithful only by expressly repenting of it.[60]

These documents contain countless corrections and omissions, which convey one now closer to, now farther from, the attitude taken by the other legislative texts devoted to the same subject. All of them are evidence of the existence of a strict rule. But it was a rule which, since it could not be rigidly applied, elicited attempts to make it flexible, even though these were interspersed by periodic reminders of earlier intransigence. As Coquin has remarked, between the *Apostolic Tradition* and the *Canons* of Hippolytus (and, one might add, between the "m" family of the latter, the most widely represented among the manuscripts, and the single manuscript R, which is nevertheless preferable on philological grounds) it was not the theoretical convictions of the Christians that had changed. It was rather the objective political situation.[61] Cooper and Maclean have concluded their discussion of the various opinions which Christians seem to have held concerning participation in military service with the following words: "Church Orders lean to the stricter view. But we cannot therefore ascribe them to sectarian bodies who kept themselves aloof from ordinary Christian life; they, like many other teachers, only lay down precepts which it is impossible to follow strictly."[62]

Other texts also demonstrate this tendency. The Synod of Elvira, which was held just before 314, remained silent on the problem of the army; but in Canon 56 it declared that the believer who had accepted the position of *duumvir* could not be admitted to the Church while in office.[63] Hefelé argued that this decision was provoked by the idolatry which was connected with the *duumvir*'s duties.[64] But Dale, who had made a detailed study of the synod and its context, considered it rather to be an explicit repudiation of violence and coercion.[65]

At the end of the fourth century St. Basil—with his well-known inclination toward monasticism—wrote, "Many gain glory from the valor they show in battle. They go so far as to boast of the murder of their brothers. Indeed military courage, and the triumphal arches erected by a general or the community, exist only through the magnitude of the murder."[66] Elsewhere Basil recognized that the Church Fathers—through leniency—had been compelled to show indulgence regarding acts of war and capital punishment and had not always bluntly categorized them as murders.[67] But he nevertheless required that the soldier "with unclean hands abstain from communion for three years."[68] The twelfth-century canonist Balsamon rightly observed that this text entailed the virtual excommunication of soldiers throughout the duration of hostilities; and since there were continual wars during this period, it must at least theoretically have separated them from the Church throughout their years of military activity.[69] In order to find justification in tradition for this interpretation, Balsamon cited the following example. When the emperor Phocas wished to account as martyrs certain soldiers who had been killed in battle, the bishops refused, expressly basing their refusal on St. Basil's disciplinary order.[70]

Did Basil derive his position from Canon 12 of the Council of Nicaea, which excommunicated "those who, called by grace, had first proclaimed their faith by doing away with their belt, but who later, like dogs returning to their vomit, even give money and presents to be readmitted into the service"?[71] Despite the conclusions of G. Fritz, I am dubious that this canon applied to conscientious objection.[72] Canon 11, to which in some old versions Canon 12 had been added as an appendix, seems indeed to leave no alternative to Hefelé's conclusion that this condemnation applied only to those men who had served with Licinius against Constantine. "Therefore one must not believe that the Council forbade military service in general."[73] On the contrary, the Council employed exclusion from Christian sacramental fellowship—a heavy cudgel indeed—solely as a means of punishing its political opponents.

Finally, let us examine the canons of the Synod of Arles (which, if we had been proceeding in a strict chronological order, we should have come to somewhat earlier).[74] The Synod, which had been convoked by Constantine, included among its decisions one which numerous scholars have recognized as the act whereby the Church, in return for governmental protection, at last wholeheartedly accepted the civil and military obligations that the state was entitled to demand of any citizen.[75] "The third [canon]," we read in *Catholicisme*, "excommunicated soldiers who refused to do service in time of peace or who rebelled against their leaders. The seventh declared that Christian officials should not be excommunicated *ipso facto*, but only if they committed an act of paganism. Thus the Church acknowledged for its faithful the perfect lawfulness of serving the state."[76] This is an elegant example of a statement which, although more or less true, nonetheless gives a false impression. In fact things were not this simple.

We may pass rapidly over canon 7:

> Christian magistrates who have acted contrary to Church discipline shall henceforth be excluded from the congregation. The same applies to those who wish to make a start in public life.

I would merely remark that this canon was not dealing specifically with idolatry, but more generally with any offense against church discipline; and, as we have seen, in this area Church discipline had required abstention from all murderous violence.

Canon 3 will detain us longer. It reads:

> *De his qui arma projeciunt in pace, placuit abstineri eos a communione* (Concerning those who throw away their arms in time of peace, it is fitting that they should not be admitted to communion).

Some manuscripts have deleted this canon, apparently without according special significance to this omission.[77] However, other manuscripts—and we shall see that this *was* significant—replaced the word *pax* by either *bellum*[78] or *proelium*.

We must give additional consideration to two expressions

in this canon's concluding sentence. First let us examine *arma
projicere*. Some scholars have understood this to mean the act
of hurling arms on someone, of killing him; canon 3 would
thus declare that anyone who killed another person in time of
(military) peace was a murderer. If this had been the case, the
canon would not apply to the problem of war, but rather to
private murder and perhaps especially to gladiators. Indeed,
the two following canons excommunicated chariot-drivers and
actors.[79] This privatizing of canon 3 would be a very attractive
thesis—were it not for the fact that in all Latin literature,
classical and religious, the phrase *arma projicere* never
denoted hurling arms on someone to kill him; it always signified throwing down one's arms in front of the military authorities to show that one refused to go on fighting. So we are
forced to conclude that the canon refers to cases of repudiation
of military service.

The other crucial expression is *in pace*, which means "in
time of peace." At first sight this is a strange qualification.
One scholar has attempted to explain it by suggesting that the
fate of those who deserted in time of war was always settled by
the direct and definitive application of military discipline.
Thus their fate, unlike that of peacetime deserters, never became a problem for the religious authorities.[80] But this would
imply an unthinkable dereliction of moral responsibility on
the part of the Church. Other scholars have suggested that
these words applied solely to the religious peace, not to
international peace. According to Harnack, "In any case the
words *in pace* raise difficulties. We could understand them to
mean 'in time of peace;' but they might also signify the peace
which had just been established between the empire and the
Church. Against the second interpretation, it might be objected that the meaning does not flow naturally from the
words. With Aubespine and Hefelé, however, I prefer the latter interpretation to the former, because otherwise *in pace*
seems superfluous."[81]

I agree with Harnack that the meaning of "peace between the Church and state" does not flow naturally from *in pace.* I would go even further and assert that this phrase, like the words which precede it, can have only one conceivable meaning for anyone who, instead of twisting its sense by abstracting it from its normal usage, takes the trouble to view it within the context of the ecclesiastical legislation that we have been studying. The phrase's obvious meaning is "international peace." Harnack rejected this because he found the qualification *in pace* to be superfluous. But he could only make such a judgment because, like most writers on the subject, he had first stated categorically, "The Church at Arles not only condemned, but placed under the formidable sanction of excommunication, the action, frequent prior to this, of Christian soldiers who deserted in the name of their religious convictions."

If we follow Secrétan's thesis, however, things become clear, and the phrase *in pace* ceases to be superfluous. "Under the influence of the persecutions," Secrétan noted,

> an opportunist party, in order to render the persecution less harsh and continuous, conceded that the Christian who had been enrolled by force might remain in the army as a so-called pacific soldier; i.e., he might carry out all the maneuvers and work which were required of a noncombatant, in time of peace, on condition that he would not become an officer, since an officer might be called upon to pronounce the death penalty.[82]

But even this opportunist party never admitted that the Christian might shed blood. The canons of Arles thus represented yet another concession—another departure from the *Apostolic Tradition* and the texts which were derived from it in which the ecclesiastical authorities had only grudgingly conceded that a Christian might be a soldier at all (*militare*). The third Arles canon, however, condemned those soldiers who would not respect the rules of the game: in peacetime, if one was in the army, one had to stay there and not cause a scandal. This canon was indeed a triumph for the opportunist doctrine. It "refused communion to the Christian who threw down his arms in time of peace, that is, in a period in which he would not have an absolutely imperative motive of conscience; for in time of peace he would not use his arms to shed blood." But "the prohibition of shedding blood was a principle over which the Christianity of the first four centuries did not compromise." For that reason, even at Arles, "it remained impossible to censure the soldier who, in a campaign, refused to use his arms."[83] Far from being superfluous, the qualification *in pace* was essential, since in wartime it was always permitted—and even recommended—that the Christian refuse to bear arms.

For many centuries, as a sort of reminder of the early teaching, the Church continued to impose penance on those who killed a man in war, "even in a just war, even in legitimate self-defense." A. Vanderpol, whom I am quoting here, cited as examples of this the penitential ordinances of St. Egbert (ca. 750) and of Regino (ca. 915), as well as the decision of the provincial Council of Reime in 923 and of the regional Council of Winchester in 1076.[84]

The correction whereby copyists replaced "in time of peace" with "in time of war" demonstrates that the former had been the inescapable meaning of the Arles canon. By the end of the Middle Ages the provisional agreement between the Church and state had long been replaced by an organic connection. Thus to copyists of that era the Arles decision—far from appearing to be a surrender to the state—seemed on the contrary to be incomprehensibly reticent. It is unlikely that the correctors intentionally distorted the canon. But its contents were so hard for them to grasp that they thought it best to interpret it by changing the crucial word—"peace"— to its opposite. For it seemed obvious to them that deserting in battle or in time of war was a far more serious matter than refusing obedience in time of peace.[85]

This is the slippery slope of compromise. The canons of Arles, like the ecclesiastical legislation which had preceded them, demonstrate that when Church discipline manifests tolerance, human weakness will exploit it to the utmost. Of course, Christians were not supposed to be soldiers at all; nevertheless, in certain precisely defined circumstances, it was possible to tolerate this as a lesser evil. After all, as long as it was solely a matter of parades, things were not very serious. But alas, these events indicate that those who consent only to *militare* soon find themselves being drawn to *bellare*. Once a little finger has been caught in a cogwheel, it is not long before the whole body is enmeshed in the works.[86]

Before attempting to explain why the ecclesiastical authorities—who were certainly not naïve and who must have had some genuine insight into human nature—allowed themselves to be caught in this trap, we must advance a final proof of the "nonviolent" character of the early Christian soldiers. Let us remember that just prior to the official recognition of Christianity a terrible persecution had taken place, which had begun with the expulsion of all Christian soldiers from the army. If these had been "normal" soldiers, who were accustomed to regarding military violence as just and salutary, this dismissal would certainly have led to civil war or at least to attempts at armed resistance. Admittedly, as St. Augustine recalled, the Christians' civic duty was such that even under Julian they never refused their military duty.[87] But at that time the situation was very different from what it had been under the Severi and their successors. Although Julian for the time being broke Christianity's religious monopoly, he refused to play the part of a bloody persecutor. In the face of savage persecution, however, it seems certain that a community convinced of its strength, of the justice of its cause, and of the legitimacy of violence in defending just causes, would have reacted by taking up arms to fight against those who wished to destroy it. It must therefore be admitted that the Christian community—in whose eyes the emperor had legitimacy only insofar as he was "a servant for good"—nevertheless could not conceive of using arms to defend that good. If the Christians had been able without qualification to serve the empire, they would also have been able to overthrow it; and the moral inhibition which prevented them from fighting it with armed force is also proof that they could not really serve it in that way.[88]

The best example of the Church's impossible attempt to maintain a "balanced" position which distinguished between two types of homicidal violence is provided by the legend of the Theban Legion.[89] According to this legend, Christians, who were forbidden to engage in violence against the emperor, were permitted to commit acts of violence in his behalf and were even praised for doing so. When one recalls that many people viewed the empire as the universal framework of order and peace, this position is understandable. But its balance remained precarious; in fact, it could not be maintained for long. For history tells us that, once the Christians generally admitted that they were justified in taking up arms to defend certain values, bloody religious conflicts broke out everywhere—between believers and nonbelievers, and even within Christendom itself.

But let us return to Arles and to the misunderstanding which later distorted its meaning. The year 314 represents a compromise, a bargain which the Church struck with the emperor in exchange for his protection. Not only did it now allow soldiers who were in the army in peacetime to stay there; it now urged them to stay there in order to avoid scandal. In doing this, the Church carefully calculated what it took to be the lowest possible price; and in the Arles canon it held back from giving permission to kill one's neighbor. Thus, in the first official document in which the Church appeared to reject conscientious objection, it remained resolutely silent concern-

ing conduct in wartime. For if it had said anything, it would
have been compelled to give an injunction which the state
would have found most uncongenial. The Church, however,
soon ceased to understand the significance of its own silence
on this point. In fact, in good faith Christians later corrected
the text of the Arles canon to convert it into something that it
certainly had not been originally—an unambiguous and unqualified condemnation of conscientious objection.

The roots of this misinterpretation may perhaps be traced
to the early Fathers, who in rhetorical passages had developed
the image of the *miles Christi*. But it was above all in Eusebius
(and to some extent in Lactantius) that this transformation of
meaning took place.[90] Eusebius reported without surprise, and
with a hint of approval, that the Christians of Armenia—when
the emperor Maximinius Daia tried to make them renounce
their faith—took up arms and inflicted a severe defeat on
him.[91] For Eusebius, as we have already had occasion to note,
the victories of Licinius and Constantine over Maximinius
Daia and Maxentius, and then of Constantine over Licinius,
were the very work of God. "Constantine . . . and Licinius . . .
were stirred up by the King of kings, God of the universe and
Savior, two men beloved of God, against the two most impious
tyrants; and when war was formally engaged, God proved
their ally in the most wonderful manner."[92] "Calling in prayer
upon God who is in heaven, and his Word, even Jesus Christ
the Savior of all, as his ally, he [Constantine] advanced in full
force, seeking to secure of the Romans their ancestral
liberty."[93] After Licinius's triumph over Daia, the victorious
troops—whom the Christians were then supporting—committed all sorts of atrocities. But Eusebius did not dream of
censuring them.[94] In these events he saw a just retribution for
the sufferings that the believers had had to endure.[95] In
Chapter 10 of Book IX of his *History of the Church*, whose
title "On the Victory of the God-beloved Emperors" revealed
its overall design, Eusebius contrasted the death of Daia, who

expired in misery "like an impious enemy of God," with the death of generals on campaign, who "contend bravely on behalf of virtue and friends, and with a good courage meet a glorious end in battle."[96] Finally, Eusebius was convinced that the eventual war between Licinius and Constantine had been a war between paganism and Christianity. For Licinius, who had come to fear the "Sign of Life" in which Constantine had put his trust, had apostatized.[97]

The same general tendency is to be found in Lactantius. He reported, for example, that at the very moment when Daia was vowing to Jupiter that he would completely wipe out the Christians, an angel was revealing to Licinius the words of a prayer for his army to recite.[98] Lactantius's attitude was not an individual view, which the Church would reject as a matter of principle. For shortly thereafter—after Licinius had changed sides, many Christians had deserted him, and Constantine had given a benevolent welcome to these selective objectors—the Council of Nicaea itself (as we have already noted) threw the weight of its authority into the balance. It excommunicated those who had returned to the service of the one whom it now considered to be the Christians' enemy.[99]

Henceforth the Church—with the exception of a few rare individuals—distanced itself definitively from its former position. As Canon Bavaud observed on the subject,

> The history of this disciplinary development is very significant. To incarnate the faith, it is necessary to be aware of the *practical circumstances.* Before Constantine, the Christian could renounce having to deal with weapons since the refusal did not endanger the empire's stability. However, during the period when the totality of the population was becoming Christian, it became necessary to accept a job which Jesus had not condemned.[100]

About eighty years after the Council of Arles, an event of vast dimensions gave to this development a quite different emotional significance: the first barbarian invasion. As P. Courcelle has rightly emphasized, the empire was then confronted with a grave danger, which awakened among the Christians an unprecedented patriotic sentiment.[101] For these barbarians were genuinely brutish.[102] In fighting against them one could with some reason think that one was defending peace and civilization.[103] The Christians were all the more likely to do so because they had gained "control of all the nerve centers of public life, in an empire ... that had come off its hinges."[104] Thus they had the power either to defend it directly or to destroy it indirectly. No longer could they desire the empire to resist its enemies, while themselves refusing to take up arms.

The perfect representative—and primary ideological architect—of this new attitude was St. Augustine.[105] To be sure, one can still detect in him certain echoes of Lactantius: "Justice being taken away, then, what are kingdoms but great robberies? For what are robberies themselves, but little kingdoms?"[106] He also quoted the pirate who was said to have told Alexander the Great, "Because I take possession of the sea with a small boat, I am a brigand. Because you do it with a large fleet, you are called an emperor."[107] "But," he concluded, "to bring war on one's neighbors, then from there to expand further and further, to destroy nations from whom one has received no offense simply to satisfy one's ambition, what can that be called except an immense brigandage?"[108]

Behind St. Augustine's denunciation of the unjust war, however, we can detect his implicit acceptance of the so-called just war. He cited the cases of Moses, who "slew the Egyptian, without being commanded by God," and of St. Peter, who, after he had cut off the servant's ear with his sword, was told by Jesus, "He who takes the sword shall perish by the sword." Concerning Moses' action, Augustine commented, "It was wrong for one who had no legal authority, even though he [the Egyptian] was a bad character, besides being the aggressor." And concerning Peter he asserted, "To take the sword is to use weapons against a man's life, without the sanction of the constituted authority."[109] In the context, however, St. Augustine was indulgent toward Moses and St. Peter, who had acted from good motives, but had unfortunately been insufficiently enlightened by God. Furthermore, it is important to note that in both cases Augustine's condemnation of private murder brought with it the complementary assurance that a killing carried out in an official capacity would have been perfectly legitimate. For, he argued, "Peace is the end sought for by war."[110] Thus he could also conclude,

> If to kill a man is murder, this may happen sometimes without any sin. When a soldier kills the enemy, when a judge or an executioner kills the criminal . . . I do not think they sin by killing a man. . . . When a soldier kills the enemy he is enforcing the law, and so has no difficulty in carrying out his duty without passion.[111]

Furthermore, it was not only defensive war that was legitimate: in certain cases offensive war was legitimate as well.[112] In any case the soldier did not have to ask himself questions. Once he had been officially ordered to do so, he could— indeed he must—kill, with an untroubled conscience.[113]

Roughly contemporary with Augustine was St. Ambrose of Milan, who, even before the theoretical development of the new attitude, was virtually an incarnation of it.[114] Ambrose had begun his career as a high official and provincial governor. Since his official residence was in Milan, he was called upon to calm the dissensions which on the occasion of a disputed episcopal succession were arising within the Christian community there. To everyone's surprise, he himself was then appointed bishop, even though he had not even been baptized. This decisive change in status in no way diminished his political importance.[115] For during the second half of the fourth century Milan was the customary residence of the emperors, and Ambrose was able, throughout the twenty years of his episcopacy, to exercise a dominating influence in their councils.[116]

To be sure, Ambrose made efforts to guide the emperor into more humane policies:[117] the episode of the penitence of Theodosius has remained famous.[118] But Ambrose clearly felt a complete identification with the imperial power. He marveled at the transformation whereby "the princes, masters of the Roman universe, have been able to become the preachers of the gospel, they who were once accustomed to be its persecutors."[119] As regards military service, he was content to recall the words of John the Baptist exhorting soldiers to be satisfied with their pay and not to extort additional sums by unlawful means.[120] Elsewhere he asserted that "courage, which in war preserves one's country from the barbarians, or at home defends the weak, or comrades from robbers, is full of justice."[121]

At the beginning of the invasions by the Goths, Ambrose was convinced that he could apply exactly to his own age a theology of history which he derived from the Old Testament. On the basis of Ezekiel 38 and 39 he explained that the emperor of the East, Valens, was the victim of the barbarian invasion because of his Arianism. But the good Catholic armies of Gratian, the emperor of the West, would come to redress the situation, thereby saving civilization and illustrating the true faith.[122] Unfortunately for Ambrose's predictions, the impatient Valens went into battle without waiting for Gratian. In a disastrous defeat Valens was killed, and the Western army had to withdraw without fighting.[123]

Athanasius, who had been born before the Church Peace, made an even clearer statement of the new position in a letter on a quite different topic which he wrote to the monk Amun.[124] In an effort to demonstrate that the morality of an act depended upon the agent's intention, and not upon the nature of the deed itself, Athanasius wrote,

It is not lawful to kill. But to destroy adversaries in war is legal and worthy of praise. Thus those who distinguish themselves in battle are considered worthy of great honors and monuments are erected to recall their exploits. So much so that the same act, if considered from a certain angle and when performed unseasonably, is unlawful; whereas when it is considered from another side and performed in its proper time, it is lawful and normal.[125]

And in 416 the Emperor Theodosius II issued a decree whereby henceforth only Christians could be in the army.[126]

This was a long distance from the uneasy tolerance that the Church had gradually come to show toward anyone whom adverse circumstances had forced into the profession of arms, which it had always condemned in principle; it was a long distance from the terrible lucidity of St. Basil, who a few years earlier was still emphasizing the moral responsibility of the man of war; it was a long distance also from the attitude which—in the same period—St. Martin and his group of friends were taking.[127] The gigantic misunderstanding, which had led to the quasi-*concordat* of the beginning of the fourth century, had now falsified everything.

Constantine, who had a superficial knowledge of the Christians, was interested in them as possible allies in his struggle for power. As allies, they would be valuable both for their numbers and for their spirit of self-sacrifice and courage, which he had seen demonstrated during the time of the most recent persecution. Such an imperial alliance with the Christians was perhaps inevitable. Since the third century the emperors had reached the conclusion that, if they did not have sufficient power to destroy the Church, they must tolerate it. All of the emperors who were contemporary with Constantine had gone one step further and had adopted the idea of relying on the Christians.[128] Constantine—primarily because he proved to be the strongest—was merely the emperor who succeeded in gaining their support. In the end, in order to strengthen his new supporters' attachment to him, he was officially and politically converted. His armies, for whom he was a god, followed him blindly in this and became Christian by pure idolatry. One is reminded of one of Chiang Kai-shek's generals, who in the 1930s had his troops baptized by hosepipe.

Hobhouse, who has perhaps written the definitive pages on the mass conversion under Constantine, has shown that two elements operated in the same direction. In the first place, the Church had already lost much of its early vitality because most of its members were no longer converts who had made an individual choice. By now they had come to be second-generation adherents who happened to be born into Christian families; thus they were less likely to possess strong personal belief. Gaps of time, which were much broader than we—at a distance of many centuries—can now realize, extended between one persecution and the next. During these periods of relative toleration the Church increasingly came to be burdened by "social" members, who lacked strong personal commitment.[129] Second, when people became Christian not only by the fact of their birth but as a result of sheer coercion, the original situation was completely reversed. When pagans were compelled to join the Church, the Church itself was bound to become pagan.[130]

The leaders of the Church, for whom God was the only Lord of history, discerned his hand in the almost miraculous imperial conversion. Thus they were no more surprised by the sudden favor which they were receiving than they had been by persecution. The same faith which had steeled them to remain constant under fire now opened itself to receive catechumens in their thousands. For God's merciful plan must not be thwarted. Combès readily admitted that "the empire was a military monarchy. If one wanted one day to conquer it, one must not be too haughty toward the army. So the Church clamped down—this was certainly its greatest sacrifice—on its warnings against war. How could it have acted otherwise? The legions were filled with Christians."[131] An uncompromising purity, which would have rejected this unique historical occasion, would probably have been irresponsible. But, on the other hand, the Church leaders were playing a dangerous game. Under the pretext of making a tactical concession which at a later date would give them a decisive influence, they were ready to conceal the most obvious implications of the Christian faith in order to lessen the friction with the ignorant pagan world.

This judgment may seem overly severe, but in fact it is substantially the same as that of P. Monceaux. Although he did not share my sympathy for Maximilian, Monceaux acknowledged that only a refusal of military service was "in accord with the teachings of the gospel and the spirit of primitive Christianity." He then stated what he considered the sole cause of the Church's change of attitude—the Christian leaders' acceptance of the fact "that a religion cannot live without sacrificing a little of its ideal."[132]

Among the theologians of the period, only John Chrysostom realized that the superficial christianization of the empire had enervated the Church more than it had transformed the state.[133] He had no illusions as to the moral worth of the soldiers who served this so-called Christian empire. It is ironical to read—from the pen of a patriarch of Constantinople, only a few years before the decree of Theodosius II—that soldiers knew only violence, excess and brigandry, that they were "like wolves, never clean from offences." Infected by all the vices, they treated as enemies those who appealed for their protection.[134] Toward magistrates the patriarch was no more indulgent. "Those who decide questions of law," he asserted, "have indeed the name of jurymen, but are really thieves and murderers."[135]

After the initial period of Caesaro-papism, S. L. Greenslade has argued, there was a period in which the Church was relatively independent of the state. From St. Ambrose onward, however, there was a complete reversal of the situation, as the Church came to reign over the state instead of being dominated by it. Thus the Church's original acceptance of submission had been tactically successful, since afterwards it enabled a complete triumph.[136] But this triumph, it seems to me, was only ostensible. The very fact that the Church was then seeking temporal power and dominion—and was gaining it—proves that it had allowed its own theology to be infected by non-Christian thinking. If it could outwardly submit to the state, this was because it had first allowed *raison d'état* deeply to impregnate its own soul.

As we have seen, the rejection of the cult of the emperor was not an isolated phenomenon; it rather was an external manifestation of a deeper conflict. As soon as Christians lost sight of this fundamental contradiction, there was an irresistible tendency for them to accept the emperor cult as well. Cerfaux and Tondriau showed in masterly fashion that "Constantine's conversion did not change much in the fundamental concept of empire."[137] The emperor expected his "divine right" to entail an obedient acceptance of all his decisions, however arbitrary they might be. The Christians had always viewed political power as dependent on God. Formerly this had compelled them to judge it by divine standards, and therefore to refuse to obey it when it gave an order contrary to God's law. From now on, however, Christians abandoned this attitude. At the same time they accepted the pictorial representations[138] and liturgical formulae[139] which they had previously rejected, if necessary at the cost of their own blood.

The Christians' changed way of thinking actually helped to divert Roman law into a more totalitarian direction. In the age of paganism the emperor had become a quasi-divinity because men had agreed to place him above themselves. Originally at least, the emperor's will, however absolute, was seen as emanating from the people. By the mid-fourth century, on the other hand, the emperor's political power had come to be viewed as descending directly from above. Thus its divinization was far more absolute than it had been in earlier emperor cults. In 366, St. Optatus of Milevis could write without a qualm that anyone who allowed himself to have opinions different from those of the emperor—even in the area of religion—was a megalomaniac who thought he was God himself. Since only God was above the emperor, only God could dispute with him. Just prior to this, while in the same frame of mind, Optatus had declared, "For the state is not in the Church, but the Church is in the state, that is to say, in the Roman Empire...."[140]

The conception of civil authority which the Christian theologians adopted in the fourth century was not all that different from that which the emperors' "Epiphaneia" had manifested in the pagan empire.[141] The latter was a very late phenomenon, however, and the wave of soldier martyrs at the time has been viewed as a reaction to its scandalous contradiction of the Christian faith.[142] The extent of the Christians' capitulation is clear.

This worldly-wise surrender was especially serious, for it was connected with the appearance and development within the Church of a new idea which was not derived from the gospel—the "degrees of perfection." At first the reaction against the general relaxation of ethical earnestness had taken the form of anarchic asceticism of the Montanist type. Soon, however, this was superseded by a more moderate, more organized form of asceticism which established an ontological distinction—no longer merely one of function—between the various categories of believers.[143] Irenée Marrou, who has superbly described the correlation between the phenomena of the "concordat" and of monachism, saw the latter as the consequence—which he felt was inevitable and spiritually salutary—of the former.[144] I would be inclined to transpose the terms[145] and to see in monachism, which Protestants have al-

ways denounced as theologically erroneous, the source of
ethical decline.[146]

The origins of this idea were already latent in what
Maurice Goguel called "old catholicism," in two notions
which were apparently far removed from each other and from
our subject. One of these was the idea of a diffuse sanctification of temporal structures, whereby the Church would be
able "to organize the life of humanity on earth and to serve as
a framework for it."[147] In addition, there was the idea of a specialized clergy, which was needed in order to fight effectively
against heresy but which led to a hierarchical and priestly conception of the Church[148] which was exactly opposite to the
"company of the faithful" (whose meaning Calvin was later to
restore). From these two preliminary ideas a third conception
developed: that there was a small class of perfect Christians—
the clergy and especially the regular clergy—to whom all the
demands of Christian morality applied. Priests were thus (and
have remained to be) strictly forbidden to shed blood. If they
were in the army, they had to take all possible precautions not
to appear to identify with its violence. Indeed, it was even forbidden for ex-soldiers later to become priests. As early as 313,
Constantine had granted exemption from all official responsibilities to the Catholic clergy, first of all in Africa and later
throughout the empire. The state thus permitted certain of its
subjects to live according to the requirements of an un-
restricted Christian ethic. In return, the Church conceded that
it would not require the great mass of simple believers to
practice heroic virtues. They could not possibly attain these,
and their attempt moreover would jeopardize the present
order of the world, within which some compromise with evil
was necessary. The fruitful tension of faithfulness within the
world was thereby replaced by a new, more relaxed position,
in which obedience was segregated from the world.

It is perhaps significant that the *Constitutions* and the *Didascalia*—the only church orders without a disciplinary con-

demnation of the soldier—both contain a mysterious passage which may be best interpreted as reintroducing the prohibition of military service for the bishops, and as stressing that it was this which distinguished them from the laity:

> Bishop, it is not right, since you are the head, that you should obey the tail, that is the laity, which fights for the purpose of destroying others, but on the contrary you should obey God alone.[149]

The same prohibition also occurred in the Arabic development of the *Tradition,* where it was linked with a demand that the believers respect the temporal power. Clearly in Christian political thought there was no longer the slightest tendency to question political authority as such. It is worth quoting this text in full:

> That the bishop, the priest or the deacon cannot serve in the army. That they must not despise the king.
> Anyone who pledges himself to the army and wishes to carry out two functions at once, a human command and the ministry, shall be deposed, for it has been said: "Render unto God what is God's and unto the king what is the king's."
> Anyone who, against all justice, scorns the king or the magistrate, shall be punished with deposition if he is of the clergy, and with excommunication if he is of the laity.[150]

From the end of the fourth century onward, more and more texts stated—and restated as often as appeared necessary—two prohibitions: not only of being a priest and a soldier at the same time, but also of receiving someone into the clergy who had earlier been in the army. Let us note, however, that the meaning of the word "army" had been enlarged by that time. From the fourth century onward the imperial civil servants wore a belt identical to the military belt; indeed, *militia* could signify all public office.[151] According to one authority, even the verb *militare* did not have a purely military significance.[152] These facts confirm two tendencies which are often discernible in the texts that we have been studying. On the one hand, the prohibition of military service appears to have been linked, especially when it was confined to the clergy alone, to a general lack of interest in the world's temporal affairs and therefore to an escape from strictly political responsibilities. But conversely, the Christians who adopted the stance of social participation could very well serve in the *militia* without functioning in a manner that a later age would understand as being military service in the specialized sense of the term.[153] However that may be, already in 378 the Council of Sirmium declared that "the priests and deacons must be completely irreproachable and not come from the magistracy or the imperial army (apo tou boulētriou kai stratiō-tikēs archēs)."[154]

Soon the bishops of Rome as well were taking an increasingly clear position. Prior to the beginning of the twentieth century, scholars had attributed the first of the texts that indicate this either to Innocent I[155] or to Siricius.[156] We now know, however, that their predecessor Damasus had in fact penned it.[157] This text, which we must therefore date between 366 and 384, still did no more than recommend that the Church not accept ex-soldiers into the ministry. But it justified its position explicitly by noting the character of the military profession, which was something to be condemned in itself.[158] Siricius, Damasus' successor, was the first pope to persuade a Roman council to take a categorical stand on the matter. In a letter of January 6, 386, he communicated the decision of this Council to the bishops of Africa: "If anyone, after the remission of sins, has taken the belt of the earthly army, he must not be admitted into the clergy" (Canon 3).[159] In September 400 the Council of Toledo softened this rule a little by prescribing that "anyone who had been a soldier and has worn the chlamys or the belt after being baptized, even if he has done nothing worse (*etiam si graviora non admiserit*), if he has been admitted into the clergy, let him not receive the dignity of the diaconate" (Canon 8).[160] The Roman Council of 402 must be expunged from the pages of history, since the canons attributed to it were really those of Damasus; but Pope Innocent I nevertheless confirmed in its full vigor the rule which his two predecessors had set forth. Indeed, about 404, writing to a group of bishops who had met again at Toledo, Innocent urged them to return to their former firmness: "No one who has belonged to the army after his baptism ought to be received into the clergy." He admitted, however, that his decision should not have a retroactive effect. Nor should it apply to those who, by benefit of canon 8 (quoted above), had during the four preceding years been ordained to minor orders in Spain.[161] Innocent's admonition, which I have just cited, recurred verbatim in canon 6 of a fuller communication which he may have addressed to a Council which had purportedly been held in Toulouse.[162] But it seems likely that there has been a confusion between Toulouse and Toledo (*Tolosena* and *Toletana*),[163] and that the text supposedly addressed to the Council of Toulouse was in fact only a distorted amplification of the letter to the Spanish bishops. This is all the more probable because Innocent—in his famous letter of February 20, 405, to Exuperus of Toulouse—did not breathe a word about the question of military service.[164] He did, however, reaffirm his position on other occasions. In a letter of February 15, 404, to Victricius, bishop of Rouen (who had himself formerly suffered and nearly been executed as a conscientious objector), Innocent repeated word for word the canon of Siricius.[165] Similarly, in his letter to Felix, bishop of Nuceri in Spain, Innocent drew up a list of persons who were forbidden to become ministers. At the very top he put the Christian who had been a soldier ("*Si quis fidelis militaverit....* ").[166]

In these texts, as earlier in the documents connected with the *Apostolic Tradition*, there has obviously been cross-pollination between the various texts. But this is significant in itself. It shows that the Church received and accepted the stance which Damasus had first taken—and which his successors had reinforced—not as isolated dicta but as the authoritative teaching of the papal seat. Although it now applied solely to the clergy, this legislation still bore witness to the former teaching: that military service was inappropriate for *all* Christians. Indeed, this legislation was not content with forbidding military service to anyone who had become a priest; it viewed past military service as an indelible stain which disqualified a former soldier forever from entry into holy orders.

As time went on, tradition retained the regulation prohibiting a person who was already a cleric from carrying out a military act. But it abandoned the notion of a lasting stain on someone who had once been a soldier. Only on the present incompatibility between the "life of perfection"—which should be that of the clergy—and participation in military life did it remain firm. As the author who systematically studied this matter throughout the Frankish period in the West, from the sixth to the ninth centuries, pointed out, "Exemption from military service in arms remained a right of the clergy as it had been in the preceding age."[167] We can see this in the Ecumenical Council of Chalcedon in 451,[168] in the Council of Angers in 453,[169] in the councils of Agda in 506,[170] of Lerida in 524,[171] of Macon in 583,[172] in the fourth Council of Toledo in 633,[173] and in the councils of Bordeaux[174] and of St. Jean de Losne[175] in the second half of the same century. Similarly, this was one of the essential preoccupations of those who in the middle of the eighth century were seeking to reform the Church in the Germanic territories. St. Boniface, at the suggestion of Carlomen, in 742 wrote to Pope Zacharias denouncing "bishops . . . given . . . to fighting in the army like soldiers and by their own hands shedding blood, whether of heathens or Christians."[176] In his reply, the pope expressed complete approval of Boniface's position. He likened the ecclesiastics who took part in warfare to adulterers or bigamists;

henceforth, he declared, they should be excluded from the ministry.[177] The Germanic Council of April 21 in the same year endorsed this policy.[178] So also did the Frankish General Council of 747.[179] And in 813, in the great reforming Council of Mainz, a similar position was adopted which from that time onward was to be the official doctrine of the Church: the laity had the right, and possibly the duty, to bear arms; but this was not the case of clerics or of those who had left the world, both of whom were only allowed to wield the arms of the Spirit.[180] In the last quarter of the ninth century Pope John VIII, in a letter to the Empress Angilberga, enthusiastically took up the defense of his namesake, Bishop John, who was refusing to perform military service for her. Recalling that the practice of this world's soldiery was contrary to the ecclesiastical status, he pointed out that "to defend the country or direct battles belongs to the arms of the temporal power."[181] After quoting this passage, Hildesheimer, upon whose study these paragraphs are based, concluded: "It was only by an abuse and contempt of the law that a cleric could be constrained to fight, even when it involved the sacred duty, which was particularly important in the eyes of his contemporaries—defense of the land when it was invaded."[182]

Constantine—from precisely 313 onward—granted to the Catholic clergy a progressively widening exemption from all public duties.[183] This was also to be the normal pattern in the future. For example, Charlemagne in person promulgated a decree prohibiting clerics from bearing arms;[184] and Charles the Bald, at the plaid of Epernay in June 846, confirmed the decisions which the Church Assemblies of Meaux and Paris had just made on this point.[185] Thus the state ordered—even compelled—certain of its subjects to live outside the world according to the demands of a perfect life;[186] the rest of its subjects it required to live within the world largely bound by the rules of sin, but redeemed by the sanctity of the former.

John Chrysostom, for example, from time to time de-

nounced the empire's excesses and exhorted the faithful to live
as citizens of heaven and soldiers of God. But his tone is different from the one which we have heard earlier. For him, the
exemplars of heavenly citizenship were the monks, who, leaving the sinful world behind them, had fled into the desert.
"Those who lead a good life and have true faith go away into
the mountains and abandon us as one flees from strangers and
enemies." [187] Elsewhere he wrote, "We pay no attention to the
ants which swarm about at our feet. Similarly, hermits pay no
attention to us, for, even less interesting than the innocent
insects, we are rather modelled on the wild beasts." [188]

Similarly, after noting the synchronization between the
development of monasticism and the peace concluded between Church and state, Louis Bouyer commented,

> There was certainly a very close link between these two his-
> torical facts, contemporary with each other. When a world in
> which Christians as such were isolated and proscribed people
> was succeeded by a world where they were honored—without
> the world's spirit being much changed thereby—then instinc-
> tively the best of the Christians would choose freely the state of
> being proscribed, although it was no longer imposed on them by
> circumstances. In a world which no longer treated them as
> enemies, they felt obliged to live as enemies of the world. They
> felt all too surely that otherwise they would quickly become its
> slaves. [189]

As a logical response to this new situation, monasticism appeared spontaneously and simultaneously in various parts of
the Christian world.

It would be interesting to analyze the causes and the consequences of the movement which has tended—especially
quite recently in the West—to confer priestly orders on monks
and to prescribe for the secular clergy an almost monastic rule
of life. In my opinion the causes and consequences of these
developments have been ecclesiastically and morally unfortunate, but to pursue this argument would take us too far

from our subject. I would merely make one general observation. It is perhaps precisely because there is a clerical order which is unsullied by compromise, and which is regarded as the only valid representation of the Church, that the Church has been able to close its eyes to what its other believers have been required to do as citizens.[190]

St. Augustine, for example, was able to explain calmly that, by virtue of a true division of labor, some believers fought by prayer against demons while others fought by arms against the barbarians.[191] It was important that each of these two functions should be preserved. That was why, when the tribune Boniface wished to become a monk, Augustine politely but firmly urged him to stay in his civic position.[192] An indirect proof of the connection between the segregation of the clergy from secular society and the church's abandonment of the antimilitarist position has been provided by the persistence with which some have tried, against all the evidence, to justify St. Martin's attitude by the monastic vows which he had allegedly already taken in his heart.[193]

Article 121 of Canon Law directs the cleric not to fight personally, even in a just war. It has been suggested that the Church has attempted thereby to maintain its prophetic testimony by displaying concretely in the present world, through the lives of a few men, the law of the coming kingdom.[194] But surely the primary ecclesiological difference between us Protestants and Roman Catholicism lies in our belief that apart from Christ's unique priesthood there has henceforth been only one universal ministry. According to such a view the entire life of every believer is called through the power and wisdom of God to become a sign and a witness, and in the eyes of men to be a scandal and a folly.

In this connection, it is worth reflecting upon the humanly engaging but theologically questionable figure of Synesios of Cyrene. Synesios was a philosopher and pagan poet, an important municipal personage in Numidia, whom the inhabitants of Ptolemais appointed archbishop without worrying about the content of his faith. He accepted this position under duress—but only after writing an open letter to the patriarch of Alexandria stating conditions: that he intended to keep his legitimate wife;[195] and that he neither could nor wished to share the "popular" faith, but would continue to adhere to his neo-Platonist beliefs.[196]

Synesios was, in fact, very much a representative of the nationalist aristocracy. In North Africa there had already been conflict between the colonists who were anxious to preserve their possessions and the destitute masses who were determined to dispossess them. Before being elevated to the archiepiscopacy, Synesios had been one of the organizers of self-defense groups. He had declared loudly that he scorned the imperial laws and regulations which forbade the establishment of private armies and the settling of private scores. "Let us defend our skins and impose peace, and after that we shall happily obey the laws"—such was the gist of his fulminations.[197]

Synesios went further than this. When sent as an ambassador to Constantinople to defend local interests before the emperor, he caused a considerable stir by a sonorous speech. The emperor, he declaimed, was "the craftsman of wars," and his soldiers were "the tools of his craft."[198] He then demanded of the emperor a rigorous purge of antinationalist elements from the army, from public offices,[199] and ultimately from the empire[200]—for all disasters were the result of their treason.[201] These were demands for blood-letting. In fact, they were part of a collective hysteria which five years later led to the juridical murder of General Stilicho, brother-in-law of the emperor Theodosius and then guardian and father-in-law of his son Honorius. The hysteria also resulted in the massacre of entire families of barbarian auxiliary troops who were stationed in Italy.

While Synesios was archbishop, it was he who addressed

the provincial assembly of Cyrenaica congratulating the general who commanded the troops.[202] Shortly thereafter he complained that attempts were being made to reduce the small elite corps of Unnigardes (a kind of foreign legion, ferocious but effective) to the same level as the native troops.[203] My concern here is not to criticize Synesios. The fearsome sacking of Cyrenaica by the barbarians in 411, by which time military protection had become inadequate, shows how real and terrible the danger was. Moreover, Synesios' excommunication of the governor Andronicus[204] shows that there had been nothing servile in his respect for power. Furthermore, his intercession on Andronicus's behalf after the latter's fall was genuinely Christian.[205] It was no coincidence, however, that the same Synesios was both the most extreme advocate within the Church of the abandoning of biblical theology in favor of Hellenistic philosophy and the Church's most vigorous exponent of military and colonialist nationalism. A single sentence reveals the essence of his attitude. When implored to intercede for a guilty man, he refused, saying, "The executioner's sword makes no less contribution to purifying the city than the holy water at the church doors."[206] Let us note in addition that Synesios had devoted an entire treatise, the *Dio* (which he probably finished in 405), to defending Hellenic culture against the Egyptian monks, whom he labeled barbarians. Synesios clearly regarded Greek humanism as the only authentic ideal; and he accepted the archbishopric not because he had altered his views but because he had come to believe that he could use it as a means of furthering that ideal.[207]

Commenting on Origen's eschatological views, Cardinal Daniélou once wrote, "Man is placed in a thorny situation, divided between an anachronistic world which has outlived its time and a catachronistic world which does not yet fully exist." In a footnote he added that one could discern an echo of this dilemma in the mistake of the conscientious objectors. "They are right to protest in the name of the gospel against war as corresponding to an outdated world. But they forget that this world nevertheless exists."[208] In another work of the same period, after he had described how the Church had passed from the prohibition of military service for all Christians to the exemption from military activities of the clergy alone, Daniélou commented, "The only difference is that whereas the whole Church was originally a small minority group in the pagan city, a special group was now a small minority in the Christian city."[209] At this point the role which the "christianization" of temporal structures played becomes emphatically clear. And the change to which this led—the position of the late Jesuit scholar and Cardinal to the contrary—was far from insignificant. For the Church, believing it was conquering the empire, was instead conquered by it. It conceded that the game of politics could retain its own rules, and it made its betrayal all the worse by christening as Christian a system which remained fundamentally pagan.[210] As Daniélou observed in 1955,"From a Christian point of view, conscientious objection can be justified only as a vocation to sanctity."[211] The regrettable thing is that, under the pretext of bringing in the masses and of "baptizing" power, the Church has forgotten that the Christian vocation has always been a vocation to sanctity.[212] A decade later Daniélou produced an astonishing book,[213] in which he, no longer content with recognizing the factual existence of "social conformity," virtually became its apologist. "Christianity as a religion" seemed totally to have taken precedence over "Christianity as revelation."[214]

In conclusion, it is interesting to note that both Jacques Moreau and Léon Homo, in their studies of the compromise which was eventually reached between Church and state, advanced the thesis that this compromise would have been possible from the outset; but "fanatics" and "blunderers" had continually upset things by their rejection of military service.[215] The authority of these two writers, as regards the purely his-

torical side of the period under consideration, is incontestable.
We can therefore believe them when they tell us that, from
the outset and repeatedly thereafter, the heart of the conflict
between Church and state was over the Christians' refusal to
conform as citizens. By eventually surrendering on this point,
the Church no doubt gained much on the temporal level. It
thereby ensured, however, that the gospel would be the real
loser.

   "As the church increased in influence," St. Jerome la-
mented, "it decreased in Christian virtues."[216] How much
truer spiritually this sad observation is than the delirious enthusiasm of the courtier Eusebius.[217]

Chapter 6

The Faith of Constantine and the Theology of Eusebius

Forty years ago almost everyone took at face value the accounts of Lactantius and Eusebius, who led them to believe that Constantine was converted to Christianity after a vision in which he had received the sign of the cross as a token of victory.[1] This story explained the abrupt and complete reversal of imperial policy toward the Christians. It also explained the disappearance of the Church's reservations about the army, since a military victory was inextricably intertwined with the victory of the true faith. Constantine's conversion implied as well that he, as a new believer, should after 312 have led an edifying life—or at least one that was morally acceptable. The Eastern Church continues on May 21 to venerate Constantine as a saint, hailing him with the titles of "equal to the apostles" and "crowned by God."[2] And in Rome the inscription by Sixtus V still stands: "Constantine, who was victorious thanks to the cross and was baptized here by St. Sylvester, was the propagator of the cross's glory."

Today, however, many scholars are far from concurring in this general consensus. In fact, Constantine's spiritual condition has become one of the most disputed topics among historians.[3] Let us briefly note the extreme positions which they have adopted. At one extreme was Alföldi, for whom the emperor remained a perfect Christian, struggling with a pagan Senate and creating Constantinople for the express purpose of having a Christian capital in counterpoise to Rome.[4] At the other extreme was Grégoire, who during the last thirty years of his life devoted his energies to disproving the classical view. His great manifesto was a paper of 1930 entitled "La 'conversion' de Constantin," with eloquent quotation marks. In 1938 he further developed his arguments in four papers in *Byzantion,* the most important of which referred once again to the "conversion" of the emperor. In this paper Grégoire announced a book entitled *Constantine: History and Legend,* which was to be published by the University of California Press (Berkeley) but which never appeared. In many articles and reviews, however, he had opportunity to return to the subject. Some of his views were too strong; but a great deal of credit must undoubtedly go to him and to Piganiol for seriously trying to find out the truth about Constantine.[5] New documentary evidence—the works of the historian Philostorgos (ed. Bidez) and the *Latin Panegyrics* (ed. Galletier)— has supplied further support for this reappraisal.

Certain points now seem to be beyond dispute: (1) Constantine's "conversion" brought about no abrupt or complete reversal. By the time he acceded to power, all of the leaders, old and new, of the empire had come to realize that it was futile to persecute the Christians; only by favors could they be conquered. After his "conversion," on the other hand, Constantine—at the same time that he was extending benevolence toward Christianity—continued to protect and patronize pagan cults. Indeed, for some time it appeared that he would be the ethical purifier of pagan religion, not its theological destroyer.[6] To the end of his life, he wanted to be the head, not only of the Christian Church, but also of the pagan church.[7] In an edict addressed to a certain Maximus, who was probably the pretorian prefect of Gaul from 327 to 337, he stated explicitly, "To insist on the ancient institutions is the

rule for the times to come. Therefore, when they do not conflict with the public interest, the things which have been kept
until now must at all costs be vindicated."[8] Moreover, in the
imperial chancellery at Trier—and perhaps also in the one at
Rome—remained groups of officials who were opposed to
Christianity, and who displayed this by promulgating laws little in keeping with their master's official religious policy.[9]

(2) Not only is the evidence from Lactantius and Eusebius obscure; it is, strictly speaking, contradictory.[10] Grégoire
ultimately rejected the authenticity of the *Life of Constantine*
almost in its entirety, for he found it inconceivable that Eusebius, who was a contemporary, could have been responsible
for the flagrant misstatements which occur in the text.[11] I
wonder if this solution is not too radical. To a large extent,
Eusebius's propensity to retouch the past is a result of his
apologetic purpose; he wanted his portrait to be one of the
ideal Christian emperor, regardless of Constantine's actual
features.[12] Eusebius also had a shrewd sense of the benefits
which might accrue to him through flattery of the emperor.
His lyrical enthusiasm nevertheless diminishes the confidence
that one can place in the evidence which he provided.

(3) Contrary to the views which Grégoire and Piganiol
upheld only a few years ago, Constantine's vision itself seems
actually to have occurred;[13] it cannot be identified with the
Apollonian revelation of 310.[14] Indeed, Gagé has shown that
the vision corresponded to the appearance on October 10, 312,
of an extraordinary constellation which was visible to Constantine in the Via Flaminia.[15] At that time, moreover,
Constantine was—and remained—an adept of a syncretist
solar monot.... On coins and medals prior to 318 the image
of the sun occurred just as frequently as the *labarum*. In fact,
the sun continued to appear on coins as late as 325.[16] Furthermore, within the column which supported Constantine's
statue in the Forum at Constantinople an oratory was
erected—for the simultaneous use of Christian and solar

worshipers.[17] Only the Christians attempted to interpret the event of the Milvian Bridge in their favor, attributing to their God something that no one previously had construed as his work.[18] The pagans—led by Constantine—interpreted it in exactly the opposite way.[19] To the end of Constantine's life, moreover, he continued to perform definite acts in favor of paganism; one of these, according to Gagé, had to do with the "sign" itself—an interpretation which, though tempting, is still conjectural.[20] J. Moreau has argued that the most exact parallel to Constantine's attitude was that of Napoleon. For Napoleon simultaneously upheld the Catholic and Muslim cults and viewed religion, like the army, as a means of acquiring and maintaining power.[21] Constantine's son went even further than his father in the political exploitation of religion.[22] It appears probable, therefore, that there was an attempt at mutual annexation, in which the emperor hoped to integrate the Christians into his solar cult, and the Christians within the Church strove for a similar synthesis.

Eventually, it is true, Constantine did tie his political fate to the Church. Delaruelle was quite happy to accept the classical date of 312 for this "gamble," as he himself called it. I would contend, however, that we can at most give this date for Constantine's decision to make use of Christianity; he did not thereby reject paganism. If in 312, 313, or even 321 Constantine had been clearly ranged on the side of the Christian religion, the panegyrics of those years could never have been produced in their actual form.

But our most important concern must be to discover what spiritual reality there was behind his conversion. Both before *and after* his decision in favor of Christianity, Constantine killed off many of his own family. In 310 he had Maximian put to death, whose daughter Fausta he had married three years before and who had obtained for him the title of Augustus.[23] This first murder, as one of his admirers could not help noting, "opened to Constantine the road to the supreme power."[24]

Maxentius, the only of his victims to die in battle (he was killed at the Milvian Bridge in 312), was the brother of the same Fausta. In 314 Constantine executed the ephemeral Caesar Bassianus, after having a little earlier given him one of his sisters in marriage. In 324 he ordered the execution of Licinius, another of his brothers-in-law (husband of his sister Constantia), although Licinius had surrendered only after Constantia had secured a promise that his life would be spared. For good measure, Constantine at the same time ordered the killing of their son—his young nephew—Licinianus. We may note in passing that the war which had such an epilogue originated solely because of Constantine's thirst for conquest.[25]

In 326 it was the turn of Crispus, Constantine's son by his first wife, Minervina, whom he had repudiated in 307 in order to marry Fausta and so to advance within the imperial family. Crispus, who was at least nominally a Christian, was brought for trial before the still predominantly pagan Roman Senate, which sentenced him to death under the accusation of having courted Fausta. He died by poison. Fausta herself did not have long to wait. In the same year (326) she was killed by being plunged into a bath of boiling water. Her alleged crime was unfaithfulness to her imperial husband with a slave.[26] These last two murders were committed while Constantine was staying in Rome, at the very time at which later tradition was to date his baptism by Pope Sylvester.[27] This coincidence would have been highly symbolic; but in actuality Constantine was baptized only on his deathbed.[28]

Heinz Kraft has recalled that although "clinical" baptism was not favored by the Church, it was widely practiced by the early Christians. He argued, therefore, that at the time of the Council of Nicaea Constantine [who, although as yet unbaptized, was functioning practically as the temporal head of the Church] considered himself already to be a member of it. But Kraft neglected to point out that the "Christian emperor" also continued to view himself as the head of another religion. On his deathbed, almost immediately after his long-deferred baptism, Constantine was still willing to give written confirmation to the colleges of the emperor cult. Thus it is not at all surprising that, in addition to his Christian funeral, the Senate decreed for him the honors of pagan apotheosis, and that the crowds of Constantinople gathered on their own accord in front of his statue to worship Constantine-the-Sun.[29] It has been conclusively shown that until 379 the Christian emperors kept the title of *Pontifex Maximus;* but this in no way proves that under Constantine the title was already a purely formal one.[30] It would rather seem to indicate that the emperor's religious ambiguity was deep-seated enough to survive Constantine.

We know why some folk postponed their baptism as Constantine did. Since the sacrament purported to cleanse the recipient from every previous sin, superstitious people attempted to receive it as late as possible—after they had committed all of their sins—so that they would be clear of the punishment they would have risked bringing upon themselves in the other world.[31] According to Zosimus, this was precisely the argument which was decisive in persuading Constantine to become a Christian: even his worst crimes could be wiped out through the sacraments which the Church alone was able to dispense.[32] The emperor preferred to give himself plenty of scope.

This was not enough, however, to make Constantine forget his suspicions and grudges. At the very time of his baptism by Eusebius of Nicomedia, he is said to have confided to his personal chaplain Eutakios his last wishes.[33] These included the order, which was to be transmitted to his sons, for the liquidation of his brothers, whom he held responsible for his death.[34] The sons made no mistake about getting rid of their uncles and their families, thereby radically simplifying all questions of succession. In the light of this, it is understandable that Julian, one of the two persons who escaped from the massacre, felt little admiration for this kind of Christianity, even though he was the pupil of Eusebius of Nicomedia (who was then appointed to Constantinople).[35] Admittedly, dynastic marriages had little to do with feelings of human affection; and Constantine's victims would no doubt have done the same to him had occasion offered. But in such an atmosphere, the prayers and pious ceremonies which according to Eusebius punctuated court life reek of blasphemy.

It would be an anachronism, however, to imagine Constantine as a skeptic or a rationalist unbeliever. He certainly believed in mysterious forces, and was doubtless caught up in the role that he was playing.[36] Christian spokesmen assured him that their God wanted him to gain victory after victory and to reign over them. These are things which princes have little trouble in believing or pretending to believe. Indeed, the exaltation of the emperor as conqueror formed the center of the imperial liturgy, Christian as well as pagan.[37]

Was it not, however, a sign of Constantine's sincerity that at the time of his conversion there was no political justification for it, since neither his army, nor Rome on which he was marching, had a majority of Christians?[38] Grégoire did not think so. He demonstrated convincingly that the most astonishing changes in religious policy which all of the rivals made were rooted in a similar motivation.[39] When attacking their adversaries, they were above all concerned to outclass them in their own domain. Maxentius, for his part, had always been favorable toward the Christians and was consistently ahead of his adversaries in granting them the legal benefits that they desired.[40] The sign of the Milvian Bridge was a masterstroke precisely because it deliberately maintained ambiguity. It possessed an almost magical, victory-eliciting power; but everyone could interpret it in such a way as would attribute that victory to his own deity. The sign anyhow had no precise resemblance either with the cross—with which it was only identified much later—or with the monogram of Christ.[41] Later on, when the eastern and western parts of the empire were struggling for dominance, the value of the sign as a rallying point for the Christians was even more obvious. In the East a majority was already Christian, and after 320 Constantine's propaganda constantly attempted to make him appear more "Christianophile" than his rival Licinius, in the eyes of the latter's subjects.[42] Grégoire, who took as his starting point the first edict of toleration, under Gallienus, wrote, "In 260, as in 311, as in 313, as in 324, anyone who wanted the East had to be, if not Christian, at least pro-Christian. There is nothing clever about my theory; it is as flat as a fact."[43]

However, as I have remarked earlier, Constantine, if not a Christian, was certainly some sort of believer. Without a doubt he was superstitious. Once again, Gagé's astronomical explanation is very tempting, all the more so because it shows the persistence of the same themes in the foundation of Constantinople and in the decoration of St. Sophia. In 335 the emperor is said to have celebrated his thirty years' reign—which celebration gave rise to an amazing address by Eusebius—as a fulfillment of the Apollonian prophecy of 310 which the heavenly sign of 312 confirmed.[44] In any case it is probable that at the end of his life Constantine believed in good faith that he had enlisted the divine power under his own standards.[45] Stauffer declared that Constantine became converted for political reasons, and that to the very end he scarcely understood the Christianity that he was professing. But he relied on the assurance of his divine right to justify his power and to excuse his crimes, which were probably more numerous than those of any other emperor.[46]

The neophyte Constantine was no doubt not the only person responsible for his moral and spiritual confusion. For example, at his side there was the mysterious figure of Ossius, bishop of Cordova, who from the beginning of 313, and possibly even from 311, enjoyed his complete confidence. This

man certainly played an essential part in Constantine's
spiritual evolution.[47] The little that we know of Ossius includes the facts that he had great admiration for Platonism
and that in the end he lapsed into Arianism.[48]

Eusebius of Caesarea, about whom we are much better
informed, had similar theological tendencies. In his book the
Praeparatio Evangelica (most notably in Books 11 and 12), he
presented the Christian faith as a kind of natural theology, in
which there was room for both Platonism and astrology as well
as for Judaism.[49] He had also completely lost the eschatological perspective. Deeply influenced by unhappy memories of the persecution, he practically deified the imperial
power from the moment the emperor accepted the name of
Christian.[50] It is not certain that Eusebius had effectively
sacrificed to idols during the last great persecution, as his adversaries—the bishop Potamon of Heracleopolis and St.
Athanasius—alleged.[51] But it is clear that, so far as he could be
said to have any coherent theological position at all, he was a
determined and impenitent Arian,[52] exactly like his namesake
and close friend, Eusebius of Nicomedia, who finally baptized
Constantine on his deathbed in 337.[53] Arius, after his first condemnation, had fled to Caesarea, where Eusebius gave him
asylum and from whence he interceded for him. As a result
Eusebius was himself summoned to the Council of Nicaea as
an accused person; only by a formal theological surrender to
Alexander and Athanasius could he save himself.[54] Eusebius of
Nicomedia faced the additional drawback of having been a religious counselor to Licinius; following the Council he was
even banned on the charge of conspiracy.[55] But the two men
had managed to attract the attention of the emperor, who was
quick to recognize in Eusebius of Caesarea someone who
would be willing to put all of his ecclesiastical authority and
theological skill at the service of the imperial ideology.
Constantine likewise rehabilitated Eusebius of Nicomedia,
whom he recalled from three years of exile to assume, on

Constantine's behalf, the identical role of religious counselor which he had already successfully played on behalf of the emperor's ill-fated rival Licinius. The two Eusebii then used their privileged official positions to launch severe purges against their enemies, who were supporters of the Nicaean faith. Eusebius of Caesarea's theological opinions were thus somewhat questionable. But above all, as Grégoire put it, he was "a party to all the doctrinal pliancies called for by Constantine's unitary system."[56] Throughout the second part of Constantine's reign, he was one of the preeminent personages of the court, a veritable propaganda minister, as Setton has remarked.[57] He was especially active in the "ideological offensive" which Constantine engineered to prepare for his campaign of 324 against Licinius, most notably in cloaking it in the garb of a "crusade."[58] This was quite an achievement, for Licinius had been the first to initiate a clear Christianophile propaganda. Licinius had had the idea, for instance, of posing as a descendent of the family of Philip the Arab, whom many regarded as having been a Christian.[59] In fact, it was Licinius that Grégoire styled—perhaps with some exaggeration—as "the first of the crusaders."[60] Licinius's stance toward Christianity, not historical scruple, compelled even Eusebius to recognize that before becoming a bad emperor, Licinius had been a good one.

Sirinelli, who has produced one of the most recent and most interesting surveys of Eusebius's thought, has credited him with a strong and attractive personality.[61] This assures us that the modern scholar has had some sympathy for the ancient writer whom he has studied. But Sirinelli's study gives us ample grounds for concluding that Eusebius was without depth of thought or responsible theology. Having spoken of Eusebius's "militant rationalism" and asserted that his theology was "revealing by its very inanity," Sirinelli went on to characterize it as a "theology of circumstance"—a crass attempt to find justification for rallying the empire.[62] This was, of course, not new: as Pichon had emphasized, Eusebius was both dependent upon Lactantius, and inferior to him.[63] But Eusebius compensated for his lack of originality with enthusiasm. In his writings, he combined frenzied praise of the emperor with thoroughness in chronicling his vicissitudes; both of these served as substitutes for theological reflection.[64] Eusebius was therefore bound to recognize in the accession of Constantine to the imperial throne "the characteristics of a privileged instance, *the* providential instance *par excellence* in history."[65] Underlying his view was the assumption that the kingship of Christ would not begin at the end of time; with the founding of the Church it had already commenced.[66] But Eusebius also showed an "extreme discretion . . . concerning anything related to Christ's life and preaching."[67] As Sirinelli commented, "He passed from the idea of a Word of revelation to that of a Word of administration."[68] Furthermore, for him "God was absent from history" and did absolutely nothing within the world.[69] Sirinelli acknowledged that Eusebius's view of history had no room for certain tenets which were the very soul of the Christian faith (i.e., the doctrine of original sin); he commented, "Since the Word had become a civil servant in charge of education, there was a gradual increase in enlightenment."[70] Eusebius "invested Christianity with the civilizing virtues which were exactly those which imperial propaganda attributed to the empire."[71] It was easily possible for him to do this, for "he had a conception of civilization which reminds us of a deist's in the Enlightenment period."[72] Indeed, his conception of the true religion identified it with the victory of reason without the inconvenience of qualifications imposed by supernatural revelation.[73] In Eusebius, therefore, we are dealing with a philosophical historian, an astute politician, but certainly not with a responsible Christian theologian.

As to Constantine's actual conversion, J.-R. Palanque has rightly observed that the emperor was anxious "to deal tactfully with the pagans of his empire and uncultivated enough to practice an *unconscious syncretism.* This is the only way to reconcile the contradictory systems—each of which no doubt reveal a part of the truth—which were built up on Constantine's Christianity."[74] For the nature of the conversion, we need only refer to the assessments of writers who have been most favorable to Constantine. Greenslade described Constantine ambiguously as "a Christian genuinely converted within certain limits."[75] De Clercq spoke of "a firm but imperfect Christian belief."[76] Parker conceded that although his conversion was sincere, "his personal piety was, no doubt, crude."[77] Foakes Jackson even observed, "It is hardly too much to say that the Christ, who appeared to him in a dream . . . cannot be regarded by us as the Christian Christ."[78] And Hobhouse, commenting on the "extreme vagueness" of Constantine's theology, recognized that most of his statements could have been uttered "by any philosophical monotheist of the day."[79] In the original German edition of his *History of the Councils,* Cardinal Hefelé argued—in opposition to Hieronymus's *Chronicle*—that Constantine's Arian baptism was insufficient proof that he had had Arian convictions. But on this point the French translator Leclercq differed vigorously from Hefelé. Maintaining that Constantine was indeed an Arian who had been officially admitted into a sect which the Christian Church fought energetically, Leclercq went so far as to write, "It seems likely that the first Christian emperor was never truly a Christian, a point perhaps which was not of much interest for him."[80]

    Such was Constantine—the man whom some have seen as the ally and first lieutenant of the God of Jesus Christ,[81] the man who summoned councils and directed their progress[82] just as if they had been sessions of the Roman Senate.[83] Eusebius called him the Bishop of the Outside World.[84] This expression has classically been understood to mean that the emperor was the bishop of the pagans, i.e., he had the duty of leading them toward an increasingly purified monotheism.[85]

We should rather understand the term to signify a sort of ecclesiastical "foreign minister." Whereas the bishops took care
of spiritual matters, Constantine was responsible for temporal
matters, concerning Christians and pagans alike.[86] But his
power was also proclaimed to be universal; he actually ruled
even in the strictly theological domain.[87] Even though
unbaptized he acted as a judge—almost always with unfortunate results—in doctrinal conflicts such as those with the
Donatists and Arians.[88] The close relationship between
Church and state, moreover, was an ultimate cause of most of
the great schisms of the Church. This was not only because of
the state's clumsiness or brutality. It was also because na-
tionalists would henceforth find that the most convenient
method of asserting local autonomy was by proclaiming as
their own a form of faith which the imperial court rejected.[89]
Thus Constantine was "an outstanding benefactor of the
Church, but also the initiator of the oppressive Caesaro-
papism from which the Church was often to suffer during the
ensuing centuries."[90]

Let us conclude this chapter by listening to the words of
E. Laboulaye, a respected Roman Catholic writer of more
than a century ago:

> Constantine—murderer of his wife and his son, doubtful
> Christian, pagan pontiff at the same time as external bishop—
> may be forgiven everything. For was he not the man who had
> the Church seated near to the throne of Caesars? Why would
> you speak of the adulteries of Louis XIV, his ambition and his
> boundless luxury? Did he not defend the unity of the faith by
> crushing the Protestants? What in another prince would be
> called violence or tyranny, was it not in the great king a great-
> hearted struggle which justified Bossuet in proclaiming him a
> new Constantine and a second Theodosius?[91]

This is the kind of Christianity that Constantine symbolizes.
But it is also the kind of Christianity against which Christ
himself stands as an uncompromising accuser.

Chapter 7

Conclusion: Christian Patience and Hope

There was thus a progressive "slide" in the Church's attitude during the early centuries of its history. Successively it forgave the repentant soldier, tolerated the nonviolent soldier, and pardoned the homicidal soldier; finally it urged the believer to hide his deepest feelings—a recantation indeed! These successive concessions, however, did not stop people, in periods of crisis, from accusing Christianity of weakening the state. This is hardly surprising, for once one starts using violence, one invariably calls for more of it. After the fall of Rome in 410, for instance, Volusianus, although the uncle of St. Melania, hurled accusations which have been preserved for us in a letter from Marcellinus to St. Augustine. Volusianus was convinced that the gospel maxims, which had led the Christians to espouse pacifism, were deadly for society. "It is obvious," he wrote, "that the observance of their religion by the Christian emperors to the best of their ability is the reason why such great misfortunes have come upon the state."[1]

This "slide," which in the end proved futile, was especially unfortunate because during these centuries Tertullian, Origen, and Lactantius were developing a doctrine of positive nonviolence which could have avoided the temptations of surrender. According to this doctrine, the use of homicidal vio-

lence to defend even the highest values was radically opposed
to the very foundations of Christianity. This certainly did not
mean that Christians must give up the idea of influencing
history; it did not mean that they were resigned and defeated
in advance. It rather was rooted in the Christian affirmation
that there was another power[2] besides that of brute force:
"Every word that goes out of your mouths in faith and love
will bring conversion and hope to many."[3] Such confidence
rested on an all-embracing vision which saw God as the source
of that power and anticipated its fulfillment in his eternal
kingdom. The believers' contribution involved allowing God's
power to act and placing trust in it; it involved enduring the
present evil with the certainty of a final victory over it. In
Latin, both classical and Christian, this attitude was called
patientia, for which our word "patience," although I use it for
the sake of convenience in this chapter, is not really an adequate translation.[4] *Patientia* was, in fact, what we today call
nonviolence.[5]

The first outlines of such a conception can be found in
the earliest Christian writings.[6] Tertullian then developed the
idea into a systematic and perfectly clear position. This position dealt with the problem of behavior toward both personal
and national enemies; it discussed unambiguously the question of the Christian in the army; and it indicated how the
believers might resist injustice without thereby having to
resort to unjust methods. Tertullian declared that since the
Christians were sons of peace, they could not attempt to
avenge themselves for wrongs which might be done to them
personally nor even to intervene to avenge the wrongs which
were done to others.[7] He also indicated that, if the Christians
had been willing to defend themselves by arms, their numbers
would certainly have ensured their victory; but "in our doctrine we are given ampler liberty to be killed rather than to
kill."[8]

This opened up another possibility, in which we can

perhaps detect the first approximation of modern methods of nonviolent resistance:

> Why! Without taking up arms, without rebellion, simply by standing aside, by mere ill-natured separation, we could have fought you! For if so vast a mass of people as we had broken away from you and removed to some recess of the "world apart," the mere loss of so many citizens of whatever sort would have brought a blush to your rule—yes, that it would, and punished you, too, by sheer desertion! Beyond doubt, you would have shuddered at your solitude, at the silence in the world, the stupor as it were of a dead globe. You would have had to look about for people to rule.[9]

But even this the Christians would not do, for to do so would have meant yielding to the spirit of surrender and thereby in some measure delivering the world over to the devil. Instead by the weight of their nonviolent determination they would act upon the city's own heart. Brute force could always be crushed by another force that was more powerful than it. But the violent would find themselves disarmed against a movement which was strong enough radically to reject impure means.

Tertullian—in his admonition to the proconsul Scapula— recalled a historical precedent. In Asia, under Arrius Antonius, the Christians had responded to persecution by going *en masse* to the tribunal to be condemned. The persecutor's embarrassment and confusion had been comical. What would Scapula do if "thousands of those under his administration, men and women of all ages and conditions, were to come and offer themselves voluntarily for martyrdom?" This threat, which was primarily an instinctive reaction of self-defense, was nevertheless based upon the faith. As the conclusion of the treatise declared triumphantly,

> We have no master save God alone. He is before you, he does

not hide himself away, and yet you are powerless against him. Moreover, those whom you look on as your masters are men, and they too will die one day. But our sect will never be destroyed. You know that it builds up the more it seems to be defeated. Indeed everyone, seeing such endurance, is drawn as if by a magnet to look into what it is all about. And when he knows the truth, he too follows it. [10]

In *De Patientia* Tertullian elaborated the same idea in more leisurely fashion. Patience, he argued theologically, was the only valid posture for Christians. He began by taking his stand on the terrain of divine revelation, for he knew that neither the wisdom of philosophers nor the prudence of men could provide authentic guidance. [11] From the vantage point of divine revelation, there was no difference between the man who was the aggressor and the man who took vengeance. The former was the first to do evil. But the latter in reaction was doing the same thing, and was just as guilty. The Christians must therefore never return evil for evil; they were rather commanded to sacrifice their honor to God by surrendering the right to defend themselves according to their own inclination. [12] Since the believers were not ready even to defend their faith by violence, they would all the more refuse to use this means in matters of secondary importance. Throughout chapter 6 of this treatise Tertullian propounded a veritable theology of patience (nonviolence). It was closely bound up with the faith which it preceded and followed. This patience, which had already been present in the old covenant, was placed above the whole law by the new covenant which was founded on grace. For it was Jesus Christ himself who was the originator and Lord of patience, and he admonished his disciples that they could be sons of their heavenly Father only in so far as they obeyed the commandment of patience. "The universal rule of patience is contained in this essential commandment: we may not do evil even when it might seem justifiable." [13]

In his *Contra Celsum* Origen wrote,

> If a revolt had been the cause of the Christians existing as a separate group (and they originated from the Jews for whom it was lawful to take up arms in defense of their families and to serve in wars), the lawgiver of the Christians would not have forbidden entirely the taking of human life. He taught that it was never right for his disciples to go so far against a man, even if he should be very wicked; for he did not consider it compatible with his inspired legislation to allow the taking of human life in any form at all. Moreover, if Christians had originated from a revolt, they would not have submitted to laws which were so gentle, which caused them to be killed "as sheep," and made them unable ever to defend themselves against their persecutors.[14]

In another passage he reasoned,

> Concerning the Christians, on the other hand, we say that they have been taught not to defend themselves against their enemies; and because they have kept the laws which command gentleness and love to man, on this account they have received from God that which they could not have succeeded in doing if they had been given the right to make war, even though they may have been quite able to do so.[15]

He continued by showing that God, while allowing some martyrdoms to take place as examples of faith, had nevertheless protected the Christians from complete destruction and had thereby discouraged their persecutors.

Origen argued that when Jesus Christ came as "reformer of the whole world," he had no need to use the methods of violence which had been in favor under the old covenant, for the force of his teaching was enough to spread the Word everywhere.[16]

> It was impossible for Christians to follow the Mosaic law in killing their enemies or those who acted illegally and were judged to be deserving of death by fire or by stoning. . . . Again,

> if you took away from the Jews of that time, who had their own
> political life and country, the power to go out against their
> enemies and to fight for their traditional custom and to take life,
> or at any time to punish adulterers or murderers or people who
> had committed any such crime, the inevitable consequence
> would have been their complete and utter destruction when
> their enemies attacked the nation, because by their own law
> they would have been deprived of strength and prevented from
> resisting their enemies.... [But] the same Providence which
> once gave the law, has now given the gospel of Jesus Christ.

It has itself destroyed the former Jewish system and, despite
all obstacles, it has allowed Christian preaching to win success
throughout the world. By the grace of God "all human machi-
nations against the Christians have been frustrated. The more
the emperors and the leaders of nations and of peoples in
many parts of the world have tried to humiliate them, the
more their number has increased, so that they *have become
exceeding strong*."[17] "We are not fools," Origen declared
resolutely, "and we do not expose ourselves without good
reason to the wrath of an emperor or governor who could
bring down on us beatings, torture, or even death." But even
if one could purchase the good-will of men by committing
murders and acts of licentiousness, savagery, or idolatry, this
would be too high a price to pay.[18]

Minucius Felix likewise bore witness to the Christians'
absolute revulsion from even judicial killing: "For us it is not
permissible either to see or to hear of human slaughter; we
have such a shrinking from human blood."[19] Nonviolence was
also the theme of Cyprian's *De Bono Patientiae*, in which he
proved himself to be a faithful disciple of Tertullian. The same
theme recurred in his *Ad Demetrianum*. "None of us, when he
is apprehended, makes resistance, nor avenges himself against
your unrighteous violence, although our people are numerous
and plentiful.... We may not hate, and we please God more
by rendering no return for wrong.... We repay kindness for

your hatred."[20] Lactantius's position was similar to that of the other writers whom we have been quoting:

> Thus it comes to pass that a just man is an object of contempt to all; and because it will be thought that he is unable to defend himself, he will be regarded as slothful and inactive; but if anyone shall have avenged himself upon his enemy, he is judged a man of spirit and activity—all honor and reverence him. And although the good man has it in his power to profit many, yet they look up to him who is able to injure rather than to him who is able to profit. But the depravity of men will not be able to corrupt the just man, so that he will not endeavor to obey God; and he would prefer to be despised, provided that he may always discharge the duty of a good man, and never of a bad man. Cicero says in his *De Officiis:* "But if any one should wish to unravel this indistinct conception of his soul, let him at once teach himself that he is a good man who profits those whom he can, and injures no one unless provoked by injury." Oh how he marred a simple and true sentiment by the addition of two words: For what need was there of adding these words, "unless provoked by injury"? that he might append vice as a disgraceful tail to a good man and might represent him without patience, which is the greatest of all the virtues. He said that a good man would inflict injuries if he were provoked: now he must necessarily lose the name of a good man from this very circumstance, if he shall inflict injury. For it is not less than the part of a bad man to return an injury than to inflict it. For from what source do contests, from what source do fightings and contentions arise among men, except that impatience opposed to injustice often excites great tempests? But if you meet injustice with patience, than which virtue nothing can be found more true, nothing more worthy of a man, it will immediately be extinguished as though you should pour water on a fire. But if that injustice which provokes opposition has met with impatience equal to itself, as though overspread with oil, it will excite so great a conflagration, that no stream can extinguish it, but only the shedding of blood.[21]

Elsewhere in the *Divine Institutions* Lactantius observed, "For he who endeavors to return an injury, desires to imitate that very person by whom he has been injured. Thus he who

imitates a bad man can by no means be good."[22] In a later
passage, he added,

> It is the part of a wise and excellent man not to wish to
> remove his adversary, which cannot be done without guilt and
> danger, but to put an end to the contest itself, which may be
> done with advantage and with justice. Therefore patience is to
> be regarded as a very great virtue; and that the just man might
> obtain this, God willed . . . that he should be despised as slug-
> gish. For unless he shall have been insulted, it will not be known
> what fortitude he has in restraining himself. Now if, when pro-
> voked by injury, he has begun to follow up his assailant with vio-
> lence, he is overcome. But if he shall have repressed that emo-
> tion by reasoning, he altogether has command over himself: he
> is able to rule himself. And this restraining of oneself is rightly
> named patience, which single virtue is opposed to all vices and
> affections.[23]

Even St. Ambrose—although as we have seen he was
partly responsible for the theoretical acceptance of military
violence—courageously practiced the opposite method when
he directed the popular opposition to the Arian heresy.[24] St.
Augustine as well devoted an entire treatise to patience. His
definition of the patient person is memorable: one who
"prefers to endure evil so as not to commit it rather than to
commit evil so as not to endure it."[25]

J. Fontaine, whose appraisal of the present book was
highly critical, has nevertheless lucidly demonstrated that the
idea of victory without bloodshed through nonviolence was a
very ancient Christian idea which the ascetics of Gaul in the
fourth century merely revived. He even went so far as to suggest that St. Martin's bloodless martyrdom—i.e., his full
readiness to give up his life, though in the end this was not required of him—may conceivably be considered, at least implicitly, to have been superior to actual martyrdom. For
Martin's action did not compel other men to shed the blood of
the very martyr who had himself objected to the shedding of
human blood.[26]

Yet the Fathers were not so naive as to imagine that the exercise of Christian patience infallibly and at a minimum cost would bring temporal victory. At the other extreme from the admonitory tale which Tertullian recounted for the consideration of Scapula are the *Acts* of the Coptic martyrs of Akhim. After Arianus, the governor of the region, had massacred some Christians in the church at Akhim, a group of their coreligionists presented themselves before him. Far from being perturbed, Arianus simply had them executed as well. Two monks from the mountain nearby then came forward and underwent the same fate. Finally forty soldiers making up the garrison of a fort in the district also appeared. "The governor could only dispose of them by having them beheaded."[27] Similarly, St. Martin, who was being taken to task by soldiers whose horses he had unintentionally startled, learned that on occasion gentleness and patience—far from calming ruffled tempers—can have the effect of enraging them still further.[28] This is a good place to recall that ethically the cross of Christ has a double meaning for Christians. First of all, it shows the heavy and cruel price which they must sometimes be ready to pay if they wish to follow their Master. But it also proclaims that the most complete defeat in men's eyes can in the end be the only true victory.[29]

With the Christian method of nonviolence remaining before us, we have come to the end of our historical investigation. Let us turn from an examination of the past in order to examine ourselves. Or rather, let us allow the past to examine each one of us and the whole Church. The question that I am posing here belongs to the order of ethics—which is derived from the faith—and not to the necessary core of the faith itself. History itself provides evidence of this. For despite the terribleness of their imprecations against the heretics, the early Church's regulations—and even the most fiery of the Fathers—always proved to be forgiving toward those who had had the weakness to get ensnared in the military system. For the person who earnestly wants to be a Christian, indeed, the acceptance of homicidal violence does not derive from a false faith; it simply indicates a weakness which prevents him from fulfilling in practice all of the demands of that faith. We must never forget that the Christian is saved by Christ's grace alone, not by any human attitude whatsoever, and not by a technique of action which always needs to be forgiven and reconsidered.[30] Nevertheless, this weakness, which prevents the faith from manifesting its fruits in transformed behavior, has serious consequences. Already in the second century the anonymous editor of the second epistle which was attributed to Clement of Rome could note that pagans, when they heard of the Christians, were full of admiration for their doctrine of loving the enemy. But when they saw the Christians at work they were exceedingly disappointed, for they observed that the believers never really put the theory into practice.[31]

Moreover, since we are dealing with a matter of method, we must always remember to take into account the historical context before making an ethical decision in this area. When the first Christian Church rejected military service, it was not assuming major responsibility for its own believers, who were unlikely to be compelled into such service. Nor was it assuming major responsibility toward the state, for the state's survival would hardly be jeopardized by the abstention of small communities of Christians. It is sufficient simply to mention the former point. For if an ethical principle is valid, it must be observed regardless of the cost. And in any case, as we saw in Chapter 4, the early believers were ready when necessary to pay the full price of fidelity.

The latter point—concerning the survival of the state— will detain us longer, for here we are really at the heart of the problem. Most early Christian writers, it would seem, regarded the state as necessary and even providential. They also believed that it of necessity had to use force, even of a homicidal nature, in order to maintain itself and to have its laws respected. They then resolved their contradiction by leaving the execution of this task, which they refused to undertake, to non-Christians. Since my approach to the Church's history is one of considered criticism rather than blind commendation, I can say candidly that implicit in this position were great dangers: of hypocrisy, if one rejoiced secretly when something got done which one did not dare do oneself; or of betrayal, if one abandoned concern for what might happen to the world. But although the fourth-century Christians were right to react against these dangers, they did so unwisely. Overreacting against their former position, they adopted a worse one, ignoring the signs pointing to a different road which they might have taken.

As far as participation in social responsibility was concerned, the effects of this change of attitude initially appeared positive. Under the early empire the international situation and public opinion were such that the Christians, who were growing increasingly numerous, could see the army as an administrative organism which ensured public order and security. Indeed, the Christian military men that we know of before Constantine all had titles and functions which make us think more of magistrates or policemen than of officers or soldiers.[32] On this level we must no doubt welcome, at least in part, the evolution which was taking place in Christian practice and acknowledge that there could be a real vocation in the police service.[33] As St. Ambrose said, the person who, when he can, does not repel the injustice that is threatening his brother,[34] is as guilty as the person who commits the injustice.[35]

The position of Christians during the previous period had implied, as Bayet wittily put it, that "the pagans will go and fight, and the Christians will pray that the pagans may fight well."[36] Clearly this was not a position which could be maintained. But we must immediately make two qualifications, one of substance, the other of method. As to substance, it is easy to mislabel any military operation as a "police action." At most, however, this term should be reserved for limited measures taken against a person or small group of persons whom the public conscience unanimously acknowledges to be harmful and antisocial. The early Christians' conception of an all-encompassing empire also has significance for us. It reminds us that—in the present situation of a world divided into national and antagonistic sovereign states—it is impossible to appeal to the idea of maintaining an international order. The tragedy of our current situation is that millions of men of equally good faith can hurl themselves against each other, each side cherishing the conviction that it is the administrator of justice and that its opponents are brigands. As to method, we should never forget that the essential objectives of a true police force include the reeducation of the offenders and their reintegration into normal social life. It is therefore not unreasonable to demand that a true police force, in order to be recognized as such, should observe the principles of "patience" which I have set out at the beginning of this chapter.[37]

It was, however, at the level of the Christian's public responsibility that the change of attitude took a radically disastrous course. At the root of the problem was the illusion that a "Christian empire," in the strict sense of both words (i.e., a political unity embracing all believers), could and must exist in the world. The state was thereby automatically sanctified, while those who stayed outside were no less automatically ranged among Satan's creatures. This was the tragic error of the Middle Ages and of the Crusades.[38] Its horrors were best symbolized by the soldier monks,[39] who piously defended and extended "Christendom" by slaughtering as many unbelievers as possible, and by the Inquisitors, at whose behest secular and spiritual authorities acted in concert—by fire and the sword—to maintain doctrinal unity.

The Church could have liberated itself long ago from this error; for example, it knew—as we are often reminded today—how to acclaim the new order in the West and to abandon the "Christian empire" to its slow and unedifying agony. Some of its leaders, however, had justifiable pangs of conscience. At the beginning of the fifth century, Bishop Orientius of Auch described the following situation: "In villages and estates in the countryside, at crossroads and in hamlets, and scattered all over the highways—all one sees everywhere is death, pain, destruction, disaster, burning, sorrow. The whole of Gaul is nothing but a burning stake."[40] Similarly, in distant Bethlehem St. Jerome—when he heard of the fall of Rome, which Alaric had captured on August 24, 410—could not withhold the outpouring of his sorrow. He wrote: "Who can tell that night of havoc, who can shed enough of tears for those deaths? The ancient city that for many a hundred years ruled the world comes down in ruin. . . ."[41] Each of the catastrophes of the day, the fall of princes and the overthrow of the empire, left a deep and painful mark on him. In his famous letter to Heliodorus, he consoled himself with the thought that the young Nepotianus, whose funeral oration he had delivered, had not lived to see these calamities which both marked the end of the world and signified the universal precariousness of human existence.[42] But in the midst of this desolation, which clearly caused him to suffer with all his soul, Jerome suddenly recovered his balance. With the full assurance of the Christian he declared, "The Roman world is falling, and yet we hold our heads erect instead of bowing our necks."[43]

During recent decades some Christian writers have exhorted the Church not to link its destiny yet again to a particular social order which has become outdated. In doing so they have recalled the fifth century, in which the Church "went over to the barbarians."[44] But, we may well ask, was the fifth-century experience one of true liberation and dispossession? Is it not more likely that in it the Church simply adopted a new myth? If that was indeed the case, then its theologians had merely fallen into the old trap: subservience to worldly ideologies. Throughout the Christian centuries this has happened recurrently. The trap's enticing bait—the dream of a terrestrial "holy city"—has been irresistibly alluring. This has partly been a result of the postponement of the Second Coming, which has led believers to attempt—according to purely human expectations—to carry forward the great and as yet unrealized Christian hope. This has also had destructive consequences, ensnaring believers in violence and cruelty which have been all the more repugnant because they have been cloaked in pious language. At long last, however, the Church is becoming aware, at least in Europe, that the Constantinian age is finished—and for good.[45] This is a momentous reversal, which implies a severe judgment on the illusions of the past. But it is also an opportunity to rediscover the ancient and authentic hope of the faithful.

Appendix

The Former Historical Doctrine

I shall first of all examine the position on the early Church and war which Fliche and Martin have taken in their *Histoire de l'Eglise*, which because of its consistency and comprehensiveness will remain a classic reference work for many years to come.° I shall then present the arguments of other writers on the subject, classifying them under the four headings which I listed in the Introduction (pp. 13-14). Because these historians have done their best to be honest, they have often contradicted their own premises. Passages in which these contradictions are evident are cited in notes to the second part of the Introduction (p. 251).

I. *Histoire de l'Eglise* (Vol. I-II in Engl. transl. by E. C. Messenger in 4 vols.)

The question which concerns us was treated by Jacques Zeiller. Under the heading "Christians Did Not Object to Military Service," he wrote, "Tertullian . . . confirms that the Christian faith did not exclude the calling of a soldier. His own mind may have changed on this point, and the opposite idea and the conduct it leads to will find its disciples. But until the end of the second century, a 'conscientious

---

°K. S. Latourette, in his famous *A History of the Expansion of Christianity*, I, *The First Five Centuries* (New York, 1937), 268-269, has taken a rather balanced view of our subject. But the immense scope of his *magnum opus* has prevented him from studying it in detail. I have therefore not included his work in my discussion, and have instead concentrated my attention upon the writings of more specialized historians.

objection' against bearing arms is no more a theme of discussion in
literature than it is a current fact in Christian practice" (II, 422).

Later on, under the heading of "The Question of Military
Service" (IV, 1028-1032), Zeiller returned to the subject under three
significant subheadings:

(1) "Christians in the army: . . . from the end of the second to
that of the third century, despite a current of hostility to the
profession of arms fortified by the intransigence of Tertullian, a
'conscientious objection' was not felt by the majority [of Chris-
tians]."

(2) "The 'Conscientious Objection' of the Intellectuals: . . .
Tertullian was responsible for this in the first place, by reason of the
evolution which led him on to an ever greater intransigence." Zeiller
then cited the Montanism which he supposed was the explanation of
such a development. Even though his exhortations in the *De Corona*
and the *De Idololatria* came from a heretic's pen, their ostensible
logicality made an impression on the intellectuals. But it was only
the intellectuals that they impressed, because ordinary believers saw
that their logic was specious. "Starting with Tertullian, then, the
question of military service was one which presented itself to Christians, and it was generally answered in his sense." (*Sic.* The last part
of the sentence, in which we should have expected to find a negative, appears to contradict Zeiller's argument. This was a misprint in
the first French edition which, although corrected in subsequent
French editions [Fliche et Martin, II, 433], Messenger accurately
and uncritically rendered in his English translation.)

(3) "Opposition between Theories and Practice": The cases of
refusal were isolated. Although there is no evidence that large numbers of Christians were in the army, some of them certainly were.
"The reasoning of Tertullian, or even of Origen, which the ecclesiastical magisterium did not adopt as its own, cannot therefore have
had a far-reaching effect . . . the good sense of the people resisted
these theories or ignored them. . . . It would therefore be a great
exaggeration to say that the ordinary practice of Christians was to
refuse military service. Such a theory was, for a century, a theory of
moralists, not the teaching of the ecclesiastical magisterium, and not
the ordinary reaction of the faithful to the question when it arose."
Zeiller concluded, in astonishing fashion, by minimizing the prob-

lem. At that period, he asserted, "people did not become soldiers unless they wished to do so." Thus the conscientious objection of some Christians admittedly created some popular prejudice against them, but their position was "not one which made them rebels in the ordinary course of things." This last remark would seem to indicate that the early Christians had the right to be conscientious objectors because the state had not forbidden this, but that in case of conflict it would be better to obey men than God!

Finally, Zeiller adopted the classical method of disposing of Tertullian's position by attributing it to Montanism, an argument which is untenable for the reasons which I have advanced above (p. 283).

From edition to edition Fliche and Martin's general position has remained identical; Gerest ("Les premiers chrétiens," 16 n.) was therefore wrong in claiming to detect some sort of development there. I can only hope that in the next edition we shall find some changes!

II. Positions Held by Other Historians

(a) Only a small minority of the early Christians refused military service. At the end of a paragraph headed "Aversion to Military Service," H. Leclercq wrote, "Studied separately, they [the facts which he had just adduced] do not prove a general antipathy to military service among believers. They rather provide evidence of personal aversions so irreducible that some preferred death to a profession which they considered to be damaging to their eternal welfare. One has sought to support these deeds by the confirmation of statistics. And E. Le Blant has concluded, on the basis of Séguier's index (which included, out of 4,734 Christian inscriptions, only 27 soldiers), that the Christians had manifested an extreme repulsion for the military profession. But we believe that this is too much to say." After having acknowledged the typical cases of antimilitarism, Leclercq continued, "If they [the antimilitarist Christians] seem to form a tradition, it is easy to bring up an opposite tradition which, although less articulate, was indeed prevalent in the Church" ("Militarisme," col. 1130). Vanderpol likewise declared (*Doctrine scolastique*, 171; cf. also 192) that those who refused military service "were never more than a very slender minority beside those who thought it compatible with the Christian religion."

(b) Christian antimilitarism was a position which appeared only very late and as a result of the influence of pagan philosophy. Bethune Baker declared (*Influence*, 31) that conscientious objection dated only from the end of the third century, "when the practical life and example of Christ and the apostles was receding far in the background." W. Cunningham also asserted (p. 253), "There seems to have been an increasing aversion to military service on the part of the Christians of the third century."

(c) Never did the Church as such sanction the attitude of antimilitarism. To establish this point, A. Tanquerey (p. 213) and P. Batiffol ("Les premiers chrétiens," 25), followed by Leclercq ("Militarisme," col. 1127) and Bayet (*Pacifisme*, 97), quoted the following sentence from H. Delehaye's *Les Légendes* (p. 2): "There was thus no incompatibility, as has often been pretended, between the profession of arms and the religion of Christ; and the Church did not bring to bear on the military calling the severe judgment of some rigid moralists." But by citing this passage these authors misrepresented Delehaye completely. For in it he was not summarizing his own findings; he was simply restating the customary position of historians who had been impressed by the number of soldier saints. In fact, as I have indicated in Chapter 4, one of the central conclusions of Delehaye's book was that this position was manifestly erroneous, for only at a much later date did the mechanistic process of hagiography turn the saints into "soldiers."

After having shown how the arguments of Lactantius and Tertullian were superseded by later theologians, Leclercq finished his paragraph by remarking (col. 1154) that although these ideas had caused a stir they had never had more than a minimal effect. Ramsay (II, p. 718) similarly observed, "Many authorities, such as Tertullian and Clement of Alexandria, absolutely forbade that Christians should be soldiers or bear arms, but the Church as a whole never sanctioned this prohibition or called on its converts to abandon the ranks or on its adherents to refuse to enter them." Cadoux (*The Early Christian Attitude*, 233 n.), basing his contention on the *Stromata* (IV, 14, 96), has indicated that this judgment is excessive as regards Clement. I hope that in Chapter 5 I have proved that it is equally false with reference to the Church's official attitude.

The same applies to A. Vanderpol's assertion (*Doctrine scolastique*, 186) that "If the Church had thought war was always and absolutely prohibited, it would have excommunicated soldiers; but there is no documentary evidence which can be adduced to this effect." If falsehoods are repeated often enough, they gain general acceptance. Ryan (p. 31), for instance, was of the opinion that not a single council or decree came out against military service. The same position was repeated by *ASS*, October, XII, p. 533. Gaubert (p. 19) stated that all the Fathers and councils invariably demanded that the Christians should, if required, serve in the army.

(d) The decisive reason for refusing military service was the army's idolatry. E. Vacandard "La Question du Service", for whom this was the essential motive, saw a secondary motive in the army's violence. But his language was so confused there that one can never know whether he meant the violence which is intrinsic to any military organization or the gratuitous violence of a Roman army which was particularly brutal (pp. 131, 132, and 139). Leclercq ("Militarisme," col. 1148) observed that after the defeat of Licinius, once the empire itself had become Christian, "the ideas which the Christians hitherto had had against military service inevitably came to be modified," because the reason behind their negative judgment—idolatry—had now completely disappeared. In the following column, however, he quoted cases of persistence in refusal from later in the fourth century, without appearing to notice that these cases contradicted what he had just written. M. Lods likewise thought that even Tertullian was not opposed to military service in principle, but only in so far as it conflicted with the service that was due to God alone (p. 22; Lods's phrase, however, is rather ambiguous). Lods also followed Seston's explanation (which I have presented on pp. 131-136) concerning the African soldier saints of 295 to 303. These saints, Lods contended, were responding to a development of the emperor cult, which was becoming something which it had not been before—clear-cut idolatry: "The texts do not mention either a conscientious objection against the necessity of shedding blood, or a refusal to take part in pagan ceremonies. But in each case they show us a Christian soldier: who refused to receive on himself the emperor's *signum*, for it would have signified that he belonged to a divine being; who would not take the oath of enlistment, the *sacramentum*, which had become the mark of membership in a demonic cult; who revolted against the idea of holding in his hand the *vexilum* bearing the emperor's images, which he had come to view as blasphemous" (p. 26).

Father M. D. Chenu declared summarily (pp. 78-79), "During the first three or four centuries . . . the Christian officers and soldiers who underwent . . . martyrdom, were not put to death for refusing enrollment in the Roman legions, but for rejecting participation in pagan ceremonies." Vanderpol had already asserted (*Doctrine scolastique*, 171, 193) that "that which alienated a certain number of Christians from military service was—far more than war itself— certain obligations which it involved, even in peacetime." In another passage (p. 189) he had expressed his thinking on the matter by saying that, after Constantine had accomplished his *volte-face*, "since all danger of taking part in pagan ceremonies had disappeared, the Christians no longer found any difficulty in serving."

As one of the most recent representatives (Vicaire) of this old orthodoxy accurately summed it up in his 1961 review of the present book (p. 391), what I have been attempting to undermine is "the common opinion among Catholic historians that Christianity before Constantine was in general not antimilitarist and that conscientious objection was only the attitude of a few intellectuals following Tertullian, chiefly because of their fear of idolatry."

Postscript to the Revised Edition

When this book originally appeared (in French in 1960 and in German in 1963), it was the subject of a quantity of reviews which—considering its rather specialized topic—was gratifyingly large. I am much beholden to all those who have generously devoted their attention to my work and given it the benefit of their criticisms and suggestions.

In this new edition I have taken many of these critical comments into account. But I have not thoroughly recast the book—as some had suggested that I should—either by distinguishing more clearly between two opposite and complementary themes[1] (the primacy of the Christian conscience, versus the submission of Christians to the state), or by delineating more finely the currents and situations "in the infinite diversity of both documents and men of various generations and regions within the empire."[2] One reason why I have been unable to accept these suggestions is practical: they would have meant my writing another book instead of merely publishing a revised edition of this one. A second reason is methodological. A. J. Visser was absolutely right in deploring the fact that the title of the German edition, *Politische Entscheidung in der Alten Kirche,* might lead one to think that there was a single, clear line of political thought among Christians from the beginning (or even, I would be ready to add, that there might be such a line of political thought today).[3] But then among the early believers there were not two such lines either—whether parallel or contrasted—as the construction of two symmetrical records would inevitably have suggested.

It is, I think, fair to say that my "passionate interest"[4] in this subject was aroused as I was forced to confront a whole complex of thought, in an inquiry in which the very illogicalities and contradictions are a continuing sign of life and creative tension.[5] If I really do not like Eusebius of Caesarea, as one reviewer has justly observed,[6] it is because I find him to be the clear symbol of the end of the era of responsible and dangerous thinking in the Church. In contrast to Eusebius, I am convinced that the function of theology is to be both critical and comforting. Its task is always, on the one hand, to awaken the Church, to help it to pull itself out of the torpor of its pervasive habits. On the other hand, its task is to point out to the Church the only solid ground on which it—in face of temptations and seductions of every sort—can confidently root its faithfulness. But here I am anticipating. Let us return, therefore, to the methodological question.

I have not composed two symmetrical accounts; on the contrary, I have tried to read the testimonies as they appeared in all their complexity and possible ambiguity. However, if I have thus sought to give as honest and complete a record as I can, I have also attempted to supply an interpretation, to discover the total significance and orientation of the Christians' collective behavior. Of course, to understand and interpret is always to simplify and generalize. The historian can never proceed without doing these things, if he intends to be more than a mere chronicler. This is all the more true in the domain of ancient history, in which the survival of documents is always rare and fragmentary. Therefore, the historian must reconstruct a coherent whole from a few surviving elements, exactly as the paleontologist reconstitutes a prehistoric animal on the basis of an assortment of vestigial bones. As it happens, the question of the early Christian attitude to the state is not badly documented; it is one of the topics on which we are best supplied with evidence. Everything which scholars have discovered about other aspects of the life and thought of the early Christians they have learned by starting from bases which are at least as full of evidential gaps as those which we have encountered in our study of the present subject. If this fact led to a skepticism on other matters similar to that which some have expressed concerning the possibility of reaching objective conclusions on my subject,[7] it would be virtually impossible to arrive at a coherent historical interpretation of any aspect of early Christian thought, practice, or discipline. But what in fact is striking about my topic is the convergence of characteristics which are evident in different strata. It is because the same themes recur— in very varied contexts—from Tertullian to Lactantius, and from Egypt to Gaul, that we are entitled to reach a conclusion on the Church's attitude. To be sure, this attitude was adopted in differing conditions, and it led to somewhat different patterns of behavior. Nevertheless it was significantly homogeneous.

I would also like to say a word on the "anachronism" of some of my comparisons. Father Roques, who like several others was worried by it, has apparently been the only one of my reviewers to see clearly—perhaps because he had had opportunity to consider my first attempt to reflect upon the reviews which my book received— that it was not simply confused thinking or sectarian propaganda on my part. It was a carefully selected method.[8] If history is really "a coming and going between the present and the past, in order to enable them to confront each other,"[9] then such an approach becomes legitimate, "even if it tends to understand men differently from the ways in which they understood themselves."[10] It is significant that a far from conventional Marxist writer, in a study of the history of the First Republic in France, has undertaken to justify this method under the title "Battle for Our Mother".[11] This "Mother," which for the committed French man of politics is the French Revolution, for the Christian is the Church of the first centuries. So this similarity in method of interpretation should cause no surprise. As Gabriel Monod said over sixty years ago in an article which has become a classic, what "for the superficial observer may be a formidable cause of error through making him distort the past by unwarranted assimilations with the present ... becomes, on the contrary, a precious guide for the scrupulous historian who is endowed with critical insight."[12] I myself once wrote,

> At the level of pure history, there is a method of systematic anachronism or shocking comparison, which is not only justifiable but very fruitful, provided that it is carried out in complete

awareness of what is being done and of the method's limits.
Nothing is more illuminating, for the understanding of a situation, than to project onto it another situation in which *nothing* is
like it except the *situation* itself.[13]

It is, of course, for the reader to judge whether I have used the
"precious guide" of which Monod spoke with sufficient scruple and
critical insight.

It was another Catholic reviewer who grasped most clearly that
this book deals with two general problems—one of them strictly historical, the other theological—which can be assessed separately from
each other.[14] In fact, the inquiry out of which this book emerged was
originally set in motion by a double question:

(a) What attitude should twentieth-century Christians hold
toward the legal obligation which forces them blindly to take part in
the organized slaughter of international conflict?

(b) What was the attitude of Christians in the past toward that
obligation?

At the start, the second question was secondary for me. It
sprang from the fact that I was very much inclined to think—amidst
the tumults of the Second World War which during my adolescence
were excruciatingly painful to me—that faithfulness to the gospel
could not mean indiscriminate participation in the massacring of
human groups which antagonistic governments had designated as
the "enemies" of the moment. But the answer which I received,
from both sides of the firing line, was an invocation of the constant
testimony of Christians throughout the ages. Never, I was assured,
had Christians—except for a few "eccentrics" and "mystics"—
allowed themselves to be influenced by the thought that "render
unto Caesar" might mean anything other than that men with a
perfectly clear conscience should carry out all the bloody tasks which
the *de facto* political power had commanded. Such an objection was
persuasive to me. For, without necessarily asking for the optimistic
ubique, semper, ab omnibus of Vincent of Lerins in order to establish a decision of Christian conscience, I could scarcely imagine
that, even in the derivative sphere of morality, the right Christian affirmation could be one which no believer anywhere had previously
held.

So the historical question, although it remained subsidiary, necessarily became the one which I had to tackle first. As soon as I made a serious start on it, however, I realized that I could not honestly answer it without addressing myself to a much wider problem—the attitude of the Christians of the first centuries to the times in which they lived. It is to answering this larger question that I have devoted the present book. But throughout my study the prior question has remained in my mind, and I have put it to the men and situations which I have "met" in my researches. To clarify the debate, however, let me now try to separate the two questions and to see what response reviewers have accorded to each of them.

Let us start with history. What credence can be given to the historical thesis which I advance in these pages? You will excuse me, I trust, if I quote at length from a favorable testimony, which is all the more valuable because its author made it clear that he was in total disagreement with my answer to the theological question:

> M. Hornus, who does not hide his personal repugnance for all the manifestations of violence, has nevertheless carried out his work very objectively. I am quite ready to believe, with him, that the refusal of military service, and still more the refusal to kill, was a doctrine and an instruction very widespread in the ancient Church, even to the point where it could be considered a normal doctrine—and indeed up to the triumph of Christianity at the beginning of the fourth century. With him I also believe that the Church's decisions of an official and canonical character, like those of the *Apostolic Tradition* and the several councils, were in the same direction; and finally that this refusal of military service was not solely based on the danger of idolatry inherent in a military career, but also on a fundamental attitude of nonviolence and respect for life, which can be counted among the basic values of Christianity. M. Hornus observes finally— and the fact is indisputable—that the mentality and discipline in the Church changed during the fourth century, while maintaining an aversion in principle.[15]

Similarly we may no doubt accord particular value to the honest acknowledgment by H. Chavannes—one of the most recent defenders of the classical military position among contemporary Christians—that my book convinced him historically, even though he could not accept its ethical conclusions. "The antimilitarist attitude of the Church of the first centuries is indisputable," he conceded.[16] This point, in fact, now seems to be generally accepted, so that I have been able to change the title of the Appendix. Whereas previously I had to refer to "the common historical doctrine," I am now able to speak of "the former historical doctrine." Take for example a recent popular survey of Christian attitudes to war. Throughout Christian history, the author observed, whenever Christians have faced the contradiction between the gospel of love and the world's resistance to it, they have been forced to choose: either to protest against violence, to compromise with it, or to sanctify it. And, the author concluded, "Of the three historical attitudes we have been considering, there can be no doubt that protest is the most authentic in the light of the primitive tradition."[17] Similarly, a large-scale work of systematic basic thinking, which distinguished three ages of Western Christianity—the pre-Constantinian era, the Constantinian era, and the post-Constantinian era into which we are beginning to grope—reproduced quite fully the account which I established for the first of these epochs; it even, although much less exclusively, adopted the basic themes of my interpretation of the transition between the first era and the second.[18] I would not, of course, attribute to myself exclusive credit for this development. But if the present book has contributed, as it seems to have done, to the settlement of a point which had hitherto been contested, then in all future histories of the ancient Church a small paragraph will have to be written a little differently.[19] This is not much, no doubt. But it is the only and highest reward that a scholar can desire.

At this point we turn from historical inquiry to ethical reflection. As soon as we come to recognize that the Constantinian era had ended, it seems to matter less whether the compromises which characterized it could have been avoided or whether they were intrinsic to the very nature of that stage of development in the Church's historic incarnation. A little over a century ago it was still possible to write, "The fourth century was the great epoch of the primitive Church.... In the social order it was then that the Church established itself and became a public power."[20] These sentences could not be written today. For there is a growing consensus that the

Church which was "established" in the fourth century is dead in the twentieth. And this awareness has enabled us increasingly to realize the continuity which links us to the gospel through the history of the earliest Christian centuries. Once again Christians today are being called to live as a small minority bearing witness to a faith which is not a sanctified part of the social landscape.

Interestingly enough, Roques—one of the two reviewers with real historical competence who could not conscientiously agree with me on that level—was also the reviewer who agreed most completely with my "theological conclusions. He is a Roman Catholic priest; I am a Protestant theologian writing primarily for my own community. Even though I was no doubt justified in beginning with Protestant principles of church doctrine and exegetics, our agreement gives ground for hope that we shall find increasing opportunity to build a joint Church doctrine, and thereby to give common testimony. And who knows? Perhaps some day we shall testify—from within the same ecclesiastical structures—to a faith which increasingly appears to be fundamentally the same. Another Roman Catholic theologian, Joseph Comblin, observed,

> There is more continuity than appears at first sight between the Church before and the Church after Constantine. The cleavage between a prophetic elite which withdrew from the temporal law of war and the common run of humanity which remained subject to it—this cleavage, which had separated the Christians from the Romans, after Constantine was imported into the Church itself. The Church did not surrender its prophetic testimony. But it reserved it for the priests and the monks.[21]

As a Protestant thinker I am no doubt duty bound to denounce this new cleavage as the central heresy against which my own tradition has borne testimony. But Evangelical and Roman Catholic thinkers alike must concede that "with or without a hierarchical clergy, with or without monks, the temptation of all religious faiths will invariably be to obtain *protection* from a *benevolent* state, often at the cost of abdications in practice and even in doctrine."[22] Indeed, the history of the Evangelical churches affords some of the most lamentable examples of the confusion of the temporal with the spiritual.

But there are grounds for hope. As Comblin proceeded to remark, "Perhaps the end of the Constantinian era will one day oblige us to look again at this over-rigid cleavage which, if one may so express it, reserved the 'better part' exclusively for the clergy, to the detriment of the laity."[23] More and more facts are forcing us to recognize that this day is rapidly dawning within the Roman Catholic Church. We are therefore free to join together with them in seeking patterns of fidelity for a single "people of God," a minority people all of whom will have borne the same witness (whether before or after Constantine) within a non-Christian world.

For reasons given above, my book only sketches the outlines of this second—theological and ethical—problem. It nevertheless is the problem which justly holds greatest interest for moden man.[24] I would therefore like to amplify and clarify my thinking on this matter as well. Since A. Dumas—Professor of Ethics in the Protestant Theological Faculty in Paris—made the most profound comments on this problem as I have treated it in this book, I will use his reflections as the primary basis for my discussion.

Dumas rightly chose as his starting-point the idea of the Concordat.[25] We are not referring, to be sure, to the disgraceful bargain whereby the state places its sword and purse at the Church's disposal while the Church in exchange subordinates its teaching and intercession to the state. Not even such a Concordat, offensive though it is, is able completely to stifle the gospel of grace. Even in Constantine's empire and in Franco's Spain the gospel has miraculously survived—despite the Concordat, and not at all because of it.

The reality of the Concordat, however, goes much deeper than such caricatures. It has consisted of the obligations of both Church and state to recognize each other's reality as such. This reality cannot be eradicated, and it implies a reciprocal acknowledgement that each "partner" will operate according to standards which are rigorously different from those of its counterpart. Thus, there is inevitably a certain amount of "reciprocal support." This is the place in which one can find a sound theology of the state as well as a correct juridical recognition of the specific status of the ecclesiastical collectivity. According to the well-known formula, which might (had it been accepted by both sides) have prevented some of the struggles between clerical and anticlerical factions in France during the last century, a "free Church" must be recognized in a "free state." This should not be taken as a "divorce by mutual consent," but rather as a decision to respect in the other partner the particular mystery of its existence. The Church's mystery is forgiving love; the state's is compelling power. Their coexistence has to be assumed as long as historical time continues even after the "it is finished" of Calvary. Precisely this is the locus of the Christians' difficult faithfulness in the world.

Believers betray this faithfulness, however, when they reach the point of considering the temporal itself as eternal. They thus no longer have the possibility of uttering a prophetic word in time, since time will never know the suspension which would have challenged its whole importance. If the kingdom of God is not for this earth, the earth may well continue to rotate forever according to its own rhythms; and faith will thereby be reduced to the contemplative activities—on the part of certain mystical souls—of celestial visions which will allow them remorselessly to abandon the rest of humanity to the powers of this world. Such a sanctification of the secular, which some regard as God's will, is defenseless against Marxist criticism. In complete contrast to this view, on the other hand, is the eschatological view. Even though Marx himself made eschatology his first target, because the spectacle presented to him by the Christians of his time did not allow him to get a glimmering of its real significance, this view is unaffected by his criticism precisely because Christian eschatology should not transfer ideal values into an imaginary world. On the contrary, it must take seriously in the present an order which will not be fully manifested until the end of time.[26]

Several reviewers commented that they could not understand the distinction which I drew on this point between Eusebius and Lactantius.[27] It is true that both men adopted a tone of besotted praise of the state. But for Eusebius nothing else remained; he no longer was looking forward to the day when all the earthly powers would pass away. God himself existed only as servant of the state. Lactantius, on the contrary, knew that there would be an end of time; there would be a judgment in which the transcendent order finally would break in. Thus, although his respect for the state was extreme and extended to the point of adulation, the state's existence in time did not permit him to forget that the honor which was due to Caesar was temporary and that God's Court alone would be final. In the name of that High Court, therefore, Lactantius remained capable of delivering warnings which are all the more forceful because— in the context of his homage to temporal power—the reader is unprepared for them.

Christian faithfulness can also be illusory when some believers, instead of forgetting the kingdom of God, suppose that in the present age they can make a colony of it, actualizing it in the form of a social structure. They then are tempted either to assume for themselves as a religious society the coercive powers which in the name of the gospel they had refused even to the state—or to discharge on to an external state the "dirty work" which they recognize is indispensable but are not themselves willing to undertake.[28]

This brings us back to the basic idea of the Concordat, toward which the Christian continues to be in an uneasy relationship. The Concordat, in fact, does not put him exclusively in either of the two realities; on the contrary, it forces him to take both of them seriously. The believer, who gives witness to his eschatological hope by offering acts of love and forgiveness, also bears testimony to God's present faithfulness by helping to establish and defend the structures of order and justice. So for the believer, as Jean-Marie Domenach excellently expressed it, "The question is never violence or nonviolence, but always what sort of violence, up to what point, and with what consequences"[29]—a formula which could also be acceptable to intelligent nonbelievers, and on a purely pragmatic basis.

Our ancestors in the faith made attempts, no less groping and unskillful than our own, to find a not too unhappy medium between the violence which one must accept and the violence which one must reject. An initial product of our investigation has been the realization that they did not recognize, any more than we do, the convenient criterion according to which acceptable violence will always and automatically be violence which the temporal state commands. Our forefathers knew that God does not discharge the conscience of an individual when the state gives him a categorical order. This new insight is essential, for innumerable oversimplified catechisms[30]—whose scandalous results disfigure both ancient and modern history—have been used to make Christians believe exactly the opposite.

The early Christians articulated the concept of the Concordat in three successive forms. First they stated that the believers might recognize the legitimacy of state violence, but only if it was exercised by pagans—not by themselves. They next stated that Christians might themselves participate in the system of violence, but only on condition that this participation remained purely formal and fictitious. Believers thus were allowed to be soldiers, but not to take part in actual fighting. Finally they stated that the mass of Christians could on governmental orders use violence, provided that an elite, which was set apart, would carefully abstain from it and would thus continue loudly and clearly to assert an ideal. But from now on this ideal would be impossible for all believers fully to obey.

These three formulas are interesting because they indicate that the early believers had an enduring repugnance at the use of violence. But none of the formulas is capable of standing up to rigorous ethical examination. They are false solutions to a real problem.

There is, however, a fourth solution—one which the Christians of old glimpsed but did not fully discern. This is the solution upon which we may legitimately take our stand: we must make a thorough distinction between the work of the police and the work of war. It is here that Dumas has completely missed the point which underlies my thought.[31] I do not believe that the distinction between *militare* and *bellare* is important in the sense that it would effectively solve our problems, but rather because it explains the apparent contradictions in the behavior of the early Christians. I do not claim that the distinction between the policeman and the soldier would be a good one for us because the early believers had clearly grasped it. In fact, their presentiment of it—in their dual attempt to be responsible to society and to be obedient to the law of perfection—was rather confused. But this distinction is important for us because, by articulating it more plainly, we can apply it more consistently. Thus it can become a valid ethical position for our time. I would argue that no Christian can legitimately refuse, if he is compelled or even without compulsion, to take part in police duties—i.e., to participate in the use of a violence that is as limited as possible in order to restrain a violence that is worse. But I am unable to understand how some

Christians can still tolerate being brigaded into military "duties"—into blind participation in one of two equally unjustifiable complexes of violence. For the Christians in both camps claim to justify their side's violence as a protection against the violence of the other side.

The concrete application of my distinction is at times problematic, for there is an imperceptible transition from the "large-scale" police operation to the "minor" war. And the propagandists have always justified the worst examples of international banditry as police-like operations which were necessary to reestablish order. But on the continuous road which leads without a break from the best to the worst, moral responsibility consists precisely in laying down a limit somewhere and saying—"so far and no further." An effective criterion is to ask oneself, "Could I, in good faith, be on the other side?" If one discovers that, for all intents and purposes, there are millions of honest men who are actually "on the other side," one can only conclude that one is faced, not with the legitimate maintenance of order, but with the absurdity of war.[32]

But what if our potential enemies fail to see the same point? Are we not then back in the old dilemma? It is here that another intuitive insight of the pre-Constantinian Christians is worthy of attention, and of amplification far beyond the resonance which they themselves gave it—the advocacy of noncollaborating patience as a technique of conversion. Such a method has a profound affinity with the Christian faith, for it evokes the themes of victorious self-sacrifice and of weakness transformed into strength. Let us consider this method, however, only at the psychological level. It disarms the person or group of persons who believe that they are one's enemy; but it does so by refusing either to yield to them or to fight them. The "enemy" thus suddenly becomes uncertain of the righteousness of his cause, for he is faced only by his own violence, which he can no longer justify or excuse by the presence of a violent opponent.

Not only will this form of struggle be less costly in the end for the community in whose behalf one is using it; it will also allow a true conquest over the enemy by persuading him to share one's point of view instead of by annihilating him.[33] Obviously this presupposes that one's cause is the right one. But here the mainspring of action is precisely the conviction that one's cause is "so completely right" that one no longer needs physical violence to establish it. The person who starts a fight is usually the person who is not sure of the validity of. his arguments. "Nonviolence" is not the best term for this method, for what I am in fact advocating is the transferral of violence to another—spiritual—level. And, admittedly, such a method is effective only insofar as we in this way carry doubt and distress into the mind of the "enemy."

In this postscript I have attempted to make clear that the Christian refusal of military service does not necessarily imply the intellectual naïveté or the political utopianism with which its opponents customarily seek to denigrate it. There is, of course, the risk that we may at times lapse into such divagations. But these possible erroneous courses, which I myself repudiate energetically, still seem venial in comparison with the moral laxity which for the past fifteen centuries has been the regular consequence of the opposite position. So let Christian conscientious objectors stop talking in absolute terms, for their position must remain both human and relative. But let other Christians also decide to take—in concrete form—the same position. For in the face of the madness of international war, this attitude is the only one which is reasonable and effective.

Beirut, Lebanon/Cairo, Egypt
Spring, 1970

Abbreviations

AB	*Analecta Bollandiana*, Brussels, 1882 ff.
ACO	*Acta Conciliorum Oecumenicorum*, ed. E. Schwartz, Berlin, 1925 ff.
ACW	*Ancient Christian Writers*, ed. J. Quasten and J. C. Plumpe, Westminster, Md., 1946 ff.
ALMA	*Archivum latinitatis medii aevi (Bulletin du Cange)*, Paris, 1924 ff.
ANL	*Ante-Nicene Christian Library*, Edinburgh, 1864-1872
ASS	*Acta Sanctorum*, Antwerp, Brussels, Paris, 1643-1925
AUS	*Annales Universitatis saraviensis*, Saarbrücken, 1952 ff.
BALAC	*Bulletin d'ancienne Littérature et d'Archéologie chrétiennes*, Paris, 1911-1914
BARB	*Bulletin de l'Académie royale de Belgique, Classe des Lettres*, 5th ser., Brussels, 1911 ff.
BLE	*Bulletin de littérature ecclésiastique*, Toulouse, 1899 ff.
BTAM	*Bulletin de Théologie ancienne et médiévale*, Louvain, 1929 ff.
Byz	*Byzantion*, Paris-Liège, 1924 ff.
CCL	*Corpus Christianorum, Series Latina*, Turnhout-Paris, 1953 ff.
CIL	*Corpus Inscriptionum Latinarum*, Berlin, 1863-1936

CS	*Christianisme Social*, Paris
CSEL	*Corpus scriptorum ecclesiasticorum latinorum*, Vienna, 1866 ff.
CUF	*Collection des Universités de France* (Budé), Paris, 1920 ff.
DAL	*Dictionnaire d' Archéologie chrétienne et de Liturgie*, ed. F. Cabrol, H. Leclercq, and H. I. Marrou, Paris, 1907-1953
DCB	*Dictionary of Christian Biography, Literature, Sects and Doctrines*, London, 1877-1887
DDC	*Dictionnaire de Droit canonique*, ed. R. Naz, Paris, 1924-1965
DHGE	*Dictionnaire d' Histoire et de Géographie ecclésiastiques*, Paris, 1912 ff.
Diehl	E. Diehl, *Inscriptiones latinae christianae veteres*, Dublin-Zürich, 1967-1970
DS	*Dictionnaire de Spiritualité*, ed. M. Viller, A Rayez, *et al.*, Paris, 1937 ff.
DTC	*Dictionnaire de Théologie catholique*, Paris, 1889-1972
EL	Jean-Michel Hornus, *Evangile et Labarum*, Geneva, 1960
Fliche et Martin	A. Fliche et V. Martin, eds., *Histoire de l'Eglise depuis les origines jusqu'a nos jours*, Paris, 1938 ff.
GCS	*Die griechischen christlichen Schriftsteller der ersten drei Jahrhunderte*, Leipzig-Berlin, 1897 ff.
Hamman	A. Hamman, ed., *La Geste du Sang*, Paris, 1953
Hefelé	C. J. von Hefelé, *Histoire des Conciles*, 2nd Fr. ed. (vols. I-X trans. by H. Leclercq), Paris, 1907-1952
HL	H. Hemmer and P. Lejay, eds., *Textes et Documents pour l'Etude historique du Christianisme*, Paris, 1901-1914
HThR	*Harvard Theological Review*, Cambridge, Mass., 1908 ff.
JEH	*Journal of Ecclesiastical History*, London, 1950 ff.
JS	*Journal des Savants*, Paris, new ser., 1903 ff.
Knopf	D. R. Knopf, ed., *Ausgewählte Martyrerakten*, 3rd ed., Tübingen, 1929
LCC	*Library of Christian Classics*, ed. J. Baillie, J. T.

	McNeill, and H. P. van Dusen, London-Philadelphia, 1953 ff.
LCL	*Loeb Classical Library*, London-Cambridge, Mass., 1912 ff.
LFC	*Library of the Fathers of the Holy Catholic Church*, ed. E. Pusey, J. Keble, J. H. Newman, Oxford, 1838-1888
LV	*Lumière et Vie*, Lyon, 1952 ff.
MAH	*Mélanges d'Archéologie et d'Histoire*, Rome, 1881 ff.
Mansi	J.D. Mansi, *Sacrorum Conciliorum Nova et Amplissima Collectio*, Florence, 1759 (facsimile reproduction, Paris-Leipzig, 1901)
MGH	*Monumenta Germaniae historica*, Hannover-Berlin, 1823 ff.
Monceaux	P. Monceaux, *La Vraie Légende dorée*, Paris, 1928
MSR	*Mélanges de science religieuse*, Lille, 1944 ff.
Musurillo	H. Musurillo, ed., *The Acts of the Christian Martyrs*, Oxford, 1972
NPNF	*A Select Library of Nicene and Post-Nicene Fathers*, ed. H. Wace and P. Schaff, Oxford-New York, 1890-1900
NRTh	*Nouvelle Revue théologique*, Tournai, 1879 ff.
PG	*Patrologiae Cursus Completus, Series Graeca*, ed. J. P. Migne, Paris, 1857-1866
PL	*Patrologiae Cursus Completus, Series Latina*, ed. J. P. Migne, Paris, 1844-1864
PO	*Patrologia Orientalis*, ed. R. Graffin, F. Nau, and F. Graffin, Paris, 1903 ff.
PSt	*Patristic Studies*, ed. R. J. Deferrari, Washington, 1922 ff.
RACh	*Reallexikon für Antike und Christentum*, Leipzig-Stuttgart, 1941 ff.
REAN	*Revue des Etudes anciennes*, Bordeaux, 1899 ff.
RELA	*Revue des Etudes latines*, Paris, 1923 ff.
RH	*Revue historique*, Paris, 1876 ff.
RHDF	*Revue historique du Droit français et Etranger*, Paris, 4th ser., 1922 ff.
RHE	*Revue d'histoire ecclésiastique*, Louvain, 1900 ff.
RHEF	*Revue d'histoire de l'Eglise de France*, Paris, 1915 ff.

RHL	*Revue d' Histoire et de Littérature religieuses*, Paris, new ser., 1910-1921
RhM	*Rheinisches Museum für Philologie*, Bonn, 1827 ff.
RHPR	*Revue d' Histoire et de Philosophie religieuses*, Strasbourg, 1921 ff.
RHR	*Revue de l' Histoire des Religions*, Paris, 1883 ff.
RPh	*Revue de philologie, de littérature et d'histoire anciennes*, Paris, 3rd ser., 1927 ff.
RSPT	*Revue des sciences philosphiques et théologiques*, Paris, 1907 ff.
RSR	*Recherches de Science religieuse*, Paris, 1911-1940
RSRUS	*Revue des Sciences Religieuses*, Strasbourg, 1921 ff.
RTAM	*Recherches de théologie ancienne et médiévale*, Louvain, 1929 ff.
RTP	*Revue de Théologie et de Philosophie*, Lausanne, new ser., 1913-1950
SAB	*Sitzungsberichte der Preussischen / Deutschen Akademie der Wissenschaften*, Phil.-hist. Klasse, Berlin
SCH	*Sources chrétiennes*, eds. H. de Lubac, J. Daniélou, C. Mondésert, Paris, 1941 ff.
Sirinelli	J. Sirinelli, *Les Vues historiques d' Eusèbe de Césarée*, Dakar, 1961
SP	*Studia Patristica*, papers presented to the International Conference on Patristic Studies, Oxford (*TU* 63 ff. [Berlin, 1957 ff.])
ThZ	*Theologische Zeitschrift*, Basel, 1945 ff.
TS	*Theological Studies*, Baltimore, 1940 ff.
TU	*Texte und Untersuchungen*, Leipzig-Berlin, 1883 ff.
VC	*Vigiliae christianae*, Amsterdam, 1947 ff.
VSB	*Vies des Saints et des Bienheureux*, Paris, 1935-1956
ZKG	*Zeitschrift für Kirchengeschichte*, Stuttgart, new ser., 1890 ff.
ZkTh	*Zeitschrift für katholische Theologie*, Innsbruck, 1887 ff.
ZNW	*Zeitschrift für die neutestamentliche Wissenschaft und die Kunde der älteren Kirche*, Berlin-Giessen, 1900 ff.

Notes

Introduction

1. As J. Daniélou has rightly remarked ("La Non-violence selon l'Ecriture et la Tradition," *Action Chrétienne et Non-violence*, Compte rendu du Congrès national Pax Christi, Paris, March 19-20, 1955 [Paris, 1955], 9), "Almost all [the books on Christian nonviolence] are falsified by their justificatory aims, whether they are trying to justify war or to defend conscientious objection. So long as we stay at this level, we shall be lost in sterile debate."

2. The first few pages of A. Philip's pamphlet, *Le Christianisme et la Paix* (Paris, 1933) were a revelation to me, even though they made no claim to be scientific. I had not previously realized that in this area the first Christians had in any sense been "nonconformist." Then there was G. J. Heering's famous book, *The Fall of Christianity: A Study of Christianity, the State, and War* (New York, 1943), the original Dutch edition of which was analyzed by F. J. Leenhardt in an article ("Le Christianisme primitif et la guerre," *CS*, 43 [1930], 331-337) which was both insightful and objective. More recently, the article by Mgr. H. F. Davis ("The Early Christian Attitude to War," *Blackfriars*, 30 [1949], 477-482) asked whether the time was not ripe for a renewal of conscientious objection. One may sympathize with his approach, but as a historical study it was not very strong. Among the recent authors who, broadly speaking, have defended the traditional Christian attitude to war, special place must be given to E. A. Ryan ("The Rejection of Military Service by Early Christians," *TS*, 13 [1952], 1-32) and to H. von Campenhausen ("Christians and Military Service in the Early Church," in his *Tradition and Life in the Early Church: Essays and Lectures in Church History* [London, 1968], 160-170). Both Ryan and von Campenhausen have come to the same general historical conclusions as I have. But both of them were convinced that the political and social developments following Constantine's conversion completely transformed the situation, thereby justifying the adoption by Christians of very different and apparently opposite answers to the questions of war and military service. Although I cannot follow these scholars in their ethical conclusions, their presuppositions concerning historical method seem to me to be the only ones possible. I was also delighted to read in a book by a Mennonite author (H. A. Fast, *Jesus and Human Conflict* [Scottdale, Pa., 1959]) that Christian nonviolence must not be made into a code for automatic application.

3. J. Lasserre, *War and the Gospel*, transl. O. Coburn (London and Scottdale,

Pa., 1962). Also noteworthy are F. Leenhardt, *Le Chrétien doit-il servir l'Etat?* (Geneva, 1939) and O. Cullmann, *The State in the New Testament,* rev. ed. (London,1963). Both of these authors adopted an approach which is slightly different from that of Lasserre. They were also less concerned to draw concrete conclusions.

4. Examples of this method of interpreting the facts will be found in the Appendix to this volume.

5. H. Leclercq ("Militarisme," *DAL,* XI [1933], cols. 1108-1181, which at points is virtually a verbatim rendering of P. Batiffol, "Les Premiers Chrétiens et la Guerre," *Revue du Clergé français,* 67 [1911], 222-242), attempted to contrast the teaching of Tertullian the Catholic (who in 197 purportedly accepted military service) with that of Tertullian the "Montanist" heretic after 210. But Leclercq was then forced to admit, "On the first occasion following the proclamation of the gospel on which a Christian writer declared himself on the subject of war, he condemned it in the name of the gospel." A. Vanderpol asserted even more clearly *(La Doctrine scolastique du Droit de Guerre* [Paris, 1925], 180) that "one cannot find in any of the Christian writers prior to Constantine a word of praise for the military profession, or even a passage stating plainly that it was permissible for Christians to fight."

6. Vanderpol, *Doctrine scolastique,* 171; Campenhausen, "Christians and Military Service," 162.

7. In contrast to the numerous writings which forbade Christians to take part in war and which denounced it as an evil, there is not a single surviving text from the same period which invited Christians to take part in it or which recommended it as a lesser evil. In his review of the French edition of this book (henceforth cited as *EL),* M. Villey (*RHDF,* 40 [1962], 268) wrote that "for all his good intentions, M. Hornus cannot avoid hiding under a bushel the texts which may be advanced against his theory." But with all his good intentions in the opposite direction, Villey was unable to produce a single one of the patristic texts which I had purportedly disregarded. He fell back upon "the Holy Scriptures which are the origin of tradition," but confined his scriptural citations to those (Matthew 8; Acts 10) referring to the two centurions. He also recommended that I take St. Augustine's *City of God* more seriously than Hippolytus's *Canons.* Villey's last prescription would lead to an astonishing methodology for discovering the position of the pre-Constantinian Church! All that one can find in the relevant patristic texts is either a consciousness of membership in an empire which also had soldiers, or an acknowledgement of the presence of some Christians in the military camps. But while these Christians were not always explicitly denounced for this, never was their behavior in any sense commended. Significantly, too, the early Christians never conjoined the two subjects—of living in the empire, and of being in the army; they would surely have done so had the latter been the normal consequence of the former.

8. *ASS,* October, XII (1867), 533-536, provides a detailed discussion of this contradiction, with specific reference to the case of Ferrutius. The author of the article considered the attitude of conscientious objection to have been not so much the exaggerated viewpoint of certain intellectuals as the unintelligent stance of certain recent converts. After citing as examples of this (p. 533) the three Gallic saints, Martin, Victricius, and Paulinus (see below, pp. 142-152), he went on to state more broadly (p. 536) that those soldiers who took literally the commands "Thou shalt not kill" and "No man can serve two masters" were uninstructed peasants *(viri utique agrestes et non eruditi).* But in the same sentence he stated that these soldiers' error came from their having read Origen, St. Cyprian, Lactantius, and Titus of Bostra, and from having detected in these writings the echo of Tertullian. Of course, they heard this echo wrongly (p. 536). But on p. 533 our author had seemed to take the opposite

point of view when he conceded that before "the Church Peace" some learned Christians had shared Tertullian's position on this matter. Who can these men have been if not those named above? It is admittedly difficult to conceive of these unlettered peasants who were simultaneously patristic scholars. But if they had indeed existed, they would be proof that the "rank and file" in the Church was far more open to conscientious objection than is often conceded.

9. Without realizing that he was thereby destroying the rest of his argument, Vanderpol wrote (*Doctrine scolastique*, 180), "The end of military service, war, is the shedding of blood; and even if this happens without guilt, it defiles the one who is responsible for it or who executes it.... And the early Church ... had a horror of bloodshed."

Chapter 1

1. M. Lods, "L'Eglise du IIIe Siècle devant le Service de l'Etat," *Bulletin de la Faculté libre de Théologie protestante de Paris*, 13, no. 35 (1950), 18; L. Homo, *Les Empereurs romains et le Christianisme* (Paris, 1931), 42n.; M.D. Chenu, "L'Evolution de la Théologie de la Guerre," *LV*, 7, no. 38 (1958), 78-79; M. Durry, *Les Cohortes prétoriennes* (Paris, 1938), 349. On the general question of military service in this period, see C. J. Cadoux, *The Early Church and the World* (Edinburgh, 1925), 116 and especially 116n. In his review, Villey (pp. 267-268) stressed how completely different the situation of the early Church was from that of our own times, in which in many countries conscription has become an accepted tradition.

2. J. Lebreton and J. Zeiller, *The History of the Primitive Church*, transl. E. C. Messenger (London, 1942-1948), IV, 1028; Ryan, "Rejection," 9-10; W. Seston, *Dioclétien et la Tétrarchie* (Paris, 1946), I, 300; F. Lot, *Nouvelles Recherches sur l'Impôt foncier et la Capitation personnelle sous le Bas-Empire* (Paris, 1955), 28; A. J. Visser, "Christianus sum, non possum militare, Soldatenmartyria uit de derde eeuw," *Nederlandsch Archief voor kerkelijke Geschiedenis*, 48 (1967), 18. This has been studied in particular in connection with the three cases to which I shall be referring later: those of Maximilian (see p. 287 for bibliography), Victricius (E. Vacandard, *Saint Victrice, Evêque de Rouen* [Paris, 1903], 7), and Martin (Sulpicius Severus, *Vita Mart.*, 2, 5, which episode has been studied in detail by A. Régnier, *Saint Martin*, 6th ed. [Paris, 1925], 34-35). See also P. Ménard, "Profil de Saint Martin," *Revue de l'Université de Laval*, 8 [1953], 9; H. C. Babut, "Saint Martin de Tours," *RHL*, 1 (1910), 173; and now J. Fontaine, *SCH*, CXXXIV, 453-460. It must be remembered that the system of veterans consisted of settling former soldiers on the empire's boundaries by making them owners of land given by the state. This was not primarily a matter of rewarding them for past services but of providing a permanent cover for the frontiers. The law of Septimius Severus, which ordered the confiscation of an aging veteran's land if the veteran's son upon reaching manhood refused to enlist (*Scriptores Historiae Augustae, LCL*, 58), was therefore perfectly logical. No doubt this arrangement was accompanied by moral and social pressures which made enlistment practically compulsory. Constantine, however, in the second half of his reign still left a choice between the army and the onerous civil office of decurion (*Cod. Theod.*, VII, 22, 2). The strict obligation for the son to enlist, which imposed sanctions upon the father if the son failed to do so, dates from 365 (*Cod. Theod.*, VII, 1, 8).

3. Josephus, *Antiquities*, XIV, 10, 6; Batiffol, "Les premiers Chrétiens et la Guerre," 223. Ryan ("Rejection," 4) stated that the exemption of the Jews from service in the Roman army was not a matter of their avoiding killing but merely of

their escaping from the pagan law. This is beside the point. He also remarked that J. Juster (*Les Juifs dans l'Empire romain* [Paris, 1914], II, 268ff.), who admitted that this exemption had been in effect in 49 BC, was of the opinion that it was later withdrawn by Augustus or Tiberius. But Ryan, even though he did not specifically discuss this thesis, did not seem himself to be in agreement with it.

4. Josephus, *Antiquities*, XVIII, 5. Even the Christian emperor Valens, in a moment of fury, resorted again to this punishment against recalcitrant monks (L. Duchesne, *Early History of the Christian Church* [London, 1922], 412)

5. M. Goguel, *The Life of Jesus*, transl. O. Wyon (London, 1933), 464-467; idem, *Jésus*, 2nd ed. (Paris, 1950), 385-386, and 392-393 for the appendix which traces the development of this tradition through primitive Christianity; see also the same author's "Juifs et Romains dans l'Histoire de la Passion," *RHR*, 62 (1910), 165-182, 295-322, and his *The Birth of Christianity*, transl. H. C. Snape (London, 1953), 440-442. Oscar Cullmann (*The State in the New Testament*, 34-39) gave the historical background to the controversy and firmly supported the position of H. Lietzmann (first argued in "Der Prozess Jesu," *Sitzungsbericht der preussischen Akademie der Wissenschaften* [1931], 313 ff.) on the essential point—that it was the Romans, not the Jews, who condemned Jesus. M. Simon (*Verus Israël* [Paris, 1948], 147) also showed how this distortion of the accounts of the Passion was designed to spare Rome. More recently, Miss A. Jaubert (*La Date de la Cène* [Paris, 1957], 128) has argued that the solution which she proposed would restore "to the Jewish trial, in accordance with the synoptic tradition, a legal character which scholars had denied." This solution remains very much in dispute. Even if we were to accept it, we would still have to insist that Roman law would have started the trial all over again, and would not merely have ratified the sentence which had already been pronounced. The same intention of acquitting the Roman state—this time without placing the blame on the Jews—is also to be found in "the popular legend which has Jesus struck during the Passion not by a Roman soldier but by an *Ethiopian*" (F. Lovsky, *Antisémitisme et Mystère d'Israël* [Paris, 1955], 152, quoting John Moschus, *Pratum Spirituale*, 30). The strange silence of Acts 28 concerning the death of St. Paul has also sometimes been explained by the author's desire not to make it obvious that the apostle was condemned to death by Roman justice.

6. Simon, *Verus Israël*, 127-128; Fast, *Jesus and Human Conflict*, 200. W. H. C. Frend, "The Persecutions: Some Links between Judaism and the Early Church," *JEH*, 9 (1958), 142, maintained that this confusion lasted until the end of the second century, at least in the mind of the ordinary public.

7. S. Case, *The Revelation of John* (Chicago, 1919), 31; Goguel, *Birth*, 500-504; W. Hobhouse, *The Church and the World in Idea and in History* (London, 1910), 41-48; Homo, *Les Empereurs*, 50-51; P. H. Menoud, *L'Evangile de Jean*, 2nd ed. (Neuchâtel-Paris, 1947), 63; Ryan, "Rejection," 7; Simon, *Verus Israël*, 144-145. The last of these, relying essentially on Justin, attributed to the Jews alone the initiative for the rupture. The responsibility for the persecution, Simon contended, was therefore theirs.

8. Frend, "Persecutions," 142-148, 155.

9. *Ibid.*, 157.

10. *Ibid.*, 153.

11. *Ibid.*, 158.

12. Ryan, "'Rejection," 16, 30.

13. *Ibid.*, 11.

14. Arnobius, *Adv. Nat.*, 4, 7.

15. Archelaus, *Controversy*, 1 (end).
16. Clement of Alexandria, *Stromata*, VI, 18, 167.
17. Ignatius of Antioch, *Letter to the Romans*, 5, 1.
18. *Mart. Pol.*, 6, 2 [Hornus transl.].
19. *Mart. Pionii*, 15 (Musurillo, 157).
20. *Ibid.*, 21 (Musurillo, 163).
21. *Passio Mariani*, 2, 2-4 (Musurillo, 195-197).
22. *Ibid.*, (Musurillo, 197).
23. *Ibid.*, 2, 4-5 (Musurillo, 199).
24. Eusebius, *Martyrs*, 4, 8-13, and 7, 2.
25. See, for example, the case of the virgin Ennathas of Scythopolis, who suffered an appalling martyrdom solely as a result of the initiative of the tribune Maxys (Eusebius, *Martyrs*, 9, 7).
26. *Ibid.*, 11, 6. "Barbarous" can here be understood in both the ethnic and the moral senses of the term.
27. Eusebius, *HE*, V, 1, 17 ff.
28. *Ibid.*, VII, 3, 4, in which there is a detailed description; or VIII, 10, 3 ff. and VIII, 11, 1, which tells of a terrible massacre in Phrygia.
29. *Ibid.*, VIII, 14, 3.
30. Lactantius, *De Mort. Pers.*, 27, 5 ff. As a matter of fact, in this passage there is also some trace of an opposition between the Dacian patriotism of Galerius and the strict "Romanism" of Lactantius. See J. Moreau's notes in his edition of *De Mort. Pers.*, *SCH*, XXXIX, ii, 256, 360-361.
31. *Didascalia*, V, 1, 1.
32. Clement of Alexandria, *Paedagogus*, II, 13, 121, slightly misquoting Homer, *Iliad*, II, 872-873.
33. Seston, *Dioclétien*, 261, 295; Moreau, *La Persécution du Christianisme dans l'Empire romain* (Paris, 1956), 112.
34. Lactantius, *De Mort. Pers.*, 7, 5. On Diocletian's army, see Moreau's footnote in *SCH*, XXXIX, ii, 234-235.
35. Lactantius, *De Mort. Pers.*, 37, 5.
36. See Chapter 2 below, p. 68 ff.
37. *Acta Carpi*, 4 (Musurillo, 33).
38. *Acts of St. John*, 6.
39. *Martyrdom of Perpetua*, 9, 16, 21 (Musurillo, 117, 125, 131).
40. Pontius, *Vita Cypriani*, 16.
41. Eusebius, *HE*, VI, 41, 16.
42. Gregory the Wonder-Worker, *Panegyric to Origen*, 5, 67-72.
43. A. Hamman, ed., *La Geste du Sang* (Paris, 1953), 324. Here, as in similar cases elsewhere, it is not clear whether it was the sight of the martyrs which brought about the soldiers' conversion or whether the converts were former Christians who were recalled to faithfulness by seeing the sacrifice of their brethren.
44. For this question in general, the work by L. Cerfaux and J. Tondriau (*Un Concurrent du Christianisme, le Culte des Souverains* [Tournai, 1958]) takes precedence over the bibliography which I provided in my "Etude sur la Pensée politique de Tertullien," *RHPR*, 38 (1958), 14n. See also Seston, *Dioclétien*, 212-228; Homo, *Les Empereurs*, 204-206, 211, 226-227; E. Stauffer, *Christ and the Caesars* (London, 1955), 208-211.
45. K. M. Setton, *Christian Attitude Towards the Emperor in the Fourth Century* (New York, 1941), 17; Cerfaux and Tondriau, *Concurrent*, 262-267.
46. Cerfaux and Tondriau, *Concurrent*, 395.

47. Roman tolerance is shown precisely in the fact that Judaism was recognized as a *religio licita* and that the Jews were exempt from a ceremony which would have offended their religious feelings (Cerfaux and Tondriau, *Concurrent*, 384-386). "But the Christians were in quite a different situation: they were either Jews by birth or converted Gentile subjects of the empire. So officially they had the choice only between the God of the Jews and the gods of the empire" (Homo, *Les Empereurs*, 51). At the beginning of this chapter I demonstrated that for opposite reasons Jews and Christians alike refused to consider Christianity a Jewish sect. As a result, the Christians' anomalous position was bound to give rise to question; and the Roman authorities would have needed extraordinary prescience to allow to a small Galilean sect the same privileges which they allowed to Judaism, an ancient religion already practiced extensively throughout the empire (M. Goguel, *Les Chrétiens et l'Empire romain à l'Epoque du Nouveau Testament* [Paris, 1905], 23). Moreover, the exemption of the Jews was essentially an empirical measure, for experience had shown that this was the best way to obtain peace and order in the regions where they lived. This exemption could not apply to a religion which was new and universalist and thus would inevitably be on the offensive and cause upheavals (T. M. Parker, *Christianity and the State in the Light of History* [London, 1955], 33).

48. Jerome wrote, "Pagans commit the error of considering as a god any man who rules over them" (*Commentary on Daniel*, 3, 46). See Cerfaux and Tondriau, *Concurrent*, 439-440, and R. Schilling, *La Religion romaine de Vénus depuis les origines jusqu'au temps d'Auguste* (Paris, 1954), 316-317, the latter of whom gave detailed references to Cicero, Varro, and Lucretius. R. Mehl ("Le Christianisme primitif et le problème de la guerre," *Le Monde*, December 26, 1961), on the other hand, wrote, "It seems difficult for us to accept the idea that in pagan antiquity there was no radical difference between gods and men, and that, therefore, to proclaim the divinity of the emperor meant merely to recognize the scope of his power." He then went on to comment that "for Christian sensibility . . . to swear a religious oath to the emperor . . . meant an impossible betrayal."

49. "The cult of the emperor is only the mark of an exceptional respect for a man above other men. It does not necessarily imply faith in the reality of his divinity" (P. Monceaux, *Histoire littéraire de l'Afrique chrétienne* [Paris, 1901-1902], I, 27n.). It is true, however, that pagan manifestations tended to center increasingly on the person of the emperor. But at the same time official paganism was increasingly losing its strictly religious character. See H. Mattingly, "The Later Paganism," *HThR*, 35 (1942), 171-179.

50. Stauffer, *Christ and the Caesars*, 211; D. van Berchem, "Le 'De Pallio' de Tertullien et le Conflit du Christianisme et de l'Empire," *Museum Helveticum*, 1 (1944), 102.

51. Setton, *Christian Attitude*, 21.

52. Van Berchem, "Le 'De Pallio,' " 102.

53. A. D'Alès, *Théologie de Tertullien* (Paris, 1905), 394; Homo, *Les Empereurs*, 28; Stauffer, *Christ and the Caesars*, 236.

54. I. T. Beckwith, *The Apocalypse of John* (New York, 1919), 198.

55. Detailed studies of this double terminology occur in Setton, *Christian Attitude*, 18-21, and in Cerfaux and Tondriau, *Concurrent*, 446-451. The latter pointed out, however, that this factor, although it undoubtedly existed, should not be overestimated. Similarly, C. Mohrmann ("Epiphania," in *Etudes sur le latin des Chrétiens*, 2nd ed., I [Rome, 1961], 249), showed that since the time of the Ptolemies the terms *Epiphania* and *Parousia* were frequently used to indicate the arrival of a visiting political ruler, who was himself referred to as *Sōter*. But these words did not go with

any strictly religious ceremonial. They were simply the technical vocabulary of imperial etiquette. It was precisely for this reason, because for him Christ is the Lord, that St. Paul borrowed these words, which originally had applied to the Hellenistic rulers (*Ibid.*, 253).

56. Setton, *Christian Attitude*, 18, 22; Cerfaux and Tondriau, *Concurrent*, 449; Ryan, "Rejection," 11. [Cf. Arthur Darby Nock, "The Roman Army and the Roman Religious Year," *HThR*, 45 (1952), 187-252.]

57. Because the crowns have been inaugurated by the false gods, believers should scorn them as the work of the devil (*De Corona*, 7). Furthermore, because the crowns, in the very ceremony of the *donativum*, have been explicitly related to the idols, they have become repugnant to the Christian (*Ibid.*, 10-12). There has been a good deal of debate about the validity of these arguments. Monceaux (*Histoire*, 271), followed by d'Alès (*Théologie*, 414), considered them to be one long sophism and rejected them completely. But if the Christians did not refuse military service because they rejected idolatry, it must have been because they rejected violence; and this is something which the above authors do not seem to realize. For in the last resort, no matter how much one accuses Tertullian of false reasoning, the fact remains that there actually were soldier martyrs, and men do not die for a sophism. E. Vacandard, on the other hand ("La Question du Service militaire chez les Chrétiens des Premiers Siècles," *Etudes de Critique et d'Histoire religieuse*, 2nd ser. [1910], 139), took exactly the opposite line to Monceaux, declaring that to take part in a *donativum* was to declare oneself a pagan. Finally, A. von Harnack (*Militia Christi: Die christliche Religion und der Soldatenstand in den ersten drei Jahrhunderten* [Tübingen, 1905; repr., Darmstadt, 1963], 66-68) saw the action by the hero of this story as merely reclaiming for Christianity a privilege already allowed to the initiates of Mithras. The last lines of the treatise, on which Harnack relied exclusively, do have this sense. But it would be a mistake to treat the whole treatise solely along these lines. On this point one may refer to a short note by G. de Plinval ("Tertullien et le Scandale de la Couronne," *Mélanges de Ghellinck* [Gembloux, 1951], 183-188) which recalled the precedents of Clement of Alexandria and Minucius Felix, and which showed how a Christian soldier might be tempted, where the crown was concerned, to imitate his fellow soldiers who were initiates of Mithras.

58. Eusebius, *HE*, VI, 5, 3-6.

59. Seston, *Dioclétien*, 211-230; Lods, "L'Eglise," 25.

60. Seston, "A Propos de la Passio Marcelli Centurionis," in *Aux Sources de la Tradition chrétienne, Mélanges M. Goguel* (Neuchâtel, 1950), 244. See also Moreau, *La Persécution*, 115.

61. Lods ("L'Eglise," 24) thought that this measure was only applied effectively in the armies of the Danube and Asia Minor, both of which were under the direct control of Galerius.

62. Epiphanius, *Panarion*, 68, 2.

63. Homo, *Les Empereurs*, 80. The relevant texts are: Eusebius, *HE*, VIII, 1, 7; VIII, 4, 2-3; Lactantius, *De Mort. Pers.*, 10.

64. Cerfaux and Tondriau, *Concurrent*, 392-396.

65. *Acta Fructuosus*, 2, 2-3 [Hornus transl.].

66. Lods, "L'Eglise," 15. G. Giannelli ("La Primitiva Chiesa cristiana di Fronte alle Persecuzioni e el Martirio," *Nuovo Didaskaleion*, 3 [1949], 5-22) indicated clearly that the refusal of the cult was something important, but he failed to bring out its full significance.

67. Clement of Rome, *Letter*, 60, 4.

68. J.-R. Palanque, *Le Christianisme et l'Occident barbare* (Paris, 1945), 2.

69. Parker (*Christianity and the State, 37*) contended that the apocalyptic tendency was to be found chiefly among the "lower-class" Christians, while believers from more cultivated circles tried theologically to justify their emotional attachment to a society in which they were among the privileged. I do not feel that such a sociological interpretation applies convincingly in the present case. See the excellent remarks of Hobhouse (*The Church and the World*, 64) on the differences between the political approaches of the Book of Revelation and the writings of St. Paul.

70. In Chapter 2 I shall deal at greater length with this prayer, its bases, and its development in Christian thinking.

71. Hippolytus, *Commentary on Daniel*, III, 24, 7.

72. Origen, *Contra Celsum*, VIII, 65.

73. Origen mentioned in passing the problem raised by the fact that some kings betray their mission. In this passage, however, he did not try to solve it. He simply referred the reader to his commentary on the Epistle to the Romans.

74. The title had already been used by Justin during the reign of Antoninus, Marcus's predecessor (Justin, *Second Apology*, 2). See Setton, *Christian Attitude*, 36-37, on the care with which the apologists addressed the emperors by their official titles and on the great hopes which they placed in Marcus's intelligence and kindness.

75. Athenagoras, *Legatio*, 37. As Moreau (*La Persécution*, 73) wrote, "During the first two centuries of the empire the Christians lived in a hostile world which hated them. But Roman peace and order ensured for them the minimum of security which allowed the Church to expand and consolidate; so it can be said without paradox that the state protected them more than it persecuted them." See R. L. P. Milburn, *Early Christian Interpretations of History* (New York, 1954), 54-55, for the persistence in the third century, before the Church Peace, of this view "of the good order and political stability which had favored the growth and expansion of the missionary Church."

76. Legei gar toi dikaiōs ho kurios (Hermas, *Similitudes*, 1, 4). See the discussion of this text on p. 100 below.

77. Justin, *First Apology*, 12, 1; 16, 14.

78. Justin, *Second Apology*, 9, 1 [Hornus translation].

79. *Acta Achatii*, 3, 2.

80. Tertullian, *Apology*, 4, 5.

81. *Ibid.*, 4, 13. Tertullian (*ibid.*, 10) labeled as *stulta* (idiotic) the law which punished the name of Christian.

82. This divine law is to some extent the Decalogue, for God, the universal Creator, gave his law through Moses for all peoples according to his lovingkindness. However, this ancient law despite everything has a historical character, i.e., it has full validity only for a certain time and place. Taking the concrete example of circumcision, Tertullian showed that this is contingent upon God's sovereign grace and upon the believer's loyal obedience to him, which alone are normative. The true and immutable law is the newly revealed law of mercy and love (*Adv. Iud.*, 2-3).

83. Origen, *Contra Celsum*, V, 37 and VIII, 56. W. A. Banner ("Origen and the Tradition of Natural Law Concept," *Dumbarton Oaks Papers*, 8 [1954], 49-82) showed clearly the apologetic function which this natural law had for Origen and traced its origins in pagan philosophy. His examination of these sources led him, however, unduly to minimize Origen's originality.

84. Basil of Caesarea, *Homilies*, XII (*in Princip. Proverb.*), 2.

85. G. Bardy, in the notes to his French edition of Theophilus (*SCH*, XX, i [1948], 69 n.), pointed to parallel passages in *Mart. Pol.*, 8, 2; *Acta Cypriani*, 2; *Acta Apollonii*, 3; Tertullian, *Apology*, 28, 3, and 32, 2-3. An infinite number of other

references could be adduced on a question of this importance. I would mention only the dialogue, which I shall quote below (p. 82), between the martyr Achatius and his judge Marcian, a dialogue which has a very direct bearing on the *pax Romana* and the army. Achatius ended his comments by saying, "I pray to the great and true God for the safety of the emperor, but he cannot demand sacrifice of us and we cannot give it to him. Who indeed could offer sacred honors to a man?" (*Acta Achatii*, 1, 5 [Hamman, 107]).

86. Theophilus of Antioch, I, 11. The quotation at the end is from Proverbs 24:21-22.

87. Irenaeus, *Adv. Haeres.*, II, 32, 2. Again Origen conceded to Celsus that "probably . . . in the so-called wars of the bees there lies teaching that among men wars, if they are ever necessary, are to be just and ordered" (*Contra Celsum*, IV, 82).

88. Irenaeus, *Adv. Haeres.*, IV, 30, 3. Cf. *DTC*, VII (1923), col. 2440.

89. Irenaeus, *Adv. Haeres.*, IV, 36, 6.

90. *Ibid.*, V, 24, 1-3. For comment on this long and very important text, see *DTC*, VII, ii, col. 2440, and P. Allard, *Histoire des Persécutions pendant la Première Moitié du IIIe Siècle* (Paris, 1886), 152.

91. Hippolytus, *Commentary on Daniel*, III, 23, 1-3.

92. Tertullian, *Scorpiace*, 14.

93. Tertullian, *De Anima*, 33, 6.

94. Tertullian, *Apology*, 30, 1-2.

95. *Ibid.*, 5, 2 and 21, 2.

96. *Ibid.*, 5, 6.

97. Tertullian, *Ad Scapulam*, 4. In the same chapter, as proof of the benevolent attitude of Severus towards the Christians, Tertullian cited the fact that the emperor always kept near him a certain doctor who had once saved his life, although he was well aware that the doctor belonged to the sect. But as C. Guignebert (*Tertullien* [Paris, 1901], 111) remarked, such action was by no means a proof of his benevolence towards Christianity: "It was mere gratitude and also prudence." In all this Tertullian's aim seems clear: he was harassing the local authorities, who were still directly responsible for the persecution, and hoped thereby to make them hesitate before taking measures of which the emperor might disapprove; he was also clearing the Christians from the *a priori* suspicion of guilt which would arise if the supreme authority had condemned them beforehand; finally, he was allowing the believers to resist persecution without thereby having to assume the attitude of rebels. On these three objectives of Tertullian, see my "Etude," 15-16. Many Christian apologists prior to and including Eusebius attempted to excuse the emperors as far as possible from any direct responsibility in the persecutions. For Eusebius, however, the primary object was no longer to secure relief for the Christians but to remove any suspicion that the imperial authority itself might have been wrong (J. Sirinelli, *Les Vues historiques d'Eusèbe de Césarée durant la Periode prénicéenne* [Université de Dakar, Faculté des Lettres et Sciences Humaines, Publications de la Section de Langues et Littératures, X] [Dakar, 1961], 414-416).

98. Van Berchem, "Le 'De Pallio,' " 110.

99. *Ibid.*, 104.

100. Hornus, "Etude," 38.

101. Clement of Alexandria, *Stromata*, I, 26 and I, 168.

102. Pseudo-Melito, 10.

103. This may seem to be a rather broad generalization, but in its justification I would mention that: (a) Cyprian was a fervent disciple of Tertullian, whose position on this point is beyond doubt (see below, p. 284); (b) Cyprian was the master who

inspired the martyr Maximilian, who was executed for refusing to bear arms, and whose mother brought his body back for burial at the foot of Cyprian's tomb; (c) Cyprian's writings contain both positive and negative statements which are exactly congruent with the position of conscientious objection.

104. Cyprian, *Testimonia*, III, 13.
105. Cyprian, *Ad Dem.*, 3 and 17.
106. Origen, *Contra Gelsum*, IV, 83. (See above, p. 258).
107. Eusebius, *Praep. Ev.*, 6, 6. Eusebius's text, which I quote here, attacks the doctrine of destiny which would render such punishment and reward impossible. I felt entitled to remodel the sentence and to formulate it in a positive way.
108. *Ibid.*, 4, 2. See also *HE*, IX, 5 ff.
109. Eusebius, *Praep. Ev.*, 2, 6. Half a century later—or earlier if we take into account the periodoi Petrou of which they are only a summary (Cadoux, *Early Church*, 457)—the *Clementine Recognitions* were just as practical and pessimistic as Eusebius in their estimate of human nature: "Who is there among men that does not covet his neighbor's goods? And yet they are restrained, and act honestly, through fear of the punishment which is prescribed by the laws. Through fear, nations are subject to their kings, and armies obey with arms in their hands" (*Recognitions*, IX, 15).
110. Eusebius, *HE*, VII, 30, 19 [Hornus translation]. On the real significance of Aurelian's expulsion of Paul from the see of Antioch, see G. Bardy, *Paul de Samosate*, 2nd ed. (Louvain, 1929), 358-363.
111. Eusebius, *HE*, VIII, 1, 2.
112. *Ibid.*, VI, 5, 3 and VI, 21, 4. See also p. 22 above.
113. *Ibid.*, VIII, 14, 11.
114. *Ibid.*, IX, 10, 3.
115. The excessiveness of Eusebius's eulogies of Constantine is obvious (Milburn, *Early Christian Interpretations*, 66 ff.). As to Licinius, he was the initial object of Eusebius's flattery when he, at a time when Constantine's position was still undecided, appeared to be the Christians' real protector (Moreau, *La Persécution*, 129, 133 ff.). But afterwards, when Constantine had come out in favor of the Christians and Licinius had thus been led to acts which the Constantinians presented as religious persecution, no insult against Licinius could be too caustic. Milburn praised Eusebius for historical honesty in not deleting the eulogies of Licinius from the later editions of his *History of the Church*, to which he however added some vehement attacks upon the former emperor. It is true that Eusebius inadvertently failed to delete some plural pronouns which imply praise of Licinius (e.g., *HE*, X, 4, 60 [quoted by Milburn, 201 n.], or X, 2, 2). But in most cases Eusebius revised his work quite drastically. This applies to *HE*, IX, 9, 1, which however is the only example (apart from the one cited above) that Milburn gave of Eusebius's objectivity (Milburn, 201 n.). It also applies to *HE*, IX, 10, 3: whereas later editions read "the prince of that time," the first edition unambiguously spelled out "Licinius." Identical corrections occur elsewhere in the *HE* which have been indicated in the editions of G. Bardy and E. Grapin (HL, II, xxiv-xxxvii, especially xxxi-xxxiii): *HE*, VIII, 17, 5; table of contents of book IX (Bardy, III, 43; Grapin, HL, XVII, 304); IX, 9a, 12; IX, 10, 3; IX, 11, 8. Eusebius has deliberately deleted the text which later came to be called the Edict of Milan, whose author was Licinius (*HE*, X, 5, 1-14; see J. Moreau, "Notes d'Histoire romaine," *AUS*, 2 [1953], 103). In at least one other case there is evidence that he has "arranged" history (cf. J. Moreau, "Vérité historique et Propagande politique chez Lactance et dans la *Vita Constantini*," *AUS*, 4 [1955], 95-96; see also R. Laqueur, *Eusebius als Historiker seiner Zeit* [Berlin-Leipzig, 1929]). The references to Licinius which Eusebius expunged from the later editions of the *HE* can fortunately be restored thanks to the

survival of certain manuscripts which he had not corrected. In sum, it is clear that the so-called "objectivity" which others have eulogized in Eusebius's work was manifestly only the result of his failure systematically to carry out his *damnatio memoriae*. Sirinelli (pp. 23-24), who reviewed once again the difficult question of the chronology of the various editions of the *HE*, argued that Eusebius must have finished the first editing by 312 and the last editing by 324. During these twelve years "out of a simple ecclesiastical chronicle, it [the *HE*] became a study of contemporary politics as well as a reflection on the meaning of history in the making" (Sirinelli, 434-436).

116. E. Honigmann, *Patristic Studies* (Vatican City, 1953), 6.

117. J. Moreau, "Les Litterae Licinii," *AUS*, 2 (1953), 100-105; Moreau, "Notes," 102-105. H. Grégoire had already pointed out ("La 'Conversion' de Constantin," *Revue de l' Université de Bruxelles*, 36 [1930-1931], 259, 261-263) that it was only in 313 that a clear confrontation between paganism and Christianity took place, "but that the champion of Christianity was not Constantine; it was Licinius." It was the latter who at Nicomedia posted the edict which has been "commonly called ... the Edict of Milan and obstinately attributed to Constantine." But J.-R. Palanque, who espoused this view with certain shades of difference in two works ("A propos du Prétendu Edit de Milan," *Byz*, 10 [1935], 607-616; J.-R. Palanque, G. Bardy, *et al.*, *The Church in the Roman Empire*, transl. E. C. Messenger [London, 1949-1952], I, 10-12), has shown a tendency to return to the classical thesis in his "Constantin, Empereur chrétien, d'après ses Récents Historiens," *Etudes médiévales offertes à M. le Doyen Fliche* (Montpellier, 1952), 134. A similar traditional assessment is found in H. Dörries, *Constantine the Great*, transl. R. H. Bainton (New York, 1972), 44-47.

118. See below, pp. 208-211.

119. Eusebius, *HE*, IV, 26, 6-11.

120. See above, p. 32.

121. Origen, *Contra Celsum*, II, 30. On the connections between the *Pax Romana* and the gospel, which for some authors was a positive relationship and for others (particularly Hippolytus, with whom I shall be dealing later) was decidedly negative, see E. Peterson, *Der Monotheismus als politisches Problem* (Leipzig, 1935), especially 66 ff. For even more extensive treatments of this subject, see E. Preuschen, *Analekta*, I: *Staat und Christentum bis auf Konstantin*, 2nd ed. (Tübingen, 1909); H. Berkhof, *Kirche und Kaiser* (Zürich, 1947); W. Hartke, *Römische Kinderkaiser* (Berlin, 1951); and Parker, *Christianity and the State*.

122. Pseudo-Justin, *Exhortation*, 17.

123. Sirinelli, 111-113, 133-134. We shall again encounter this lack of responsible theological thinking in Eusebius.

124. Eusebius, *Demonstratio Evangelica*, III, 7, 35, quoted by Sirinelli, 450.

125. Eusebius, *Demonstratio Evangelica*, VI, 20, which Sirinelli (p. 451) dated from 315 or a little later. Sirinelli devoted a chapter (pp. 388-411) to the theme of this "coincidence between empire and incarnation." Reluctant though he was to recognize any major significance in Eusebius's thought on this point, he traced with clarity the outlines of the entire tradition.

126. John Chrysostom, *Commentary on Isaiah*, 2, 4.

127. *Idem, Homilies on St. Matthew*, 75, 2.

128. Lactantius, *De Ira Dei*, 17, 6-7. See also the remainder of chapter 17.

129. *Ibid.*, 23, 10.

130. Lactantius, *Div. Institutiones*, I, 1, 15. From the context it is clear that Lactantius meant this sentence to indicate that God was siding with Constantine and against his adversaries.

131. "Daia . . . obtained authority to trample underfoot and oppress the empire of the East; a person ignorant alike of war and of civil affairs, and from a herdsman become the leader of armies" (Lactantius, *De Mort. Pers.*, 19, 6).

132. Lactantius, *Div. Institutiones*, I, 1, 13.

133. Lactantius, *De Mort. Pers.*, 18, 10.

134. A good summary of the period 306-323, during which the system of the Tetrarchy collapsed in confusion, can be found in Moreau, *La Persécution*, 125 ff.

135. Lactantius, *De Mort. Pers.*, 44-48. See Moreau's edition of this work (*SCH*, XXXIX, ii [Paris, 1954], 433-436) for a discussion of the meaning of the *signum Dei* on the Milvian Bridge. The bibliography on this subject is too extensive to summarize here; Moreau treats it especially well in his edition. For his discussion of the Edict of Milan, see ibid., 458. In Chapter 6 I shall comment further on the historical falsity of Lactantius's views.

136. Lactantius, *Div. Institutiones*, V, 9, 15-17.

137. Basil of Caesarea, *Moralia*, 79, 1-2; *idem*, *Homilies on the Psalms*, 1, 14.

138. Mansi, I, col. 46.

139. *Mart. Pol.*, 10, 2 (Musurillo, 11).

140. John Chrysostom, *Commentary on the Psalms*, 148, 4-5; *idem*, *Homilies on the Epistle to the Romans*, 23, 2.

141. Origen, *Contra Celsum*, I, 3.

142. Sirinelli, 417. At this stage Eusebius was merely quoting the explanations put forward by the Christian communities of Lyons and Smyrna. He never adhered to these himself. What interested him was already solely the prowess of the martyrs (*Ibid.*, 418).

143. *Ibid.*, 445.

144. *Ibid.*, 439. The sole exception was Maximinus, against whom Eusebius had a highly personal argument.

145. *Ibid.*, 440.

146. Eusebius, *Demonstratio Evangelica*, III, 7, 39.

147. Sirinelli, 452 ff.

148. Lactantius, *Div. Institutiones*, V, 12.

149. For an excellent survey (with exhaustive bibliographies) of the empire's persecutions of the Christians, see J. Vogt and H. Last, "Christenverfolgung," in *RACh*, II, cols. 1159-1228. Another lucid recent study of manageable proportions is J. Moreau, *La Persécution*. An important work by H. Grégoire (*Les Persécutions dans l'Empire romain* [Brussels, 1951]) stimulated a constructive debate with E. de Moreau ("Le Nombre des Martyrs des Persécutions romaines," *NRTh*, 73 [1951], 812-832). Both authors further developed their points of view under the joint title of "Nouvelles Observations sur le Nombre des Martyrs," *BARB*, 38 (1952), 37-70. Personally I subscribe to the finely worked out views of Parker, who regretted that a sort of Hegelian dialectic had led from one obviously false thesis (of Christians undergoing three centuries of uninterrupted terror) to an antithesis which was just as false (of Christians during the same period enjoying a wonderful life free from all difficulties) (Parker, *Christianity and the State*, 22 ff.). Parker then proceeded to give several historical examples of what the life of the whole community within a hostile state may really have been like (*Ibid.*, 26-28).

150. Lactantius, *De Ira Dei*, 20, 7.

151. Cyprian, *Ad Dem.*, 11.

152. *Ibid.*, 2 and 5.

153. Pseudo-Cyprian, *Quod Idola*, 4 ff.

154. Origen, *Contra Celsum*, IV, 70, 72.

155. Pseudo-Melito, 10.
156. Irenaeus, *Adv. Haeres.*, V. 30.
157. *Ascension of Isaiah*, 4, 2, 6, 7, 8, and 11. The *Sybilline Oracles*, III, 63, also made a close connection between Belial as the future manifestation of Satan and the emperors. Commodian (*Carmen Apologeticum*, 805 ff., 887, 891, 933, 935) also saw Nero as an eternal symbol of the bloody dictator, whose imminent return he proclaimed—for an exemplary punishment.
158. *Apocraphal Acts of St. John*, 36 (end).
159. Cadoux (*Early Christian Attitude*, 241) did not exclude this hypothesis in this particular case.
160. Eusebius, *HE*, VIII, 6, 8.
161. Tertullian, *Ad Nat.*, II, 9. Here, as often, Tertullian—who in the present case was depending upon Horatius—made use of a theme which he had already found in the Latin pagan writers.
162. Tertullian, *Adv. Iud.*, 9. Cf. his *Adv. Marc.*, III, 13, where he already used the same expressions.
163. Tertullian, *De Fuga*, 12.
164. "Whatever is not God's can belong to nobody but the devil," Tertullian commented, speaking of the pagan magistrates. "The demons are the magistrates of this world. They [i.e., the magistrates and demons] carry the *fasces* and wear the purple of one and the same college" (*De Idololatria*, 18). Tertullian also stated (*De Spec.*, 7) that Rome was the place where the demons assembled. For an important study of Tertullian's convictions concerning Christian participation in military service, see W. Rordorf ("Tertullians Beurteilung des Soldatenstandes," *VC*, 23 [1969], 105-141; for comment upon *De Idol.*, 18, see pp. 108-109), which was published too late for me to use it in this revised edition.
165. Tertullian, *De Corona*, 13. For the significance of *pompa diaboli*, see J. H Waszink, "Pompa Diaboli," *VC*, 1 (1947), 15-41.
166. G. Bardy, intro. to Hippolytus of Rome, *Commentary on Daniel*, SCH, XIV (1947), 24.
167. Hippolytus, *Commentary on Daniel*, III, 8, 9.
168. *Ibid.*, IV, 8, 7-8.
169. *Ibid.*, IV, 9, 2. In striking contrast, Eusebius maintained that, even if the devils had had total dominion over pre-Christian history, their reign had been wholly ended by the coming of Jesus (Sirinelli, 323-326).
170. Hippolytus, *Commentary on Daniel*, IV, 35; Eusebius, *Demonstratio Evangelica*, VIII, 2, 9-45.
171. On the various patristic exegeses of these seventy weeks and the consensus which was finally reached to make them end with the birth of Christ, see *DTC*, IV (1911), cols. 75-79.
172. Sirinelli, 464. With reference to the exegesis of the "seventy weeks" (pp. 459-465), Sirinelli showed that if Eusebius borrowed the eschatologists' interpretation, while their earlier adversaries had rejected it, it was in order to deprive the eschatologists of one of their most effective weapons. While accepting that the last "week" did not end with the birth of Christ, Eusebius made it end with his death. After Jesus Christ's time, therefore, history was all that remained for the future. As a result, there was no external standpoint left from which to judge history. It is beyond dispute that apocalyptic illuminism can at times lead to puzzling mistakes (see, for instance, Bardy's intro. to Hippolytus's *Commentary on Daniel*, SCH, XIV, 11 ff.). But Hippolytus was writing precisely to provide a safeguard against such divagations. His interpretation was thus not that of an irresponsible fanatic. It was that of a theolo-

gian who, however learned, remained aware that the history of the present world was to culminate in an end which was already judging it.

173. We are not dealing here with biblical theology. Let us merely recall that in 2 Thessalonians 2:6-7 Paul speaks of the thing and the man whose actions for a moment restrain "the mystery of lawlessness." Most commentators, from the early Fathers onwards, have seen these as the empire and the emperor (Goguel, *Birth*, 445). O. Cullmann has been almost alone in seeing them as the preaching of the gospel to the heathen and as the man carrying this out (i.e., St. Paul himself) ("Le Caractère eschatologique du Devoir missionaire et de la Conscience apostolique de Saint Paul," *RHPR*, 16 [1936], 244-245; *idem, Christ and Time: The Primitive Christian Conception of Time and History*, rev. ed. [London, 1962], 164-165; *idem, The State*, 52 n.). The two interpretations, however, are not as much in conflict as appears at first sight. In fact, the unity of the empire, with the material and intellectual opportunities for communication which it afforded and which I have stressed above, provided a providential framework for the propagation of the gospel (cf. E. F. Scott, *Man and Society in the New Testament* [New York, 1946], 171). So it can be admitted that for St. Paul the empire was opposed to the Antichrist, whether because it was itself the "restrainer" which gave time for the spread of the preaching of the gospel, or whether it simply enabled preaching, the activity of which may also have been the primary meaning of the word "restrainer." For the non-Christian context of this idea, see Cerfaux and Tondriau, *Concurrent*, 389.

174. Tertullian, *Apology*, 32, 1. See also his *De Res. Carnis*, 24, which in effect amounts to a repetition with a few verbal alterations of the text of 2 Thessalonians 2 along with some glosses, all of which is suffused with the clear intention of transforming a rather enigmatic text into a direct and unequivocal designation of the Roman empire. On Tertullian's political position in general, see the interesting remarks of Ryan, "Rejection," 17-18.

175. M. Dibelius, "Rom und die Christen im ersten Jahrhundert," in his *Botschaft und Geschichte, Gesammelte Aufsätze*, ed. G. Bornkamm (Tübingen, 1953-1956), II, 186-187. Dibelius viewed Tertullian's position as a misunderstanding of St. Paul's thinking and as a very unattractive "petit bourgeois" search for quietism. Certainly St. Paul was far less precise than Tertullian in his identification, and certainly the whole of his thinking was directed toward the dynamism of the preaching of the gospel, not toward the problem of preserving a political reality. I find, even so, that Dibelius overstated his case and that Tertullian's contentions contained real insights into Pauline thought.

176. "The Antichrist will be proud, he will feed on war and be a bold enough tyrant to raise himself above God. He will swell with pride because of his army, he will sack the fortresses of his enemies.... He will utter monstrous words against God, and he will want everyone to adore him alone, like the one God." He will destroy Tyre, Egypt, Libya, Ethiopia, and will reign over Jerusalem. He will declare himself king of the Jews. "It is he whom the unbelievers adore as God. They will bend the knee before him, taking him for the Christ because they will not remember the word of the prophet who called him an imposter and cheat" (Hippolytus, *Commentary on Daniel*, IV, 49, 1, 4-5). Several of these points could be applied to the empire. The passage which I quote in the main text, immediately after this footnote (*Commentary on Daniel*, IV, 17, 7-8), however, proves that they referred not to the empire but to one of its adversaries.

177. Hippolytus, *Commentary on Daniel*, IV, 17, 8.

178. *Ibid.*, IV, 17, 7.

179. *Ibid.*, IV, 21, 3. The word ὁ πλάνος, with which Hippolytus designated

264 Notes for pages 49-52

the Deceiver, is precisely the term used in 2 John 7 as the equivalent for the Antichrist.
180. Bardy, intro. to Hippolytus, *SCH*, XIV, 25.
181. Goguel, *Birth*, 440; Cullmann, *The State*, 46.
182. Parker, *Christianity and the State*, 40.
183. Tertullian, Apology, 21, 24. For penetrating comment upon this general attitude, see Cadoux, *Early Christian Attitude*, 212-213. He showed that for St. Paul and the Fathers the sovereign who could be called just, whom they recognized must employ violent means, was invariably a pagan sovereign. This meant that the non-Christians did not escape from God's sovereignty; but that fact could not justify the Christians in using methods available only to those who did not yet know Jesus Christ. On this point see Campenhausen, "Christians and Military Service," 160-161; Daniélou, "La Non-Violence," 21-22; Guignebert, *Tertullien*, 38-42; Setton, *Christian Attitude*, 17; Hornus, "Etude," 11.
184. Hobhouse, *The Church and the World*, 65.
185. A. Molnár, "L'Eschatologie contre l'Impérialisme romain," unpublished lecture given at the pastoral meeting of the Union of Czech Brethren, January 30—February 3, 1955, reported in *Protestant Churches in Czechoslovakia*, 2, No. 2 (1956), 13. [For Molnár's treatment of eschatological themes in a later period of church history, see his *A Challenge to Constantinianism: The Waldensian Theology in the Middle Ages* (Geneva, 1976), ch. 3.]
186. Sirinelli (p. 485) wrote that Eusebius found "this present age, which was constituted politically by the empire and religiously by the Church, substantial enough, rich enough, exciting enough for him not to need to disparage and negate it by continual reference to the future." For Eusebius all the prophecies of the Old Testament had already been fulfilled, and a second coming of the Lord was of no interest whatsoever (Sirinelli, 465, 465 n., 466-467, 470-484).
187. *Ibid.*, 410 n.
188. See J. Turmel, *Histoire des Dogmes* (Paris, 1931-1936), IV, 213-215, and also Turmel's very detailed study "L'Eschatologie à la fin du Iv^e siècle," *RHL*, 3 (1900), 97-127, 200-232, 289-321. It is unlikely, however, that Eusebius would have been bold enough to write plainly, as Didymus the Blind later did: "The Day of the Lord, in all probability, is the enlightenment produced in the soul by the true light" (*Commentary on the Second Epistle to the Corinthians*, 1, 13).
189. See Sirinelli, 51, 455-458, 468.
190. J. Daniélou, *Les Anges et leur Mission d'après les Pères de l'Eglise*, Collection Irénikon, new ser., V, 2nd ed. (Chevetogne, 1953), 176.
191. J. C. Bennett, *Social Salvation* (New York, 1935), 141. Similarly, Sirinelli wrote (p. 455): "The end of history, the end of the world, is one of the problems in which the opinions of an historian who knows something about theology can be seen most clearly."
192. Cullmann *The State*, 11-12, 49.
193. *Ibid.*, 67. Cf. also pp. 44-45, 55.
194. *Ibid.*, 55-56; Hornus, "Etude," 3.

Chapter 2

1. See, among other texts, Irenaeus, *Demonstration*, 20, 27 and 29; Cyprian, *De Zelo*, 5; pseudo-Cyprian, *Adv. Iud.*, 6; Hippolytus, *Commentary on Daniel*, I, 8, 3. My purpose here is not to examine the Old Testament directly, but merely to note how the Fathers understood and utilized its texts. For clear and concise general

analysis of the bellicose passages of the Old Testament, see A. M. Brunet, "La Guerre dans la Bible," *LV*, 7, no. 38 (1958), 31-47.

2. Tertullian, *Adv. Marc.*, I, 24, and IV, 29.
3. (Adamantius), *Dialogus*, I, 9-16, 18.
4. Clement of Rome, *Letter*, 12, 7.
5. Exodus 17:8-13.
6. Barnabas, *Letter*, 12, 2. Similarly, Cyprian wrote (*Testimonia*, II, 16): "Amalek was overcome by Jesus [Joshua], that is, the devil was overcome by Christ."
7. Numbers 21:6-9.
8. Barnabas, *Letter*, 12, 5-7.
9. Numbers 23:18.
10. Barnabas, *Letter*, 12, 8.
11. Exodus 17:14.
12. Barnabas, *Letter*, 12, 10.
13. It was a standard argument, which Clement as well as Tatian, Theophilus, Tertullian, and Eusebius borrowed from Josephus, that since Moses was even more ancient that Homer he had greater authority.
14. Clement of Alexandria, *Stromata*, I, 24, 158, 1.
15. *Ibid.*, I, 24, 158, 2.
16. *Ibid.*, I, 24, 159.
17. *Ibid.*, I, 24, 160.
18. Irenaeus, *Adv. Haeres.*, IV, 27, 1.
19. Origen, *De Princ.*, IV, 2, 8. See also IV, 1, 9 (end).
20. Origen, *Homilies on Joshua*, 15, 1.
21. U. Treu, "Etymologie und Allegorie bei Klemens von Alexandrien," *SP*, IV (*TU*, 79 [Berlin, 1961]), 200-211. In addition, see below, p. 111.
22. Philoxenus of Mabbug, *Letter Sent to a Friend*, 61. The expression "the Egypt of evil" recurs in sections 6, 10, and 36.
23. Origen, *De Princ.*, II, 4, 4.
24. Aristides, *Apology*, 8.
25. *Ibid.*, 10.
26. Arnobius, *Adv. Nat.*, *1, 6.*
27. *Didascalia*, VI, 19, 1.
28. Barnabas, *Letter*, 16, 4.
29. *Ibid.*, 6-10.
30. Origen, *Homilies on Joshua*, 17, 1. This passage was cited in a slightly different form by Lovsky, *Antisémitisme*, 463.
31. Lovsky, *Antisémitisme*, 125.
32. *The Ascension of Isaiah*, 7, 9-12; see also 10, 29-31.
33. Victorinus of Pettau, *Commentary on the Apocalypse*, 19.
34. Cyprian, *De Mortalitate*, 2.
35. Minucius Felix, *Octavius*, 33, 3.
36. (Adamantius), *Dialogus*, I, 10, 12, 13.
37. Irenaeus, *Adv. Haeres.*, III, 17, 3.
38. Hippolytus, *Commentary on Daniel*, IV, 40, 3.
39. Basil of Caesarea, *Treatise on the Holy Spirit*, 16, 39.
40. Tertullian, *Scorpiace*, 3.
41. Theophilus of Antioch, *Three Books*, III, 11.
42. Pseudo-Cyprian, *Quod Idola*, 10; see also 12.
43. Tertullian, *Apology*, 26, 3.
44. Tertullian, *Adv. Marc.*, III, 23.

45. *Mart. Pionii*, 4, 18 (Musurillo, 141).
46. Hippolytus, *Commentary on Daniel*, IV, 58, 3.
47. Hippolytus, *On the Antichrist*, 30.
48. Justin, *First Apology*, 47.
49. Justin, *Dialogue with Trypho*, 110, 6.
50. *Ibid.*, 139, 3.
51. Origen, *Contra Celsum*, IV, 73.
52. *Ibid.*, VIII, 42. See also I, 47; II, 8, 13, 34, 78; IV, 32; V, 43; VII, 26; VIII, 47, 69.
53. *Ibid.*, IV, 22.
54. Minucius Felix, *Octavius*, 33, 5.
55. (Adamantius), *Dialogus*, I, 11.
56. Pseudo-Cyprian, *Adv. Iud.*, 6-8.
57. Eusebius, *Praep. Ev.*, 1, 3.
58. *Sybilline Oracles*, IV, 115-118, 125-127. See also Cadoux, *Early Christian Attitude*, 185.
59. Augustine, *Discourse on the Psalms*, 74, 17.
60. Pseudo-Cyprian, *De Pascha Computus*, 15.
61. Lactantius, *Div. Institutiones*, IV, 21, 5.
62. J. Isaac, *La Dispersion d'Israël, Fait historique ou Mythe théologique* (Algiers, 1954), 26 ff. On the Christian interpretation of the disaster of AD 70, see Goguel, *Birth*, 546-547.
63. Lovsky, *Antisémitisme*, 72.
64. *Ibid.*, 150.
65. Cited by Eusebius, *HE*, II, 23, 18.
66. Origen, *Commentary on St. Matthew*, 10, 17; *Contra Celsum*, I, 49; II, 13. Later on John Chrysostom combined the two traditions (*Homilies on St. Matthew*, 69, 1): he argued that the catastrophe of AD 70 was indeed the punishment for the death of Christ, but that God in his mercy had not punished the Jews immediately. But events such as the murders of James and Stephen had finally exhausted his patience.
67. Theophilus of Antioch, *Three Books*, II, 36.
68. Tertullian, *Apology*, 20, 2.
69. Tertullian, *Adv. Marc.*, IV, 39.
70. Clement of Rome, *Letter*, 8, 4.
71. Commodian, *Instructions*, II, 9-10.
72. Jerome, *Ep.*, 60, 17. On the events to which Jerome was referring, see L. Halphen, *Les Barbares*, 3rd ed. (Paris, 1936), 15; G. Bardy, *L'Eglise et les Derniers Romains*, 8th ed. (Paris, 1948); and P. Courcelle, *Histoire littéraire des Grandes Invasions germaniques* (Paris, 1948).
73. Eusebius, *HE*, VIII, 1, 8-9.
74. Tertullian, *De Idol.*, 19.
75. Irenaeus, *Adv. Haeres.*, IV, 36, 6, which has already been mentioned on p. 32.
76. On the theme of the *de morte persecutorum* in Eusebius, see Sirinelli, 420, 433, 444. In the last of these instances, Eusebius also applied this theme to Maxentius, who had never persecuted the Christians but who received judgment as a bad ruler. For Eusebius, however, this theme was less central than it was for Lactantius; in fact, Eusebius ultimately abandoned it altogether (Sirinelli, 439).
77. Eusebius, *HE*, VI, 41, 9. On Eusebius's occasional extension to a whole group of the punishment which he viewed as that of the responsible individuals, see Sirinelli, 442-443.

78. Eusebius, *HE*, IX, 9, 1.
79. Eusebius, *HE*, IX, 10, 13 and 15.
80. *Ibid.*, X, 1, 7.
81. Lactantius, *De Mort. Pers.*, 44-48.
82. *Ibid.*, 49.
83. *Ibid.*, 50, 1.
84. *Ibid.*, 52, 4.
85. See below, pp. 184-187.
86. E. Grapin, introduction to Eusebius, *HE*, HL, II, xii. On Lactantius, see Moreau, "Vérité historique," 93.
87. Cyprian, *De Bono Patientiae*, 21.
88. Lactantius, *Div. Institutiones*, VI, 18, 11.
89. F. Casavola, "La Politiche dei Cristiani pregiustinianei," *Labeo*, 1 (1955), 55-73.
90. Romans 6:13, 23; 13:12; 16:7; 1 Corinthians 9:7, 25; 2 Corinthians 6:7; 10:3-6; 11:8; Ephesians 6:12-18; Philippians 2:25; Colossians 4:10; 1 Thessalonians 5:8; 1 Timothy 1:18; 4:12; 2 Timothy 2:3; 4:7; Philemon 2, 23. "Whereas in the Old Testament infidelity was called adultery, in the New Testament and the early Church it is described as desertion" (R. H. Bainton, "The Early Church and War," *HThR*, 39 [1946], 189).
91. E. Nielsen, "La Guerre considérée comme une religion et la religion comme une guerre," *Studia Theologica*, 15 (Aarhus, 1961), 109.
92. H. Edmonds, who devoted an article ("Geistlicher Kriegsdienst: der Topos der Militia spiritualis in der antiken Philosophie," in O. Casel, ed., *Heilige Überlieferung*, suppl. vol. to *Beiträge zur Geschichte des alten Mönchtums und des Benediktinerordens* [Münster, 1938], 21-56; repr. in Harnack, *Militia Christi* [1963 ed.], 133-162) to the study of the theme of the *militia spiritualis* in pagan philosophy, contended that the *militia Christi* was simply a later application of this classical theme.
93. Harnack, *Militia Christi*, 35. See also J. Gagé, " Stauros nikopoios , La Victoire impériale dans l'Empire chrétien," *RHPR*, 13 (1933), 395; Rordorf, "Tertullians Beurteilung," 130-138; [and J. Auer, "Militia Christi," *DS*, X (1979), 1213-1217].
94. It is enough to point out that a patrology such as that of F. Cayré (3rd ed. [1945], II, 904) has in its "doctrinal table" no fewer than seventeen lines of patristic references under the heading of "spiritual battle." See also J. Lortz, *Tertullian als Apologet* (Münster, 1928), II, 30-54; *DS*, III (1954), art. "Démon", esp. cols. 150-152, 177-196, 204-208, 216-219; J. Daniélou, *Essai sur le Mystère de l'Histoire* (Paris, 1953), 57-60; J. Fontaine, *SCH*, CXXXIV, 417-419.
95. C. Mohrmann, "Statio," *VC*, 7 (1953), 244. See also F. J. Dölger, "Sacramentum Militiae," in his *Antike und Christentum: kultur-und religionsgeschichtliche Studien* (Münster, 1930), II, 268-280.
96. E. Malone, "Martyrdom and Monastic Profession as a Second Baptism," in A. Mayer, J. Quasten, and B. Neunheuser, eds., *Vom Christlichen Mysterium* (Festschrift O. Casel) (Düsseldorf, 1951), 115. See also C. Mohrmann, "Sacramentum dans les plus anciens textes chrétiens," in *Etudes sur le latin des Chrétiens*, 1 (Rome, 1958), 233-244, which demonstrates how Tertullian played upon the ambiguity of the word *sacramentum* in popular Latin in which military enrollment simultaneously had religious and legal meanings. But the extreme linguistic artificiality of this play on words is an indication of the significance of this idea in the history of thought.
97. Clement of Rome, *Letter*, 45, 7.

98. *Ibid.*, 36, 6-37, 4. On Clement's admiration for the Roman army, see Guignebert, *Tertullien*, 191 n.; Harnack, *Militia Christi*, 18 ff., 52 ff.; H. Weinel, *Die Stellung des Urchristentums zum Staat* (Tübingen, 1908), 26.

99. Clement of Rome, *Letter*, 21, 4.

100. II Clement, *Ep.*, 7.

101. Ignatius, *Epistle to Polycarp*, 6, 2. P. Lelong, in the notes to his edition of Ignatius (HL, XII, 2nd ed., [1927]), remarked on the presence at this place in the Greek text of three "technical terms of [Latin] military language." He speculated that Ignatius was familiar with these terms because of his constant contact with soldiers following his condemnation. The close similarity with Eph. 6:13-17 is unmistakable.

102. Ignatius, *Epistle to the Smyrnaeans*, 1, 2.

103. *Mart. Pol.*, 3.

104. Harnack, *Militia Christi*, 40-43.

105. Cadoux, *Early Christian Attitude*, 166-167. We should especially note the *Passio Mariani*, 1, 3; 3, 4; 8, 4; 10, 3; *Passio Montani*, 1, 1; 4, 6; 6, 3-5; 14, 5; *Acta Fructuosus*, 7. H. Leclercq, *Les Martyrs* (Paris, 1902-1911), I, lv, made a close study of the comparison between the martyr and the soldier.

106. Minucius Felix, *Octavius*, 37, 1-3.

107. E. Demougeot, "Remarques sur l'Emploi de 'Paganus,' " *Studi in Onore di H. Calderini e R. Paribeni* (Milan, 1956), I, 337-350.

108. Cadoux, *Early Christian Attitude*, 167; *idem, Early Church*, 409, 569. Cf. C. Mohrmann, "Encore une Fois 'Paganus,' " *VC*, 7 (1952), 109-122. See also p. 73. The articles of Mlles. Demougeot ("Remarques") and Mohrmann ("Encore") are full of fine nuances, and the linguistic evolution of the term *paganus* is complex. The line of development which I indicate here, however, is one of its certain components.

109. *Acts of Paul*, 4.

110. *Ibid.*, 3, 4, 6.

111. Justin, *Dialogue with Trypho*, 131, 2.

112. Simon, *Verus Israël*, 145.

113. Justin, *First Apology*, 55, 6.

114. *Ibid.*, 39, 5.

115. Pseudo-Justin, *Discourse*, 5.

116. Irenaeus, *Adv. Haeres.*, III, 16, 4; IV, 24, 1, frags. 18, 44; *idem, Demonstration*, 20, 27, 29. All of these are cited in Cadoux, *Early Christian Attitude*, 174.

117. Irenaeus, *Adv. Haeres.*, II, 2, 3; IV, 20, 11, frag. 21.

118. Clement of Alexandria, *Protrept.*, X, 93, 2.

119. *Ibid.*, XI, 116, 1-4.

120. Clement of Alexandria, *Stromata*, II, 20, 110.

121. *Ibid.*, I, 11, 3, 6.

122. The word ἀντιμαχησις is to be preferred here, but scholars are by no means fully agreed on this point. Indeed, unless we keep in mind the strictly military context of much early Christian language, other terms might seem more appropriate than this to indicate temptations.

123. Clement of Alexandria, *Stromata*, II, 20, 120.

124. Clement of Alexandria, *Excerpta ex Theodoto*, 72, 1-2.

125. It is clear that in Clement's terminology this term was equally applicable to the Christians.

126. Clement of Alexandria, *Excerpta ex Theodoto*, 85, 3. Cadoux (*Early Church*, 409 n.) cited the following passages in which Clement used the military metaphor to describe a Christian's life: *Stromata*, IV, 4, 14-16; 8, 60; 13, 91; 22, 141;

VI, 12, 103; 14, 112; VII, 3, 21; 11, 66; 13, 83; 16, 100; *Qui Dives*, 25 and 34.

127. Jerome, *De Vir. Ill.*, 53.

128. Tertullian, *Apology*, 50; *De Cultu Fem.*, II, 5; *De Fuga*, 10; *Adv. Marc.*, V, 5. Malone ("Martyrdom," 116) wrote of Tertullian: "Not only was the life of the Christian a true military service, but it was one which in the eyes of many Christians was also incompatible with actual military service in the armies of the Roman empire." See also R.C. Gerest, "Les premiers chrétiens face à leur monde," *LV*, 12, no. 73 (1963), 18-19.

129. Tertullian, *De Anima*, 31.

130. Tertullian, *De Fuga*, 10. See also the similar affirmations of a much later date that the Lord is really commander, master, and king (*Homélies anonymes dans la tradition d' Origène*, ed. P. Nautin, *SCH*, XXXVI [1953], I, 19).

131. Tertullian, *Adv. Marc.*, III, 13-14; IV, 20; V, 18; *Adv. Iud.*, 9; *De Res. Carnis*, 20. See also Cadoux, *Early Christian Attitude*, 183; idem, *Early Church*, 409. In Tertullian's *De Corona*, 11, there is the following untranslatable play on words: "*Apud hunc tam miles est paganus fidelis, quam paganus est miles fidelis.*" (A rough rendering of this into English is: In Christ, the civilian who is one of the faithful is a soldier-of-Christ, in similar manner to the soldier who, faithful to his calling, is a civilian-pagan non-Christian.) For a contrasting of the concept of *paganus*=civilian with that of the *miles Christi*, see Hobhouse, *The Church and the World*, 371-372.

132. See, for example, Origen, *Homilies on Exodus* (*SCH*, XVI, 273), in which a significant number of texts are listed under the heading of "spiritual combat."

133. Origen, *De Princ.*, III, 2, 5.

134. Cyprian, *Ep.*, 73, 10 (*ANCL* ed., 72, 10).

135. Cyprian, *De Bono Patientiae*, 12.

136. Cyprian, *Ad Fortunatum*, 13; *Testimonia*, III, 117; *De Zelo*, 2. J. Capmany ("*Miles Christi*" *en la Espiritualidad de San Cipriano*, Collectanea San Paciano, Serie Teológica, I [Barcelona, 1956], demonstrated, with numerous details and quotations, that this idea of spiritual combat was the key to St. Cyprian's thought. He unfortunately, however, did not seem even to conjecture that the sources of this conception might have been St. Paul and the earliest Fathers.

137. Pseudo-Cyprian, *De Pascha computus*, 10.

138. Commodian, *Instructions*, II, 12.

139. *Ibid.*, II, 22. One could also cite II, 9-11, 20. The allegorization in these passages at times becomes so obscure that it is hard to know precisely what the author is talking about, but the general vision clearly remains one of hideous apocalyptic combat.

140. *Didascalia*, II, 6, 6-11.

141. Lactantius, *Div. Institutiones*, Epilogue (73).

142. Eusebius, *HE*, V, 1, 18.

143. *Ibid.*, VI, 41, 16.

144. Eusebius, *Martyrs*, 11, 22.

145. Athanasius, *Letter on Love and Temperance*, 288; see also 290, 291.

146. Basil of Caesarea, *Homilies on the Psalms*, 7. In a curious fashion, this text associates "the injuries received in battle" with "blemishes and traces of sin." Thus the sanctity which will allow entry into the kingdom consists not so much in having fought valiantly as in having been able to avoid battle to the very end. Nor does this text imply (as some have argued) that Satan collaborates actively with God in judgment. Cf. S. Giet, *Les Idées et l'Action de Saint Basile* (Paris, 1941), 179.

147. John Chrysostom, *Letters to Olympias*, VIII, 9b.

148. *Ibid.*, XVII, 2b. The author is addressing these strictures to Jeremiah.

270   *Notes for pages 76-80*

149. *Ibid.*, XV, 1a and 1b.
150. Aphrahat the Syrian; *Demonstrationes*, VU, 18.
151. *Life of Pachomius*, ed. and transl. L. Th. Lefort, *Bibliothèque du Muséon*, XVI (Louvain, 1943), 2. The editor commented (p. 2 n.) that the Coptic word for legion has a meaning which is exclusively military.
152. Malone, "Martyrdom," 118.
153. Frend, "Persecutions," 141.
154. Cyril of Scythopolis, *Life of Sabbas*, 92-93.
155. This is the origin of the Eastern clergy's obligation to wear beards.
156. Cyril of Scythopolis, *Life of Euthymius*, 25-26.
157. Cyril of Scythopolis, *Life of Theodosius*, 239. If here as elsewhere there was no clear distinction between military and sporting contests, it is because there was a deep psychological resemblance between them. See J.-Y. Jolif, "Pourquoi la Guerre?" *LV*, 7, no. 38 (1958), 13.
158. R. Génier, *Vie de Saint Euthyme le Grand* (Paris, 1909), 164.
159. W. K. L. Clarke, ed., *The Ascetic Works of St. Basil* (London, 1925), 56.
160. *Ibid.*, 55 n.
161. John Chrysostom, *Homilies on St. Matthew*, 69, 3.
162. A. Vanderpol (*Doctrine scolastique*, 204-206) summarized this treatise and quoted extensively from it.
163. Sulpicius Severus, *Dialogue*, I (2, 11). The text specified that St. Martin was requiring a common pursuit of the monastic life, which entailed the exclusion of all sexual relationships. The Basilian *Preliminary Sketch*, as we have just seen also stipulated the abandonment of feminine companionship as a prerequisite for the life of both the soldier and the monk. But it further stressed that the woman, for her part, could also "serve as soldier" for Christ.
164. Jerome, *Ep.*, 58, 8.
165. Gregory the Great, *Morals on the Book of Job*, Preface, 1, 7; I, 9-11, 35, 49; II, 2, 13, 19, 32, 70, 73, 79.
166. Diehl, I, 198 (no. 1,041).
167. H. Rahner, "Pompa Diaboli," *ZkTh*, 55 (1931), 239-273.
168. Waszink, "Pompa Diaboli," *passim*.
169. See, for example, A. Bayet, *Pacifisme et Christianisme aux Premiers Siècles* (Paris, 1934). For Bayet's treatment of the apocalyptic wars see pp. 20-25 and 118-120. For a representative sample of his general method and interpretation, see his p. 53, n.1.
170. James Moffat, "War," in J. Hastings, ed., *Dictionary of the Apostolic Church* (Edinburgh, 1915-1918), II, 657.
171. Lactantius, *Div. Institutiones*, VI, 4, 14-24.
172. *Ibid.*, VI, 4, 11.
173. *Ibid.*, VI, 20, 16 ("*neque militare iusti licebit cuius militia est ipsa iustitia*"). For the context to this passage, see below, pp. 219-220.
174. Chenu, "L'Evolution," 82. This "spiritualization" is no doubt very bad exegesis. We should note, moreover, that the same method would lead, in the opposite direction, to taking the concrete meaning out of the Old Testament prophecies of peace, the importance of which I shall shortly be demonstrating. Thus, in Cyril's *Life of Sabbas* (p. 99, lines 12-18), Micah 4:2-4 became an invitation to stop *fighting* wicked thoughts, which the saints henceforth were to defeat definitively in their own hearts, and to begin *cultivating* the masses of people, whose souls had been neglected.
175. John Chrysostom, *Commentary on Isaiah*, 2, 3.
176. Eusebius, *HE*, VII, 11, 20.

177. This would have been the logical place for Dionysius—like the earlier Christian writers—to insert a clause commenting that these soldiers had passed from the vain conflicts of this world to the real conflict, from obedience to the world's leaders to obedience to the one true Lord, etc.; but he failed to do so.

178. "You who are a soldier, work to the same end as the gospel. Fight the good fight against the evil spirit, against the desires of the flesh. Put on the whole armor of God, so as not to allow yourself to be imprisoned in the affairs of life, and so as to be agreeable to him [God] who chose you for the army" (Basil of Caesarea, *Homilies*, 3, 4).

179. *Ibid.* See Giet, *Idées*, 173.

180. Tertullian, *Apology*, 31, 2.

181. Clement of Rome, *Letter*, 60,4-61,3. Goguel (*Birth*, 552-553) studied intensively the astonishing manner in which the bishop of Rome minimized as mere disagreeable "incidents" the terrible persecutions of Nero and Domitian.

182. See H. Hemmer, intro. to vol. II of *Pères apostoliques*, HL, X, liii. See also Cullmann, *The State*, 65.

183. *Acta Apollonii*, 6-7.

184. In this passage there is perhaps something reminiscent of the Tertullian quotation which I have just cited (in n. 180 above). In any case, no state cares very much for the spiritual insight on the part of its subjects, when they come to recognize that it, too, needs forgiveness.

185. Arnobius, *Adv. Nat.*, 4, 36.

186. Polycarp, *Letter to the Philippians*, 12, 3. By a careful exegesis of the Latin version of this text, which is its only extant version, Goguel (*Birth*, 551) was confident that he could prove that it is identical with Tertullian's thinking. I agree that this is likely (but unprovable). Polycarp concluded: "The Roman authorities are to be prayed for because they are enemies of the Christians." Cullmann, commenting (in *The State*, 47) on the key text concerning submission to the authorities (Romans 13: 1-7), reminded his readers to keep in mind the context of this passage, which proves that "the matter under discussion at this point is the Christian commandment of love— evil is not to be rewarded with evil, rather one is to do good to his enemy. This stands in Romans 12 immediately before the section about the state in Romans 13:1 ff.; and directly afterwards, in verse 8, the same theme is resumed."

187. Justin, *First Apology*, 17, 3.

188. Tertullian, *Apology*, 30, 4. See also 31, 3; 37, 9; 39, 2.

189. *Ibid.*, 40, 13.

190. *Acta Achatii*, 1, 3.

191. Cyprian, *Ad Dem.*, 20.

192. Basil of Caesarea, *Letters*, 155.

193. Eusebius, *HE*, X, 8, 10.

194. *Ibid.*, VIII, 12, 42.

195. Origen, *Contra Celsum*, VIII, 68-70. Van Berchem ("Le 'De Pallio'," 193) made some useful remarks concerning the seriousness of Celsus's arguments. See also Gerest, "Les premiers chrétiens," 15, 20-21.

196. Origen, *Contra Celsum*, VIII, 73 (beginning). See also VIII, 68, 74-75.

197. What is the exact meaning of this "righteous" (just) cause? Cadoux (*Early Christian Attitude*, 208) adduced this text—among others—as proof that for Origen the non-Christian empire had a lawful right to make war.

198. Origen, *Contra Celsum*, VIII, 73. This translation of this vitally important passage is that of Chadwick (p. 509). (For French equivalents, see Lods, "L'Eglise," 23, and Leclercq, "Militarisme," col. 1128.) At a later date, St. Jerome wrote sadly of

the barbarians' overthrow of the empire and recalled the way in which Israel's heroes had conquered—by intercession rather than by the sword. Then he remarked, "If we wish to be lifted up, let us first prostrate ourselves." If we were to do so, he added, the disgrace of the Roman army's rout would end immediately. "Then we should see the enemy's arrows give way to our javelins, his caps to our helmets, and his nags to our chargers" (Jerome, *Ep.*, 60, 17).

199. Origen, *Contra Celsum*, VIII, 74. This was to claim for the entire Christian community a function which—as we shall see in Chapter 5—later came to be restricted to a specialized clergy. During the thirteenth century, however, the founding of a lay Third Order gave that ideal a new lease on life, even for laymen. The Rule of the Franciscan Brethren of the Third Order states that the Tertiaries "shall not receive nor carry with them any weapon which could kill someone" (VI, 3, quoted by P. Lorson, *Défense de tuer* [Paris, 1953], 21). Although popular reaction was enthusiastic, those in power were not amused. In time an interplay of casuistry and practical pressures progressively weakened the Rule.

200. Most of the patristic texts which follow have been collected more or less in the same order by Cadoux (*Early Christian Attitude*, 61-63). Daniélou ("La Non-violence," 13, 17) emphasized that the Christian authors of the first two centuries were unanimous in finding in the pacifism of Christians a conclusive proof that this prophecy had indeed applied to Jesus Christ.

201. ἡδέως, ὁμολοζουντες τὸν Χριστὸν, ἀποθνήσκομεν (Justin, *First Apology*, 39, 1-3.).
202. Justin, *Dialogue with Trypho*, 109; 110, 3.
203. Isaiah 66:5.
204. Matthew 5:44-46.
205. Theophilus, *Three Books*, III, 14.
206. Irenaeus, *Demonstration*, 61.
207. *Idem, Adv. Haeres.*, IV, 34, 4.
208. Origen, *Contra Celsum*, V, 33.
209. (Adamantius), *Dialogus*, I, 10.
210. Pseudo-Cyprian, *Adv. Iud.*, 9.
211. Cyprian, *De Habitu Virginum*, 11 [Hornus transl.].
212. Tertullian, *Adv. Iud.*, 3.
213. *Idem, Adv. Marc.*, III, 21. See also IV, 1.
214. Sirinelli, 57 n., 164-170.
215. Eusebius, *Praep. Ev.*, I, 4, and VI, 1.
216. Athanasius, *De Incarnatione Verbi*, 52, 4-6.
217. *Ibid.*, 53, 1.
218. *Ibid.*, 53, 3-5.
219. John Chrysostom, *Commentary on Isaiah*, 2, 4-5.
220. Clement of Alexandria, *Paedagogus*, I, 12, 98; II, 2, 32; II, 4, 42.
221. Clement of Rome, *Letter*, 8, 4 (already quoted on p. 64).

Chapter 3

1. Eusebius, *Praep. ev.*, 1, 4; 4, 16-17; 5, 1; 5, 4.
2. Tertullian, *De Idol.*, 19.
3. *Mart. Pol.*, 3; Tertullian, *Adv. Marc.*, V, 17; *idem, De Spec.*, 8.
4. Tertullian, *De Spec.*, 25.
5. *Ascension of Isaiah*, 10, 13.
6. Ignatius, *Eph.*, 19.
7. Arnobius, *Adv. Nat.*, 2, 1.

8. Tatian, *Oratio*, 11.
9. Tertullian, *Traité du Baptême*, ed. R. Refoulé, *SCH*, XXXV (Paris, 1952), 49-50, includes a note which provides both a listing of other passages in which Tertullian develops this theme and a bibliography of recent scholarly work. See also above, p. 69.
10. Ignatius, *Rom.*, 6, 1.
11. Hippolytus, *Commentary on Daniel*, IV, 9.
12. Sulpicius Severus, *Vita Mart.*, 4, 3 (*SCH*, CXXXIII, 260).
13. *Mart. Pionii*, 3, 2-5 (Musurillo, 139).
14. Irenaeus, *Adv. Haeres.*, V, 26.
15. Origen, *Contra Celsum*, VII, 70.
16. *Ibid.*, IV, 70.
17. Gregory of Nazianzus, *Discourse 43: in honor of Basil the Great*, 48. Giet (*Les Idées*, 358) quoted the Greek text, and commented: "There are two reasons for the refusal: a. All God's creatures are equal, at least in this respect. So there is no reason why one person should surrender his liberty and rights to another; b. The Christian, who has been called by grace to share in the divine nature, least of all can accept this degradation."
18. Gregory of Nazianzus, *Discourse 43*, 48.
19. Tertullian, *Apol.*, 33.
20. Eusebius, *Vita*, I, 16 ff.
21. Basil, *Ep.*, 99, 1.
22. *Ibid.*, 299.
23. Tertullian, *De Cultu fem.*, II, 11. Tertullian qualified this, however, by instructing them not to follow Roman fashions of dress.
24. Tertullian, *De Idol.*, 16.
25. *Ibid.*, 18.
26. Tertullian, *Apol.*, 36, 1.
27. *Ibid.*, 41, 1.
28. *Ibid.*, 44, 1.
29. Tertullian, *De Idol.*, 17. Tertullian took his stand on the concrete example of Joseph and Daniel, who had been able to fill the highest public offices without trespassing the borders of idolatry. The Christian of his day could still do the same, if it were at all thinkable that such a thing might be possible (*si haec credibile fieri posse*). These words seem to have meant that Tertullian considered that this eventuality, although it might have been realizable in theory, was illusory in practice in the world of his own time.
30. Tertullian, *Ad Nat.*, I, 17; *idem, Apol.*, 30, 3; 32, 2.
31. Tertullian, *Adv. Marc.*, I, 13.
32. Tertullian, *De Spec.*, 15.
33. *Anonymous Homilies*, III, 18.
34. Eusebius, *HE*, VIII, 9, 6.
35. This was a familiar theme in John Chrysostom's preaching. In the *Homilies on St. Matthew* (9, 7), for example, he argued that the flight of the infant Jesus and his family into Egypt had implicitly confronted every believer with the question, "Why do you pride yourself on your country, when I am commanding you to be a stranger to the whole world?" Again, in the *Homilies on St. John*, he wrote that those who listened to the apostle's preaching "could no longer be mere men nor remain upon earth, [but] would dwell on earth just as if it were heaven" (1, 1). In a later homily on the same gospel, he declared that "thou art a stranger and a sojourner ... for thou hast a city whose artificer and creator is God, and the sojourning itself is but for a

short and little time. . . . We are citizens of heaven, registered for the country which is above" (79, 3). In his *Homilies on Ephesians* he quoted, "So then you are no longer strangers and sojourners, for you are fellow-citizens with the saints" (VI, 1). But elsewhere he corrected the evasive impression which such statements might leave. Should Christians claim privileges by virtue of their heavenly citizenship so as to avoid obedience to earthly magistrates? Not at all. Precisely because they were "strangers and sojourners" on earth, believers were required to obey the governing authorities. The effects of the Christians' liberation would only be realized in the future (*Homilies on Romans*, 23, 2).

36. *Mart. Pionii*, 18, 7 (Musurillo, 159). Pionius was the priest in charge of the group of martyrs.

37. St. Augustine, *Confessions*, IX, 11, 28.

38. Eusebius, *Martyrs*, 11, 8-12. This scorn of the name given by parents, because it represented the natural man and not the Christian, was often to be found in the records of the martyrs. E.g., *Acta Tarachii*, 1, and *Acta Dasii*, 6.

39. Sirinelli, 144. See also 151-157, 219, 250.

40. Clement of Rome, *Letter*, 1, 1. There is an identical greeting at the beginning of the *Letter* of Polycarp.

41. Irenaeus, *Contre les Hérésies*, ed. F. Sagnard, *SCH*, XXXIV, 9.

42. P. de Labriolle, "παροικία , Paroecia," *RSR*, 18 (1928), 60-72. On p. 61 Labriolle simply identified πάροικοι with μέτοικοι , the "parishioners" with the "metics" or the "people without a country." This is a theme which should have saved us from slogans like "For Christ and France," "For God and Country," etc. See also Giet, *Les Idées*, 317 n., who refers to Labriolle, "Paroecia," *ALMA*, 3 (1927), 196-205, and *L'Année philologique*, 2 (1927), 321.

43. Cyril of Scythopolis, *Life of Euthymius*, p. 8; *idem, Life of Theodosius*, p. 235; and, in a slightly different form, *idem, Life of Sabas*, p. 86, l. 27. In each case, as if to accentuate the contrast, Cyril then provided information on the human origins (familial and national) of the hermit.

44. John Chrysostom, *Homilies on St. Matthew*, 69, 4 (end). On the consequences of this qualification, see pp. 193 ff.

45. Hermas, *Similitudes*, I, 1-6. Here it is the verb katoikō which is used, but with the immediate specification epi xenēs. In his edition of this text, P. Lelong wrote (HL, XVI [Paris, 1912], 138 n.), "The 'earthly city' is the world. Yet [T.] Zahn (*Der Hirte des Hermas* [Gotha, 1868]) was not altogether wrong to understand the 'earthly city' to mean Rome and its empire. For in the eyes of many Christians Rome . . . was the kingdom of the devil, and the emperor was his minister."

46. II Clement, *Ep.*, 5, 1.

47. *Ibid.*, 5, 4.

48. *Ibid.*, 5, 6-7.

49. *Ibid.*, 6, 1.

50. *Ibid.*, 6, 3.

51. Tertullian, *De Corona*, 13.

52. Tertullian, *De Idol.*, 15; *idem, De Fuga*, 12; *idem, Adv. Marc.*, IV, 38; *idem, Scorpiace*, 14.

53. Tertullian, *Apol.*, 31, 2.

54. Tertullian, *De Spec.*, 30.

55. Tertullian, *De Patientia*, 15.

56. See especially Tertullian, *Ad Scapulam*, 3.

57. Tertullian, *Apol.*, 1, 2.

58. Van Berchem ("Le 'De Pallio,' " 103) contrasted this conciliatory view with

the attitude of complete rupture which he thought to find in the treatise *De Pallio*. He rightly noted, however (p. 113), that this contrast—independent of Tertullian's movement towards Montanism—did not represent a complete contradiction; it was rather a tension between complementary viewpoints, as was shown by the existence in the *Apology* itself of texts as stern as the one I have just quoted. It seems at any rate that for Van Berchem the most characteristic stance of the first Christians was one of rejection. He wrote (p. 101), "They acknowledged a leader who was not the emperor. They announced the establishment on earth of a new empire, which was to replace that of Rome, and they pleaded for this change in their suffrages and their prayers. So it might reasonably have been wondered whether they were not the sworn enemies of the empire."

59. Cyprian, *De Mortalitate*, 26.

60. Clement of Alexandria, *Protrept.*, X, 108, 4. See also his *Paedagogus*, III, 8, 1.

61. Fragment quoted in Clement of Alexandria, *Stromata*, VI, 5, 41.

62. H. I. Marrou (*L'Epître à Diognète, SCH*, XXXIII [Paris 1951], 132) showed that Aristides took up this idea (*Apology*, 2) without, however, putting Christians in a different category from other men. Marrou rejected the facile argument that if Christians were recognized to have the characteristics of a *people*, they could claim the right to live, like any other people, in accordance with their own laws, *ta patria* (a remark inspired by Simon, *Verus Israël*, 136); even if the Christians were few and isolated, "they nevertheless represented by right a universal society, immanent in the whole universe." A year after the publication of the French edition of this book (*EL*) and without any knowledge of it, Sirinelli (pp. 140-141) developed the same argument on the basis of Marrou's points, in a strikingly parallel form. He convincingly demonstrated (pp. 140-143) the special importance of this idea for Eusebius, who was struggling on two fronts: with the Greeks, to show them that Christianity was more rational than their own systems; with the Jews, to prove that Christianity was the legitimate historical heir of the promises; and with both, to convince them that Christianity could not be reduced to either of them. Instead, Eusebius argued, Christianity "is neither a form of Hellenism, nor of Judaism, but is a religion of its own characteristic stamp.... This is not anything novel or original, but something of greatest antiquity, something natural and familiar to the godly men before the times of Moses.... "(*Demonstratio Evangelica*, I, 2, 8). On the problems with which Eusebius had to struggle in regard to this idea of the *tertium genus*, see Sirinelli, 248-249.

63. Minucius Felix, *Octavius*, 8.

64. Origen, *Contra Celsum*, VIII, 2. On the subject of the accusations brought against the Christians, see Hornus, "Etude," 6.

65. Origen, *Contra Celsum*, VIII, 75. The rest of the chapter is a continuation of the same theme. It demonstrates that the essential tasks are mutual edification within the Church and evangelization, in order to lead the rest of mankind as well into this community of redeemed sinners.

66. *Anonymous Homilies*, III, 6.

67. Giet, *Les Idées*, 158-165.

68. Basil of Caesarea, *Ep.*, 51; 74, 3; 75; 76; 104; 165; all of which were mentioned by Giet, *Les Idées*, 368.

69. Basil of Caesarea, *Ep.*, 87.

70. Giet, *Les Idées*, 164. It is curious, however, that Basil borrowed the very expression of this idea from the pagan Euripides.

71. Basil of Caesarea, *Homilies on the Psalms*, 59, 3.

72. *Ibid.*, 48, 1; *idem, Ep.*, 66, 2.

73. Gregory of Nazianzus, *Discourse 43: in honor of Basil the Great*, 49.

74. In the text which Sozomen supplied of this interview, Basil explained the contradiction by saying, "I dwell on the earth as a traveler" (*Ecclesiastical History*, VI, 16).

75. See Giet, *Les Idées*, 165, 358-361.

76. *Epistle to Diognetus*, 5, 4-5.

77. *Ibid.*, 5, 8-9.

78. *Ibid.*, 6, 1-3. One can find the same theme, not only in the authors whom I have already quoted, but also in a letter in which St. Jerome exhorted St. Paulinus to turn away from the earth and to strive toward the heavenly Jerusalem, the city in which the apostle "rejoices to have his citizenship with the righteous (*se municipatum cum iustis habere)*" (*Ep.*, 58, 2). In the ensuing paragraph Jerome expanded upon the idea that God was the same everywhere and that therefore there could be no place that was specially privileged. The example of the monks confirmed this view, for they did not need to travel to the earthly Jerusalem to be holy (*Ep.*, 58, 3).

79. *Epistle to Diognetus*, 6, 7-8.

80. Hans Lietzmann, *A History of the Early Church*, transl. B. L. Woolf (London, 1961), II, 53.

81. Pontius, *Life of Cyprian*, 11.

82. Tertullian, *Apol.*, 38, 3. Although he did not expressly quote this text, Father Chenu ("L'Evolution, 80) considered this thought to be the natural sentiment of any "evangelistic theologian." In this connection he quoted (p. 95) the remark of Vitoria, the great Spanish theologian of the sixteenth century: "Since a state is a part of the whole universe, if a war is profitable for a state but detrimental to the universe . . . I am of the opinion that the war thereby becomes unjust." On Vitoria, whom I can only mention here, the interested reader should consult Lewis U. Hanke, *The Spanish Struggle for Justice in the Conquest of America* (Philadelphia, 1959), as well as A. Vanderpol's contributions to P. Batiffol, *et al.*, *L'Eglise et la Guerre* (Paris, 1913).

83. Philippians 3:20. Insofar as they are balanced by other complementary affirmations, we may take as a faithful gloss on these words St. John Chrysostom's expression, "Their true citizenship is in the heavens," which referred to the life of the ascetics (*Letters to Olympias*, VIII, 9d).

84. It should be noted, however, that this criticism by Karl Marx was directed at a Christianity which rendered its adherents indifferent to the present social order and thus made them accept any form of society, thereby stifling revolutionary inclinations. The opposite accusation, such as Guignebert made against Tertullian, of destroying society by indifference instead of preserving it, is excessive, but seems to me to be better founded. This is a danger about which the thinking of responsible Christians, as well as the practice of casual Christians, must remain on the alert.

85. Ignatius, *Rom.*, 6, 2.

86. Job was a typical example of these persons.

87. Gregory the Great, *Morals on the Book of Job*, I, 20, 24, 36, 34.

88. Commodian, *Carmen Apologeticum*, vv. 805 ff., 887-892, and esp. 920-926, which read:

> "And the brutes no longer know in what age they are living.
> Once she [Rome] rejoiced, but all the world groaned;
> And yet she has scarcely received as much as she deserved.
> She will weep for eternity, she who has flattered herself that she was eternal,
> And her tyrants will be judged at last by the All-High.
> Smouldering Rome, the time has at last been fulfilled;
> And the wages shall be paid to each according to his deserts."

In his *Instructions* (I, 34), Commodian rejected both the vain struggles and the empty joys of this world, so that he could turn himself toward the heavenly city:

"Here below they fight, then they sing of love instead of psalms.
You think that life consists of amusements, and these are the things that you are hunting for.
You are gathering ashes, you foolish ones that seek gold."

89. Eusebius, *HE*, III, 5, 3. Similarly, Sirinelli (pp. 113-115) was of the opinion that Eusebius had assigned a preeminent place in his *Chronicle* to the Jewish kingdom solely to accord greater importance to its final downfall, which exemplified the end of a "national" people of God.

90. Daniélou, "La Non-Violence," 19. St. John Chrysostom interpreted the Jews' hostility to the new faith very much along these lines. "Priests and Pharisees," he wrote, "feared that if everyone believed in Christ there would be no one left to defend the city of God and the Temple against the Romans. They thought, therefore, that Christ's teaching was directed against the Temple and against their traditional laws" (*Homilies on St. John*, 49, 26).

91. Eusebius, *HE*, VII, 32, 7-11.

92. *Mart. Pionii*, 5, 3-5 (Musurillo, 143).

93. G. Florovsky ("Eschatology in the Patristic Age," *SP*, 2 [Berlin, 1957], 245, 249), recalling that Celsus had called the Christians philosōmaton genos (Origen, *Contra Celsum*, V, 14), showed that it was true that the Christians, in contrast to the philosophers, were attached to earthly life and considered death to be a catastrophe. As an example he pointed to Tertullian, who declared in strong terms that death—far from being natural, normal, or pleasant—was the dramatic consequence of sin (*De Anima*, 52).

94. Athenagoras, *Legatio*, 35, 4.

95. Yet this was the position of both Cardinal F. J. von Hefele (*Beiträge zur Kirchengeschichte, Archäologie und Liturgik* [Tübingen, 1874], I, 21) and J.F. Bethune-Baker (*The Influence of Christianity on War* [Cambridge, 1888]); the latter's arguments were quoted and discussed by Cadoux (*Early Christian Attitude*, 100-103. A. Bigelmair (*Die Beteiligung der Christen am öffentlichen Leben in vorkonstantinischer Zeit* [Munich, 1902], 166), on the other hand, limited himself to the insinuation that such a broadening of the meaning of the text could not be ruled out completely. On the significance of these last words "even justly," see Cadoux, *op. cit.*, 214.

96. Athanasius, *Letter on Love and Temperance*, 282.

97. Basil of Caesarea, *Ep.*, 63. Most of this sentence is a word-for-word translation of Euripides (Giet, *Les Idées*, 165).

98. Basil of Caesarea, *Ep.*, 199 and 217.

99. Isidore of Pelusium, *Ep.*, IV, 200 (to Ophelius).

100. Clement of Alexandria, *Stromata*, II, 18, 88. Clement went on to give two picturesque examples: one was the female captive, whom a specific biblical law protected against a possible conqueror's lust to have intercourse with her (*ibid.*, 89; see also 82); the other was our enemy's beast of burden, which our Lord has commanded us to succor. He had taught us "not to indulge in joy at our neighbors' ills, or to exult over our enemies, in order to teach those who are trained in these things to pray for their enemies" (*ibid.*, 90).

101. Arnobius, *Adv. Nat.*, 3, 26. This argument had appeared as early as Justin, who had used it to accuse the wicked angels, and their descendants, the demons, of

being those who "sowed among men murders, wars, adulteries, and intemperance, and every kind of vice" (*Second Apology*, 5, 4).
102. Tertullian, *De Patientia*, 4.
103. *Idem, De Anima*, 33.
104. *Idem, Apol.*, 28, 3; 30, 1.
105. *Ibid.*, 9, 5.
106. *Ibid.*, 39, 7-8.
107. *Ibid.*, 8, 1-5.
108. *Idem, Adv. Iud.*, 7.
109. *Idem, De Corona*, 12. Theophilus (*Three Books to Autolycus*, III, 14) already observed that the Christians were not "kindly disposed . . . only towards those of our own stock, as some suppose."
110. Tertullian, *Adv. Marc.*, V, 17, in which passage he followed the text of Paul's epistle to the Ephesians.
111. See the penetrating remarks of Refoulé (*SCH*, XXXV, 15) on the identity between death, sin, and Satan in the thought of Tertullian as well as that of all the Fathers of the earliest centuries. See also the paragraph on "the prohibition of shedding blood" in Rordorf ("Tertullians Beurteilung," 124-130). In his review of *EL*, Roques (p. 241) thought that he was raising an objection to my interpretation when he wrote: "When the Christian clearly and definitely refuses to kill, he does not do so without reference to God's order, which must prevail over all human injunctions. The absolute primacy of God constitutes, therefore, the cardinal motivation of the Christian conscience, even when Christian behavior seems directly to take into consideration only respect for human life." I entirely agree with this interpretation: and I simply cannot understand where it fails to tally with my own.
112. Tertullian, *Apol.*, 9, 8.
113. The law to which it leads is simple and unequivocal: "The Christian does not do evil, even to his enemy" (Tertullian, *Apol.*, 46, 15). That is why I could not follow Seston when he remarked ("A propos de la Passio," 244) that "the compromises which qualified Tertullian's anti-militarism" were to be explained by the fact that his rejection of the army had nothing to do with a refusal to shed blood but only with a repudiation of certain pagan acts.
114. Tertullian, *Apol.*, 50, 1-2.
115. John Chrysostom, *Letters to Olympias*, X, 3f-g. It must be said, however, that this argument rings of dubious rhetoric when one realizes that it leads to a final assertion that sadness is even more fearsome than death! Cullmann (*The State*, 35-36) has felicitously emphasized how "the purely human dread which Jesus feels in the face of death" reveals a choice in the realm of values which Christians should emulate: "Jesus is not a Greek philosopher. Death for him as for St. Paul is the last enemy." This acknowledgement of the horror of death was also, as a matter of fact, in the philosophical tradition of the Aristotelian school. K. Giocarinis ("An Unpublished Late Thirteenth-Century Commentary on the Nicomedian Ethics of Aristotle," *Traditio*, 15 [1959], 317) has shown rightly that the Christian commentators on Aristotle's *Ethics* prior to the Middle Ages have a true understanding of the text when they "freely and frequently refer to death as the *malum maximum, maximus defectus, terminus totius*. Death is the supreme object of fear; through it man loses all the goods of his life."
116. John Chrysostom, *Homilies on St. John*, 79, 3.
117. *Idem, Homilies on Romans*, 14, 5-end.
118. There may be an allusion here to the tradition whereby Diocletian, according to a prophetess's intimations, "only wanted to obtain the empire, although he had

a desire for it, by killing in the boar-hunt." This tradition, which is obviously apocryphal, was developed in detailed form in the middle of the fourth century, when it was seen to be necessary to find an explanation for the murder through which Diocletian—who by then had become the symbol of Roman order and legitimacy— had come to power. The pretorian prefect, who was accused of having killed the previous emperor, Numerian, in order to set himself up in Numerian's place, and who in turn was put to death by Diocletian, was in fact called Aper (which in Latin means wild boar). See Seston, *Dioclétien*, 48.

119. I.e., to the temples.

120. Lactantius, *Div. Institutiones*, I, 18, 8-10. A little later (*ibid.*, I, 19, 6) he returned to the argument, saying that the so-called gods of mythology had not even been good men, for one could relate all sorts of weaknesses and wickedness about them, not least the fact that they engaged in warfare.

121. *Ibid.*, VI, 6, 18-24. A little earlier in the same chapter Lactantius had forbidden the resort to arms even defensively and in a just cause. For, he observed, it was not always the better side which won; quite the contrary. War was in fact nothing but a bloody game of chance, which if anything favored the wicked.

122. *Ibid.*, II, 6.

123. *Ibid.*, II, 9, 63.

124. *Idem, De Opificio Dei*, 2, 6. The same argument in almost the same words occurs in his *Div. Institutiones*, VII, 13-14.

125. *Idem, Div. Institutiones*, II, 10, 23.

126. *Ibid.*, V, 9, 2.

127. *Ibid.*, VI, 11, 1 ff.

128. *Ibid.*, VI, 18.

129. *Ibid.*, VI, 20, 10, 15-17.

130. E.g., see Tertullian, *Adv. Iud.*, 2-3.

131. Jerome, *De Vir. ill.*, 80. See R. Pichon (*Lactance, Etude sur le Mouvement philosophique et religieux sous le Règne de Constantin* [Paris, 1901], 2, 454), who wrote of Lactantius that "his name is inseparable . . . from the appearance of the first Christian government." He occupies a "double situation of philosopher respected in the Church and personal friend of the prince." Moreau ("Vérité historique," 93) was convinced that Lactantius was privy to Constantine's confidential decisions and that the *De Mortibus Persecutorum*, for example, must thus have been published a few months before the measures of January 1, 321, to prepare public opinion for them.

132. If we reflect on this attitude with care, it becomes clear that it was founded on the tension between the believer's waiting for the full manifestation of the kingdom and his daily presence in the world. A. Molnár ("L'Eschatologie," 13) has rightly pointed out that the eschatological perspective saved Lactantius from lapsing, like Eusebius, into complete servility toward Constantine. Cullmann ("Le Caractère eschatologique," 210-245) had already shown that the active expectation of Christ's return was at the heart of St. Paul's missionary ardor; and he had contended that it ought to animate today's Church in the same way. Lactantius gives us an idea of how this expectation could and should foster in the Christian a prophetic political attitude, which would not refrain from living out the gospel in the world, but would never forget that the criterion of earthly success can never be final in the eyes of faith. (In addition to the Lactantius texts quoted above, see his *Epitome*, 52.) Such reflections have been suggested by H. I. Marrou in "La Fin du Monde n'est pas pour Demain," *LV*, 2, no. 11 (1953), 77-99. I find, however, that the earlier remarks of E. Peterson (*Le Mystère des Juifs et des Gentils dans L'Eglise* [Paris, n.d.], 77-82, 88-89, 97) went too far. So did the late Cardinal Daniélou in his *Le Mystère du Salut des Nations*

(Paris, 1946). But Lactantius was convinced that the Christians knew about the beginning and the fulfillment of history (*Div. Institutiones*, VII, 14), whereas for Eusebius—who had no time for transcendent origins or culminations—the only thing that mattered was history itself (Sirinelli, 38-41, 51, 62, 455). Eusebius's only "theological" aim was "to prove the historical superiority of Christianity" (p. 135) and to convince those who still hesitated that if they joined the Christian group they would be swimming with the tides of historical development (p. 26).

Chapter 4

1. Paris, Bibliothèque nationale, MSS. Parisini lat. 16929-16935.
2. E. Le Blant, *Manuel d'Epigraphie Chrétienne d'après les marbres de la Gaule* (Paris, 1869), 15-16: 5.42 percent of the pagan inscriptions were of soldiers, compared to only 0.55 percent of the Christian inscriptions. See also Le Blant, *Inscriptions chrétiennes de la Gaule* (Paris, 1856), I, 84.
3. Leclercq, "Militarisme," col. 1130.
4. *Ibid.*, cols. 1155-1167.
5. *Ibid.*, cols. 1167-1170.
6. *Ibid.*, cols. 1170-1179. Leclercq provided significant details about only a few of these.
7. *Ibid.*, col. 1155 (italics mine).
8. *Ibid.*, col. 1164, no. 47; Diehl, no. 277; *CIL*, VI, no. 37273. Its first modern rendering was in O. Marucchi, "Lavori nelle catacombe romane," *Nuovo Bullettino di Archelogia Cristiana*, 6 (1900), 338. Leclercq dated it without hesitation from the diarchy of Septimius Severus and Caracalla (198-211). Diehl was unsure whether to date it in this period or in the diarchy of Marcus Aurelius and Commodus (177-180).
9. C. Mercurelli, "Il sarcofago di un centurione pretoriano cristiano e la diffusione del cristianesimo nelle coorti pretorie," *Rivista di Archeologia Cristiana*, 16 (1939), 73-99. The author's thesis—that there were numerous Christians among the praetorian troops—is too bold. But one must bear in mind the inscription from which he began. It reads as follows, with Mercurelli's interpretations (p. 84):

AELIUS MARTINUS	Aelio Martino [centurioni]
COHIPR ET STATIAE	cohortis primae praetoriae et Statiae
MOSCHIANETI CONIV	Moschianeti coniu
CIETUS ET STATIAE MAR	gi eius et Statiae Mar
TINAE FILLAEORUM	tinae filiae eorum
AELIUS VERINUS EVOK AUGGN	Aelius Verinus evokatus Augustorum nostrorum
FRATRI BENEMERENTIBUS	fratri, benemerentibus
FECIT	fecit

That this inscription was that of a Christian is clear from certain characteristic details in the imagery of the bas-relief. Mercurelli conjectured that this could have been the same Aelius Martinus who had already buried a first wife, Aurelia Julia, and their son, Aelius Martinus, aged ten, while he was centurion to the Legion 22a *Primigenia* at Mainz. Their inscription (Diehl, no. 735) was recognized to be crypto-Christian, because it used the expression *Innocenti spirito* for the child.

Another praetorian centurion's epitaph, which is full of lacunae, was found at Rome in the Christian cemetery in the Viale Regina Mergherita, to the left of the Via

Tiburtina (*Rivista di Archeologia Cristiana*, 11 [1934], 247, no. 198; *L'Année épigraphique* (1935), i.e., *Revue Archéologique*, 6th ser., 6 [1935], ii, 245, no. 155). But the fragment itself contains nothing which distinguishes it as a Christian inscription, and the place of its discovery is arguably not sufficient evidence for regarding it as one.

10. G. Mihailov, *Inscriptiones Graecae in Bulgaria repertae* (Sofia, 1966), III, i, 80, no. 80. See the first commentaries by Jeanne and Louis Robert, "Bulletin épigraphique," *Revue des Etudes Grecques*, 75 (1962), 175, and in "Séance du 4 Mai 1962," *Comptes rendus de l'Académie des Inscriptions et Belles-Lettres pour 1962* (Paris, 1963), 115, which Louis Robert quoted and developed in his *Noms indigènes ènes dans l'Asie-Mineure gréco-romaine* (Paris, 1963), 364 n.

11. W. M. Ramsay published this inscription for the first time in "The Cities and Bishoprics of Phrygia," *Journal of Hellenic Studies*, 4 (1883), 428 ff. In the notes below I shall cite the more recent editions of the same inscriptions.

12. Aurēlioi Gaios kai Mēnophilos apo sstrateiōn, paides Aur . . . hōs mēdeni heterō(i) exeinai episenenkein ē theinai xenon nekron ē sophon monois gnēsiois hēmōn teknois, ktl. W. M. Ramsay, *The Cities and Bishoprics of Phrygia* (Oxford, 1897), II, 717.

13. This inscription, which has often been reproduced (e.g., the bibliography of it in *DAL*, V (1922), col. 742, no. 19), has been systematically studied by Louis Robert (*Noms indigènes*, 360-365). See also *Hellenica*, 11-12 (Paris, 1960), 399.

14. This inscription, which was first published by G. B. de Rossi (*Inscriptiones Christianae urbis Romae* [Rome, 1861], I, no. 9), is reproduced in *DAL*, III (1914), col. 146, and in Diehl, no. 3332. See also Cadoux, *Early Church*, 392 n., for the epitaph of Prosenius, and 421 n., for the addition of Ampelius.

15. One of the points under discussion was whether these were physical tortures, as W. M. Calder ("Studies in Early Christian Epigraphy," *Journal of Roman Studies*, 10 [1920], 53) and H. Grégoire ("Les Inscriptions hérétiques d'Asie Mineure," *Byz*, 1 [1924], 695-710) believed, or merely moral torments, as A. Wilhelm ("Griechische Grabinschriften aus Kleinasien," *Sitzungsberichte der Preussischen Akademie der Wissenschaften*, Phil.-Hist. Klasse, 27 [1932], 792-865) and F. Halkin ("Faux martyrs et inscriptions hagiographiques," *AB*, 67 [1949], 90) asserted.

16. The value of this inscription had already been well demonstrated by C. M. Kaufmann (*Handbuch der altchristlichen Epigraphie* [Freiburg/Breisgau, 1917], 114). The remaining pages in which Kaufmann discussed other Christian soldiers (*Handbuch*, 114-118) dealt above all with the period after Constantine. He devoted pp. 249-251 to Eugenius. The translation which I use is Calder's ("Studies," 45), with slight modifications. The primary authorities on this inscription—in addition to Calder himself—have been Grégoire ("Les inscriptions," 695-699) and Wilhelm ("Griechische Grabinschriften," 834-847).

17. H. Grégoire ("Notes épigraphiques, IV," *Byz*, 8 [1933], 68-69) argued that Eugenius could not have left the service at once and that he was obliged to sacrifice. This epitaph would thus have been the clear echo of the justification which Eugenius could give—according to Canon 3 of the Council of Ancyra—in order to escape excommunication and, *a fortiori*, to become a bishop.

18. W. M. Calder, "The Epigraphy of the Anatolian Heresies," in *idem* and W. H. Buckler, eds., *Anatolian Studies presented to Sir William Mitchell Ramsay* (Manchester, 1923), 59-91. See also H. Grégoire, "Les inscriptions," 695-710, which sums up and substantially confirms Calder's work, but which does not accept the identification between our Julius Eugeniús and the heretic Eugenius who is attested by another inscription.

19. Leclercq, "Militarisme," col. 1157, no. 12; Diehl, no. 400; *CIL*, XIII, no. 5383, add. 71. But the titles of legionary centurion and quaestor are only attested by the ligatures, of which the reading is not absolutely certain.

20. *DAL*, IV (1921), cols. 63-64; Diehl, no. 280; *CIL*, III, no. 8752, add. 2261. It will be noticed that, if the soldier mentioned in this case was|the|husband|of the deceased, he was not the man who erected the monument.

21. Leclercq, "Militarisme," list in cols. 1155-1165, no. 5 (*DAL*, XI, col. 1156); Diehl, no. 396; *CIL*, III, no. 8754, add. 1510; *DAL*, IV, col. 39.

22. Leclercq, lists as in n. 21 above, no. 30 (*DAL*, XI, col. 1162); Diehl, no. 414; *CIL*, VI, no. 32691. M. Durry (*Cohortes prétoriennes*, 355) recognized this inscription as valid, even though his general thesis (pp. 348-358) was that the Christians were not present among the praetorian troops. He was also inclined (p. 354) to think that inscriptions 24 and 32 were Christian, while G. Lopuszanski ("Les Chrétiens dans l'armée romaine," unpub. PhD thesis, Faculté de Philosophie et Lettres, Brussels University, 1949) considered them to be doubtful. Inscription 24 is the description of the beneficiary Maritus (Diehl, no. 409; *CIL*, VI no. 32971), which Bainton ("Early Church," 192-193) accepted as going back to the period before Constantine. Inscription 32 is a description of the soldier Pyrrus (Diehl, no. 415a; *CIL*, VI, 32979). Durry (p. 355) identified the inscriptions in Diehl, nos. 414, 2199 (*CIL*, VI, nos. 32980, 32654) as referring to Christian praetorians. But these inscriptions are too badly damaged to be deciphered with certainty.

23. Diehl, no. 398b; *CIL*, VI, no. 2873, add. 3377.

24. Diehl, no. 402, where it is dated 384; *CIL*, VIII, no. 9967, add. 976.

25. Diehl, no. 403, where it is dated 372; cf. references in *CIL*, VIII, no. 21634.

26. Diehl, no. 411, where it is dated 408; *CIL*, VI, no. 33712.

27. Diehl, no. 412, where it is dated as well after the beginning of the Christian empire.

28. Diehl, no. 423, where the date of 583 is hazarded; *CIL*, VIII, no. 9870, add. 2059.

29. Diehl, no. 394; *CIL*, VIII, no. 9909, add. 2065. According to Lopuszanski ("Les Chrétiens," 46), it is not even certain that this is a Christian inscription.

30. Diehl, no. 397; *CIL*, VI, no. 32974.

31. Diehl, no. 401; *CIL*, III, no. 4190, add. 1751.

32. Diehl, no. 407; *CIL*, VI, no. 2870, add. 3377. Only the appearance of this (probably pagan [Diehl, IV, 407] inscription indicates as possible third century dating.

33. Diehl, no. 406; *CIL*, VIII, no. 9964; *DAL*, IV, col. 1450.

34. Diehl, no. 410; *CIL*, VI, no. 2704, add. 3370.

35. Diehl, no. 416; *CIL*, VI nos. 3565 and 32975.

36. Diehl, no. 426; *CIL*, VI, no. 33010.

37. Diehl, no. 428; *CIL*, VI, no. 3450.

38. Bainton, "Early Church," 193.

39. The teaching of John the Baptist (Luke 3:14), the centurion whose faith Jesus admired (Matthew 8:5-13), the centurion Cornelius (Acts 10:1-7), and the jailor at Philippi (Acts 16:27-34).

40. Bainton, "Early Church," 191. A. J. Visser ("Christianus sum," 17) and A. Benoît (review of *EL*, *RHPR*, 42 [1962], 341-342) were upset by this sentence and emphasized that other historians have drawn the opposite conclusion from this silence. But these critics do not seem to have noticed that, in the very next sentence, I have dealt with precisely that alternative interpretation. It is true, as Benoît rightly remarked, that in the French edition I dealt "a little too quickly" with the question of "the witness of the stones." As a response to this fair criticism, the present edition in-

corporates a more fully developed study of that topic.

41. Cadoux (*Early Church*, 440 n.) quoted and then refuted the writings of those who considered Christian conscientious objection to have been a late phenomenon. Even Ryan ("Rejection," 11) maintained that until the middle of the second century those who were converted while in the army did what they could to leave it, and that those who were already Christians did not join it. He went on to maintain that Christian soldiers became more numerous at the end of the third century (cf. pp. 11 and 23; there is surely a misprint here, and we should read *second* century) "despite the unfavorable attitude of the Church and of the body of the Christian people" (p. 15).

42. In the following chapter I shall demonstrate that the divergence of the two attitudes which the early Christians took toward the military profession originated here, and only here. Some believers, starting from the Church s constant principle which forbade the seeking out of martyrdom, believed that, provided both that they had been constrained by external forces and that they were not called upon to commit homicide, they could don the military uniform without its being—strictly speaking— a denial of their faith. Others who, like Tertullian, were more rigorous, rejected this concession to adverse circumstances. It is clear that these two points of view are still very close to each other. It is not fair, with D'Alès (*Théologie*, 414-415), to account for Tertullian's intransigent antimilitarism by identifying it with the Montanism of his final years. In fact, it is a viciously circular argument to reject his firmest text on this subject on the grounds that they emanated from his final and heretical period, and for that reason to dismiss them as being unrepresentative of the thought of the Church. For, in general, the only means of dating the works of Tertullian is by the extent of their unbending severity, a quality which many have assumed that he increasingly manifested as he advanced in age. But it is hardly a fair procedure to advance a hypothesis (i.e., severity) as a criterion for chronological classification, and then to claim to prove this hypothesis on the basis of the classification which had only been assumed. Moreover, in my opinion Tertullian's position was far more consistent— from the start to the finish of his writings—than many have alleged. This is also the point of view of Visser ("Christianus sum," 7), who has boldy written that according to the alternative interpretation, which for him is exemplified by Leclercq's article in the *DAL* ("Militarisme"), Tertullian would have thought—during his first, Catholic, period—"more or less like a contemporary French patriotic Catholic *à la De Gaulle*."

Writing of Tertullian's attitude to human wisdom, A. Labhardt ("Tertullien et la Philosophie ou la Recherche d'une Position pure," *Museum Helveticum*, 7 [1950], 166-167) observed that in this area there was "a line of thought which [he] had never abandoned for one moment in his spiritual development after his conversion. The orthodox thinker's convictions were the same as those of the Montanist afterwards, the disciple of Montanus's views just like those of the defender of orthodoxy." This judgment could easily be applied as well to his position regarding military service. Moreover, other Fathers, who have never been accused of Montanism, shared his point of view on this question. As Daniélou stated categorically ("La Non-Violence," 20), "The texts here are clear and must not be minimized. The military profession was shown to be incompatible with the profession of Christianity." If Tertullian was the first to articulate that opinion clearly, this can certainly in no way be attributed to his heresy. In fact, according to Daniélou, "it is certain that it was only the echo of the Church's regulations."

Cyprian, who in the years immediately following Tertullian's time was bishop of Carthage and primate of Africa, and whose catholicity has never been questioned, regarded Tertullian with reverence as his master in Christian thinking. Cyprian's former private secretary recalled that Cyprian "was accustomed never to pass a day without reading Tertullian, and that he frequently said to him, 'Give me the master,' meaning by this Tertullian" (Jerome, *De Vir. ill.*, 53). In particular, Cyprian was in total agreement with Tertullian's views concerning the emperors and the army. P. Monceaux *(Saint Cyprien* [Paris, 1914], 170-180) showed that the saint based his whole attitude on Tertullian, although he never quoted him because Tertullian had died a schismatic and thus Cyprian "could not have quoted his master's name without condemning his memory" (p. 175).

43. Lactantius, *De Mort. Pers.*, 10; *idem, Div. Institutiones*, IV, 24. See also Fliche et Martin, II, 462; Lods, "L'Eglise," 24; and above all Moreau, "Notes," 89-92.

44. On this point, see J. Fontaine's critical edition of the *De Corona* (Coll. Erasme, XVIII [Paris, 1966], 11, 18).

45. Tertullian, *De Corona*, 1.

46. *Idem, Apol.*, 37, 4; 42, 3.See also *idem, Ad Nat.*, I, 1-2; in addition, for the number of Christians especially in the province of Africa, but without special reference to the army, see *idem, Ad Scap.*, 5, 2-3. Concerning what one should make of these statements, see my "Etude," 4, and Visser, "Christianus sum," 7.

47. Clement of Alexandria, *Protrept.*, X, 100 (end).

48. Leclercq, "Militarisme," cols. 1125 n. and 1130. There is a marked difference, for no obvious reason, between the two translations which Leclercq quoted. The first of them reads: "The gnosis has taken hold of you when you were in service; obey the righteous orders of your leader." The second of them is different: "The Christian faith has taken hold of you while under warlike arms; listen to the captain whose rallying cry is righteousness." Could Leclercq possibly have been in doubt between one interpretation, whereby the soldier, once he had become a Christian, could still obey the "righteous orders" of his superiors but would henceforth have to disobey unrighteous orders, and another interpretation—which in my view in the context is infinitely more probable—whereby the soldier who had become a believer has passed from submission to a human leader to obedience to the only true Leader, who was God? I am convinced that the text can only be understood through the spiritual transformation of military terminology which we have considered at length in chapter 3. A parallel can be adduced in the declaration of Speratus, the martyr of Scilli, who told the proconsul, "Never have we uttered a curse; but when abused, we have given thanks, for we hold our own emperor in honor." But he also asserted, "I do not recognize the empire of this world, *ego imperium huius seculi non cognosco" (Passio Scillitanorum,* 2, and 6). Cadoux *(Early Christian Attitude,* 76) was eminently justified in glossing, "We pay heed to our emperor (i.e., Christ)." Visser ("Christianus sum" 18 n.) explicitly expressed his inability to accept the interpretation of the passage from Clement which I am here advancing. Bayet *(Pacifisme,* 112-113), on the other hand, contended that Clement in this text would have preferred to refer to Christ, but that at the same time he did not want to upset Christians who had accepted military service.

49. "It will perhaps be objected that, when speaking to the soldier, Clement does not tell him explicitly to continue, as he does the two others, and indeed that the imperfect tense instead of the present might indicate a different idea. But the close connection with the two others would seem to exclude any hesitation, and this triple admonition is, in truth, only a paraphrase of the words of St. Paul: 'Let every man abide in the same calling in which he was called' (1 Cor. 7:20)" (Lebreton and Zeiller, *History of the Primitive Church,* IV, 1031 n.).

50. Cadoux *(Early Church,* 418 n.), who quoted this passage (A. von Harnack, *The Mission and Expansion of Christianity in the First Three Centuries,* 2 vols.

[London, 1908], II, 55 n.) without comment, was apparently in agreement with it.
   51. Cadoux, *Early Christian Attitude*, 233 n., with reference to Ramsay, *Cities and Bishoprics*, II, 717.
   52. Clement of Alexandria, *Stromata*, III, 12, 91.
   53. *Ibid.*, II, 11, 117; IV, 14, 96.
   54. Romans 8:38-39.
   55. Clement of Alexandria, *Stromata*, II, 18, 82.
   56. Cyprian, *Ep.*, 39, 3.
   57. Leclercq, "Militarisme," col. 1132.
   58. Basil of Caesarea, *Various Homilies*, 18, 7. One cannot help sensing in these lines an element of self-justification against the prevalent opinion that there was a contradiction between military service and the Christian faith.
   59. This martyrdom, which was supposed to have taken place in 320, had inspired many other well-known homilists (*DAL*, XIV [1948], col. 2004). In reality, however, it was a legend which was based on the incidents which occurred in the army of Licinius after 315 when he had reverted to paganism and tried to force his soldiers to sacrifice (Cadoux, *Early Christian Attitude*, 242). At least two cases of refusal to enlist, those of Marcellianus and Theogenes, occurred in the same period and the same circumstances, although it is hard to disentangle the various motives for their refusal (*ibid.*, 260; *idem, Early Church*, 591).
   60. Basil of Caesarea, *Various Homilies*, 19.
   61. Giet, *Les Idées*, 163.
   62. Basil of Caesarea, *Ep.*, 116.
   63. *Ibid.*, 106. Although Basil was one of the propounders of the then-emerging view that monasticism was the only certain route to a perfect Christian life (by departing altogether from the preoccupations of the present world), it is notable that in this passage he argued the opposite case. In Sulpicius Severus (*Vita Martini*, 2, 8) one finds the same conditional approval of involvement in worldly affairs. Cf. Fontaine, *SCH*, CXXXIV, 468-473, 501-503.
   64. Basil of Caesarea, *Homilies on the Psalms*, 1, 6.
   65. H. Delehaye, *Les Légendes grecques des Saints militaires* (Paris, 1909), 2. Thus a "former naval chaplain," the Abbé C. Profillet, delighted in compiling—for purposes which can easily be guessed—a martyrology of military saints (*Les Saints militaires, Martyrologe, Vies et Notices*, 6 vols. [Paris, 1891]), of which approximately one hundred pages were crammed with names and dates alone. H. Gaubert (*Les Saints sur les Champs de Bataille* [Paris, 1941]) had the same idea. But after St. Martin, whose case caused Gaubert some embarrassment (see n. 150 later in this chapter), the first saint whom he found on a battlefield was St. Léger in the seventh century.
   66. Delehaye, *Les Légendes*, 112. It is true that on the following page he also mentioned the opposite case of the "demilitarization" of saints who had probably originally been soldiers.
   67. *Ibid.*
   68. H. Delehaye, "Saints de Thrace et de Mesie," *AB*, 31 (1912), 265-268; *idem, Les Passions des Martyrs et les Genres littéraires* (Paris, 1921), 321-328. See also J. Dubois, "Dasius," *Catholicisme*, III (1952), col. 471.
   69. *Acta Dasii*, 6-10.
   70. D. van Berchem, *Le Martyre de la Légion thébaine* (Basel, 1956), 46, which cited the various passages in which Delehaye had provided this evidence.
   71. In all the military legends "one can recognize one and the same pattern and an identical purpose" (Delehaye, *Les Légendes*, 118). See also B. de Gaiffier, "Saint

Marcel de Tanger ou de Léon," *AB*, 61 (1943), 132 n. [On the extension of military imagery in Christian iconography and pastoral care, see Charles Pietri, *Roma Christiana* (Rome, 1976), I, 316, 541 ff.]

72. See the studies by J. Guey: "La Date de la Pluie miraculeuse (172 après J. C.) et la Colonne aurélienne," *MAH*, 60 (1948), 105-127, and 61 (1949), 93-118; and "Encore la Pluie miraculeuse," *RPh*, 23 (1948), 16-62. For Bardy's controversy with Guey on this subject, see *SCH*, XLI, 30 n.-31 n.

73. Fliche et Martin, I, 316; Leclercq, "Militarisme," col. 1131; *DAL*, V, cols. 2692-2703; Cadoux, *Early Christian Attitude*, 230. It is astonishing to observe that all of these authors—even though they recognized that there was no historical basis for the tale of a *Christian* legion which prayed for rain, had its prayer heard, and *for that reason* had received the name *Fulminata*—nevertheless concluded that the account proved that during that period there were numerous Christians in the army. Cadoux's only reservation was that no doubt the religious authorities had not approved of this.

74. Eusebius, *Chronicle*, 238 olymp., xiii (pp. 206-207); *idem, HE*, V, 5, 3 ff.; Tertullian, *Apol.*, 5, 6; *idem., Ad Scapulam*, 4.

75. For a sound and detailed study of this passion, see *ASS*, November, III (1910), 748 ff. Its main arguments can be found more conveniently in two works of H. Delehaye: "Le Culte des Quatre Couronnés à Rome," *AB*, 32 (1913), 64-71; and *Etude sur le Légendier romain, les Saints de Novembre et de Décembre* (Brussels, 1936). The learned Bollandist has shown that nothing can be made of the *Passio Romana*, which tells of five soldiers as martyrs at Rome, and that the most that can be accepted is the Greek version which speaks of stone-cutters who were put to death in Pannonia. It was probably the word "coronati" which encouraged the "militarization" of these stories. See also *DAL*, XIV, cols. 2009-2014. [Dom Dubois has recently suggested (*Annuaire de l'Ecole pratique des hautes Etudes* [Paris, 1972], 503-505) that this confusion arose from the fact that these men were said to be working "*in comitatu*," which meant "at the court," but which has been misinterpreted as meaning "in the imperial army."]

76. They are known only through the martyrdom of Symphorosa and her seven sons. She, who was supposed to have been the wife of Getulius and the sister-in-law of Amantius, has declared to the emperor Hadrian: "*Vir meus Getulius, cum fratre suo Amantio, tribuni tui cum essent, pro Christi nomine passi sunt diversa supplicia, ne idolis consentirent ad immolandum.*"

77. *VSB*, XI (1954), 207.

78. *Ibid.*, 332.

79. There is no historical basis for the martyrdom. But it is rooted in an ancient tradition, since in 514 Severus of Antioch devoted an entire homily to the two saints. Cf. *VSB*, X (1952), 191-197.

80. B. Aubé, *L'Eglise et L'Etat dans la Deuxieme Moitié du IIIe Siècle* (Paris, 1886), 377.

81. Eusebius, *HE*, VI, 41, 11. I mention this fact here because of the close contact which existed between the state and the army. Later, for instance, during Diocletian's persecution, one of the martyrs was to be Philoromos, "who had been entrusted with an office of no small importance in the imperial administration at Alexandria, and who, in connection with the dignity and rank that he had from the Romans, used to conduct judicial inquiries every day, *attended by a bodyguard of soldiers*" (*HE*, VIII, 9, 7). On the spread of Christianity throughout the upper strata of Roman society, in connection with the legend related by Eusebius (*HE*, V, 21) of the Senator Apollonius, see both the note in G. Bardy's edition of the *HE* (*SCH*, XXXI [1952], 63) and the comments of M. Lods ("L'Eglise," 17).

82. Eusebius, *HE*, VI, 41, 22.

83. I say "perhaps," because, although the text of the martyrdom of Julian speaks of Ferreolus, the best recension of the martyrdom of Ferreolus does not refer to Julian. References to him occur only in the recension reproduced by *ASS*, September, V (1857), 764-765. On the nature of the post filled by these two men, see below, p. 318.

84. Eusebius, *HE*, VII, 15.

85. *Ibid.*, VIII, 1, 7.

86. *Ibid.*, VIII, 4, 2-3. A similar "purge" was also undertaken soon thereafter by Galerius (*ibid.*, VIII, app. 1).

87. See the unpublished thesis of A. Mascaux ("Les Martyrs militaires en Afrique à la Fin du IIIe Siécle" [Faculty of Protestant Theology, Paris, 1925]), which was entirely devoted to these texts, and the more recent work of Visser ("Christianus sum," 8-11 and 16-17 dealing with Maximilianus, 11-13 with Marcellus, and 15-16 with Julius).

88. Lods, "L'Eglise," 25-26.

89. The italics are mine. The minimizing of the emperor's divinity prior to 291 is essential to Seston's thesis, as is the overrating of it after that date.

90. Seston, "A propos de la Passio," 241.

91. *Ibid.*, 243.

92. For the details of this evolution, see Seston, *Dioclétien*, 212-230, 354-355. I follow him completely in his rejection of H. C. Babut's thesis concerning the *adoratio* (*L'Adoration des Empereurs et les Origines de la Persécution de Dioclétien* [Paris, 1916], 21); but I can no longer follow him in his suggestion that the increase in the emperor's religious status, which he described superbly, constituted not only an increase but also a radical change in conception from the thinking which had been prevalent since Augustus (*Dioclétien*, 356). The same thesis had been put forward already in *ASS*, October, XII (1867), 535.

93. P. Allard (*La Persécution de Dioclétien*, 3rd ed. [Paris, 1908], I, 97-98) was of the same opinion as other authors against whom I am arguing—that the antimilitarist attitude was confined to Africa, where it derived from the Montanist teaching of Tertullian, and that it had been clearly excluded from the teaching and practice of the Church. Allard's originality lay in his insistence that this attitude survived, as a sort of family tradition, in certain circles which otherwise returned to complete orthodoxy. He apparently did not see an unsurmountable obstacle in the fact of a father, who was himself a soldier, bringing up his son in antimilitarist *family* tradition (*ibid.*, 100). Monceaux began his study (*La Vraie Légende*, 249) by speaking of Maximilian in these terms: "An uncompromising Christian, by virtue of a personal conception which was contrary to the Church's traditions and teaching, he was convinced that he must refuse military service. But he was not punished as a Christian. If he had consulted his bishop, he would not figure among the martyrs. His story is nevertheless very touching." Allard's opinion (*La Persécution*, 105-106) was much the same. But I have already demonstrated that the tradition of the Church on this point was not what Monceaux assumed; and in the next chapter I shall show that the same applied to its teaching. I can imagine that such a contention may have seemed strange to someone who belonged to a community which claims to be a Church with an infallible and unchangeable teaching; for clearly with time the tradition and regulations of the Church on this point have altered considerably. On the essential historical fact, however, I am in agreement with Monceaux. Maximilian was condemned *as a conscientious objector*, not as an atheist (in the Roman sense). Cadoux too, whose historical honesty was punctilious and in no way was distorted by his personal religious convictions, wrote

(italics mine): "It is fairly clear from the martyr's own words that his objection was largely, if not solely, to the business of fighting. *The question of sacrificing to idols or to the emperor is not mentioned by either party"* (Cadoux, *Early Christian Attitude,* 149; *idem, Early Church,* 585). [See the recent study of Paolo Siniscalco (*Massimiliano: un obiettore de coscienza del tardo impero* [Turin, 1974], 134-135) who, after citing a whole list of authorities, pronounced firmly: "The question of sacrificing to idols does not play a noticeable part. As a matter of fact, nowhere in the entire *Passio* is it even expressly mentioned." He added (p. 135 n.), however, that he did "not feel [that he could follow] *in toto* and *per totum"* the position elaborated in the present paragraph, which he quoted from the French edition. Unfortunately, he did not specify the nature and extent of his dissatisfaction.]

94. This Fabius Victor was *temonarius.* [For a full discussion of the hypotheses of various authors concerning the precise meaning of this almost unknown Latin word, see Siniscalco, *Massimiliano,* 10-11, 39-40.]

95. *Mihi non licet militare, quia Christianus sum. (Acta Maximiliani,* 1-2 [Hornus trans.])

96. Seston, "A propos de la Passio," 242.

97. *Non possum militare; non possum malefacere. Christianus sum.*

98. Lods, "L'Eglise," 21.

99. *Non milito . . . non milito saeculo, sed milito deo meo.*

100. *Militia mea ad Dominum meum est. Non possum saeculo militare. Iam dixi, Christianus sum.*

101. If Seston's explanation were right, how could the Church have avoided condemning these new idolators? And why did the martyr not reply to his interrogator that if they remained in the army, they would thereby lose any right to be called Christians? [See D. F. O'Reilly, "The Theban Legion of St. Maurice," *VC,* 32 (1978), 201.]

102. Cadoux *(Early Christian Attitude,* 150 n.) wrote: "Ruinart . . . tells us that this last question and answer are absent 'in editis,' the reason for the omission apparently being that the words contradict the traditional Roman Catholic view of war. Ruinart inserts the words but suggests that they mean that Maximilianus 'did not reject military service as if it were evil in itself, but on account of the opportunities of sinning which soldiers often meet with.' This is clearly insufficient to account for the language used; and the Roman Catholics remain faced with the awkward fact that one of the canonized saints of the Church died as a conscientious objector! It is significant that Bigelmair, throughout his full treatment of the early Christian attitude to military service, makes no mention of Maximilianus at all. He is certainly an awkward martyr for a Romanist to deal with, but doubly so for one who is both a Romanist and a German." In *Early Church,* 585 n., Cadoux was more lenient in his judgment. He also removed the anti-German bias, which was obviously nothing more than an inverted nationalism.

103. Especially M. Meslin, review of *EL, Archives de Sociologie des Religions,* 10 (1960), 184, and Jacques Fontaine, "Sulpice Sévère a-t-il travesti S. Martin de Tours en martyr militaire?" *AB,* 71 (1963), 43 n.

104. See above, pp. 25-26.

105. Roger Mehl was convinced—wrongly, to my mind—that Seston had overstressed the importance of the innovation of 291. He wrote ("Christianisme primitif"), "The refusal of idolatry has played a major part since the beginning. The human Caesar's claim to be Lord collided head-on with the Christian conviction that Christ alone is Lord." (For subsequent lines of this passage, see ch. 1, n. 48.).

106. Monceaux, *La Vraie Légende,* 257-258. See also his earlier and more

detailed work, "Etude critique sur la Passio Tipasii," *Revue archéologique*, 4, no. 4 (1904), 267-274.

107. Or before, if we accept that this episode had been added to Tipasius's *Passio* at a later date in order to make the position less absolute—for after Constantine's concordat conscientious objection was no longer generally maintained.

108. This introduction, which comes from the M 2 family of MSS, is of a later date. B. de Gaiffier ("Saint Marcel," 116-139) does not reproduce it. It can be found in *AB*, 41(1923), 261; Knopf, 87; Musurillo, 250-251.

109. I.e., a week earlier.

110. *Sacramenta huic militare non posse* (MS. M.). *VSB*, X, 990—following the Madrid MS, supplied by de Gaiffier, which reads *huic officio militare non posse*—translates this as "I could not serve him as an officer," something of a mistranslation.

111. The Madrid MS has "to act as you have done," whereupon it breaks off.

112. "*Molestiis saeculi militare*" (MS. N). [This is to be preferred to the formerly accepted text of "militia saecularibus militare." See F. Dolbeau, "A Propos du texte de la 'Passio Marcelli Centurionis'," *AB*, 90 (1972), 331, who has finally settled the question.]

113. *AB*, 41 (1922), 277-278.

114. Leclercq, "Militarisme," col. 1142.

115. "*Septies* in bello *egressus sum, et post neminem retro steti nec alicuius inferior* pugnavi" (*Passio Iuli Veterani*, 2, 2). I stress in *bello* and *pugnavi*, for these two terms directly contradict the thesis which I shall be advancing in the next chapter. But this may be why Julius goes on to say that he had strayed (*errare*) when agreeing to become a part of the army (see below, n. 117).

116. "I have always adored the God who made heaven and earth. I still try to serve him today" (2, 3).

117. *In vana militia quando uidebar errare* (2, 1).

118. Eusebius, *Martyrs*, 11, 20-21: "He had served in the army ... [He] belonged to a picked band of young men in the army; and of those who held positions of rank among the Romans had attained to no small distinction." In the second recension of the text Eusebius added in the following paragraph (22): "He displayed himself a true soldier of Christ."

119. In the *Acta Tarachii* there are many episodes, of which I quote only one, from the first chapter. "The Governor Maximus: 'What is your name?' Tarachus: 'I am a Christian.' Maximus: 'Don't say that impious word, tell me what your name is.' Tarachus answered again in the same manner. Then, after being slapped, he continued: 'The name I have given you is indeed the one I bear personally. But if you want the name which is in common use, I was called Tarachus by my parents, and while I was a soldier, I was given the name Victor.' Maximus: 'Where do you come from?' Tarachus: 'I am of Roman and military race, born at Claudopolis in Isauria.' " Then Tarachus explained how, because he was a Christian, he had asked for and obtained his discarge from the army. The Greek words here are nun paganeuein hē (i)retēsamēn, which the old Latin version rightly translates as *renuntiavi militare*. In Chapter 2, I showed how the use of military metaphors in Christian parlance was purely spiritual. Here we have an exact counterpart, in what to modern ears sounds like a spiritual metaphor given a military connotation: "to become pagan" means to cease to be a soldier.

120. E. Amélineau, *Les Actes des Martyrs de l'Eglise copte* (Paris, 1890), 26-29, 42, 48, 49, 58, 59, 97.

121. *Ibid.*, 103.

122. *Ibid.*, 34, 36, 37, 75-77, 104.

123. *Ibid.*, 76.

124. *Ibid.*, 77.

125. *Ibid.*, 112.

126. Cf. above, p. 131.

127. Moreau, "Notes," 94.

128. I.e., the rival imperial claimants.

129. Life of Pachomius, *Codex sahidicus*, 7 (ed. Lefort, 293); *Codex bohairicus*, 7 (ed. Lefort, 83); *Vita prima*, 4 (ed. Halkin, 3).

130. *Ibid.*, *Codex bohairicus*, 8 (ed. Lefort, 83); *Vita prima*, 5 (ed. Halkin, 3-4).

131. E. Misset, *Pourquoi Saint Martin refusa-t-il de combattre: Pugnare mihi non licet et le 74,^{e} Canon d' Hippolyte* (Paris, 1907), 12. Apart from Misset, nobody to my knowledge has used or discussed this episode, even in cases in which it would have been most relevant. Ménard ("Profil," 5) merely stated that the conversion of Pachomius occurred after he had been "released from military service."

132. E.g., by Louis Bouyer, *La Spiritualité du Nouveau Testament et des Pères* (Paris, 1960), 389.

133. N. K. Chadwick, *The Age of the Saints in the Early Celtic Church* (London, 1961), 107 n.

134. A. de Vogüé, *La Communauté et l'abbé dans la Règle de St. Basile* (Paris, 1961), 23.

135. P.-T. Camelot, "Bulletin d'histoire des doctrines chrétiennes," 751 n. [Jean-Marie Vianney, the "Curé d'Ars," was a famous nineteenth-century French saint who deserted rather than "serve" during the Napoleonic wars.]

136. See above, p. 252.

137. Sulpicius Severus, *Vita Mart.*, 2 (*SCH*, CXXXIV, 254-257).

138. *Ibid.*, 3, 5 (*SCH*, CXXXV, 258).

139. In *SCH*, CXXXIII-CXXXV (Paris, 1967-1969), Jacques Fontaine has published a careful edition and French translation of the *Vita* and the *Letters* of Sulpicius Severus, in which he has also provided an illuminating introduction and detailed annotations. Although Fontaine was right in emphasizing the importance of Severus's use of literary "clichés" which must not be taken at face value as historical accounts (a theme which he had already developed in "Verité et Fiction dans la chronologie de la Vita Martini," *Studia Anselmiana*, 46 [1961], 189-236; "Une Clé littéraire de la Vita Martini de Sulpice Sévère: la typologie prophétique," in *Mélanges Mohrmann* [Utrecht, 1963], 84-95; and "Sulpice Sévère," 31-58), he has probably overstressed this necessary corrective. [All the Severian textual information concerning Martin has now been published in a handy popular edition of the latest French translations (by Fontaine and Monceaux) (Luce Pietri, ed., *Saint-Martin, textes de Sulpice Sévère*, supplement to the *Lettre de Ligugé*, nos. 172-173 [July-October, 1975]).]

140. Gregory of Tours, *Historia ecclesiastica francorum*, I, 34.

141. Sulpicius Severus, *Vita Mart.*, 2, 2, and 3, 6 (*SCH*, CXXXIII, 225, 259).

142. H. Delehaye, "Saint Martin et Sulpice Sévère," *AB*, 38 (1920), 19-33, and esp. 26, 31; Lecoy de la Marche, *Saint Martin*, 3rd ed. (Tours, 1890), 109-110; A. Régnier, *Saint Martin*, 36, 42). Gaubert (*Les Saints*, 17), no doubt inadvertently, put it under Constantine II; Ménard ("Profil," 18 n.) dated it under Constantius, as also did J. Christophe (*Saint Martin, le soldat pacifique* [Lyon, 1966], 27).

143. H. C. Babut, *St. Martin de Tours* (Paris, 1913), 168-170. On this promising historian (who was killed on February 28, 1916, at the early age of thirty-eight during the battle for Verdun) and his contrubution to our subject, see J.-R. Palanque, "Un anniversaire," *Le Monde*, March 3, 1966.

144. For example, E. Griffe, in the first edition of *La Gaule chrétienne* (Paris-

Toulouse, 1947), 203-204, suggested that one should read *vicennium* instead of the *biennium* which is universally evidenced, not only by the MSS, but also by Paulinus of Perigueux only a century after the events to which the passage was referring. In subsequent works ("La Chronologie des années de jeunesse de Saint Martin," *BLE*, 63 [1961], 114-118; and *La Gaule chrétienne*, 2nd ed. [Paris, 1964], 277 n.), Griffe suggested an ingenious change of punctuation, whereby the reference to two years of waiting could be made to apply to something other than military service, and the reference to adolescence would apply to the date of his entering the service and not to its duration. J. Fontaine, for his part, was convinced that Sulpicius Severus, for apologetic reasons and at the cost of what must strictly be called a masking of historical truth, had intentionally attempted to give the reader the impression of as short a period of military service as possible (*SCH*, CXXXIII, 205; *SCH*, CXXXIV, 501; "Sulpice Sévère," 38; and especially the entire paper "Vérité et fiction").

145. B. de Gaiffier, "Sub Juliano Apostata dans le martyrologe romain," *AB*, 74 (1956), 41; Fontaine, "Sulpice Sévère," 36. Paulinus of Périgueux (I, 139-177), who gave a detailed account of St. Martin's refusal, did not even mention Julian, although by that time his name had become a byword for the persecuting pagan emperor. Nor did Paulinus give the slightest hint that in Martin's attitude there might have been anything connected with the rejection of idolatry. These omissions are all the more conspicuous since Sulpicius Severus was no doubt influenced by the projection onto the still-Christian Julian of 356 in the West of the characteristics which he demonstrated in 362 in the East (e.g., the sad story of Juventinus and Maximinus, two Christian officers of his guard. See the thorough study of this incident in Fontaine, "Sulpice Sévère," 49).

146. *Christi ego miles sum: pugnare mihi non licet* (Sulpicius Severus, *Vita Mart.*, 4, 3 [*SCH*, CXXXIII, 260]). After reciting this statement, Paulinius of Périgueux (I, 35 ff.) contrasted the chains of the *miles Christi* with those of the worldly soldier, and then continued with a long antithetical elaboration upon that classical theme.

147. Sulpicius Severus, *Vita Mart.*, 4, 5, and 7 (*SCH*, CXXXIII, 260).

148. Ménard, "Profil," 18. Note 58 on the next page suggests, however, that Ménard was scarcely convinced by his own explanation.

149. It is astonishing, for example, to find Courcelle (*Histoire*, 214 n.) wondering, with reference to passages in Severus and Paulinus dealing respectively with Martin and Victricius, "whether such formulations were really an apology for conscientious objection, or whether they were not simply customary circumlocutions to say that an officer had embraced the religious life." As we shall see, the "circumlocution" of Victricius entailed the execution squad. For reasons of charity I shall refrain from quoting the amazing passage in *VSB*, 11 (1954), 338, which is devoted to St. Martin. The only prior reference to his desertion was in this delectable summary on p. 337: "He received baptism and finally he was freed." The most recent popular biographies of St. Martin (G. Hünermann, *L'Apôtre des Gaules*, transl. E. Saillard [Paris, 1964], 90-93; and Marguerite Jardel, *Le soldat du Christ, Saint Martin de Tours* [Paris, 1967], 54-57) have both respected historical truth on this point. The former, however, did not give any explanation for the saint's behavior. The latter was convinced that up to the time of his leaving the army St. Martin, although already an old soldier, had never had any occasion to take part in a battle. Then, at the decisive moment, "Martin sensed that he must obey; he knew that a Christian must bear arms to defend the soil which is his. But he wanted to become a monk, and the Church forbade monks to make war. If he were to fight, the Church would perhaps refuse to ordain him. And yet he must fight ... since he was an officer." Two pages later (p. 59)

Jardel also invoked an argument of "providential convenience" which, to say the least, is unexpected. The foes of the moment were Franks. But now, "many centuries later . . . Gaul was to become France. It would have been most improper for the saint who was to be its protector to have triumphed over it in the first place by arms."

150. Christophe, *Saint Martin*, 27; Jardel, *Soldat du Christ*, 57; Lecoy de la Marche, *Saint Martin*, 112. The essential argument in the last of these works is that the expression *miles Christi* was a technical term used only for monks. As we have seen earlier (p. 76), the term did apply to monks; but it had also been used prior to the advent of monasticism and thus it bore a much broader meaning. Sulpicius Severus (*Vita Mart.*, 2, 2) indeed spoke of the attraction which Martin had felt since his infancy for monachism; but this was an obvious anachronism on the part of his biographer (Delehaye, "Saint Martin," 88; Fontaine, *SCH*, CXXXIV, 441-446, who followed his usual pattern of interpretation in seeing in this passage a projection of hagiographic stereotypes). Gaubert (*Les Saints*, 18) observed that the modern historians' resort to a monastic explanation is a clumsy and futile attempt to escape from an embarrassing situation. But his own escape route is even worse. He began by observing (p. 17) that so-called Christian conscientious objection made its first appearance in recent times, "amidst American and Anglo-Saxon sects which, for want of sufficient theological culture, divert certain biblical texts from their precise meaning." But then on pp. 19 and 22 he was forced to acknowledge that St. Martin must have allowed himself to be carried away by the same "somewhat hazardous personal interpretation." He was quick, however, to rehabilitate the saint by recalling that a sin committed through imprudence is a venial sin. One is tempted to rejoice upon finding that a Catholic author considered it only a venial sin to share a theological point of view with "American and Anglo-Saxon sects;" but one is prevented from doing so by the recollection that the venial sin consisted in diverting biblical texts from their precise meaning. The only way that one can escape from perplexity in harmonizing these different statements is by attributing to St. Martin the ideas of a nineteenth- or twentieth-century American theologian!

151. *ASS*, October, XII (1867), 53, stated that the three saints—Martin, Victricius, and Paulinus—*persuasum fuerit licitum non esse sanguinem humanum fundere etaim in justo bello, imperantibus christianis principibus*. But it went on: *terni adhuc erant laici, in doctrina christiana parum eruditi*. In the *In Sulpicium Severum observationes* which G. da Prato added to his Verona edition (1741) of the works of Severus, he likewise stressed (p. 325) the identity in the situations of the three "chained enlisted men"—Maximilian, Pachomius, and Martin. Vanderpol (*Doctrine scolastique*, 185) grouped together Maximilian, Martin, Victricius, and Paulinus, and judged them in the same expeditious way as did the *ASS*. This enabled him to dispose of the testimony of three bishops and a martyr in exactly eight lines—no mean achievement in a book of 534 large pages, all of them devoted to the Christians' attitude to war. If Sulpicius Severus, *Vita Mart.*, 10, 6 (*SCH*, CXXXIII, 274) actually said that St. Martin was unlettered, it was only in comparison to himself and Paulinus, who were extremely well educated. Nor should we forget that St. Martin was "the founder of a training center at Marmoutier, out of which emerged the elite of the Gallic episcopate" (Ménard, "Profil," 6). Fontaine (*SCH*, CXXXIV, 676 n.) went even further in refuting the argument of *ASS* and Vanderpol when he showed that in Severus's vocabulary the word *ars*, far from denoting intellectual activity, was always used for manual work.

152. E. Griffe, "Saint Martin et le monachisme gaulois," *Studia Anselmiana*, 46 (1961), 3. One may suppose, but only on a conjectural basis, that Martin had met

monasticism in the East and was therefore himself a kind of "bridge" between the two parts of the Christian world of his day. This would indeed fit with the place of his birth. See Willy Schatz, "Studien zur Geschichte und Vorstellungswelt des frühen abendländischen Mönchtums" (unpub. thesis, University of Freiburg/Breisgau, 1957), to which M. Fontaine has called my attention.

153. For example, Bouyer (*Spiritualité*, 384), commenting upon St. Anthony and his time, wrote that "the primitive monk did not appear at all as a kind of specialist . . . he was simply a Christian, and more precisely a pious layman who merely took the most radical means to make his Christianity all-embracing."

154. "St. Martin's life as a soldier . . . seems traced—exactly traced—on the 14th canon of Hippolytus" (Misset, *Pourquoi Saint Martin*, 12). Leclercq ("Militarisme," cols. 1150-1152), who developed the same view at length, concluded, "This prohibition of shedding blood was certainly, in the eyes of Sulpicius Severus, the explanation for St. Martin's behavior."

155. Sulpicius Severus, *Dialogue*, III, 15. In accordance with the Christian "strategy" of human relationships, St. Martin confronted this verbal violence, like all violence, with a patience which bore evil but did not accept it. The result was that this "bad monk" later became St. Brictio, St. Martin's successor as bishop of Tours.

156. Concerning Fontaine's method of interpretation in his *SCH* (CXXXIII-CX-XXV) edition of the *Vita Martini*, see my review in *RHPR*, 50 (1970), 77-79.

157. Fontaine, "Sulpice Sévère," 36.

158. *Idem*, "Vérité et fiction," 213; "Sulpice Sévère," 38.

159. In "Vérité et fiction," 213, Fontaine observed that the body of antimilitarist church laws, which we shall be studying later (pp. 161-168), had a precise application to St. Martin's case. Paradoxically, it was because Siricius was an "adversary of the new ascetic spirit"[!] (Erich Caspar, *Geschichte des Papstiums* [Tübingen, 1930], I, 259) that he viewed his harking back to an earlier tradition as a weakness in the Western monastic movement; for he could neither approve of its founder nor reject him.

160. Fontaine, "Sulpice Sévère," 39. See also *SCH*, CXXXIV, 423, 428, and esp. 441.

161. Fontaine, "Vérité et fiction," 208; *SCH*, CXXXIV, 441, 454-459.

162. Fontaine, "Sulpice Sévère," 43-46.

163. *Ibid.*, 51, 57; *SCH*, CXXXIV, 463 n.

164. *DTC*, XV (1950), cols. 2954-2956. See also R. Herval, "La Province ecclésiastique de Rouen aux IVe et Ve siècles," *MSR*, 16 (1959), 53-57, which portrayed St. Victricius as "the outstanding bishop [who] brought the Christian group in Rouen out of the darkness, and who was the first to organize upon solid foundations the religious life of the entire Second Province of Lyon."

165. *DTC*, XII (1935), cols. 68-71; *DAL*, XII (1936), cols. 1437-1455. The latter study—especially its first part—examines the entire Romano-Gallic circle with which we are concerned here. Martin, Paulinus, and Victricius first met at Vienne (Isère) in 386 (Herval, "La Province," 51). In a letter (*Ep.*, 18), Paulinus also reminded Victricius that they had formerly met at the home of St. Martin, "to whom the Lord had done the same as for you, even though you are younger." On the relationships between these personalities, see A. Baudrillart, *Saint Paulin*, 4th ed. (Paris, 1928), 33-34.

166. Paulinus, *Ep.*, 18. It is from this letter, especially para. 7, that I have derived the account of the events which followed. See also J. Mulders, "Victricius van Rouan, Leven en leer," *Bijdragen*, 17 (1956), 7-9.

167. Paulinus, *Ep.*, 25.

168. *Ibid.*, 37.

169. B. de Gaiffier, "Sub Juliano Apostata," *passim.*

170. Griffe, *La Gaule chrétienne*, 1st ed., 227.

171. Martin, who was the son of a superior officer, was placed by virtue of his name under the patronage of Mars, the god of war (Ménard, "Profil," 4). The name Victricius similarly had a military resonance, and it is virtually certain that he was the son of a veteran who had settled on the imperial frontier (Vacandard, *Victrice*, 3-4; Herval, "La Province," 54). The power of the gospel was thus stronger than the attraction of conformity to their background.

172. Vacandard (*Victrice*, 14 n., 15) demonstrated, as Paulinus had already done (*Ep.*, 18), that Victricius faithfully imitated the conduct of Martin and even of Maximilian. See also Griffe, *La Gaule chrétienne*, 1st ed., 226.

173. Sulpicius Severus, *Dialogue*, III, 11-13; *idem, Vita Mart.*, 20; *idem, Chronicle*, II, 49-51; Fontaine, *SCH*, CXXXV, 913-946. [See also H. Chadwick, *Priscillian of Avila* (Oxford, 1976), 138-148.]

174. Sulpicius Severus, *Vita Mart.*, 20, 2; *SCH*, CXXXIII, 296.

175. Priscillian and six of his companions were finally executed. See Sulpicius Severus, *Chronicle*, II, 51.

176. This charge had already been made by Ithacus, the accuser of Priscillian (Sulpicius Severus, *Chronicle*, II, 50). It has been revived in several of H. C. Babut's works ("Paulin de Nole et Priscillien," *RHL*, 1 [1910], 97-130; *Saint Martin, passim),* in which he reiterated the themes of his Sorbonne thesis, *Priscillien.*

177. A. d'Alès, *Priscillien et l'Espagne chrétienne à la fin du IVe Siècle* (Paris, 1936); J. A. Davids, *De Orosio et Sancto Augustino Priscillianistarum Adversarii* (Nijmegen, 1930); E. Dalaruelle, A. Latreille, and J.-R. Palanque, *Histoire du Catholicisme en France*, I (Paris, 1957), 53, Delehaye, "Saint Martin," esp. 108 ff.: P. Monceaux, "La Question du Priscillianisme," *JS*, n.s., 9 (1911), 70-75, 104-113; A. Puech, "Les Origines du Priscillianisme et l'Orthodoxie de Priscillien," *BALAC*, 2 (1912), 81-95, 161-213. St. Ambrose of Milan came to Trier at the same time as Martin, and the two men took precisely the same position on the controversy.

178. Delehaye, "Saint Martin," 88.

179. F.-L. Ganshof, "Saint Martin et le Comte Avitianus," *AB*, 67 (1949), 203-223.

180. Griffe, *La Gaule chré*tienne, 1st ed., 228.

181. Paulinus, *Ep.*, 19, 4.

182. *Pariter spectantes jussa tyranni.* The elliptical style peculiar to inscriptions makes this text almost impossible to translate. One could easily lapse into a paraphrase in an attempt to make the meaning explicit. To my mind it means that the two martyrs at first believed falsely that one could serve God and Caesar *on equal terms.* Then they realized that a choice between the two was necessary; this is the meaning of the phrase "they turned" (were converted).

183. Diehl, no. 1981.

184. Ambrose, *Hymn* XI, in *PL*, Supplementum I (Paris, 1958), cols. 584-585.

185. Prudentius, *Peristephanon*, I, 34, 39.

186. *Ibid.*, 58-59, 61.

187. The inscription gives *suscendit*, for which an alternative reading *surrexit* has been suggested. Is it not more likely to have been *ascendit, or* possibly a falsely conjugated perfect of *succedere?*

188. On Ferrutius, see *ASS*, October, XII (1867), 530-543 (the inscription is on p. 530). The passion which follows is certainly quite unhistorical.

189. Monceaux, *La Vraie Légende*, 280.

190. Van Berchem (*Le Martyre*, 25-33) concluded, "The elements of the legend

which we have determined to be irreducible are mutually contradictory . . . and the tradition falls apart." For reviews of *Le Martyre*, see H. G. Pflaum, *RELA*, 34 (1956), 410-413; H. I. Marrou, *RHR*, 152 (1957), 236-240; and C. Roth, *Revue Suisse d' Histoire*, 1957, 511-514.

191. L. Dupraz, *Les Passions de S. Maurice d'Agaune: Essai sur l'historicité de la tradition et contribution à l'étude de l'armée pré-dioclétienne (260-286) et des canonisations tardives de la fin du IVᵉ siècle*, Studia Friburgensia, n.s., 27 (Fribourg, 1961). [For a recent re-examination of this question, see O'Reilly, "The Theban Legion of St. Maurice," 195-207.]

192. In his book (*Les Passions*, 294-295), Dupraz clearly set forth the chronological sequence of the events of the martyrdom as he understood them. He was convinced that the occasion was probably not a persecution of the Christians, but was rather an expedition to suppress a revolt of uprooted farmers called the Bagaudes. The only reason for the martyrdom of Maurice and his fellow soldiers, whom Dupraz reduced from a legion to a mere company (i.e., from 6,000 to 600 men), was their refusal to take idolatrous oaths.

193. Cf. my review of this book in *RHPR*, 48 (1968), 285-288.

194. Van Berchem, *Le Martyre*, 27, 53. In the Catholic journal of the Bernese Jura *L'Echo* (October 21, 1961) G. Bavaud—although a professor in the Higher Seminary of Fribourg—really exceeded all bounds. Under the title "Pourquoi Saint Maurice et ses compagnons ont-ils été martyrisés?" he claimed that both Dupraz's historical restoration and my own interpretation of the primitive Christian discipline are equally valid. He therefore came to the impossible conclusion that Maurice and his six hundred companions were executed *en masse* for conscientious objection. Another article by Bavaud in the preceding (October 14, 1961) issue of the same newspaper ("Les premiers Chrétiens étaient-ils objecteurs de conscience?") argued that the attitude of conscientious objection, which was salutary for all Christians as long as they were only a minority in the empire, at a later date naturally and necessarily became the sole privilege of the clergy. On this point, see above, p. 93.

195. *Passio Acaunensium*, 3.

196. *Hostis*. Ferreolus, whose case might at first glance seem similar to that of Maurice, spoke not of enemies but of the guilty. It is this which indicates the difference between the soldier and the policeman. The relevant portion of his answer is: "I served the emperors as long as religion allowed me. I promised obedience to just laws, never to sacrilegious laws. I enlisted to serve against the guilty, not against Christians."

197. *Inimicus*.

198. *Pugnavimus pro fide* (i.e., the faith which they owe to the emperor as well as their faith toward God).

199. *Juravimus primum in sacramenta divina, juravimus deinde in sacramenta regia*.

200. *Passio Acaunensium*, 9.

201. *Ibid.*, 10.

202. In these paragraphs, stylistic convenience has led me to personify the members of the Theban Legion. Quite clearly, however, what I am setting forth and criticizing here is the viewpoint of St. Eucher, who speaks through his heroes. The soldiers themselves come from the realm of pure myth.

Chapter 5

1. It was precisely at the moment at which Church policy opened its doors to

compromise that it became necessary to establish boundaries and to legislate on the subject.

2. Tatian, *Oratio*, 28.
3. Arnobius, *Adv. Nat.*, 2, 38.
4. Tertullian, *De Idol.*, 19.
5. *Idem, De Pallio*, 5.
6. Clement of Alexandria, *Paedagogus*, I, 12, 99 and II, 4, 42.
7. *Idem, Stromata*, IV, 8, 61.
8. *Ibid.*, VII, 11, 62.
9. *Ibid.*, VII, 14, 84.
10. Cyprian, *Ep.*, 73, 4.
11. *Idem, De Bono Patientiae*, 14.
12. *Idem, Ad Donatum*, 6-10.
13. Origen, *Contra Celsum*, VIII, 68, 73.
14. It is particularly important to remember this date in light of explanations such as Seston's, which I set forth in Chapter 4.
15. Kaufmann, *Handbuch*, 114.
16. E.g., Jacques Zeiller (Lebreton & Zeiller, *History*, IV, 1031).
17. The basic contributions were those of Dom R. H. Connolly and Dom Gregory Dix, which in more recent years have been incorporated in and superseded by the masterly works of Dom Bernard Botte. The article in which he most clearly expresses his general conclusions on the relationships between the various texts is "L'Authenticité de la Tradition apostolique de saint Hippolyte," *RTAM*, 16 (1949), 177-184. See also pp. xvii-xxviii of Botte's second edition of the *Apostolic Tradition* (*La Tradition apostolique de Saint Hippolyte, Essai de reconstitution*, 39ᵉ Cahier des Liturgiewissenschaftliche Quellen und Forschungen [Münster in Westphalia, 1963]). J.-M. Hanssens has advanced an opposing position. In a polemical assessment of the reviews—which were admittedly often scathing—aroused by his book *La Liturgie d'Hippolyte, ses documents, son titulaire, ses origines, et son charactere*, Orientalia Christiana Analecta (Rome, 1959), he has insisted ("La Liturgie d'Hippolyte, assentiments et dissentiments," *Gregorianum*, 42 [1961], 290-302) upon the great difficulty which scholars still face in establishing an exact line of derivation between the various Hippolytus texts.
18. Bernard Botte, "Le Texte de la Tradition Apostolique," *RTAM*, 22 (1955), 161. See also Botte's "Les plus anciennes collections canoniques," *Orient Syrien*, 5 (1960), 331-350, and R.-G. Coquin, *Les Canons d'Hippolyte*, PO, 31, ii (1966), 308-340. J. Quasten (*Patrology*, 3 vols. [Utrecht-Brussels, 1950-1960], II, 180-181) wrote of the *Apostolic Tradition*, "It is, with the exception of the *Didache*, the earliest and the most important of the ancient Christian Church Orders.... [It] has given us the richest source of information that we possess in any form for our knowledge of the constitution and life of the Church in the first three centuries." I am astonished that J. Fontaine ("Christians and Military Service in the Early Church," *Concilium*, 7 [1965], 116 n.) can still question whether "the Canons of Hippolytus, the rigorist antipope, can be taken in the form in which they have reached us as reflecting the Church's discipline without any further qualification? And how can one speak of *one* discipline of the Church at such an early date and particularly on such very controversial questions...?" These are the only points at which I sense that Fontaine's criticisms of my work went beyond healthy questioning and became somewhat arbitrary.
19. J. and A. Périer, eds., "Les '127 Canons des Apôtres: Texte Arabe," *PO*, 8 (1912), 553. See also Botte, "Les plus anciennes collections," *passim*.

20. C. C. Richardson, "The Date and Setting of the Apostolic Tradition of Hippolytus," *Anglican Theological Review*, 30 (1948), 38-44.

21. Pierre Nautin (*Hippolyte et Josipe: Contribution à l'histoire de la littérature chrétienne du 3ᵉ siècle* [Paris, 1947], attempting a reconstruction of the historical Hippolytus, found that one had to distinguish between two persons. According to his findings, one Hippolytus was an antipope, whose statue has been discovered at Rome and whose real name was Josippus; the other Hippolytus was an author, who wrote the works which bear his name but who was certainly not a Roman (p. 92). The latter Hippolytus was a mid-third-century Easterner from some area other than Syria (p. 93). It is not even certain that he was a bishop. Nautin maintained that the surviving text of the *Apostolic Tradition* was indeed written by the latter Hippolytus, and thus is distinct from the identically entitled treatise that is mentioned on the base of the Roman statue. Nautin (p. 81) thought it possible, however, that the Eastern Hippolytus used the *Apostolic Tradition* as one of his sources, which—if there *were* two such different people—seems to me not merely possible but virtually certain. In that case the primitive text (which reflected the Roman Church's discipline at the beginning of the third century and which, according to Nautin's hypothesis should be attributed to Josippus) would still be beyond our reach. The first document in our possession would thus be a revised version of the treatise emanating from the East toward the end of the first half of that century.

22. P. de Lanversin, "Une belle dispute: Hippolyte est-il d'Occident ou d'Orient?" *Proche-Orient Chrétien*, 6 (1956), 118-122; R. Salles, "La Tradition apostolique est-elle un témoin de la liturgie romaine?" *RHR*, 148 (1955), 181-213. Salles' interpretation is even more radical than that of Nautin, since it attempts to prove that the *Tradition* is evidence of an Eastern-type liturgy very different from that of Rome. But it would not basically threaten the validity of my argument; for the existence of an ancient Latin version of the *Tradition* proves in any case that this text was disseminated in the West as well as the East.

23. Cf. Quasten, *Patrology*, II, 166-169, who gave an exhaustive bibliography of the controversy, in which Marcel Richard ("Comput et chronographie chez S. Hippolyte," *MSR*, 7 [1950], 237-268; 8 [1951], 19-50) opposed Nautin's reconstruction with especial vigor. See also Richard's "Bibliographie de la Controverse: Hippolyte-Josipe," *PO*, 27, ii (1954), 271-272.

24. We should then simply have to say: "The state of the Roman discipline at the beginning of the third century was described in an *Apostolic Tradition*, the work of the antipope Josippus. Unfortunately this has been lost. But we can get quite an accurate idea of it from the identically titled work produced shortly thereafter by the writer Hippolytus, who use Josippus's work as his primary source. The relationship between Hippolytus's text and the Roman discipline is confirmed by the fact that the earliest and best evidence for this text is the Latin translation, which we will discuss

25. See, for example, Bernard Botte, ed., *La Tradition apostolique*, SCH, XI (Paris, 1946), 8.

26. H. Tattam, ed., *The Apostolical Constitutions of the Apostles in Coptic with an English Translation* (London, 1848).

27. W. Till and J. Leipoldt, eds., *Der koptische Text der Kirchenordnung Hippolyts*, TU, 58 (Berlin, 1954).

28. Périer, "Les 127 Canons des Apôtres.'"

29. H. Duensing, *Der aethiopische Text der Kirchenordnung des Hippolyt* (Göttingen, 1946).

30. E. Hauler, *Didascaliae apostolorum fragmenta Veronensia latina* (Leipzig, 1900).

31. A. Wilmart, "Le texte latin de la Paradosis de Saint Hipolyte," *RSR*, 9 (1919), 62-71.

32. This point can be demonstrated by a comparison with other surviving versions of the same text, which also guarantees that the translator has not tried to "slant" his text.

33. Botte, *La Tradition apostoloque*, *SCH*, XI, 12-13.

34. Botte, *La Tradition apostolique* (1963 ed.), 36, canon 16. H. F. Davis ("Early Christian Attitude," 478-479) vigorously asserted that it was because the Christians were not allowed to kill that "it became the official custom in Rome in the latter half of the second century to forbid . . . [them] to volunteer for certain positions." He also declared that even in the fourth century, after the empire had officially become Christian and the numbers of Christians in the army had multiplied, the Church continued to maintain a certain scruple about baptizing soldiers. But at the same time he contended that the *Apostolic Tradition* could not have applied to the case of war, because (he remarked rather naively) "it would be difficult to understand how they [the Christians] could continue in service at all . . . if the prohibition to execute included killing men in battle." If we were to follow this interpretation, we should arrive at a pecular paradox: a law based on the principle of respect for human life which did not allow the believer to take the slightest responsibility in the execution of common-law criminals but which found it normal for believers to slaughter soldiers whom only the hazard of war had made into enemies.

35. Canon 41 (Till and Leipoldt, *Der koptische Text*, 10-11).

36. Canons 27 (end) and 28 (Périer, "Les '127 Canons des Apôtres,' " 527).

37. Canons 27 (end) and 28 (Duensing, *Der aethiopische Text*, 44-45). In other MSS, these canons are numbered 28 and 29, or even 31 and 32.

38. Here, as later, I have italicized the words which differ from other texts of the same family, and have placed between brackets words not in the original text which I have added for clarity in translation.

39. The exact words are: "and if he has not left off, he will be rejected." These are the identical words that we encounter in the following canon. One might justifiably understand these words to mean that "if he does not refuse to carry out that order, he shall then not be admitted as a catechumen." But for one thing, was not the only solution for the soldier and others in the same category to give up their job before taking part in homicidal action? Furthermore, since these passages refer to someone who had already been entangled in the contradiction between the use of the sword and Christian morality, it seems that the only person to whom this could have applied was someone who at an earlier date had formally become a believer and who was dismissed when he failed to draw the logical consequences of his Christian profession. I am therefore convinced that my translation is in fact the only possible one.

40. This is why Botte, who in his 1946 edition of the *Apostolic Tradition* (p. 45 n.) had rejected the words "let him not be permitted to take the oath," restored them in his 1963 edition (pp. 36-36 n.).

41. D'Alès, *Théologie*, 415 n. The eighth book of the *Constitutions* is the one which interests us here, for it is a systematic exploitation of the *Apostolic Tradition*. The *Constitutions*, especially in their first six books, depend otherwise and just as closely on the *Didascalia*. Since the original Greek version of the *Didascalia*—like that of the *Tradition*—has disappeared, it is extremely difficult to judge whether the two works, which were almost contemporary with each other even though they came from the opposite ends of the world of that time, were completely independent of each other. In any case, the two texts are closely linked in their common canonical descent and F. X. Funk (*Didascalia et Constitutiones Apostolorum* [Paderborn, 1905]) has

provided an edition of them in parallel.

42. *Constitutions*, VIII, 32, 10: "If a soldier comes, let him be taught to 'do no injustice, to accuse no man falsely, and to be content with his allotted wages:' if he submit to those rules, let him be received; but if he refuse them, let him be rejected."

43. *Ibid.*, II, 14, 12; see below, p. 307.

44. Botte (1963 ed.) rightly regrouped these three versions along with the Bohairic under the common name of "Alexandrine versions." This canonical collection from Alexandria also contains translations of the *Apostolic Canons* (not to be confused with those of Hippolytus), of the *Apostolic Tradition*, and of the *Epitome* of the eighth book of the *Constitutions*. A similar compilation is to be found in Verona MS. Bibl. cap. LV (53) published by Hauler (*Didascaliae*). Only the English translation of the three versions by G. Horner (*The Statutes of the Apostles or Canones ecclesiastici* [London, 1904]) and the edition of the Arabic version by J. and A. Périer ("Les '127 Canons des Apôtres' ") have supplied the entire texts of these three compilations, whereas Duensing as well as Till and Leipoldt (see above, nn. 27 and 29) published only those parts which interested them. The arrangement of materials in the various versions is as follows: Sahidic (*Canons* nos. 1-30; *Tradition* nos. 31-62; *Epitome* nos. 63-78); Arabic (*Canons* nos. 1-21; *Tradition* nos. 21-47; *Epitome* nos. 49-72). The canon that we are studying here is Sahidic 75, Arabic 62, and English 63 (respectively Horner, 351; Périer, 646; Horner, 208).

45. J. And A. Périer ("Les '127 Canons des Apôtres,' " 555) assumed that the findings of Dom R. H. Connolly (*The So-called Egyptian Church Order and Derived Documents*, Texts and Studies, VIII, iv [Cambridge, 1916]) were the indisputable basis for further work on these texts.

46. Dom G. Dix, ed., *The Treatise on the Apostolic Tradition of St. Hippolytus of Rome*, rev. Henry Chadwick (London, 1968), lxiii, lxv. See also A. G. Martimort, "La Tradition Apostolique d'Hippolyte et le rituel baptismal antique," *BLE*, 60 (1959), 57-62.

47. A. Salles, ed., *Trois antiques rituels de baptême*, SCH, LIX (Paris, 1958), 7 n., 35 n. This Judaizing tendency was retained for a long time. Coquin (*Les Canons*, 52-53, 320-321) found it again in the *Canons of Hippolytus* (which I shall be discussing) in connection with the rule which is of especial interest to us—that concerning the "sin of blood."

48. Botte's review (*BTAM*, 8 [1958], 174-176) of Salles' work was scathing. Martimort's assessment (see n. 46 above), which although more moderate was still highly critical, had the merit of providing the reader with a short résumé of the hypothesis upon which Salles was working. Neither of these reviewers referred to the most obvious weakness in Salles' theory—the Ethiopic text's transparent dependence upon an earlier Arabic one—no doubt because both imagined that it was common knowledge.

49. Botte (1963 ed.), 36 n.

50. *Testament of Our Lord*, II, 2 (ed. Cooper and Maclean, 118; ed. Rahmani, 114; ed. Nau, 62-63).

51. The Arabic translation, which was made from the Sahidic Coptic and which is all we possess, dates from as late as the thirteenth century. But a Greek original must be postulated which would date from the period indicated in the text. The surviving MSS of this Arabic translation are divided into three groups: the Arabic Berlin 10181 (="R"); the *Nomocanon* of Michael of Damiette (="d"); and the Macaire Collection (="m") of which there are numerous copies.

52. This is the reading of "R". "m" reads: "let him not be received in any case."

53. "m" simply omits the entire text between n. 52 and this.

54. Once again, "m" reads, "let him not be received in any case," and thereby it refuses admission into the Church even to the "nonviolent" soldier.

55. At an early stage of his research, Coquin, arguing from the parallel text in the *Constitutions* (VIII, 32, 10, quoted n. 42 above), speculated that this clause might denote acting as an informer. This reference might then apply to the present canon, for the informer kills by his words as certainly as the soldier by his weapon and the magistrate by his sentence. By the time that he published his findings, however, Coquin had returned to the explanation which Botte had given to justify the retention in the text of the *Tradition* of the words "he shall not take the oath," even though they are attested only by the Sahidic. As Botte (1963 ed., 37 n.) argued, "The prohibition of the military oath (Sahidic text) must have appeared impossible in the era in which the empire had become Christian. Hence its omission [in the Arabic and Ethiopic versions]. The reading [of the Sahidic text] seems confirmed by [the *Canons* of Hippolytus]: he will not utter evil words. Between the prohibition of killing and that of wearing crowns, it could not have been a question of evil conversations, but rather of words which had an idolatrous meaning." This argument is unconvincing. Although the prohibition of the oath might have seemed impossible after the empire had espoused Christianity, the words which immediately preceded these—which stated bluntly that the soldier must not obey certain of the orders of his lawful superior— must have seemed even more impossible to admit.

56. *Alâmat.* This word can mean either a rank, a decoration, or a sum of money which is presented at a *donativum*. The "F" MS (a late copy which dates from the fourteenth century) repeats the word "crown": "Let those who have received a crown as a token not put the crown on their head." But this addition, which is attested by only one MS, looks too much like a clumsy explanatory interpolation for it to be retained.

57. "d" replaces these words with: "nor let him be a chief having the sword."

58. Partly because of the "d" variant quoted in n. 57 above, Coquin (*Les Canons*, 368 n.-369 n.) indicated that others had speculated that the original text had been: "The Christian must not become a soldier, unless he is constrained. Let the chief having the sword not take on himself the sin of blood." See, for example, the German translation of W. Riedel (*Die Kirchenrechtsquellen des Patriarchats Alexandrien* [Leipzig, 1900], 207). But Coquin remarked rightly that the translator's task is to render the text as it is, not to produce a text adulterated by the translator's assumptions of what may have been behind it.

59. Coquin, *Les Canons*, 367 (99)-369 (101).

60. A. Bayet, who was generally overimaginative in his interpretations of our subject, at least had the merit of seeing that "these *Canons of Hippolytus*, which at first we find so severe, are in reality only a softening of an older law" (*Pacifisme*, 77). This process becomes even clearer when we turn from the *Canons* to the *Tradition*. Of course, Hippolytus himself did not claim to be producing an original work. So probably the Ethiopian versions of the *Tradition*, like the "m" reading of the *Canons*, are an echo of the historical starting point of this development.

61. Coquin, *Les Canons*, 322 (54).

62. Cooper and Maclean, *The Testament of Our Lord*, 209.

63. Cadoux (*Early Christian Attitude*, 238) remarked that "the silence of the Synod of Illiberis [Elvira] on the legitimacy of military service is significant." But I do not grasp what he thought the significance to be. Cf. J. Gaudemet, "Elvire," *DHGE*, XV (1963), cols. 317-348.

64. Hefelé, I, i, 252. [Because of the authoritative character of Leclercq's French edition, we have preferred it to the English translation of W. R. Clark, *et al.* (*A His-*

tory of the Christian Councils, 5 vols. [Edinburgh, 1871-1896]).]

65. A. W. W. Dale, *The Synod of Elvira and Christian Life in the Fourth Century* (London, 1882), 234.

66. Basil of Caesarea, *Homilies on the Psalms*, 61, 4.

67. Obviously this admission by Basil may seem to reinforce the thesis against which I am arguing—that conscientious objection was a late development. But for the proponents of this thesis, "late" means the end of the third century, not the latter half of the fourth century; and in any case, I have elsewhere demonstrated that those who argue in this way are wrong. The testimony of St. Basil, who incorrectly believed that he was contradicting the traditional position, and who nevertheless took his stance because of faithfulness to the gospel, thereby becomes all the more authoritative.

68. Basil, *Ep.*, 188 *(canonica prima)*, 13. Earlier in the letter Basil had prepared the ground for this conclusion by discussing various cases of murder which, he stressed, were obviously more serious when intentional than when unintentional. He continued: "He who makes use of a sword or any other such weapon has no excuse. . . . And again entirely voluntary and admitting of no doubt are, for instance, the acts of robbers and the attacks of soldiers. For the former kill for the sake of money and to avoid exposure, and men in warfare proceed to slaughter openly, proposing neither to terrify nor to chastise but to kill their opponents" *(Ibid.*, 8). In this penetrating criticism of the "direction of intention," Basil, reversing the usual argument, placed the soldier-killer even lower in the hierarchy of murder than bandits and perpetrators of crimes of passion.

69. Balsamon, *Commentary on the Canons*, canon 13, II, 65.

70. *Ibid.*, 70. See G. Fritz, "Service militaire," *DTC*, XIV (1941), col. 1980. The Greek text of these different passages from Basil and Balsamon is reproduced by Giet, *Les Idées*, 167-169. L. Arpee (*A History of Armenian Christianity* [New York, 1946], 189), after noting the wary attitude of the Church toward soldiers, remarked that this was not the case with the Armenian Church—which, in fact, canonized all those who fell in the tragic defeat of Avarair in 451. But Arpee also cited a canon of St. Isaac which refused communion to soldiers as well as to drunkards and other disreputables. This provision is unique in the corpus of Armenian religious literature; but its extremely late date (426) makes it noteworthy.

71. Quoted in Hefelé, I, i, 591. See also E. Vacandard, "La Question du Service militaire," 159 n.: "[This canon] deals only with soldiers who had been expelled for their Christian feelings and who had then betrayed their faith by returning into the service under Licinius." Nevertheless, later in the fourth century Popes Damasus and Siricius understood the canon in exactly the same way as Fritz has done recently (see pp. 152, 190). It is hard to comprehend how Jean Gaudemet (*L'Eglise dans l' Empire romain [IVᵉ-Vᵉ siècles]*, Histoire du Droit et des Institutions de l'Eglise d'Occident, III [Paris, 1958], 141 n.) can have failed to reach a similar understanding of it.

72. *DTC*, XIV, col. 1978: "The canon did not forbid the Christian to be a soldier. It recalled the ancient rule which forbade him to be one voluntarily." See also Lorson, *Défense*, 35.

73. Hefelé, I, i, 592. Bayet (*Pacifisme*, 189) offered a different explanation. According to him, this canon was directed at those who had consistently refused to serve under Licinius but who would have liked to sérve again under a Christian emperor— Constantine. Thus interpreted, canon 12 would imply an indirect but genuine anti-militarism. Although it admittedly conceded the right of soldiers to remain in the army, it condemned those who, having left the service under special circumstances, wanted to return to it once these circumstances had changed. It is true that this interpretation is the one which flows most naturally from the verbal construction of the

sentence. But it does not fit properly with the canon's psychological context. And in any case, Bayet misunderstood Hefelé, citing him as the authority for his interpretation despite the fact that Hefelé's position was diametrically opposed to Bayet's.

74. [J. Gaudemet (*Conciles Gaulois du IV*ᵉ *Siècle*, SCH, CCXLI [Paris, 1977], 48-49) gives the text, with a new French translation, of the Canons of Arles, with comment.]

75. L. Sturzo (*Church and State* [Notre Dame, 1962], 33), having recalled Constantine's essential role in this synod, wrote: "This Council, acting on his inspiration, blamed the anti-militarism of Christians as prejudicial to the empire."

76. G. Bardy, "Arles (Conciles d')," *Catholicisme*, I (1948), col. 838. For similar interpretations, see Babut, *L'Adoration*, 20; Bayet, *Pacifisme*, 124; Harnack, *Militia Christi*, 88; Delaruelle, Latreille, and Palanque, *Histoire du Catholicisme*, I, 43. All of these, however, detected in the canon a departure from former teaching which the author of the passage in *Catholicisme* failed to recognize.

77. E.g., Paris, Bibliothèque nationale, cod. lat. 12097 and 1452, as well as in the MSS of Cologne and Albi. All four of these MSS have many other omissions as well.

78. E.g., Toulouse Bibliothèque municipale, cod. 364, which dates from before 666, has *bellum* as a correction in its margin.

79. Cardinal C. J. von Hefelé, in the first German edition of his *Conciliengeschichte* ([Freiburg/Breisgau, 1855], I, 186), and Bigelmair (*Beteiligung*, 182) were not adverse to this interpretation, which was also favored by Cooper and Maclean (*Testament of Our Lord*, 209) and defended vigorously by De Jong (*Dienstweigering*, 55). Bayet (*Pacifisme*, 8-9), on the other hand, mentions it only to ridicule it. The second German edition of Hefelé's *Conciliengeschichte* (I, 206), as well as the French translation by H. Leclercq ([Paris, 1907], I, i, 283), follow the interpretation which I shall discuss below, according to which canon 3 did indeed refer to possible desertions and condemned them because of the advent of peace between Church and state.

80. Dale, *Synod of Elvira*, 238 ff., 281.

81. Harnack, *Militia Christi*, 88. Kaufmann (*Handbuch*, 114) was of the same opinion. Le Blant (*Manuel d'Epigraphie*, 15n.) indicated that, despite the fact that he had at first supported this position, he had been led by a close comparison of this canon with Roman juridical texts to recognize that "the Council of Arles speaks of desertions in time of peace as opposed to those which might take place in wartime."

82. H. F. Secrétan, "Le Christianisme des Premiers Siècles et le Service militaire," *RTP*, 2 (1914), 364.

83. *Ibid.*, 360. Fritz ("Service militaire," col. 1977) vigorously upheld this interpretation; but he acknowledged that "this attitude of the Council of Arles can be characterized as bizarre." He was keenly aware of the unity of the movement which extended from Tertullian to St. Basil, and which passed without interruption through the *Apostolic Tradition*, the soldier saints, and the Arles decision. See also Rordorf, "Tertullians Beurteilung," 121.

84. Vanderpol, *La Doctrine scolastique*, 116.

85. This attitude, alas, still lives on. For example, M. Villey, in his review of the French edition of the present book (*RHDF*, 40 [1962], 268), after reciting my explanation of the words *in pace*, commented: "M. Hornus would conclude *a contrario* from this that desertion in time of war was authorized. Such an interpretation seems to me to defy sense: what would be the use of military service in time of peace, if it were to be followed by refusal to take part in war?" Such a position would indeed be useless to the state, and I am not personally advocating it as a sound ethical stance. But this has been—and still is—the solution that "reasonable people" within the Church keep urging upon young men who hear the inner call to refuse to participate in bloodshed.

In this way endless "disagreements" can allegedly be avoided without violating anyone's ethical principles.

My interpretation of the meaning of the Arles wording *in pace* was also that of von Campenhausen ("Christians and Military Service," 168 n.), who summed up the position of the Christians of the last years of the third century as follows: "Soldiers who are Christians never actually enter the field of battle, even if the emperor demands it" (*Ibid.*, 165). Gerest ("Les premiers chrétiens," 16 n.) also wrote: "It is perhaps necessary to introduce a distinction between the fact of serving and the fact of fighting (see the canons of Hippolytus and of the Council of Arles). Such a distinction would not have been absurd; during the third century one could remain in the army without taking part in fighting." Cf. the pungent comment of Ramsay MacMullen, "Many a recruit need never have struck a blow in anger, outside of a tavern" (*Soldier and Civilian in the Later Roman Empire* [Cambridge, Mass., 1963], v).

86. Cooper and Maclean (*Testament of Our Lord*, 208) provided an illustration of concessions which invariably lead to still other concessions once one has started to make them: "The *Constitution of the Egyptian Church* [i.e., the *Apostolic Tradition*] has almost the same rule as the *Testament [of our Lord]*, one which seems impossible to put in practice, that Christians are not to become soldiers. And yet the *Constitutions of the Egyptian Church* probably represents a code actually in existence. The *Canons* of Hippolytus rule is hardly less impracticable. For how can a soldier help killing an enemy in war?"

87. Augustine, *Discourse on the Psalms*, 124, 7.

88. Tertullian himself suggested this argument (*Apol.*, 37, 5): "For what war should we not have been fit and ready even if unequal in forces—we who are so glad to be butchered—were it not, of course, that in our doctrine we are given ampler liberty to be killed than to kill?"

89. See Chap. 4 above, pp. 155-157.

90. We should not forget that Lactantius, although he at times was quite as much of a "concordat man" as Eusebius, was also capable of courageous affirmations (*Div. Institutiones*, VI, 20, 10, which I quoted on p. 116 above). With reference to these passages, D'Alès (*Théologie*, 416) wrote: "One may regard as exceptional the opinion of Lactantius, who also proscribed for the Christian the profession of arms." We now know that initially all the Church Fathers shared this "exceptional opinion."

91. Eusebius, *HE*, IX, 8, 2 and 4.

92. *Ibid.*, IX, 9, 1.

93. *Ibid.*, IX, 9, 2; see also IX, 11, 9.

94. *Ibid.*, IX, 11, 2-7.

95. *Ibid.*, IX, 11, 5.

96. *Ibid.*, IX, 10, 13.

97. Eusebius, *Vita*, II, 16.

98. Lactantius, *De Mort. Pers.*, 46. In his edition of this text, J. Moreau (*SCH*, XXXIX, ii, 450) showed that this prayer, which Eusebius afterwards attributed to Constantine, has a distinctly Christian coloration, even though it remained ambiguous enough also to be acceptable to pagan soldiers. Moreau also quoted a text of a similar nature from the *Martyrdom of St. Basil of Amasea*: "Licinius, therefore, upheld by the almighty hand of our Lord Jesus Christ, gained the victory over Maximinius."

99. See above, p. 171. Cf. Harnack, *Militia Christi*, 91, and Cadoux, *Early Christian Attitude*, 260.

100. Bavaud, "Les premiers chrétiens."

101. Courcelle, *Histoire*, 13. Some of Courcelle's reservations to this statement

are, however, astonishing (see 13 n.).

102. Ambrose of Milan, *De Off.*, II, 15, 71; II, 28, 136; III, 13, 14.

103. *Ibid.*, I, 27, 129. See also Chenu, "L'Evolution," 84-86, which lays particular stress on Augustine's feeling of "Romanity" (*romanitas*).

104. Sturzo, *Church and State*, 46.

105. M. Villey (*RHDF*, 40 [1962], 268) noted, "I find it hard to conceive of a breach as complete as M. Hornus supposes between Augustine's doctrine of war and the preceding Christian tradition." But on this very point G. S. Windass (*Christianity Versus Violence* [London, 1964], 80) has indicated clearly that "St. Augustine's thought about war . . . was in a state of tension. On the one hand, he felt bound to concede, with the world, that it was possible to fight in war and yet to be a Christian; but on the other hand, he was always aware that the early Christian tradition was an important part of himself, and the teaching and example of Christ in the Scriptures, pulled in another direction." See also *ibid.*, 88, in which Windass reminds the reader of St. Augustine's classical denial of the right of "legitimate self-defence."

106. Both robberies and kingdoms, Augustine explained, have their leaders, their agreements, and their laws. This is a disconcerting idea for those who make the "maintenance of order" to be the supreme virtue of the state. For although there can be a good order, there is also an "order" which is nothing more than a well-organized brigandage.

107. Augustine, *City of God*, 4, 4. See also *ibid.*, 4, 3, which contains a parallel passage glorifying the rule of the good.

108. *Ibid.*, 4, 6.

109. *Idem, Contra Faustum*, 22, 70. See also *ibid.*, 22, 74.

110. *Idem, City of God*, 19, 12; *Ep.*, 189, 6. In *Ep.*, 47, 5, Augustine developed the distinction between public and private murder, to which St. Leo the Great also pointed (*Ep.*, 167, 12 and 14). Similarly, St. Maximus of Turin (*Homily*, 114, 1) argued that, although civil or military service should not be allowed to serve as a pretext for crimes, the fact of serving was not in itself morally objectionable: "*Non enim militare delictum est, sed propter praedam militare peccatum.*"

111. Augustine, *On the Free Will*, I, 4, 9; I, 5, 12. The same ideas recur in almost identical language in the *City of God*, I, 21 and 26. Seven centuries after Augustine bishop Rufinus wrote that "one should not be at peace [with the wicked], but one must rather make war on them. For no sensible person is unaware that this gives us a clear advance toward the good of peace itself.... It is only in order that the good should remain intact in all things that we must make war and use weapons. It is also for this reason that the laws order tortures" (*De Bono Pacis*, II, 14). Already in the ninth century Pope Nicholas I was contending that "man would tempt God" if he did not prepare arms for the defense of himself and his country (*Responsa*, 46).

112. G. Combès, *La Doctrine politique de Saint Augustin* (Paris, 1927), 284-285; R. Régout, *La Doctrine de la Guerre juste de Saint Augustin à nos jours* (Paris, 1935), 39-44; P. Monceaux, "Saint Augustin et la Guerre," in P. Batiffol, *et al.*, *L'Eglise et la Guerre* (Paris, 1913).

113. Combès, *La Doctrine politique*, 289 and esp. 290, on which he quoted many literally "scandalous" texts from St. Augustine. Before leaving Augustine, I would like to mention a question which at present divides the interpreters of his thought. Between the heavenly city and the earthly city, the latter of which is often pictured as diabolical, is there room for a third city—one which would still be human but would be good because of its subjection to God? C. Journet has written a confused article on this ("Les Trois Cités [de Dieu, de l'Homme et du Diable]," *Nova vetera*, 33 [1958], 25-48). H. I. Marrou ("Civitas Dei, Civitas terrena: num tertium quid?"

SP, 2 [Berlin, 1957], 342-350) seems to me to have been correct when he observed that in Augustine's thought the two cities existed as clearly differentiated abstract ideas; concrete reality, on the other hand, far from being a representation of the third idea, is simply a degraded expression of an intricate intertwining of the first two ideas.

114. Ambrose seems to us to have lived in an earlier period than Augustine: he died at a relatively young age—over thirty years before Augustine—and had played an important part in the latter's conversion. In fact, there was a difference of less than fifteen years between the two men. For this reason I have taken the liberty of not fully respecting chronology, in order to be able to consider the thinker (Augustine) before the man of action (Ambrose). For Ambrose's activity is a striking illustration of Augustine's style of thinking.

115. See A. de Broglie, *Saint Ambroise* (Paris, 1891), and R. Thamin, *Saint Ambroise et la Morale chrétienne au IV ^{e} Siècle* (Paris, 1895), which discuss at length this aspect of Ambrose's activity. For an authoritative treatment of the whole question, see A. Paredi, S. *Ambroglio e la sua Eta,* 2nd ed. (Milan, 1960), which clearly demonstrates Ambrose's contribution to the crystallization of the new ideology.

116. *DHGE,* II, cols. 1091 ff.

117. For example, Ambrose pleaded for and obtained a pardon from Theodosius for the partisans of Eugenius (*Ep.,* 62).

118. See F. van Ortroy, "Saint Ambroise et l'Empereur Théodose," *AB,* 23 (1904), 418 ff., and P. de Labriolle, *Saint Ambroise* (Paris, 1908).

119. Ambrose, *De Obitu Theodosii,* 48.

120. Ambrose, *Exp. in luc.,* II, 77.

121. Ambrose, *De Off.,* I, 27, 129.

122. Ambrose, *De Fide,* II, 16. R. Roques (review of *EL, RHR,* 164 [1964], 242) was offended here—as in my quotations (n. 183 below) from Eusebius (*HE,* X, 7) and the *Cod. Theod.* (XVI, 2)—by my use of the adjective "Catholic." In all three instances, however, the word occurs in the quoted texts themselves. Obviously, it is not in opposition to "Protestant," as he assumes that I am hinting, but to the heresies of that era—Arianism and Donatism. See my comments below (p. 307) concerning my solidarity as a Protestant theologian with many of the ideas of the "Old Catholicism."

123. Jerome, *Commentary on Ezekiel,* 11; *idem, Book of Questions on Genesis,* 10, 2.

124. Athanasius was attempting to prove that the "wet dreams" to which monks may be prone were not a sin.

125. Athanasius, *Letter* (48) *to Amun.*

126. *Cod. Theod.,* XVI, 10, 21, quoted by Ryan, "Rejection," 27.

127. When from time to time the Christian conscience has spoken out against violence, it has been a voice "crying in the wilderness," even though it has generally been tolerated because of its rarity. Efforts have invariably been made to neutralize it, and the sensitive conscience has been informed that it has taken the wrong road, and that only the monastic life can satisfy its desire for purity and the absolute. At the end of this chapter I shall demonstrate that monachism was one of the primary forces that were responsible for the watering down of the Christian ethic.

128. Parker, *Christianity and the State,* 41, 42; Stauffer, *Christ and the Caesars,* 244, 301. As Hobhouse has rightly stressed (*Church and the World,* 77, 91), by the end of the third century the Christians—in spite of the relative setbacks about which he had written a few pages earlier—had come to be the most dynamic element, although not yet a majority, within the empire. It was therefore to them that the future belonged, and mere political prudence dictated that one should try to rally them to one's side.

129. Hobhouse, *Church and the World*, 66-67.
130. *Ibid.*, 112-114, which are three pages of great force and conviction.
131. Combès, *La Doctrine politique*, 260. Such an admission was significant, for Combès did not conceal his personal adherence to the theory of the just war and his approval of necessary violence. Durry *(Cohortes prétoriennes*, 330-331) similarly believed that by the end of the third century the Christians had already come to be numerous—perhaps a majority—within the Roman army, in spite of the efforts of the state to prevent this. (Durry did not consider what efforts the Church might have been making, in one direction or another.)
132. Monceaux, *Histoire*, 274. G.F. Hershberger *(The Way of the Cross in Human Relations* [Scottdale, Pa., 1958], 24, 59) has delineated the interrelationship between Constantine's pseudo-conversion, the invasion of the Church by superficial initiates, and the identification (which he deplored) between Christianity, Christendom, the social order and the empire.
133. A. Puech, *Saint Jean Chrysostome et les Moeurs de son temps* (Paris, 1891), 303.
134. John Chrysostom, *Homilies on St. Matthew*, 61, 2.
135. *Idem, Homilies on St. John*, 82, 4.
136. S. L. Greenslade, *Church and State from Constantine to Theodosius* (London, 1954), *passim.*
137. Cerfaux and Tondriau, *Concurrent*, 408. Bayet *(Pacifisme*, 186) has also shown that from Claudius to Constantine the imperial government pursued exactly the same religious policy. Bayet even claimed, with some exaggeration *(ibid.*, 173, 175), that the emperors finally opted for Christianity because it was more exclusive than the other cults and thus was more congruent with their desire for totalitarian uniformity. F. J. Foakes-Jackson *(Eusebius Pamphili* [Cambridge, 1933], 48) did not go as far as this; but he nevertheless commented, "Constantine ... was the real successor of Diocletian, and though one sanctioned a cruel persecution, and the other loaded the Church with benefits, the ultimate object of both was the same, namely, to make religion the handmaid of the empire." See also Gagé, "La Victoire," 400, and the excellent little book by O. Heggelbacher, *Vom Römischen zum Christlichen Recht* (Freiburg/Breisgau, 1959). Basing his argument on references to laws and institutions in the *Ambrosiaster,* Heggelbacher has demonstrated that the first Christian empire took its stand on Romans 13 in order to reemploy Roman law and natural right for its own benefit.
138. Cerfaux and Tondriau, *Concurrent*, 409.
139. Setton, *Christian Attitude*, 24-25; Gagé, "La Victoire," 393-394.
140. Optatus of Milevis, *De Schismate Donatistarum*, III, 3. It was only at the beginning of the eighth century that what F. Dvornik has called "the idea of a single universal Church in a single universal empire" began to be questioned in the West, or rather that the submission of the Roman religious power to the Byzantine political power began to fade away, only to be replaced by another synthesis. Dvornik, who has examined all of these developments *(Byzance et la Primauté romaine* [Paris, 1964], 77-87), has stressed that, in the exchange of letters between emperor Leo III and Pope Gregory II, the pope did not yet challenge the priestly character claimed by the emperor as a part of his imperial function. But the pope reminded him that his imperial/priestly role "did not permit him to oversee the Church and to judge the clergy, nor to consecrate and distribute the holy sacramental signs."
141. Setton, *Christian Attitude*, 28.
142. See above, pp. 25-26.
143. Hobhouse *(Church and the World*, 68-69) has analyzed with clarity the

relationship between the deteriorating ethical standards of the Church, the Montanist reaction, and clerical specialization.

144. *SCH*, XXXIII, 167.

145. Marrou himself has shown (see n. 144 above), however, that observers as early as Origen and Clement of Alexandria described the cleavage between the different categories of Christians.

146. Good theology should never be unbalanced. Perhaps it is therefore necessary to specify here that a monachism freed from the idea of supererogatory merits, such as our brethren in the community of Taizé are apparently realizing, would not be subject to this criticism. It is the same in the case of the "old catholicism," with which I share a dual concern—for responsibility toward the civil community, and for order within the Christian community.

147. Goguel, *Birth*, 550, in which passage he also paid tribute to Dibelius for having shown clearly that this tendency had existed from the early days.

148. *Ibid.*, 434-435. D. E. Hall ("La Conversión del Emperador Constantino," *Pensamiento Cristiano*, 6 [1958], 149-169), whose article was otherwise mediocre, made a valuable contribution by emphasizing the connection between the ecclesiastical and the political evolutions within early Christianity. As Roger Mehl commented ("Christianisme primitif"), "It is one of J.-M. Hornus's important contributions that he noted the subtle but real link between the evolution of the Church's political attitude and a particular conception of monasticism."

149. *Constitutions*, II, 14, 12. The text of *Didascalia*, VI, 14, 10 and 12 (ed. Nau, 51-52; ed. Connolly, 44-45) is substantially identical. In *Constitutions*, VIII, 12, 42 there is also a prayer for the king, the power-holders, and the entire army, "So that all which is ours may remain in peace." But *Didascalia*, XVIII, 6, 4 (ed. Nau, 142; ed. Connolly, 158) blamed the bishops who, in order to feed orphans and widows, accepted impure offerings coming from "soldiers who act lawlessly; or from murderers; or from spies who procure condemnations; or from any Roman officials, who are defiled with wars and have shed innocent blood without trial." The text of *Constitutions*, IV, 6, 5, which Funk cited in his edition (p. 225) as a parallel, is really quite different.

150. Périer, "Les '127 Canons des Apôtres,' " II, 55. This double clause also occurs in canons 83-84 of the series of *Apostolic Canons* in Greek or in Latin, published by Hefele, *Conciliengeschichte*, 2nd ed., 285-286. Leclercq's French translation of Hefelé (*Histoire*, I, ii, 1203-1204) did not reproduce their text, but dated them in about the fifth century and commented on their wide geographical diffusion. On these Greek and Latin canons, see also F. Nau, *DTC*, II (1905), cols. 1605-1611, and G. Bardy, *DDC*, II, cols. 1288-1295.

151. A. H. M. Jones, *The Later Roman Empire* (Oxford, 1964), I, 566; MacMullen, *Soldier and Civilian*, 48 n.

152. Gaudemet, *L'Eglise*, 143. See also Fontaine ("Vérité et fiction," 211), who rightly noted that even if, as was long thought, soldiers could not be the only people to whom this law alluded, they were still included in a more general reprobation.

153. MacMullen, *Soldier and Civilian*, chap. 3.

154. Letter of the bishops of Illyria to the Eastern bishops, Mansi, III, col. 388, which Theodoret of Cyrus included in full in his *Ecclesiastical History* (IV, 8). Hefelé (*Histoire*, I, ii, 982) dated the Council in 375; Mansi (III, col. 388) put it even earlier. I have retained the date given by J. Zeiller (*Origines chrétiennes dans les provinces danubiennes* [Paris, 1918], 326-327), although Zeiller discerned in this text an opposite meaning—to the effect that only irreproachable people were to be chosen as priests, *even if* they had come from the magistracy or the army. If that reading were

correct, the significance of the decision would certainly be different from the one I have seen in it. But it would still provide evidence of a general attitude of reserve on the part of the Church toward the professions which it mentioned.

155. Hefelé, *Histoire*, II, i, 136.

156. E.g., *PL*, XIII, cols. 1181 ff., in which it was presented as the tenth letter of Siricius.

157. H. C. Babut, *La plus ancienne décrétale* (Paris, 1904), 69-87, in which the best edition of the text, which is called the *Canones ad Gallos*, is to be found. [Although Fontaine ("Vérité et fiction," 212 n.) and Gaudemet (*L'Eglise*, 220) have revived the former attribution, Pietri (*Roma Christiana*, I, 764-772) has reverted to Babut's position.]

158. Canon 7. The same attitude can be seen in canon 13, where it is mixed with a more general condemnation of the various civil offices which entailed participation in coercive power.

159. Hefelé, *Histoire*, II, i. 69; P. Jaffé, *Regesta Pontificum Romanorum ab condita ecclesia ad annum post Christum natuim 1198* (Leipzig, 1885), I, 41; Siricius, Letter (no. 5) *cum in unum*, 2 (*PL*, XIII, col. 1158; *PL*, LVI, col. 727). This letter, which Siricius addressed to the episcopate of Africa, was substantially repeated with further explanations in Siricius's ecumenical Letter (no. 6) *cogitantibus nobis*, 1, 3 (*PL*, XIII, col. 1165; Fontaine, "Vérité et fiction," 211-213).

160. Hefelé, *Histoire*, II, i. 123: "*Si quis post baptismum militaverit et chlamydem sumpserit aut cingulum, etiamsi graviora non admiserit, si ad clerum admissus fuit, diaconii non accipiat dignitatem*" (Mansi, III, col. 1000).

161. Mansi, III, col. 1064.

162. *Ibid.*, III, col. 1069; Innocent I, Letter (no. 3) *Saepe me* (*PL*, XX, col. 492a); Jaffé, *Regesta*, I, 45. This canon, like Letter 6 of Siricius which I have quoted above, borrows from Damasus, *Canones ad Gallos* in yet another erroneous attempt (cf. nn. 71-72 above) to claim the Council of Nicaea's authority for their antimilitarist position.

163. H. Wurm, *Studien und Texte zur Decretalensammlung des Dionysius Exiguus* (Bonn, 1939), 128, esp. n. 5. Wurm quoted the various available authorities, but failed to take a position as to the preferred reading. He also failed to give indication as to the likelihood and date of a Council at Toulouse.

164. Mansi, III, cols. 1038-1041; *PL*, XX, cols. 495-502.

165. Innocent I, Letter 2, 2 (4), *PL*, XX, col. 472 (also in *PL*, LVI, col. 521, and in Jaffé, *Regesta*, I, 44). A. Vanderpol attempted (*Doctrine scolastique*, 191) to evade the obvious meaning of this text (which recurred in a canon of Pope Leo I) by arguing that "remission of sins" meant not baptism but the postbaptismal penance which would have made the penitent sinner into a veritable monk for the rest of his life. *PL*, XX, col. 471 n. has made clear, however, that the most probable original meaning of this expression was baptism. The other two texts from Innocent I (to which I have referred above) enable one to assess this evasion at its true value.

166. Innocent I, Letter 37, 3 (5), *PL*, XX, col. 63 (Jaffé, *Regesta*, I, 47), which cannot be dated precisely. It is interesting to note that this part of the sentence has been deleted from the later recension of the same letter (*PL*, LXXXIV, cols. 651-654).

167. E. Hildesheimer, "Les Clercs et l'exemption du service militaire à l'époque franque," *RHEF*, 29 (1943), 17. See also the texts collected by Vanderpol (*Doctrine scolastique*, 121-122).

168. Chalcedon, Canon 7, Hefelé, *Histoire*, II, ii, 788-789.

169. Angers, Canon 7, *CCL*, CXLVIII, 138: "There is no injustice in the rejection by the Church of the clerics who have abandoned the clergy to mingle with the

secular army and with the laity."
170. Agda, Canon 20, Hefelé, *Histoire*, II, ii, 973 (mansi, VIII, col. 319), which condemned the clerics who bore arms.
171. Lerida, Canon I, Hefelé, *Histoire*, II, ii. 1063 (Vanderpol, *Doctrine scolastique*, 599), which prescribed that any priest who had shed enemy blood while contributing to the defense of a besieged place was to be excommunicated for two years and excluded from advancement in the ecclesiastical hierarhcy.
172. Macon, Canon 5, *MGH, Legum*, III, i (*Concilia aevi Merovingici*), 156, which prohibited clerics from bearing arms.
173. Toledo (Fourth Council), Canon 45, Hefelé, *Histoire*, III, i, 273.
174. *MGH, Legum*, III, i, 215.
175. St. Jean de Losne, Canon 2, *MGH, Legum*, III, i, 218.
176. *MGH, Epistolae*, III (*Epistolae Merovingici et Karolini Aevi*, I), 229.
177. *Ibid.*, 303.
178. Germanic Council (742), Canon 2, *MGH, Capitularia Regum Francorum*, I, 25: *MGH, Legum*, III, ii, 3.
179. *MGH, Legum*, III, ii, 7.
180. Mainz, Canon 17, *MGH, Legum*, III, ii, 266. To compensate for their loss of temporal weapons, clerics could at times take up these "spiritual" or intellectual weapons in a very literal sense. Thus in 833, when the troops of Lothair, accompanied by Pope Gregory IV, were advancing against Emperor Louis the Pious, Archbishop Agobard of Lyon wrote to the emperor, whose sincere partisan he was, that the priests should bring their intercessory support and spiritual resources to the laity who would be fighting with temporal arms. Whereas the one order must fight with swords, "the others contend with words so that like may be opposed with like" (*MGH*, V [*Annales, chronica et gesta aevi Salici*], 226). For other examples of the numerous prohibitions of clergy bearing arms, see the Councils of Meaux (845) and of Paris (846) (*MGH, Capitularia*, II, 407) or the Council of Tribur (895) (*ibid.*, 248).
181. *MGH, Epistolae*, VII (*Epistolae Karolini aevi*, V), 311.
182. Hildesheimer, "Les Clercs et l'exemption," 18.
183. Eusebius, *HE*, X, 7; *Cod. Theod.* XVI, 2.
184. Charlemagne, *Admonitio generalis*, canon 70, *MGH, Capitularia*, I, 59.
185. Epernay, Canon 10, *MGH, Capitularia*, II, 262.
186. Bainton ("The Early Church and War," 82) rightly called attention to this function of monastic life as an alternative to military service. The radical distinction between two entirely different types of Christians—clerics and monks on the one hand, and laymen on the other—was already present in the *Decretum* of Gratian (Part II, Causa XII, 9, 1, cvii). It is symptomatic that an entire paragraph of Jerome's letter to the monk Heliodorus (*Ep.*, 14, 2), which has been viewed as a kind of charter of Occidental monasticism, should have limited the *Militia Christi* to monasticism, which it contrasted in classical fashion to the *Militia Mundi*.
187. John Chrysostom, *Homilies on Ephesians*, 6, 4.
188. *Idem, Homilies on St. Matthew*, 69, 4.
189. Bouyer, *Spiritualité*, 371.
190. Vacandard, "La Question," 168.
191. Augustine, *Ep.*, 189, 4-5.
192. *Ibid.*, 220, 3.
193. See above, pp. 145-146.
194. *DDC*, I (1935), col. 1047; III (1942), cols. 868-869; L. Viollet, "L'Objection de Conscience," *L'Ami du Clergé*, 60 (1950), 376; A. de Soras, "Le Problème de l'Objection de Conscience," *Revue de l'Action populaire*, 36 (1950), 241.

195. Synesios even stated that he wanted to have "many fine children" by her.
196. Synesios, *Ep.*, 105 (transl. C. Lacombrade, *Synésios de Cyrène, Hellène et chrétien* [Paris, 1951], 220-223). Lacombrade contended (*ibid.*, 224-227) that Synesios eventually relinquished his archbishopric; but he certainly remained an impenitent neo-Platonist (*ibid.*, 264-265). Despite Lacombrade's censure of U. von Willamowitz-Moellendorff ("Die Hymnen des Proklos und Synesios," *SAB*, 14 [1907], 272-295) for oversimplifying matters, it is hard to see that the latter's basic thesis has really gone astray.
197. Synesios must have felt quite in his element afterwards among the clergy of Africa, where the priests, upon coming out after Mass, would form irregular bands with their parishioners and stone to death any prowlers who fell into their hands (Synesios, *Ep.*, 122).
198. Synesios, *Discourse*, 9.
199. *Ibid.*, 23.
200. *Ibid.*, 25.
201. On the meaning of this speech, see E. Demougeot, *La Théorie du Pouvoir impérial au Début du Ve Siècle*, Mélanges de la Societé toulousaine d'Etudes classiques, I (Toulouse, 1946), 205. Begin reading at line 20, and only return to the top of the page afterwards.
202. Synesios, *Catastasis*, 2. This is but one example of the general development which Hobhouse (*Church and the World*, 110) tersely described: "More and more the emperor becomes the head of the Church on earth, and more and more the bishops approximate to the position of civil administrators."
203. Synesios, *Ep.*, 78.
204. *Ibid.*, 57-58.
205. *Ibid.*, 90.
206. *Ibid.*, 121.
207. K. Treu, *Synesios von Kyrene, Ein Kommentar zu seinem "Dion,"* TU, LXXI (Berlin, 1958), 26.
208. Daniélou, *Les Anges*, 176-177. Daniélou then proceeded to assert that although internationalism had had its Christian expression in the Holy Roman Empire, in its modern guise—a secularized, post-Christian version of the Eusebian conception of a Christian empire—it had become a demonic temptation which would lead to the kingdom of the Antichrist. My own ethical position—virtually point by point—would be exactly the opposite. But then when two men—one of them now [1970] to be found on the conservative fringe of the group of French cardinals, and the other for many years a militant member of a revolutionary party—pass from the establishment of facts to the making of judgments of value and meaning, differences are inevitable.
209. Daniélou, "La Non-Violence," 26.
210. R. de Pury (*La Maison de Dieu*, Cahiers théologiques, XIV [Neuchâtel, 1946], 32-33) has splendidly denounced the self-deceit whereby the Church has believed that it has been serving its Master when it has reigned over "spiritual" spheres but has relinquished the proclamation of God's will in and for the world.
211. Daniélou, "La Non-Violence," 28.
212. An anonymous reviewer of the French original of this book ("P.M.," in *La Feuille d'Avis de Lausanne*, November 15, 1960) stated, in words diametrically opposite to those of Daniélou, that "The Christian vocation is always, as this historical study reminds us, a vocation to sanctity. Hornus tells this to us again through the Christian authors of the first centuries."
213. J. Daniélou, *Prayer as a Political Problem*, transl. J. R. Kirwan (London, 1967).

214. Cf. my review in *CS*, 74 (1966), 666-668. The book is full of interesting insights, but I disagree with its basic presuppositions.

215. Moreau, *La Persécution*, 77; Homo, *Les Empereurs*, 29. Homo was not afraid of paradox, as can be seen in his contrasting of the "fanatical" Christians "who, should occasion arise, refused military service" with "pacific" Christians who accepted it.

216. Jerome, *Vita Malchi*, init.

217. Milburn *(Early Christian Interpretations,* 70) rightly quoted the above passage from Jerome to contrast it with Eusebius's oversimplified and unscrupulous attitude.

Chapter 6

1. Lactantius, *De Mort. Pers.*, 54; Eusebius, *Vita*, I, 28.

2. On this veneration, see F. Halkin, "Une Nouvelle Vie de Constantin dans un Légendaire de Patmos," *AB*, 77 (1959), 63-107, 370-372, and the old but still basic study of F. Nève, "Constantin et Théodose devant les église orientales," in his *L'Arménie chrétienne et sa littérature* (Paris, 1886), 155-191.

3. A summary of the discussion (with bibliography) can be found in A. Piganiol, "L'Etat actuel de la Question constantinienne, 1930-1949," *Historia*, 1 (1950), 82-96. See also E. Delaruelle, "La Conversion de Constantin," *BLE*, 54 (1953), 37-54, 84-100; and J.-R. Palanque, "Constantin Iᵉʳ le Grand," *DHGE*, XIII (1956), col. 607.

4. A. Alföldi, *The Conversion of Constantine and Pagan Rome* (Oxford, 1948). H. Berkhof *(Kirche und Kaiser* [Zürich, 1947], 60 ff.) evidenced the same admiration of Constantine, as did K. Aland ("Die religiöse Haltung Kaiser Konstantins," *SP*, 1 [Berlin, 1957], 549-600). The latter (p. 575) even rejected the modest reservations about Constantine of H. Lietzmann ("Der Glaube Konstantins des Grossen," *SAB*, 29 [1937], 274). H. Dörries *(Constantine, passim)* also believed in the sincerity, if not the depth, of Constantine's religious development. R. A. G. Carson ("The Emperor Constantine and Christianity," *History Today*, 6 [1956], 20) was convinced that "despite many of his actions, the consensus of evidence indicates a genuine personal acceptance of Christianity by Constantine."

5. On the positive contribution made by Grégoire and his school, see P. Orgels, "A propos des erreurs historiques de la *Vita Constantini*," *Mélanges H. Grégoire, Revue Internationale de Philosophie* (Brussels, 1963), 575-576. Most of the disagreement between the contending parties depends on whether one believes, with the classical school, that Eusebius, *Vita*, 2, 5-17, alludes solely to the 324 war, or whether one follows Grégoire in thinking that it refers both to that war and to the war of 314 together. Orgels (pp. 592, 600, 612) was of the latter opinion, basing his conclusion on a comparison between *Vita*, 2, 11 and Zosimus, *Ecclesiastical History*, 2, 19, 1. The transition between the first war and the second would thus be in *Vita* 2, 15. See also H. Grégoire, "Nouvelles Recherches constantiniennes," *Byz*, 13 (1938), 566.

6. P. Petit, "Libanius et la 'Vita Constantini,' " *Historia*, 1 (1950), 578-579.

7. H. Grégoire, "Notes bibliographiques," *BARB*, 34 (1947), 229.

8. *Cod. Theod.*, V, 20, 1.

9. H. Ehrhardt, "Some Aspects of Constantine's Legislation," *SP*, 2 (Berlin, 1957), 114-121.

10. H. Grégoire, "La 'Conversion' de Constantin," *Revue de l'Université de Bruxelles*, 36 (1930-1931), 255.

11. *Idem*, "Nouvelles Recherches," 561; *idem*, "L'Authenticité et l'historicité de la 'Vita Constantini' attribuée à Eusèbe de Césarée," *BARB*, 39 (1953), 426-478.

12. Setton, *Christian Attitude,* 51-53; F. Vittinghoff, "Eusebius als Verfasser der *Vita Constantini,*" *RhM,* 96 (1953), 330-373. J. Moreau ("Eusèbe de Césarée," *DHGE,* XV [1963], col. 1456) has also concluded for Eusebian authorship. For persuasive arguments in favor of the substantial authenticity of the *Vita,* see A. H. M. Jones, "Notes on the Genuineness of the Constantinian Documents in Eusebius' 'Life of Constantine,' " *JEH,* 5 (1954), 196-200. P. Petit "Libanius et la 'Vita Constantini,' " 580-581), on the other hand, has provided a good summary of the critical view. One must note that Petit merely stressed that the author could not have been Eusebius in person. But he argued that the *Vita* was most probably composed before 340 by someone who had been closely connected with Eusebius, who had access to his files, and who shared his political views. Grégoire ("Nouvelles recherches," 583) proposed as a simple hypothesis that Euzoios, the Arian bishop of Caesarea who inherited Eusebius's library, was the author. It was not Eusebius himself, Grégoire contended, but rather this "second Eusebius" who made Licinius's persecution of the Christians into the cause of the wars of 314 and 324, and who referred to the celestial vision as well as to the *Labarum (ibid.,* 578). Petit ("Libanius et la 'Vita Constantini,' " 581) was of the opinion that the additions to books 3 and 4, which were made during the reign of Theodosius, simply made Constantine to appear to be more fanatically opposed to paganism than he actually had been. Grégoire ("L'Authenticité," 467-470), on the other hand, was far more radical, basing his view on "objective evidence" that before 420 none of the sources currently extant contained a single quotation from the *Vita* or showed any discernible influence of it. He nevertheless admitted that both the style and the fundamental ideology of the *Vita* are clearly Eusebian.

13. But, as A. Brasseur ("Les deux visions de Constantin," *Latomus,* 5 [1946], 35-40) has pointed out, Constantine's vision was merely an unimportant pagan dream which gave a rallying sign to the army.

14. On the latter see *Panegyric,* 7, 21, with E. Galletier's comments (Galletier, ed., *Panégyriques latins,* II, *Les Panégyriques constantiniens* [Paris, 1959], 43-46).

15. J. Gagé ("Le 'Signum' astrologique de Constantin et le Millénarisme de 'Roma aeterna,' " *RHPR,* 31 [1951], 181-223) has referred to, and corrected, an observation by F. Heiland *(Die astronomische Deutung der Vision Konstantins* [Lecture, Zeiss Planetarium, Jena, October, 1948]).

16. Carson, "The Emperor Constantine," 14-16. On this point, see the exhaustive documentation in M. R. Alföldi, *Die Constantinische Goldprägung* (Mainz, 1963). Alföldi's no. 118 (reproduced in plate 5, no. 60) is the famous coin of 313 with the triumphal entry into Rome and the text "FELIX ADVENTVS AVGG NN" on the one side; on the other side is Constantine's head in profile with the symbol of the divine sun behind him. (This coin has been reproduced and described with an analysis of its significance in Grégoire, "Nouvelles recherches," 579.) The same image is found in coins produced in the periods of 313-317 (Alföldi, nos. 479, 480, 483, 489, 492 [plate 7, no. 105]), 314-315 (nos. 491, 495), 317 (no. 486 [plate 7, no. 106]), 317-324 (nos. 481, 490 [plate 8, no. 126], 493 [plate 8, no. 125], 494 [plate 7, no. 120]), even 324-326 (no. 482). See also S. P. Kyriakides, "Kōnstantinos ho Megas kai hē autokratikē latreia", *Hellēnika,* XVII, 220-240. The important book by Jules Maurice *(Numismatique constantinienne,* 3 vols. [Paris, 1908-1912], II, xxix-xxx) provides significant information about Constantine as an apostle of the monotheistic solar cult. See also Maurice's *Constantin le Grand, L'origine de la civilisation chrétienne* (Paris, 1924), 28. But Maurice still believed that Constantine had experienced a complete Christian conversion at the Milvian Bridge. The later ambiguities he explained by the fact that with Constantine a truly Christian monarchy had taken over an empire that was still predominantly pagan. Constantine was thus like "a very Christian King of

France, governing a Muslim empire" *(Constantin, 68)*. But on the other hand, Maurice was also able to point out that as early as 313 the Tarragona mint in Spain was using the cross on the back of its coins at the same time as it was casting medals with the solar sign to commemorate the Milan meeting *(Numismatique,* II, 339). This would seem to prove that Constantine's syncretism worked in both directions and that some imperial officials soon understood this.

17. Maurice, *Constantin,* 99. Grégoire ("L'Authenticité," 465, and "Nouvelles recherches," 57) also made much of the triumphal arch with purely pagan decorative motifs which was erected in 315.

18. Delaruelle, "Conversion," 95.

19. F. Altheim, "Konstantins Triumph von 312," *Zeitschrift für Religion und Geistesgeschichte,* 9 (1957), 221-231; Gagé, "La Victoire," 386; *idem,* "Le 'Signum,' " 210; Galletier, *Panégyriques latins,* II, 112-115.

20. Gagé, "Le 'Signum,' " 209. J. R. Palanque *(DHGE,* XIII, col. 597) has also noted that initially at least Constantine's Christianity was thoroughly permeated by astrology.

21. J. Moreau, "Zur Religionspolitik Konstantins des Grossen," *AUS,* 1 (1952), 165, 168.

22. Combès, *Doctrine politique,* 304, 313.

23. Galletier, *Panégyriques latins,* II, 3, 20.

24. Maurice, *Constantin,* 22.

25. V. C. de Clercq, *Ossius of Cordova: a Contribution to the History of the Constantinian Period* (Washington, 1954), 184. It was Constantine as well who had started the war of 312 *(Panégyriques,* 9, 2).

26. A Piganiol, *L'Empire chrétien, 325-395* (Paris, 1947), 35-36. Foakes-Jackson *(Eusebius Pamphili,* 103) agreed that something terrible must have happened, but he advised against pressing details too far since they have reached us only through historians who were hostile to Constantine (Ammianus Marcellinus, *Roman History,* XIV, 11, 20; Philostorgos, *Ecclesiastical History,* 2, 4; Victor, *Epitome;* Flavius Eutropius, *Breviarium,* 10, 6; Zosimus, *Ecclesiastical History,* 2, 29). But can one cast this suspicion of prejudice against all of these sources? And what about the observer who was certainly not a prejudiced pagan—the anonymous author of the *Vita Sancti Artemii* (41, ASS, October, VIII [1853], 856)? Similar testimony is also to be found in Jerome, Orosius, Sidoine Apollinaire, and Gregory of Tours. On this bloody tale see also Maurice, *Constantin,* 22, 93, 182-190. Carson ("The Emperor Constantine," 18) has provided a detailed description of this incident, and has concluded that "these murders are often quoted as evidence of Constantine's insincere Christianity; but although they were not the acts of one who truly embraces Christ's teaching, they are unfortunately not unparalleled in acts of many who are accepted as genuine professing Christians." To this I would simply like to add that acts of this nature have certainly never been acceptable except within "Constantinian" Christianity. Carson's reasoning is therefore circular, and is yet another example of the way in which the gospel of Jesus Christ has been corrupted by the Constantinian concordat.

27. L. Duchesne, *Liber pontificalis* (Paris, 1886), I, cix-cxx, which text dates from about 500.

28. Herval, "La Province," 52.

29. Grégoire, "Notes bibliographiques," 230.

30. A. Alföldi, *A Festival of Isis in Rome under the Christian Emperors of the IVth Century,* Dissertationes Pannonicae, 2nd ser., 7 (Budapest, 1937), 36-37.

31. Parker, *Christianity and the State,* 50, citing Augustine, *Confessions,* I, 2.

32. Zosimus, *Ecclesiastical History,* 2, 2. A. Piganiol *(L'Empereur Constantin*

[Paris, 1932], 80) suggested that Ossius of Cordova was the proponent of this argument.

33. Socrates Scholasticus, *Ecclesiastical History*, 1, 39.
34. Philostorgos, *Ecclesiastical History*, 2, 16; Piganiol, *L'Empereur Constantin*, 215.
35. Julian the Apostate, *The Caesars*, 2, 336b; *idem, To the Athenians*, 3, 270c.
36. Parker, *Christianity and the State*, 46, 49.
37. Gagé, "La Victoire," 379.
38. Parker, *Christianity and the State*, 47, 48. Cf. M. Besnier, *L'Empire romain de l'Avènement des Sévères au Concile de Nicée* (Paris, 1937), 358.
39. Grégoire, "La 'Conversion' de Constantin," 234, 265.
40. *Ibid.*, 242-243.
41. Gagé, "La Victoire," 388-389; *idem*, "Le 'Signum,' " 181, 185, 206; Galletier, *Panégyriques latins*, II, 112-115.
42. Orgels, "A propos des erreurs historiques," 584-585.
43. Grégoire, "Nouvelles recherches," 588.
44. Gagé, "Le 'Signum,' " 198-199, 213.
45. Galletier, *Panégyriques latins*, II, 155-157. Jules Maurice, who was one of Constantine's most convinced admirers, listed among his hero's significant achievements "the sign of Christ attributed to the army, as legionary insignia" (*Constantin*, 49). Whether this was an achievement or a betrayal remains an open question.
46. Stauffer, *Christ and the Caesars*, 219, 271.
47. De Clercq, *Ossius of Cordova*, 148, 175, 158-160.
48. Piganiol, *L'Empire chrétien*, 293.
49. Eusebius, *Praep. ev.*, 6, 1; *idem, Demonstratio evangelica*, II, 2.
50. On this theological degeneration within Eusebius's thought, see H. Eger, "Kaiser und Kirche in der Geschichtstheologie Eusebs von Cäsarea," *ZNW*, 38 (1938), 97-115; N. H. Baynes, "Eusebius and the Christian Empire," in *idem*, ed., *Byzantine Studies* (London, 1955), 168-172; E. Peterson, "Das Problem des Nationalismus im alten Christentum," *ThZ*, 7 (1951), 81-91 (reprinted in a French transl. in *Dieu Vivant*, 22 (1952), 88-106, and as an appendix to Daniélou, *Les Anges*, 153-169); F. E. Cranz, "Kingdom and Polity in Eusebius of Caesarea," *HThR*, 45 (1952), 47-66.
51. Epiphanius, *Panarion*, 68, 8; Athanasius, *Apologia*, 8.
52. Moreau, "Eusèbe," col. 1440. Hefelé (*Histoire*, I, ii, 642 n.) has placed primary emphasis upon the fact that Eusebius was unable clearly to take sides.
53. See the excellent article on Eusebius of Nicomedia by M. Spanneut (*DHGE*, XV [1963], cols. 1466-1472). Eusebius (of Caesarea) had at first enjoyed a close relationship with Constantine's sister Constantia, and as such was one of Licinius's intimates.
54. The oft-repeated statement that it was Eusebius who made the speech which welcomed Constantine to the council (Eusebius, *Vita Const.*, I, preface; III, 11; Sozomen, *Ecclesiastical History*, I, 19; J. B. Lightfoot, "Eusebius of Caesarea," *DCB*, II, col. 312) is not in accord with the facts. Instead, this detail was added to the texts at a later date, by which time the two Eusebii had been able to win the emperor's confidence and to reverse the situation to their advantage. This is a good example of the rewriting of history which was common in Eusebius's circle. The actual speaker was probably Eustathius of Antioch (Moreau, "Eusèbe," cols. 1440-1441).
55. Theodoret, *Ecclesiastical History*, I, 20, 1.
56. Grégoire, "L'Authenticité," 471. See also Moreau, "Eusèbe," col. 1443, which emphasized that Eusebius had fully shared in this pliant doctrine.

57. Setton, *Christian Attitude*, 42.

58. The expressions between quotation marks are those of Orgels ("A propos des erreurs historiques," 586), who noted that the *Labarum* was created on precisely that occasion. Orgels also emphasized (p. 588), on the basis of Eusebius, *HE, X*, 8, 16, that what have been termed the Licinian persecutions were only police precautions against the "fifth column" which his rival was organizing.

59. Orgels, *op. cit.*, 584; Grégoire, "Nouvelles recherches," 559-560.

60. Grégoire, "L'Authenticité," 464. This does not mean that Licinius—who murdered in cold blood the two Christian princesses Valeria and Prisca, the widow and daughter of Diocletian—was any less cruel than Constantine (*idem*, "Nouvelles recherches," 565).

61. Sirinelli, 488.

62. *Ibid.*, 493, 253, 409. Sirinelli added that for this reason Eusebius had not imagined that the Church itself might colonize and organize the state according to its own principles. In this, his attitude was similar to that of Lactantius (*Ibid.*, 495). Sirinelli also pronounced the following severe judgment (*Ibid.*, 490): "[In Eusebius's writings] the stress was no longer on the Christian faith and on the hopes, new insights, and uniqueness which it implied; but it was rather on the perfect coincidence which existed between the teaching of Christian doctrine and the universe as it stood. . . . The question was not so much to demonstrate the new ideas which Christianity brought with it, but rather [to show] that Christianity did not introduce anything particularly new which would call for the renunciation of ideas which were commonly held."

63. Pichon, *Lactance*, 450.

64. I have already pointed out (Ch. 1, n. 115) that Eusebius, after Licinius's downfall, "corrected" history in order to erase most of his initial estimates of him—which had been highly positive. Grégoire ("Nouvelles recherches," 563) dated the three "editions" of the *Ecclesiastical History* as follows: 1st ed., 314-315; 2nd ed., 325; 3rd ed., after 326. On this point see also J. Vogt, "Die Vita Constantini des Eusebius über den Konflikt zwischen Constantin und Licinius," *Historia, 2* (1953-1954), 463-471.

65. Sirinelli, 410. Since the Roman Empire was the worldly system within which the Christians must live, there was "a somewhat organic unity between empire and Church" (*ibid.*, 485).

66. *Ibid.*, 483.

67. *Ibid.*, 257-258.

68. *Ibid.*, 287.

69. *Ibid.*, 253, 491.

70. *Ibid.*, 211, 494. As Sirinelli elsewhere observed (*ibid.*, 472 n.), Eusebius was "basically the holder of a natural, rational religion in which there was more room for values of organization and edification than for those of devotion, self-sacrifice, and redemption."

71. *Ibid.*, 244, 203, 240-243.

72. *Ibid.*, 238.

73. *Ibid.*, 163.

74. J.-R. Palanque, "Constantin, Empereur chrétien," 142. See also Palanque's treatment of "The Conversion of Constantine" in Palanque, Bardy, *et al.*, *The Church in the Roman Empire*, 12-24, and his article "Constantin Iᵉʳ le Grand," in *DHGE*, XIII (1956), cols. 593-608, in which he wrote (col. 599): "Doubtless motivated by superstitious reasons (he [Constantine] had *gambled* on the protection of the God of the Christians, to whom he attributed his unexpected victory over Maxentius),

his 'conversion' was never a complete one." In a similar vein, G. Downey ("Education in the Christian Roman Empire: Christian and Pagan Theories under Constantine and his Successors," *Speculum,* 32 [1957], 50) wrote: "Some students believe that Constantine experienced a true conversion and that his policy toward Christianity was based upon genuine religious conviction, while others maintain that he was a calculating statesman who concluded that Christianity offered a means of uniting the empire and saving it from the political, military, and economic dangers with which his predecessor Diocletian had been struggling . . . . It seems beyond question that there was some feeling of a *quid pro quo* in the early stages of Constantine's connection with Christianity, a feeling which is certainly visible among the Christians of the period." To be complete, we must also mention Albert Florès, "La Conversion de Constantin le Grand," Mémoire de diplôme de l'Ecole pratique des Hautes Etudes [mimeographed ed.] (Paris, 1949), which presents a moderate, rather conservative view; it was, however, already out of date at the time of its publication.

75. Greenslade, *Church and State,* 12.
76. De Clercq, *Ossius of Cordova,* 159.
77. Parker, *Christianity and the State,* 52.
78. Foakes-Jackson, *Eusebius Pamphili,* 108.
79. Hobhouse, *Church and the World,* 88-89.
80. Hefelé, I, ii, 679. See the out-of-date but thorough bibliographies on various Constantinian questions in *ibid.,* I, ii, 680-681. H. Leclercq (*DAL,* I, col. 2818)has even questioned the objective validity of Constantine's baptism.
81. F. Laufer, "O triunfo da Cruz no tempo de Constantino," *Estudios* [Brazil], 19, no. 73 (1959), 81-95.
82. Greenslade, *Church and State,* 16-18. Constantine summoned the Synod of Arles (Eusebius, *HE,* X, 5, 23-24) and the Council of Nicaea (P.-T. Camelot, "Les conciles oecuméniques des IV$^{\overline{e}}$ et V.$^{e\,|}$siècles," in *Le Concile et les conciles* [Paris, 1960], 49 ff., which was based on Eusebius, *Vita Const.,* III, 6, p. 79, on the synodic letter to the Egyptians quoted by Athanasius [Socrates Scholasticus, *Ecclesiastical History,* I, 9], and on the letter written by Constantine to the Church of Alexandria in which he claimed to have acted under "divine inspiration" [*ibid.,* col. 87]). At Nicaea it was Constantine who made the introductory speech (Eusebius, *Vita Const.,* III, 13) and imposed the *homoousios* (letter, Eusebius to his flock, q. Socrates Scholasticus, *Ecclesiastical History,* I, 8, col. 72; Opitz, *Athanasius Werke,* III, i, 43-44). At Chalcedon the situation was apparently still the same: "It does seem, as a matter of fact, that it was the emperor who presided and arbitrated at the discussions, and the bishops seem also to have found this quite natural" (Camelot, "Les Conciles," 58). The emperor Marcianus, however, who drew a parallel between the late Constantine and himself, seems in fact to have been far more respectful of Church authority than Constantine had been (Actio [VI] Concilii Chalcedonensis, in *ACO,* II, ii [Berlin-Leipzig, 1933], 140). Furthermore, a new factor at the time of Chalcedon—according to Camelot—was the development of increased authority on the part of the Roman pope.
83. F. Dvornik, "The Authority of the State in the Oecumenical Council," *The Christian East,* 14 (1934), 95-107.
84. Eusebius, *Vita Const.,* IV, 24. See the useful bibliography in Y. Congar, *After Nine Hundred Years* (New York, 1959), 105.
85. A. Piganiol, *L'Empire chrétien,* 61.
86. J. Straub, "Kaiser Konstantin als ἐπίσκοπος τῶν ἐκτός," *SP,* 1 (Berlin, 1957), 678-695.

87. Greenslade, *Church and State*, 11; H. Kraft, " διοούσιος ," *ZKG*, 66 (1955), 1-24; *idem*, "Kaiser Konstantin und das Bischofsamt," *Saeculum*, 8 (1957), 32-42.

88. G. Ostrogorsky, *History of the Byzantine State*, transl. J. Hussey (Oxford, 1956, 42-44.

89. This can already be seen in Donatism.

90. Palanque, "Constantin," *DHGE*, XIII (1956), col. 599.

91. E. Laboulaye, *Journal des débats*, October 2, 1860. It goes without saying that Laboulaye was in agreement with our condemnation. He therefore put these words into the mouths of those whom he singled out as the people who were really responsible for the alienation of so many people from the Christian faith.

Chapter 7 (Conclusion)

1. Marcellinus to Augustine, in Augustine, *Ep.*, 136, 2.

2. Bainton ("The Early Church and War," 90) has contrasted the Christian view of peace as a dynamic reality with the Roman view in which peace was static and contractual.

3. Barnabas, *Ep.*, 11, 8.

4. [See the recent and exhaustive study by M. Spanneut ("Geduld," *RACh*, IX [Stuttgart, 1976], cols. 243-294), which has convincingly demonstrated that—for the early Christians—patience involved both strength and power; and also that—for the early monks—patience, when intertwined with the hope of the kingdom, was a cardinal virtue.]

5. P. Fabre, *Saint Paulin de Nole et l'Amitié chrétienne* (Paris, 1949), 116.

6. For examples, see *Didache*, 1, 2-4; 2, 6-7; 3, 2; Clement of Rome, *Letter*, 13, 1; 19; 30, 3 and 8; Ignatius, *Eph.*, 10, 1-3; 13, 2; *idem*, *Pol.*, 1, 2; *idem*, *Tral.*, 3, 2; 4, 2; Polycarp, *Ep.*, 2, 2; 10, 2; Hermas, *Precepts*, V, 1, 1 and 5; 2, 3; 8; Tatian, *Oratio*, 19; Aristides, *Apology*, 15; Justin, *First Apology*, 11, 2; 14, 3; 15, 9; 16, 1-4; *Acta Apollonii*, 37; Athenagoras, *Legatio*, 1; 11; 34; Irenaeus, *Demonstration*, 96; *idem*, *Adv. Haeres.*, III, 18, 5-6; IV, 13, 3; Clement of Alexandria, *Stromata*, II, 1, 2; *idem*, *Qui Dives Salvetur?*, 42, 1-15; *Passio Scillitanorum*, 2 and 7.

7. Tertullian, *De Corona*, 11.

8. *Idem, Apol.*, 37, 5.

9. *Ibid.*, 6, 7.

10. *Idem, Ad Scapulam*, 5.

11. *Idem, De Patientia*, 1.

12. *Ibid.*, 10.

13. *Ibid.*, 6-7; 15.

14. Origen, *Contra Celsum*, III, 7.

15. *Ibid.*, III, 8. In his edition of the *Contra Celsum* ([Cambridge, 1953], 512), Henry Chadwick has suggested that these lines, which in the present state of the text are separated from the preceding passage by approximately a page, in the original followed it directly; he has also speculated that the gap was caused by the accidental turning over of a page in the course of binding. I concur with these hypotheses.

16. Origen, *Contra Celsum*, IV, 9.

17. *Ibid.*, VII, 26, 27. The last words, which are a quotation from Exodus 1:7, emphasize that the old Israel had made way for the new.

18. *Ibid.*, VIII, 65.

19. Minucius Felix, *Octavius*, 30, 6.

20. Cyprian, *Ad Dem.*, 17, 25. See also his *Testimonia*, III, 3, 8, 22, 23, 49, 106. For similar passages from the period between Tertullian and Lactantius, see *Di-*

dascalia, I, 2, 1 and 2; II, 6, 1; II, 45, 1; II, 46, 2; V, 14, 22; Gregory the Wonder-Worker, *Canonical Epistle*, 5; *Passio Montani*, 10, 5; Arnobius, *Adv. Nat.*, 2, 45.

21. Lactantius, *Div. Institutiones*, VI, 18, 10-20.
22. *Ibid.*, VI, 18, 25.
23. *Ibid.*, VI, 18, 29-32. Other Lactantius texts with a similar argument are: *De Ira Dei*, 20, 5 and 12; 21, 10; *Div. Institutiones*, V, 4-5, and 13-14; V, 8, 6.
24. Ambrose, *Ep.*, 20. See A. de Broglie, *Saint Ambroise*, 85.
25. Augustine, *De Patientia*, 2. See also *ibid.*, 1, 7 (6-7); 26 (22); 29 (26). See also Athanasius, *Letter on Love and Temperance*, p. 284; Basil, *Homilies on the Psalms*, 48; John Chrysostom, *Letters to Olympias*, XIII, 4d; *idem*, *Homilies on St. John*, 82, 2; *idem*, *Homilies on Romans*, 14, 7.
26. Fontaine, "Sulpice Sévère," 37, 38 n.
27. Amélineau, *Actes*, 32-34.
28. Sulpicius Severus, *Dialogues*, II, 3.
29. Hershberger's *The Way of the Cross in Human Relations* is a remarkable meditation on this problem. See esp. pp. 33-42, in which he—closely following Bonhoeffer—has shown that the cross must permeate the Christian's entire life.
30. P. Burgelin ("La Fin de l'Ere constantinienne," *Foi et Vie*, 58 [1959], 16-17), in the course of a discussion of the Christian's political behavior, has strongly and rightly emphasized that the Church's primary concern must consist of refusing to allow itself to be split at this level.
31. Clement of Rome, *Ep.*, 13, 3 ff.
32. Bainton, "Early Church and War," 86-87; Ryan, "Rejection," 15. A passage in the *VSB* (VIII [1950], 550) commented, with reference to SS. Ferreolus and Julian of Brioude, "Today their functions would be regarded as belonging more to the police than to the army." *VSB* (IX [1950], 380) added that Ferreolus's functions as a military tribune were "practically the same as those of a police inspector." Perhaps this is also the direction in which we should look for a solution to the chronological contradiction in St. Martin's life. About 336, two years after he was baptized, he transferred into a unit of the *protectores*—the nonfighting imperial police—and he stayed with them for twenty years (Fontaine, "Sulpice Sévère," 54 n.). From 334 to 336 Martin would thus have been a "soldier in name only" (Sulpicius Severus, *Vita Martini*, 3, 6; *SCH*, CXXXIII, 258). And thereafter he would no longer have been a soldier at all, for he had become a policeman (who in French is still called a "*gardien de la paix*").
33. For a discussion of the differentiation between the police and the army, which to me is ethically essential, see my paper "Dieu et la Guerre dans la Théologie de Karl Barth," *CS*, 63 (1955), 580-590.
34. The word *socius* is used, but apparently in a very broad sense.
35. Ambrose, *De Off.*, I, 36, 178.
36. Bayet, *Pacifisme*, 133. For the basis of this judgment, see above, p. 264.
37. P. Ricoeur (*Etat et Violence* [Geneva, 1957], 13-14) vigorously stressed the contrast between war and the "violence" used by magistrates. I have not quoted these passages, because they are required reading for everyone. Ricoeur did not, however, feel that this was a completely satisfactory solution to the problem, for there was still the question of the survival of the state as such. Daniélou ("La Non-Violence," 17) believed that, within the Palestinian circles closest to Jesus, the distinction was commonly drawn between the legitimate use of arms against brigands and the illegitimate use of arms for national or political struggles.
38. Cf. Chenu, "L'Evolution," 81, 87-90. Also worth consulting is Stephen Neill, *A History of Christian Missions* (London, 1964), 115, which quotes the negative judgment of Sir Steven Runciman (*A History of the Crusades* [Cambridge, 1952-1954],

III, 469, 480). See also my own article "L'Imposture des Croisades," *Communio Viatorum*, 6 (1963), 143-166. M. Villey himself concluded his review (*RHDF*, 40 [1962], 268) by remarking: "We must indeed distinguish between the Holy War, for which credentials cannot easily be found in the first Christian tradition, and the war waged by Caesar. There is no evidence that the average Christian of the first three centuries would have called for conscientious objection in opposition to this [latter form of warfare]."

39. This was a complete contradiction, for the central idea of monachism was that some people, far from the compromises of the world, should be able to live a perfect life and thereby compensate for the sins which the ordinary Christians—involved as they were in the complexities of daily life—could not help committing. Protestant theology, as I have noted, has rejected this system in principle. But it became doubly scandalous when the very people who pretended to keep their hands clean began plunging them into the blood of their brethren—apparently with a clear conscience. It is therefore not surprising that serious objections were raised when the military monastic orders were first founded. In the recently rediscovered letter *Ad milites templi*, the writer (probably Hugues of Payns, the founder of the Templars) found it necessary to react strongly against the doubts which were assailing his recruits on this point (J. Leclercq, "Un document sur les débuts des Templiers," *RHE*, 52 [1957], 86-89).

40. Orentius of Auch, *Commonitorium*, II, 181-184 (quoted in P. de Labriolle, *Histoire de la Littérature Latine Chrétienne*, ed. G. Bardy [Paris, 1947], II, 723-724).

41. Jerome, *Ep.*, 127, 12. See also *Ep.*, 126, 2 and 128, 4, all three of which are quoted in Labriolle, *Histoire*, I, 585.

42. Jerome, *Ep.*, 60, 15-16, 18.

43. *Ibid.*, 60, 16.

44. The first to use this expression in this sense was Frédéric Ozanam, in an 1848 issue of the *Correspondant* (Fliche et Martin, XXI, 42).

45. This was acknowledged unambiguously by H. I. Marrou (*SCH*, XXXIII, 176), to cite only one example. See also Burgelin, "La Fin de l'Ere constantinienne," 19-20. It is interesting to note that the Hesychasts, who in the fourteenth century were the largest school of mystics in the Greek Orthodox Church, were accused of national betrayal because they refused to identify Christian truth with the interests of the Byzantine Empire. Gregory Palamas, for example, found no difficulty in recognizing the positive aspects of the Turkish regime. The Hesychasts' humanist adversaries, on the other hand, were so dominated by the assumptions of politico-religious syncretism that they were eventually ready to sacrifice the integrity of the faith itself (J. Meyendorff, *Introduction à l'étude de Grégoire Palamas* [Paris, 1959], 158-159).

Postscript

1. As H. Rahner has done in the first part of his remarkable collection of texts, *L'Eglise et l'Etat dans le Christianisme primitif*, transl. G. Zinck (Paris, 1964), 29-38 ("Le refus opposée á l'état"), 39-47 ("L'acceptation de l'état").

2. Fontaine, "Christians and Military Service," 115. For a similar point of view, see the reviews of M. Meslin (*Archives de Sociologie des Religions*, 10 [1960], 185), R. Roques (*RHR*, 164 [1964], 241), and especially M. H. Vicaire (*RHE*, 56 [1961], 391-392), whose brief notice was not a critique—it was a summary execution. A. Dumas' complaint ("L'Eglise d'avant Constantin et la violence," *Esprit*, 29 [1961], 315), on the other hand, was that my texts "were more often thrown in than presented in an orderly manner."

3. Visser ("Christianus sum," 19). Roques (review, 241) commented that he would have preferred that the French edition's subtitle had read "the attitudes of the first Christians" rather than "the attitude of primitive Christianity."

4. Fontaine ("Christians and Military Service," 102), who had already commented upon some valuable pointers concerning the undue systematization which—in his eyes—resulted from it. M. Villey likewise remarked concerning my "passionate interest" at the beginning of his short review (*RHDF*, 40 [1962], 267). J. Daniélou also used this term in his contribution to the *Nouvelle Histoire de l'Eglise, I, Des Origines à Grégoire le Grand* (Paris, 1963), 559. But then one may be quite cool in developing a totally distorted picture and, conversely, be passionately involved in arguing a well-grounded case. Such seems to have been the view of G. Richard-Molard. In a brief review of *EL* in *Réforme* (October 15, 1960), after stressing that I had made no attempt to conceal my commitment, he maintained that "this deep feeling, far from reducing in the slightest the objectivity of the study, gives it a vigor lacking in many scientific and abstract works." I have argued elsewhere ("Christianisme et désordre établi," *CS*, 74 [1966], 666-668) that Cardinal Daniélou had his "passionate interest" too—an interest (no doubt diametrically opposed to mine) in the preservation of social conformity and of "the established order" in both politics and religion.

5. This is why I agree with Mehl and Dumas more than they seem to have thought. The former spoke ("Le Christianisme primitif") of an "ambiguity as fundamental as it is necessary in the common attitude of Christianity toward the state and its politico-military order"; the latter referred ("L'Eglise," 311) to the "constant ambiguities of a thesis [mine] which in intention claimed, on the contrary, to be purely objective." Would it be merely a play on words to say that my intention was precisely to demonstrate at least one ambiguity—that of the "Constantinian" historians in the overassurance of their clear consciences? Villey (review, 267) found in my text "many an embarrassed page and some abortive attempts to modify [my] positions." What is embarrassing in recognizing that the facts are complex? Fr. Rouquette (review, *Etudes*, 308, i [1961], 424), on the other hand, was convinced that I, as a Protestant theologian, must have been deeply troubled at having to quote from the Church Fathers as well as from the Scriptures. An excellent response to him came from the very Protestant *Fraternité Evangélique* (May 1960): "One cannot censure the author for falling into the simplifications of a fanatical pacifism. One must, on the contrary, acknowledge that he has brought us—within the limits of his discipline—a precious aid to calm reflection in the form of countless quotations from the Church Fathers. After reading this book . . . one will realize better what an anti-ecumenical sin certain Protestants commit who behave—even in the present day—as if the history of the Church had started in the sixteenth century." A similar approval of my method was expressed by P. Verseils (review, *Etudes évangéliques*, 20 [1960], 120), a spokesman of the most fundamentalist grouping within French Protestantism, who did not in the slightest degree share this book's ethical conclusions, and by P. Gagnier (review, *Bulletin du Centre protestant d'Etudes et de documentation, n.s.*, 53-54 [Aug.-Oct. 1960], 5-6), who did not share them either. Mehl, who also expressed satisfaction at the renewed interest in patristics which several of us have exemplified, explained it thus: "Admittedly, Protestantism does not accord a normative value to the Church Fathers; it subordinates their authority to that of the Scriptures, but it sees in them both an approach to the Scriptures which is profitable to the Church in all eras and a consistent attempt to incarnate the evangelical demands in the concert of history." I regret, therefore, that the journal of the French Jesuits has proved to be so ill-informed concerning what constitutes a sound reading of the Bible in its dialogue with tradition. I also wonder whether Fr. Rouquette, who has tried to confound me with

the holy wars of the Old Testament and the use of the interdict, would uphold these as moral prescriptions which current Christians ought to follow.

6. Meslin (review, 185). Hobhouse (*Church and the World*, 87) had already written, "Whatever merits Eusebius possessed as a historian ... his critical faculty deserted him in describing his hero ... and his account of Constantine is little better than a nauseous panegyric, sometimes bordering on blasphemy." Hobhouse quoted Fleury's remark that one would not go far wrong on Constantine by retaining only the ill said of him by Eusebius and the good said of him by Zosimus (chiefly, *Ecclesiastical History*, II, 28-29). But in that case, Hobhouse concluded, one would have practically nothing at all to say about the first "Christian" emperor.

7. Thus J. Newman concluded his contribution to the debate with S. Windass ("The Early Christian Attitude to War," *Irish Theological Quarterly*, n.s., 29 [1962], 248) with the following words, "The early Christian attitude to war ... is a notoriously controverted subject which it would not be profitable to pursue at length." Yet it was Newman who had trotted out all the most threadbare clichés of the traditional approach to this topic, particularly in "Modern War and Pacifism," *Irish Theological Quarterly*, n.s., 28 (1961), 187-188. Without Windass's spirited response, readers would never have been given any indication that this was in any sense a "controverted subject."

In similar fashion, Ryan began his review (*Erasmus*, 15 [1963], 453) by stating: "Whether the early Church was antimilitaristic or not is a problem which will never be solved historically." His conclusion is equally limp: "His [my] scholarly efforts have not been in vain because he has thrown much light on a problem which, however, remains unsolved, and is in fact insoluble." It thus appears that historically agnosticism is the last-ditch defense of those who for a long time professed to be certain that the Christian faith and military service had always been able to coexist happily in the same believer—and should do so in the future as well.

8. Roques, review, 242.

9. R. Aron, *Introduction à une philosophie de l'histoire* (Paris, 1938), 142.

10. *Ibid.*, 134. On the same page Aron also stated, "The historian perhaps projects his own categories into the past.... The anachronism plays a legitimate part if the action had come before the awareness of it, if the present theory illuminates a behavior which had been unconscious of it."

11. D. Guérin, *Jeunesse du socialisme libertaire* (Paris, 1959), 133-167. Guerin had previously set out his views concerning the uses and limits of anachronism in history in *La Lutte des classes sous la Première République*, 7th ed. (Paris, 1946), II, 396-399. It is to him that I owe the quotations from Aron and Monod.

12. G. Monod, "L'Histoire," in F. Thomas, ed., *De la méthode dans les sciences* (Paris, 1909), 336-337.

13. J.-M. Hornus, "Les Pères de l'Eglise et la non-violence," *Cahiers de la Réconciliation*, March 1962, 8, in which I gave two examples from very different periods of history. Here is the first: the fundamentally bourgeois and reactionary character of "Gaullism" after 1950 "became apparent far more quickly and far more clearly to those who had been the 'Gaullists of 1940' and who, having formerly exposed the Vichyist imposture, could more easily than the rest read the new version of Gaullism through the code offered them by their prior experience of having rejected Pétainism." Here is the second: "There are some of us who cannot thoroughly understand anything about the great ecumenical councils (of the first centuries) or the lacerating schisms of the Communist International, in the fury—often stupid and always revolting—of their respective major conflicts, except by illuminating through each other the behavior of the theologians and leaders of the Christian factions on the

one hand, and the Marxist theorists and authorities on the other. In each case the elements are entirely different, yet a certain structure emerges which is identical and which becomes an aid to our understanding."

14. C. Martin, in *Nouvelle Revue théologique*, 84 (1962), 1001. After having given unqualified approval to my analysis up to the developments of the fourth century, Martin was unable to follow me in my assessment of those developments themselves. "The problem," he wrote, " . . . is a matter of theology, not of history. The answer one brings will inevitably depend upon the ideas one has formed about three great factors: the Gospel, the Church, and human society; their respective nature and degree of finality; and their interrelationships. As the author's [my] positions probably do not come near to my own on these different points, my silent reservations will be easily understood. But after all, these considerations extend beyond the conclusions of the strictly historical inquiry which forms the essential part of the work."

15. Martin, review, 1000. Similarly, P.-Th. Camelot concluded his review of *EL* as follows (*RSPT*, 45 [1961], 530): "With this thesis . . . the historian can only express his agreement, at least in its main lines: the facts and texts quoted are too numerous and fit together too well for one to reject the conclusions as a whole." Gerest ("Les premiers chrétiens," 17) wrote that the "motives for this Christian antimilitarism were many. There was a dread of idolatry . . . but the most frequently mentioned reason was the horror at the shedding of blood." See also Dumas ("L'Eglise d'avant Constantin," 314-316), who was more cautious in his agreement at this level because he did not feel that he had sufficient historical qualifications. Mehl ("Le Christianisme primitif"), on the other hand, wrote of this book: "If he [Hornus] is right in his unwillingness to discard the evangelical refusal to shed blood as one of the motives for Christian conscientious objection . . . I still think that he is wrong to make it the first and most obvious motive; the rejection of idolatry operated strongly from the outset." Perhaps it is not so important to know which of the two motives was the first, once one accepts that the two coexisted. I have, in fact, indicated above that I agree with Roques in seeing the core of the Christian attitude as the recognition of "God's absolute primacy." I have also shown that I still find today—in the nation-states of the late twentieth century—the idolatry of those nations or states, even if perhaps in slightly subtler forms, to be the core of military ideology. Even Fontaine ("Christians and Military Service," 114), whose assessment of the rest of my work was rather severe, nevertheless recognized as a fact "the gradual change in the Christian attitude toward the *militia armata*." For me, at any rate, that is the basic historical point.

16. H. Chavannes, *L'Objection de conscience* (Lausanne, 1961), 71. Similarly, in a clear though rather embarrassed way, an editorial in the hyper-Constantinian *France catholique* was obliged to admit: "No doubt absolute conscientious objection can invoke the support of certain Church Fathers of the first centuries: a period in which divergencies were the sign of a thought trying to find forms of expression and to become articulate; admirable and sometimes abrupt beginnings, in minority communities, whose Christian ethic on temporal matters had scarcely been worked out. With St. Augustine and the advent of a largely Christian society, such an ethic became progressively more explicit. Absolute conscientious objection *ceased* to be allowed in the Catholic Church. . . . The Church *then retained only* the obligation to total nonviolence for certain people who were consecrated to God in the priestly or religious life" (Luc Baresta, "L'Objection de conscience," *France catholique*, no. 848 [March 1, 1963]). I have italicized *ceased* and *then retained only* because these words show how much historical ground the author had conceded with relation to the former official thesis.

17. Windass, *Christianity Versus Violence*, 126. For an account of this attitude of

"Protest," and for its extension even into the early part of the "Constantinian" period, see *ibid.*, 1-27; for a discussion of the extremely significant internal contradiction in St. Augustine's thought, see pp. 80 and 88-89. See also Gerest ("Les premiers chrétiens," 14-22), who generously sent me an offprint of his article inscribed "To M. Hornus—my presentation of this article to him is really a 'restitution.' "

18. J. Comblin, *Théologie de la Paix*, II, *Applications* (Paris, 1963), 9-19, 21-24. Visser ("Christianus sum," 8) observed, "One thing seems evident: the primitive Church never formally accepted the use of violence as a necessary evil in order to defend a just cause." For a similar statement, see L. Vischer's review of *EL* (*ThZ*, 17 [1961], 67).

19. [The recent article by John Helgeland ("Christians and the Roman Army, A.D. 173-337," *Church History*, 43 [1974], 149-163, 200), which is based on his University of Chicago doctoral thesis of 1973, indicates that, for one scholar at least, the issue has not been as definitively settled as Dr. Hornus—writing in 1970—thought.]

20. A. F. Villemain, *Tableau de l'eloquence chrétienne au IVᵉ siècle* (Paris, 1849), 81.

21. Comblin, *Théologie de la Paix*, 22.

22. Roques, review, 242.

23. Comblin, *Théologie de la Paix*, 22. Camelot (see n. 15 above) was the first of my reviewers—earlier but less emphatic than C. Martin—to perceive and state clearly that, regardless of the agreement with which he could respond to my thesis on the historical level, there remained a difference between our two ecclesiologies which he was not free to surmount. In my reply ("Les Pères de l'Eglise," 16 n.) I expressed the hope that the Catholic theologians themselves might be able to attempt a new formulation in this field. But at that time I did not dare to think that this might come to pass so soon as a result of the Second Vatican Council.

24. This contemporary ethical concern is prominent in the introduction to Rordorf's article ("Tertullians Beurteiling," 105), and also in "Problemi de non violenza," *Protestantismo* (1967), 186-187. Visser ("Christianus sum," 6) put it like this: "The problem for the Church of old, and not only for the Church *of old*, is: can a Christian in good conscience be a soldier?" Similarly, the title given by E. de Peyer to his review of my book (*Journal de Genève*, 28 June 1960) was significantly "The Church on its road towards fidelity." M. Gavillet ended his review (*Le Lien de l'Eglise évangélique du Canton de Vaud*, November 24, 1960) by referring to the pamphlet of R. Hegnauer (*Le Combattant non-violent* [Lausanne, 1960]), which is a manual for practical action today. R. Rouget's review (*Vie Protestante*, December 2, 1960) did the same. And Mehl ("Christianisme primitif") wrote that I was tackling "a problem which has lost none of its relevance and indeed seems likely during the coming decades to acquire additional topical and tragic importance."

25. Dumas, "L'Eglise d'avant Constantin," 309. This idea was borrowed from P. Ricoeur, "La merveille, l'errance, l'enigme," *Esprit*, 28 (1960), 1670. P. R. Regamey ("La conscience chrétienne et la guerre," *Cahiers St. Jacques*, no. 27 [1962]) argued that "so long as the Christians were a minority in the empire, they could be mere minors politically.... But then the responsibility for the earthly city in the *political* sphere fell to the Christians as well. Then they were obliged to reach *political* maturity." The whole problem is to decide whether that "responsibility for the earthly city" must necessarily consist of giving to it a general coat of whitewash of a vaguely religious coloration, or whether it rather should consist of working within it like the leaven and salt of which the gospel speaks. On this point, the conclusion of Dumas (p. 309) is excellent. I am also grateful to Dumas for having grasped that it was

the very complexity of the historical record which made it "a living question for us to-day."

26. On this point see the important book by B. Besret, *Incarnation ou eschatologie* (Paris, 1964) and my review of it in "Christianisme," 671-673. My original intentions in *Evangile et Labarum* were clearly perceived by M. Gavillet, in a review/editorial under the title of "Un problème a revoir" (A Problem to be Reconsidered) (see n. 22 above): "The great merit of this book lies in its being an objective study, made in the perspective of present-day theology—the eschatological perspective—and in not being a piece of special pleading. This is how he [the author] seizes the attention of his readers and wins them over. In this perspective, conscientious objection no longer appears as a flight from the world or as 'a refusal to defend one's neighbor, but rather as a confession that there was no one anywhere who was not one's neighbor.' So the 'no' is a 'yes,' a very bold one in fact to the mission given by Christ to his Church: that of being by men's side, not as judges, but as witnesses to Jesus Christ, who takes on himself the sin of his brethren." Mehl ("Christianisme primitif") also observed, "Hornus rightly emphasizes that by losing its eschatological dimensions, Christian thought has increasingly been ready to accept the regime of Caesaropapism."

27. Dumas, "L'Eglise d'avant Constantin," 312; Meslin, review, 185.

28. See my comments on these "perfectionist" experiments in "Les Pères de l'Eglise," 12, and concerning a particularly typical case in "Du côté des Mennonites," CS, 69 (1961), 698-701.

29. This set of problems has always been central to the reflections on this topic in the journal *Esprit*. See especially its issues of February 1949 ("Revision de Pacifisme") and of August-September 1954 ("Les Pacifismes et la guerre"). I can contribute a small personal anecdote to the catalog of ambiguities inherent in decisions concerning concrete political ethics. I originally wrote the article "Les Pères de l'Eglise" for *Esprit* as a rejoinder to Dumas's article. Since the editors of *Esprit* were not interested in it, I resubmitted it to the more modest *Cahiers de la Reconciliation*. But even that journal would only publish it if they could delete a whole section of the conclusion in which I argued that resistance of a violent type was inevitable in certain situations (e.g., the landing of paratroops on Paris which Michel Debré in April 1961 had announced to be imminent). For such a suggestion had contradicted the consistent nonviolence position which the editors of the *Cahiers* were dedicated to maintain. And *Paix et Coexistence*, to which I then agreed to give the same text as well so that it might appear at least once in its entirety, eventually also published the expurgated text instead!

30. This staggering over-simplification is evident in H. Chavannes' *L'Objection de conscience*. Even though he recognized the soldier's right to "Refuse to carry out certain particularly odious acts" (p. 89), he declared that basic distinction between the assassin and the soldier is that the soldier is constrained to do what he does, on pain of the most severe sanctions, and so becomes "the instrument of the state's violence" (p. 74). But this did not stop him from asserting immediately afterwards that the good soldier who dies for his country is the temporal transposition of Christ who died for the world's salvation (p. 75). Finally this pearl: "It is because the army exists that peace is assured" (p. 68). For, as everyone knows, it is the antimilitarists who start wars and wage them!

31. Dumas, "L'Eglise d'avant Constantin," 316 n.

32. Gregarious influence and propaganda are so potent—once a country is catapulted into the unknown territory of war—that almost everyone lets himself be dragged into it. Only too late do people discover the extent of their blindness, unless

they have previously and unconditionally fortified their consciences by deciding to refuse to allow their bodies and minds to participate in large-scale butchery—which is what every international war is. This psychological dimension has been neglected by the Barthian conception of the "commandment for the moment." And for that reason, although from the theological point of view it is theoretically irreproachable, it remains completely inadequate in practice (cf. my "Dieu et la guerre," 580-590). J. M. Domenach ("Les pacifismes et la guerre," *Esprit*, 22 [1954], 161-175) put forward some interesting views concerning the need for any pacifism to be sociologically rooted in the interests of a given group. He also discussed changes in the world situation which had resulted from technological "advances" in the destructive potential of weaponry. Since then "nuclear pacifism" such as his has made some progress in the Christian and humanist consciences. But I am still surprised to see it so little followed up in concrete commitment. As Mehl ("Christianisme primitif") wrote, "In the perspective of a total and ideological war using atomic weapons and involving every country in the world, it becomes futile to look for the dividing line between a just and an unjust war. The means employed are bound by their very nature to lead to corrupt ends."

Visser ("Christianus sum," 19) was ready to accept that prior to Constantine most Christians had favored total nonviolence. But he argued that that had only been because they had not realized that a government could vindicate justice only by resorting to a limited amount of violence. Therefore an "adult" Christian thought must now free itself from the naïveté—characteristic of early Christianity—of a state deprived of a "secular arm." But simultaneously, he emphasized, it must free itself from the madness of the motto *si vis pacem, parra bellum*, which motto has been inherited from the false and godless "wisdom of the nations." Domenach, on the other hand, appealed (p. 173) to nonviolent pacifists to "intervene so as to break a vicious circle—to intervene not by setting itself [pacifism] up as an absolute ideal, as [they do] . . . too often, but by becoming involved in the order of means, in the actuality of situations."

It is on this basis that one must judge the most recent problem in this field—revolutionary violence. Insofar as the revolutionary intends, by using a lesser violence, to prevent worse violence, he is morally identifiable with the policeman. But it is his duty beforehand to take as clear a view as possible of the point beyond which his violence would cease to be justifiable and would become absurd.

33. See, for example, R. B. Gregg, *The Power of Nonviolence* (London, 1961). P. Ricoeur ("L'homme nonviolent et sa présence a l'histoire," *Esprit*, 18 [1949], 229) was perfectly justified in issuing a warning against a pacifism which is overly facile in belief and practice. For pacifism is an attitude which can be costly, and its adherents must honestly assess its price. But Ricoeur was also right in regretting that we in the nonviolent Christian movement have spent so little time studying Gandhi's "techniques" in detail. In fact, the example of India's liberation, although it has no normative character (cf. the stern demystifying study of M. Biardeau, "Gandhi, histoire et légende," *Esprit*, 22 [1954], 176-214), nevertheless has value as a historical experiment. And there have been others since. Taken as a method of political effectiveness, it is through the analysis of such experiences that nonviolence must be tested, its possibilities defined, and its techniques and limitations assessed.

Systematic Table of Primary Sources *

Achatius, Acts of *(Acta Achatii)* (250)
  Knopf, 57-60; Hamman, 107-111
    1,3*(83)*; 1,5*(258)*
    3,2*(30)*
[Adamantius], Dialogue on the Or-
  thodox Faith *(Dialogus de recta in*
  Deum fide)
  Ed. W. H. Van de Sande Bak-
  huyzen, *GCS*, 4(1901)
    I, 9-16, 18*(53-54)*
    I,10(87); I,10, 12-13*(60)*;
    I,11(63)
Agaune, Passion of the Martyrs of
  (Passio Acaunensium) (ed. 5th c. by
  St. Eucher)
  MGH, Scriptores rerum merovin-
  gicarum, 3 (1896), 32-40; Mon-
  ceaux, 282-292
    3*(155-156)*; 9*(156)*; 10*(156)*
Ambrose, of Milan, St. (339?-397)
  The Duties *(De Officiis)*
  Ed. J. G. Krabinger (Tübingen,
  1850); trans. H. De Romestin,
  NPNF, 2nd ser., 10(1896), 1-89
    I,27,129(180)*(182)*; I,36,
    178(223)
    II,15,71(180); II,28,136(180)
    III,13,14(180)

On Faith *(De Fide)*
  PL, 16, 527-698
    II,16(182)
Funeral Oration for Theodosius
  (De Obitu Theodosii)
  Ed. O. Faller, *CSEL*, 73(1955),
  369-401
    48*(182)*
Hymn XI
  PL, Supplementum I (Paris,
  1958), 584-585; ed. A. Walpole,
  Early Latin Hymns
  (Cambridge, 1922), 82-86
    (153)
Letters *(Epistolae)*
  PL, 16, 875-1286; ed. O. Faller,
  CSEL, 82(1968)
    20*(220)*; 62(305)
Treatise on the Gospel of Luke
  (Expositio Evangelii secundum
  Lucan)
  Ed. M. Adriaen, *CCL*, 14,
  iv(1947), 1-400; ed. & trans. G.
  Tissot, *SCH*, 45(1956), 52(1958)
    II,77*(182)*
Ammianus Marcellinus
  Roman History
  Trans. C. D. Yonge (Bohn's

---

* The number in the parenthesis following each citation indicates the page on which we refer to the source. If the number is *italicized*, we quote the source (at least in part) ver- batim. E.g., Ambrose's *De Officiis* (I,27,129) is referred to on p. 180 and quoted on p. 182; his eleventh hymn is quoted on p. 153; etc.

Classical Library) (London,
1887).
  XIV,11,20(313)
Anonymous Homilies (in the tradition
  of Origen) (Alexandria, c. 400)
  Ed. & trans. P. Nautin, *SCH*,
  36(1953)
    I,19*(269)*; III,6*(103)*;
    III,18*(97)*
Aphrahat the Syrian (early 4th c.)
  Demonstrationes
  Ed. R. Graffin, *Patrologia
  Syriaca*, I, i(Paris, 1894); trans.
  J. Gwynn, *NPNF*, ser. 2,
  13(1898)
    VII,18*(76)*
Apollonius (martyred under Commo-
  dus, c. 180-185)
  Martyrdom of *(Acta Apollonii)*
  Knopf, 30-35; Monceaux, 148-
  157; Musurillo, 90-105
    3(257-258); 6-7(82); 37(317)
Apostolic Constitutions (end 4th c.)
  Ed. F. X. Funk, *Didascalia et
  Constitutiones Apostolorum*
  (Paderborn, 1905); trans. J.
  Donaldson, *ANL*, 17 (1870); ed.
  & trans. H. Tattam, *The Apos-
  tolical Constitutions or Canons
  of the Apostles in Coptic*
  (London, 1848)
    II,14,12(164) *(188-189)*; IV,6,
    5(307)
    VIII,12,42*(307)*; VIII,32,
    10(164) *(299)*
Archelaus
  Controversy
  Ed. C. H. Beeson, *GCS*,
  16(1906)
    1*(19)*
Aristides of Athens (mid 2nd c.)
  Apology
  Ed. J. Geffcken, *Zwei
  griechische Apologeten*
  (Leipzig-Berlin, 1907), 1-96; ed.
  & trans. J. R. Harris & J. A.
  Robinson, *Texts and Studies*, I, i
  (Cambridge, 1891); ed. & trans.
  L. Gauthier, *RTP*, 12(1879), 78-
  82

    2(275); 8*(56)*; 10(56); 15(317)
Arles, Synod of (314)
  Hefelé, I, i, 281-294; Mansi, II,
  469-477; ed. & trans. J.
  Gaudemet, *SCH*, 241(1977), 48-
  49
  Canon 3*(172)*; Canon
  7*(172)*(173-175)
Arnobius (d. c.330)
  Against the Heathen *(Adversus
  Nationes)*
  Ed. C. Marchesis, *Corpus
  Paravianum*, 62(Turin, 1934);
  ed. & trans. G. E. McCracken,
  ACW, 7-8(1949)
    1,6*(57)*;
    2,1*(93)*; 2,38*(159)*; 2,45(318);
    3,26*(110-111)*;
    4,7(19); 4,36*(82)*
Artemius
  Vita Sancti Artemii
  ASS, October, 8(1853), 856-885
    41(313)
Athanasius, St.(295?-373)
  Apology Against the Arians *(Apo-
  logia Secunda)*
  PG, 25, 241-409; ed. H. G.
  Opitz, *Athanasius Werke*, II
  (Berlin, 1938), I, 87-168; trans.
  M. Atkinson, *NPNF*, ser. 2, 4
  (1892), 97-147 8(208)
  Letter on Love and Temperance
  Ed. A. Van Lentschoot,
  Museon, 40(1927), 265-292
    282*(109)*; 284(318); 288*(75)*;
    290-291(75)
  The Incarnation of the Word *(De
  Incarnatione Verbi)*
  PG, 25, 95-197; ed. & trans. P.
  Th. Camelot, *SCH*, 18(1946);
  ed. & trans. A. Robertson, *LCC*,
  3(1954), 55-110
    52,4-5(88); 53,1*(88)*; 53,3-
    5*(88-89)*
  Letter 48, to Amun *(ad Amunem)*
  PG, 26, 1169-1176; trans. A.
  Robertson, NPNF, ser. 2,
  4(1892), 556-557
    (183)
Athenagoras (second half of 2nd c.)

A Plea Regarding Christians (*Legatio pro Christianis*)
Ed. E. Schwartz, *TU*, 4,
ii(1891); ed. & trans. G. Bardy,
SCH, 3(1943); ed. & trans. E. R.
Hardy, *LCC*, 1(1953), 300-340;
ed. & trans. W. R. Schoedel
(Oxford, 1972)
1(317); 11(317); 34(317); 35,
4(*109*); 37(*29*)
Augustine, St. (354-430)
City of God (*Civitas Dei*)
CCL, 47-48(1955); ed. & trans.
G. E. McCracken, *et al.*, *LCL*, 7
vols. (1957-1972)
I,21 & 26(304)
IV,3(304); IV,4(*180*);
IV,6(*180*)
XIX,12(*181*)
Confessions
Ed. P. Knoell, *CSEL*, 33(1896);
ed. P. de Labriolle, *CUF*, 2 vols.
(1950-1954); trans. J. G. Pilkington, in Augustine, *Works*,
14(Edinburgh, 1876)
I,2(313); IX,11,28(98)
Against Faustus (*Contra Faustum*)
Ed. J. Zycha, *CSEL*, 25, i(1891),
251-797; trans. R. Stothert, in
Augustine, *Works*,
5(Edinburgh, 1872), 145-560
22,70(*180-181*); 22,74(180-181)
Discourse on the Psalms
Ed. E. Dekkers & J. Fraipon,
CCL, 10, 2 vols.(1956); ed. &
trans. S. Hebgin & F. Corrigan,
ACW, 29(1960)
74,17(63); 124,7(176)
On the Free Will (*De Libero Arbitrio*)
Ed. W. M. Green, *CCL*, 29
(1970), 211-321; ed. & trans. M.
Pontifex, *ACW*, 22(1955); I,4,
9(*181*); I,5,12(*181*)
Letters
Ed. A. Goldbacher, *CSEL*,
44(1904), 57(1911), 58(1923);
trans. M. Dods, in Augustine,
Works, 6(1872), 13(1875).

47,5(304); 136,2(*213*); 189,4-
5(195); 189,6(*181*); 220,3(195)
On Patience (*De Patientia*)
Ed. I. Zycha, *CSEL*, 41(1900),
663-691; ed. G. Combès, *Bibliothèque augustinienne* (1937)
1,7(318); 2(*220*); 26(318);
29(318)
Aurelius Victor, Sextus
Epitome de Caesaribus
Ed. F. Pichlmayr (Leipzig,
1911)
(313)
Balsamon (1140-1195)
Commentary on the Canons
PG, 138, 571 ff.
13,II,65,70(171)
Barnabas (end 1st c.)
Letter
Ed. H. Hemmer, G. Oger & A.
Laurent, *HL*, 5, 2nd ed.(1926);
trans. E. J. Goodspeed, *The Apostolic Fathers* (New York,
1950), 19-46
11, 8(*214*); 12,2(*54*); 12,5-
7(54-55); 12,8(55); 12,10(*55*);
16,4(58); 16,6-10(58)
Basil, the Great, of Caesarea, St. (330?-
379)
Homilies on the Psalms
PG, 29, 208-494
1,6(*127*); 1,14(42); 7(*75*);
48(318); 48,1(104); 59,3(*104*);
61,4(61)
Homilies, various
PG, 31, 163-618,1429-1514
3,4(*80*) (*271*); 12,2(31); 18,
7(*126*); 19(*126*)
Letters (*Epistolae*)
Ed. & trans. R. J. Deferrari,
LCL, 4 vols. (1926-1934); ed. Y.
Courtonne, *CUF*, 1(1957)
51(104);63(109-110); 66,
2(104); 74,3(104); 75(104);
76(104); 87(104); 99,1(96);
104(104); 106(*127*); 116(*127*);
155(83); 165(104); 188,
13(*171*); 188,8(*301*); 199(110);
217(110); 299(*96*)
Moral Principles (*Moralia*)

PG, 31, 692-870
  79,1-2*(42)*
Preliminary Sketch of the Ascetic
  Life
  Ed. W. K. L. Clarke, *The Ascetic Works of St. Basil*
  (London, 1925), 55-59
  (77)
Treatise on the Holy Spirit
  Ed. & trans. B. Pruche, *SCH*, 17
  (1947); trans. B. Jackson,
  NPNF, ser. 2, 8(1895), 2-50
  16,39*(60)*
Bet Hezuyah, Martyrs of (341?)
  Ed. P. Bedjan, *Acta Sanctorum et
  Martyrum*, II (Paris-Leipzig,
  1891), 241-248; Hamman, 322-
  326.
  (22-23)
Boniface, St. (680-754)
  Letters
  MGH, Epistolae, III *(Epistolae
  Merovingici et Karolini Aevi),*
  229; trans. E. Emerton, ed. A.
  Evans (Records of Civilization,
  31) (New York, 1940), 78-83
  Letter to Pope Zacharias *(192)*
Canones ad Gallos
  Ed. H. C. Babut, *La plus
  ancienne décrétale* (Paris, 1904),
  69-87
  Canon 7 *(190)*
  Canon 13 (308)
Canon Law
  DDC, I(1935), 1047; III(1942),
  868-869
  Article 121 (195)
Carpus (Acts of Carpus, Papylus and
  Agathonicê) (under Marcus Aurelius) *(Acta Carpi)*
  Ed. H. Delehaye, *AB*, 58(1940),
  142-176; Hamman, 41-45;
  Musurillo, 22-37
  4(22)
Cassian, Acts of
  Knopf, 89-90; trans. H. Leclercq,
  Les Martyrs, II, 159-160
  (138)
Clement of Alexandria (150?-215?)
  Carpets *(Stromata)*

Ed. O. Stählin, *GCS*, 15(1905),
  17(1909); 2nd ed.(1939); ed. &
  trans. C. Mondésert & M.
  Caster, *SCH*, 30(1951) and P.
  Th. Camelot & C. Mondésert,
  SCH, 38(1954); trans. W.
  Wilson, *ANF*, 2(1885), 299-567
  I,11,3,6*(73)*; 24,158,1*(55);*
  26(36); 158,2(55); 159(55);
  160(55); 168(36)
  II,1,2(317); 11,117(125); 18,
  82*(125)* (277); 18,88*(110);*
  18,89-90(277); 20,110(72);
  20,120*(73)*
  III,12,91*(125)*
  IV,4,14-16(268); 8,60(268);8,
  61*(159);* 13,91(268);14
  96*(125);* 22,141(268)
  VI,5,41(103); 12,103(269); 14,
  112(269); 18,167(20)
  VII,3,21(269); 11,62*(159);* 11,
  66(269); 13,83(269); 14,
  84*(159-160);* 16,100(269)
Extracts from Theodotus
(Excerpta ex Theodoto)
  Ed. & trans. F. Sagnard, *SCH*,
  23(1948); ed. & trans. R. P.
  Casey
  (Studies and Documents, 1)
  (London, 1934).
  72,1-2*(73)*; 85,3*(73)*
Exhortation *(Protrepticus)*
  Ed. & trans. C. Mondésert,
  SCH, 2, 2nd ed. (1949); ed. &
  trans., G. W. Butterworth,
  LCL(1919), 2-263
  X,93,2*(72);* 100*(124);* 108,
  4*(102);* 116,1-4*(72)*
The Tutor *(Paedagogus)*
  Ed. O. Stählin, *GCS*, 12, 3rd
  ed.(1972); ed. & trans. H.-I.
  Marrou, M. Harl, C. Mondésert
  & C. Matray, *SCH*, 70(1960),
  108(1965), 158(1970); trans. W.
  Wilson, *ANL*, 4(1867), 113-346
  I,12,98(90); 12,99*(159)*
  II,2,32*(90);* 4,42*(90) (159);* 13,
  121*(21)*
  III,8,1(102)
Who Is the Rich Man That Is

Saved?(*Quis dives salvetur?*)
Ed. O. Stählin, *GCS*, 17(1909);
ed. & trans. G. W. Butterworth,
LCL(1919), 270-367
25(269); 34(269); 42,1-15(317)
Clement, of Rome, St. (end 1st c.)
Letter
Ed. H. Hemmer, *HL*, 10, 2nd
ed.(1926); ed. & trans. C. C.
Richardson, *LCC*, 1(1953), 43-73
1,1(*99*); 8,4(*64*) (*90*); 12,7(*54*);
13,1(317); 13,3(222); 19(317);
21,4(*70*); 30, 3&8(317); 36,6-
37(*70*); 45,7(*70*); 60,4(*27*); 60,
4-61,3(*81*)
Clement of Rome (Pseudo-)
Sermon Called the Second Letter
of Clement (*II Clement, Ep.*)
Ed. H. Hemmer, *HL*, 10, 2nd
ed.(1926); ed. & trans. C. C.
Richardson, *LCC*, 1(1953), 193-
212
5,1(*100*); 5,4(*100*); 5,6-7(100-
101); 6,1(101); 6,3(101);
7(70); 8(101)
Clementine Recognitions
• Ed. B. Rehm, *GCS*, 51(1954);
trans. T. Smith, *ANL*, 3(1867),
140-471
IX,15(259)
Commodian (mid 3rd c. or 5th c.)
Carmen Apologeticum
Ed. B. Dombart, *CSEL*,
15(1887), 115-188; ed. J. Durel,
Revue tunisienne, 19(1912),
369-383; 20(1913), 46-61
805 ff.(108) (262); 887(262);
887-892(108); 891(262); 920-
926(*276*); 933-935(262)
Instructiones
Ed. B. Dombart, *CSEL*,
15(1887), 3-112; ed. J. Durel,
Les Instructions de Commodien
(Paris, 1912); trans. A. Roberts
& J. Donaldson, *ANL*, 18(1870),
434-474
I,34(*277*); II,9-10(64); II,9-11,
20(269); II,12(*74*); II,22(*74*)
Coptic Church, Acts of the Martyrs
of the

Ed. A. Amélineau, *Les Actes des
Martyrs de l'Eglise copte* (Paris,
1890)
(*139-141*) (*221*)
Coronati, Passion of the Four
Ed. *ASS*, November, 3(1910),
765-784
(129)
Cyprian, St. (210?-258)
Acts of Cyprian (*Acta Cypriani*)
Ed. Monceaux, 192-198;
Musurillo, 168-175
2(257)
The Advantage of Patience (*De
Bono Patientiae*)
Ed. C. Moreschini, *CCL*, 3a,
ii(1976), 118-133; ed. & trans.
M. G. E. Conway, *PSt*, 92(1957)
12(*74*); 14(*160*); 21(*68*)
To Demetrianus (*Ad De-
metrianum*)
Ed. M. Simonetti, *CCL*, 3a,
ii(1976), 35-51; trans. R. E.
Wallis, *ANL*, 8(1868), 423-443
2(*45*); 3(36-37); 5(*45*); 11(*44-
45*); 17(36-37); 17,25(*218-
219*); 20(*83*)
To Donatus (*Ad Donatum*)
Ed. M. Simonetti, *CCL*, 3a,
ii(1976), 3-13; trans. R. E.
Wallis, *ANL*, 8(1868), 1-13
6-10(*160*)
The Dress of Virgins (*De Habitu
Virginum*)
Ed. & trans. A. E. Keenan, *PSt*,
34(1932)
11(87)
Exhortation to Martyrdom (*Ad
Fortunatum*)
Ed. R. Weber, *CCL*, 3(1972),
185-216; trans. R. E. Wallis,
ANL, 13(1869), 52-77
13(74)
On Jealousy and Envy (*De Zelo et
livore*)
Ed. M. Simonetti, *CCL*, 3a,
ii(1976), 75-86; trans. R. E.
Wallis, *ANL*, 13(1869), 39-51
2(74); 5(264)
Letters (*Epistolae*)

Ed. & trans. L. Bayard, *CUF*, 2
vols.(1925); trans. R. E. Wallis,
ANL, 8(1868), 1-332
  39,3(*126*); 73,4(*160*); 73,
  10(*74*)
On the Mortality *(De Mortalitate)*
Ed. M. Simonetti, *CCL*, 3a,
ii(1976), 17-32; ed. & trans. M.
L. Hannan, *PSt*, 36 (1933)
  2(59); 26(*102*)
Three Books of Testimonies
Against the Jews *(Testimonia)*
Ed. W. Hartel, *CSEL*, 3,
i(1868), 33-184; trans. R. E.
Wallis, *ANL*, 13(1869), 78-198
  II,16(*265*); III,13(36);
  III,117(74); III,3,8,22,23,49,
  106(317)
That the Idols Are Not Gods
(Quod Idola dii non sint)
Ed. W. Hartel, *CSEL*, 3,
i(1868), 17-31; trans. R. E.
Wallis, *ANL*, 8(1868), 443-451;
Quasten, *Patrology*, II, 364 (on
authorship)
  4 ff.(45); 10(61); 12(61)
Cyprian (Pseudo-)
Against the Jews *(Adversus
Iudaeos)*
Ed. W. Hartel, *CSEL*, 3,
iii(1871), 133-144: trans. S. D.
F. Salmond, *ANL*, 9(1869), 41-
45
  6(*264*); 6-8(63); 9(87)
The Computation of Easter *(De
Pascha Computus)*
Ed. W. Hartel, *CSEL*, 3,
iii(1871), 248-271
  10(74); 15(*63*)
Cyril of Scythopolis (6th c.)
Ed. E. Schwartz, *TU*, 49, ii(1939)
Life of Euthymius
  8(274); 25-26(*76-77*)
Life of Sabas
  86(274); 92-93(*76*); 99(270)
Life of Theodosius
  235(274); 239(*77*)
Damasus I, St. (Bishop of Rome, 366-
384)
Inscription in Memory of Nereus

and Achilleus
Diehl, no. 1981 *(152)*
Dasius, Martyrdom of *(Acta Dasii)*
Knopf, 91-95; Monceaux, 273-
278; Musurillo, 272-279
  6(*274*); 6-10(*128*)
Didache (The Teaching of the Twelve
Apostles) (probl. first half of 2nd c.)
Ed. T. Klauser, *Doctrina
Duodecim Apostolorum*, Florile-
gium Patristicum, 1 (Bonn, 1940);
ed. & trans. C. C. Richardson,
LCC, 1(1953), 161-179
  1,2-4(317); 2,6-7(317); 3,2(317)
Didascalia Apostolorum (mid 3rd c.)
Ed. E. Hauler, *Didascaliae
apostolorum fragmenta
Veronensia latina* (Leipzig, 1900);
ed. F. X. Funk (see under *Apostolic Constitutions)*; ed. & trans.
R. H. Connolly, *Didascalia
Apostolorum* (Oxford, 1929); ed.
& trans. F. Nau, *La Didascalie*,
2nd ed. (Paris, 1912)
  I,2,1-2(318); II, 6,1(318); II,6,
  6-11(*75*); II,45,1(318); II,46,
  2(318); V,1,1(21); V,14,
  22(318); VI,14,10 & 12(188-
  189); VI,19,1(*57-58*); XVIII,6,
  4(*307*)
Didymus Alexandrinus (the Blind)
(313?-398?)
Commentary on 2 Corinthians
PG, 39, 1677-1732
  1,13(264)
Diognetus, Letter to (2nd c.?)
Ed. & trans. H. I. Marrou, *SCH*,
33(1951); ed. & trans. E. H.
Fairweather, *LCC*, 1(1953), 205-
224
  5,4-5(*105*); 5,8-9(*105*); 6,1-
  3(*105*); 6,7-8(*105*)
Dionysius of Rome (Bishop of Rome,
259-268)
PL, 5, 99-136
  (80)
Elvira, Synod of (306)
Hefelé, VI, i, 221-264; Mansi, II,
1-20
  Canon 56(170)

Epiphanius of Salamis (315?-403)
Medicine Chest *(Panarion)*
Ed. K. Holl, *GCS,* 25(1915),
31(1922), 37(1930)
68,2(256); 68,8(208)
Eusebius of Caesarea (263?-340?)
Chronicle
Ed. R. Helm, *GCS,* 24(1913)
238 olymp., XIII*(129)*
Ecclesiastical History *(Historia Ecclesiastica [HE])*
Ed. & trans. G. Bardy, *SCH,*
31(1952), 41(1955), 55(1958);
ed. & trans. K. Lake & J. E. L.
Oulton, *LCL,* 2 vols. (1928-1932)
II,23,18(63); III,5,3,(108);
IV,26,6-11*(39)*
V,1,17 ff.(21); 1,18*(75);* 5,3
ff.(129); 21(286)
VI,5,3(37); 5,3-6(25); 21,
4*(37);* 41,9*(65);* 41,11(130);
41,16*(22) (75);* 41,22(130-131)
VII,3,4(21); 11,20(79-80);
15*(131);* 30,19*(37);* 32,7-11(108)
VIII,1,2*(37);* 1,7*(131)* (256); 1,
8-9(65); 4,2-3*(131)* (256)
(287);6,8*(45-46);* 9,6*(97);* 9,
7*(286);* 10,3(21); 11,1(21);
12,42*(83);* 14,3(21); 14,
11*(37);* 17,5(259); app.
1(287)
IX,8,4,2(178); 9,1*(65-66) (178)*
(259); 9,2*(178);* 9,5 ff.(259);
9a,12(259); 10,3*(38)* (259);
10,13*(66) (178-179);* 10,
15(66); 11,2-7(178); 11,
5(178); 11,8(259); 11,9(178)
X,1,7*(66);* 2,2(259); 4,60(259);
5,1-14(259); 5,23-24(316);
7(193) (305); 8,10*(83);* 8,
16(315)
Life of Constantine *(Vita Constantini)*
Ed. I. A. Heikel, *GCS,* 7(1902),
1-148; trans. A. C. McGiffert,
NPNF, new ser., 1(1890), 481-610

I,preface(314); I,16 ff.*(96);*
I,28(200); II,5-17(311);
II,16*(179);* III,6(316);
III,11(314); III,13(316);
IV,24*(211)*
The Martyrs of Palestine
Ed. & trans. G. Bardy, *SCH,*
55(1958), 121-174; ed. & trans.
H. J. Lawlor & J. E. L. Oulton
(London, 1927-1928), I, 327-400
4,8-13(21); 7,2(21); 9,7(254);
11,6*(21);* 11,8-12*(98);* 11,20-21(139) *(289);* 11,22*(75) (289)*
Preparation for the Gospel
(Praeparatio Evangelica)
Ed. K. Mras, *GCS,* 43, i(1954),
ii(1956); ed. & trans. E. H. Gif-
ford, 4 vols. (Oxford, 1903)
1,3(63); 1,4 *(88)* (92); 2,6*(37);*
4,2*(37);* 4,16-17(92); 5,1(92);
5,4(92); 6,1*(88)* (208); 6,6(37)
The Proof of the Gospel *(Demon-stratio Evangelica)*
Ed. I. A. Heikel, *GCS,* 16(1913);
ed. & trans. W. J. Ferrar, 2 vols.
(London, 1920)
I,2,8*(275);* II,2(208); III,7,
35(40); III,7,39(44);
VI,20(40); VIII,2,9-45(47)
Eutropius, Flavius
Breviarium ab Urbe Condita
Ed. F. Ruehl (Leipzig, 1887)
10,6(313)
Fabius, Acts of (c. 303)
AB, 9(1890), 123-134
(138)
Ferreolus, St., Passion of (under Decius?)
ASS, September, 5(1857), 766-767
(131) (287)
Fructuosus and His Companions, Acts
of *(Acta Fructuosii)*
Knopf, 83-85; Hamman, 132-136;
Musurillo, 176-185
2,2-3*(26-27);* 7(268)
Gregory I, the Great, St.(c.540-604)
Morals on the Book of Job
Ed. & trans. R. Gillet & A. de
Gaudemarie, *SCH,* 32(1952);
LFC, 3 vols.(Oxford, 1844-1850)

SCH, 14(1947)
I,8,3(264)
III,8,9(47); 23,1-3(33-34); 24,
7(28)
IV,8,7-8(47); 9(93); 9,2(47);
17,7(49); 17,8(48); 21,3(49);
23-24(49); 35(47); 40,3(60);
49,1,4-5(263); 58,3(61)
Ignatius of Antioch, St. (end of 1st c.)
Ed. & trans. P. Th. Camelot,
SCH, 10, 2nd ed. (1951); ed. &
trans. C. C. Richardson, *LCC*,
1(1953), 87-120
Letter to the Ephesians *(Eph.)*
10,1-3(317); 13,2(317); 19(92)
Letter to Polycarp *(Pol.)*
1,2(317); 6,2(70)
Letter to the Romans *(Rom.)*
5,1(20); 6,1(93); 6,2(107); 7(92)
Letter to the Smyrnaeans
(Smyr.)
1,2(70)
To the Trallians *(Tral.)*
3,2(317); 4,2(317)
Innocent I, St. (?-417)
Letter to Exuperus of Toulouse
Mansi, III, 1038-1041; *PL*, 20,
495-502
(191)
Letter to Felix, Bp. of Nuceri
PL,20,63; *PL*, 84, 651-654
37,3(5) *(191)*
Letter to Spanish Bishops
Mansi, III, 1064
(191)
Letter to Victricius
PL, 20, 469-481; 56, 519-527
2,2(4)(191)
Irenaeus, St. (c. 130-after 200)
Against Heresies *(Adversus Haereses)*
Ed. W. W. Harvey, 2 vols.
(Cambridge, 1857, reprinted
1949); Book III ed. & trans. F.
Sagnard, *SCH*, 34 (1952); trans.
A. Roberts & W. H. Rambaut,
ANL, 5 (1868),9(1869)
II,2,3(72); 32,2(32)
III,16,4(72); 17,3(60); 18,5-
6(317)

IV,13,3(317); 20,11(72); 24,
1(72); 27,1(55); 30,3(32);
34,4(86); 36,6,(32)(65)
V,24,1-3(32-33); 26(94);
30(45)
Fragments 18, 21, 44(72)
Demonstration of the Apostolic
Preaching
PO, 12, v(1919); ed. & trans. L.
M. Froidevaux, *SCH*, 62(1959)
20,27,29(264); 61(86); 96(317)
Isaiah, Ascension of
Ed. & trans. R. H. Charles
(London, 1900); ed. & trans. of
Ethiopic version, E. Tisserant
(Paris, 1909)
4,2,6,7,8,11(45); 7,9-12(59);
10,13(92); 10,29-31(59)
Isidore of Pelusium, St. (?-450)
Letters *(Epistolae)*
PG, 78, 177-1646
IV,200(110)
Jerome, St. (c. 342-430)
Book of Questions on Genesis
Ed. P. de Lagarde, *CCL*,
72(1959), 1-56
10,2(182)
Commentary on Ezekiel
Ed. F. Glorie, *CCL*, 75(1964)
11(182)
Commentary on Daniel
Ed. F. Glorie, *CCL*, 75a (1964)
3,46(255)
Illustrious Men *(De Viris illus-
tribus)*
Ed. E. C. Richardson, *TU*, 14,
1(1896); trans. idem, *NPNF*,
2nd ser., 3(1892), 359-384
53(73) (284); 80(116)
Letters *(Epistolae)*
Ed. & trans. J. Labourt, 6 vols.,
CUF(1949-1958); 1-22 ed. &
trans. C. C. Mierow, *ACW*,
33(1963); selected letters ed. &
trans. F. A. Wright, *LCL*(1933)
14,2(309); 58,2-3(276); 58,
8(78); 60,16(225); 60,17(64-
65) (271-272); 60,15-16,
18(225); 126,2(319); 127,
12(225); 128,4(319)

Life of Malchus *(Vita Malchi)*
  PL, 23, 53-60
  init. *(199)*
John, St., Apocryphal Acts of (second
  half of 2nd c.)
  Ed. R. A. Lipsius & M. Bonnet,
  Acta Apostolorum Apocrypha
  (Leipzig, 1891-1903), II, i, 151-
  216; ed. & trans. M. R. James,
  The Apocryphal New Testament
  (Oxford, 1924), 228-270
    6(22); 36(45)
John VIII (Pope, 872-882)
  Letter to Empress Angilberga
  MGH, Epistolae, 7 *(Epistolae
  Karolini aevi,* 5), 311
    (193)
John Moschus, St. (550?-619)
  Spiritual Meadow *(Pratum
  Spirituale)*
  Ed. & trans. Rouët de Journal,
  SCH, 12(1946)
    30(253)
John Chrysostom, St. (344?-407)
  Commentary on the Psalms
  PG, 55, 35-528
    148,4-5(43)
  Commentary on Isaiah
  PG, 56, 11-94
    2,3*(79);* 2,4(40); 2,4-5*(89)*
  Homilies on St. Matthew
  PG, 57; 58, 975-1058; ed. &
  trans. D. R. Bueno, *Bibliotheca
  de Autores cristianos,* 141,
  146(Madrid, 1955-1956); trans.
  S. G. Prevost, ed. M. B. Riddle,
  NPNF, 10(1888)
    9,7*(273);* 61,2*(185);* 69,1(266);
    69,3(77); 69,4(99) *(194);* 75,
    2(41)
  Homilies on St. John
  PG, 59, 23-482; ed. P. Schaff,
  trans. G. T. Stupart, 14(1890), 1-
  334
    1,1*(273);* 49,26*(277);* 79,
    3(114) *(273-274);* 82,2(318);
    82,4(185)
  Homilies on Romans
  PG, 60, 391-682; ed. G. B.
  Stevens, trans. J. B. Morris &

W. H. Simcox, *NPNF,*
  11(1889), 335-564
    14,5-end(114); 14,7(318); 23,
    2*(43) (274)*
  Homilies on Ephesians
  PG, 62, 9-176; ed. G. Alexander,
  trans. W. J. Copeland, *NPNF,*
  13(1889), 49-172
    6,1*(274);* 6,4*(194)*
  Homily on St. Lucian
  PG, 50, 520-526
    (97-98)
  Letters to Olympias
  Ed. & trans. A. M. Malingrey,
  SCH, 13(1947)
    VIII,9b*(75);* VIII,9d*(276);*
    X,3f-g*(113-114);* XIII,4d(318);
    XV, 1a-b *(75-76);* XVII,2b*(75)*
Josephus, Flavius (c. 37-c. 100)
  Jewish Antiquities *(Antiquitates
  judaicae)*
  Ed. B. Niese (Berlin, 1887-
  1895); trans. J. Weill, 1-2(Paris,
  1900, 1926); trans. J. Chamo-
  nard, 3(Paris, 1904); trans. G.
  Mathieu & L. Hermann,
  4(Paris, 1929)
    XIV,10,6(252); XVIII,5(253)
Julian of Brioude, Passion of (under
  Decius?)
  ASS, August, 6(1868), 173-175
    (131) (287)
Julian the Apostate (332-363)
  Ed. & trans. W. C. Wright, 3
  vols., *LCL*(1913-1923)
    The Caesars
    2,336b*(206)*
    To the Athenians
    3,270c(206)
Julius the Veteran, Martyrdom of
  (302?) *(Passio Iuli Veterani)*
  Knopf, 105-106; Hamman, 184-
  186; *VSB*, 5(1947), 525-528;
  Musurillo, 260-265
    (139) (289)
Justin (?-165?)
  First Apology
  PG, 6, 327-440; ed. & trans. E.
  R. Hardy, *LCC*, 1(1953), 242-
  289

11,2(317); 12,1(29); 14,3(317);
15,9(317); 16,1-4(317); 16,
14(29); 17,3(82); 39,1-3(85);
39,5(71-72); 47(62); 55,6(71)
Second Apology
    Ed. L. Pautigny, HL, 1(1904);
    trans. G. J. Davie, *LFC*(1861),
    57-69
        2(257); 5,4(277-278); 9,1(29-
        30)
Dialogue with Trypho
    Ed. G. Archambault, HL, 8,
    11(1909); ed. & trans. A. L.
    Williams (London, 1930)
        109(85); 110,3(85); 110,6(62);
        131,2(71); 139,3(62)
Justin (Pseudo-)
    Discourse
        Ed. & Latin trans. J. C. T. Otto,
        *Corpus Apologeticarum
        Christianorum Saeculi secundi*,
        3, 3rd ed. (Jena, 1879), 2-18
            5(72)
    Exhortation to the Gentiles
        Ed. & trans. Otto, *Corpus*, 19-
        127
            17(40)
Lactantius (after 250-after 320)
    The Death of Persecutors *(De
    Mortibus Persecutorum)*
        Ed. & trans. J. Moreau, 2 vols.,
        SCH, 39(1954); trans. W.
        Fletcher, *ANL*, 22(1871), 164-
        210
            7,5(21-22); 10(123-124) (256);
            18,10(42); 19,6(261); 27,5 ff.
            (21); 37,5(22); 44-48(42) (66);
            46(179); 49(66); 50,1(66); 52,
            4(67); 54(200)
    Divine Institutions *(Divinae Insti-
    tutiones)*
        Ed. S. Brandt, *CSEL*, 29(1890);
        trans. W. Fletcher, *ANL*,
        21(1871)
            I,1,13(42); 1,15(41)
            II, 6(115); 9,63(115); 10,
            23(115); 18,8-10(114); 19,
            6(279)
            IV,21,5(63); 24(123-124)
            V,4-5(318); 8,6(318); 9,2(115);

9,15-17(42); 12(44); 13-
14(318)
VI,4,11(79); 4,14-24(79); 6,18-
24(114-115); 11,1 ff.(115-
116); 18(116); 18,10-
20(219); 18,11(68); 18,
25(219-220); 18,29-32(220);
20,10(116) (303); 20,16(79)
VII, 13-14(279); 14(280)
Epilogue,73(75)
*Epitome Divinarum Institu-
tionum*
    Ed. S. Brandt, *CSEL*, 29(1890),
    675-761; ed. & trans. H.
    Blakeney (London, 1950)
        52(279)
God's Workmanship *(De Opificio
Dei)*
    Ed. S. Brandt, *CSEL*, 27(1893),
    1-64; trans. W. Fletcher, *ANL*,
    22(1871), 49-91
        2,6(115)
The Wrath of God *(De Ira Dei)*
    Ed. S. Brandt, *CSEL*, 27(1893),
    67-132; trans. W. Fletcher,
    ANL, 22(1871), 1-48
        17,6-7(41); 20,5 & 12(318);
        20,7(44); 21,10(318); 23,
        10(41)
Leo I, the Great, St. (before 400-461)
    Letters
        PL, 54, 551-1218; trans. C. L.
        Feltoe, *NPNF*, 2nd ser.,
        11(1896)
            167,12 & 14(304)
Marcellus, Acts of (298) *(Passio
Marcelli)*
    Ed. P. de Gaiffier, *AB*, 61('1943),
    116-139; Musurillo, 250-259
        1-5(137-138) (289)
Marianus and James, Passion of
(Passio Mariani) (259)
    Knopf, 67-74; Monceaux, 202-
    219; Musurillo, 194-213
        1,3(268); 2,2-4(20); 2,4-5(20-
        21); 3,4(268); 8,4(268); 10,
        3(268)
Maximilian, Acts of *(Acta Maximil-
iani)* (295)
    Knopf, 86-87; Monceaux, 251-

Ed. W. A. Bahrens, *GCS*,
30(1921), 286-463
15,1*(56);* 17,1*(58)*
Pachomius, St., Life of (292-346)
Greek text: ed. F. Halkin, *Subsidia Hagiographica*, 19(Brussels,
1932)
4(141); 5*(142)*
Coptic text: ed. & trans. L. Th.
Lefort, *Bibliothèque du Muséon*,
16(Louvain, 1943)
2*(76);* 7(141); 8*(142)*
Panegyrics, Latin
E. Galletier, ed., *Panégyriques latins*,
II, *Les Panégyriques constantiniens*,
CUF (1959)
7,21(312); 9,2(313)
Paul, Apocryphal Acts of (before end
of 2nd c.).
Ed. R. A. Lipsius & M. Bonnet,
Acta Apostolorum Apocrypha
(Leipzig, 1891-1903), I, 235-272;
ed. & trans. M. R. James, *The
Apocryphal New Testament* (Oxford, 1924), 270-299
3,4,6(71)
Paulinus of Nola, St. (353-431)
Letters *(Epistolae)*
Ed. W. Hartel, *CSEL*, 29(1894);
ed. & trans. P. G. Walsh, *ACW*,
35-36(1967)
18*(148-149) (293) (294);* 19,
4*(151-152);* 25(148); 37(148)
Paulinus of Périgueux (second half of
5th c.)
De Vita Sancti Martini episcopi
Ed. M. Petschenig, *CSEL*,
16(1888), 1-190
I,35 ff.(291); I,139-177(291)
Perpetua and Felicitas, Sts.,
Martyrdom of (202)
Knopf, 35-44; Monceaux, 165-
188; Musurillo, 106-131
9,16,21(22)
Phileas, St., and Philoromus, Acts of
(306)
Knopf, 113-116; Hamman, 253-
258; *DAL*, 14, i(1939), 703-709;
Musurillo, 328-354
(22-23)

Philostorgos (368?-433?)
Ecclesiastical History
Ed. J. Bidez, rev. F.
Winkelmann, *GCS*(1972)
2,4(313); 2,16(205)
Philoxenus of Mabbug (d. 523)
Letter Sent to a Friend
Ed. & trans. G. Olinder,
Göteborgs Högskolas Årsskrift,
56,i(1950)
6,10,36*(265);* 61*(56)*
Phocas, St., Acts of
ASS, July, 3(1867), 610-617; ed. &
trans. F. C. Conybeare, *The
Apology of Apollonius and Other
Monuments of Early Christianity*
(London, 1894), 103-121
(22)
Pionius, St., Martyrdom of *(Mart.
Pionii)*
Knopf, 45-57; Hamman, 89-106;
Musurillo, 136-167
3,2-5*(94);* 4,18*(61);* 5,3-5*(109);*
15(20); 18,7(98); 21(20)
Polycarp, St., Martyrdom of *(Mart.
Pol.)*
Musurillo, 2-21
3(71) *(92);* 6,2*(20);* 8,2(257); 10,
2*(42-43)*
Polycarp, St., (c. 70-c. 156)
Letter to the Philippians
Ed. & trans. P. T. Camelot,
SCH, 10, 2nd ed.(1951); ed. &
trans. E. J. Goodspeed, *The
Apostolic Fathers* (New York,
1950), 237-244
2,2(317); 10,2(317); 12,3*(82)*
Pontius, St. (d.c.260)
Life of Cyprian *(Vita Cypriani)*
Ed. W. Hartel, *CSEL*, 3(1871),
xc-cx
11*(106);* 16(22)
Prudentius (348-424?)
Peristephanon
Ed. M. P. Cunningham, *CCL*,
126(1966), 251-389; ed. & trans.
M. Clement Eagan (Washington, 1942)
I,34,39*(153-154);* I,58-59,
61*(154)*

Acts of *(Acta Tarachii)*
Ed. T. Ruinart, *Acta Martyrum*,
451-476; trans. Leclercq,*Martyrs*,
II, 258-290
1(274); 1-2(139) *(289)*
Tatian (second half of 2nd c.)
Address to the Greeks *(Oratio ad
Graecos)*
Ed. E. Schwartz, *TU*, 4, i(1888);
trans. B. P. Pratten, *ANL*,
3(1867), 5-45
11*(93);* 19(317); 28*(159)*
Tertullian (c. 155-after 220)
Apology *(Apologeticum)*
Ed. E. Dekkers, *CCL*, 1(1954),
85-171; ed. & trans. T. R.
Glover, *LCL* (1931), 2-227
1,2*(102);* 4,5(30); 4,10(30); 4,
13(30); 5,2(35); 5,6(35) (129);
6,7*(215);* 8,1-5(111-112); 9,
5(111); 9,8(113); 20,2(64); 21,
2(35); 21,24*(50);* 26,3(61); 28,
3(111) (258); 30,1(111); 30,1-
2(34); 30,3(97); 30,4*(82);*31,
2(80) (101); 31,3(82); 32,
1*(48);* 32,2(97); 32,2-3(258);
33(95); 36,1(97); 37,4*(124);*
37,5*(214);* 37,6-7(317); 37,
9(82); 38,3*(106);* 39,2(82); 39,
7-8(111); 40,13*(82);* 41,1(97);
42,3*(124);* 44,1(97); 46,
15*(278);* 50(73); 50,1-2*(113)*
On the Cloak *(De Pallio)*
Ed. A. Gerlo, *CCL*, 2(1954),
733-750; trans. S. Thelwall,
ANL, 18(1870), 181-200
5*(159)*
On the Soldier's Crown *(De Corona)*
Ed. A. Kroymann, *CCL*,
2(1954), 1039-1065; ed. & trans.
J. Fontaine, Coll. Erasme,
18(Paris, 1966); trans. S. Thelwall, *ANL*, 11(1869), 333-355
1*(124);* 7(256); 10-12(256);
11(214) *(269);* 12*(112-113);*
13*(46) (101)*
On the Dress of Women *(De
Cultu Feminarum)*
Ed. A. Kroymann, *CCL*,

1(1954), 343-370; ed. & trans.
M. Turcan, *SCH*, 173(1971);
trans. S. Thelwall, *ANL*,
11(1869), 304-332
II,5(73); II,11(96)
On Flight in Persecution *(De
Fuga in Persecutione)*
Ed. J. J. Thierry, *CCL*, 2(1954),
1135-1155; trans. S. Thelwall,
ANL, 11(1869), 356-378
10(73); 12(46) (101)
To the Heathen *(Ad Nationes)*
Ed. J. G. P. Borleffs, *CCL*,
1(1954), 11-75; trans. P.
Holmes, *ANL*, 11(1869), 416-
506
I,1-2(284); I,17(97); II,9*(46)*
On Idolatry *(De Idololatria)*
Ed. A. Reifferscheid & G.
Wissowa, *CCL*, 2(1954), 1101-
1124; ed. & trans. S. L. Green-
slade, *LCC*, 5(1956), 83-110
15(101);16*(96);* 17(97); 18*(96-
97) (262);* 19(65) (92) *(159)*
Against the Jews *(Adversus
Iudaeos)*
Ed. A. Kroymann, *CCL*,
2(1954), 1339-1396; trans. S.
Thelwall, *ANL*, 18(1870), 201-
258
2(257); 2-3(116); 3(87) (257);
7(112); 9*(46)* (73-74); 7*(262);*
8(92), 15*(97);* 25*(92);* 30(101-
102)
Against Marcion *(Adversus Mar-
cionem)*
Ed. A. Kroymann, *CCL*,
1(1954), 441-726; ed. & trans. E.
Evans, 2 vols. (Oxford, 1972)
I,13(97); 24(52-53)
III,13(73-74) (262); 14(73-74);
21*(87);* 23(61)
IV,1(87); 20(73-74); 29(52-
53); 39(64); 38(101)
V,5(73); 17(92) (113); 18(73-
74)
On Patience *(De Patientia)*
Ed. J. G. P. Borleffs, *CCL*,
1(1954), 299-317; trans. S. Thelwall, *ANL*, 11(1869), 205-230

1(216); 4(111); 6-7(216);
10(216); 15(102)*(216)*
On the Resurrection of the Flesh
(De Resurrectione Carnis)
Ed. J. G. P. Borleffs, *CCL,*
2(1954), 921-1012; trans. P.
Holmes, *ANL,* 15(1870), 215-
332
20(73-74); 24(263)
To Scapula *(Ad Scapulam)*
Ed. E. Dekkers, *CCL,* 2(1954),
1127-1132; trans. S. Thelwall,
ANL, 11(1869), 46-52
3*(102);* 4(35)·(129); 5*(215-
216);* 5,2-3(284)
Scorpiace
Ed. A. Reifferscheid & G.
Wissowa, *CCL,* 2(1954), 1069-
1097; trans. S. Thelwall, *ANL,*
11(1869), 379-415
3*(60);* 14*(34)* (101)
On the Shows *(De Spectaculis)*
Ed. E. Dekkers, *CCL,* 1(1954),
227-253; ed. & trans. T. R.
Glover, *LCL*(1931), 230-301
7(262); 8(92); 15*(97);* 25*(92);*
30(101-102)
On the Soul *(De Anima)*
Ed. J. H. Waszink, *CCL,*
2(1954), 781-869; trans. P.
Holmes, *ANL,* 15(1870), 410-
541
31*(73);* 33(111); 33,6(34);
52(277)
Testament of Our Lord
Ed. I. E. Rahmani, *Testamentum
Domini Nostri Iesu Christi*
(Mainz, 1899); trans. F. Nau, *La
Version syriaque* (Paris, 1913); ed.
& trans. J.Cooper & J.A. Mac-
lean (Edinburgh, 1902)
II,2*(166)*

Theodoret of Cyrus (393?-466?)
Ecclesiastical History
PG, 82, 882-1280; trans. B.
Jackson, *NPNF,* 2nd ser.,
3(1890), 1-348
I,20,1(208); IV,8*(190)*
Theodosian Code *(Codex
Theodosianus)*
Ed. T. Mommsen, *Theodosiani
Libri XVI,* 3 vols. (Berlin, 1905)
V,20,1*(201-202);* VII,1,8(252);
VII,22,2(252); XVI,2(193) (305);
XVI,10,21(183)
Theophilus of Antioch, St. (late 2nd c.)
Three Books of Autolycus
Ed. & trans. G. Bardy & J.
Sender, *SCH,* 20(1948); trans.
M. Dods, *ANL,* 3(1867), 53-133
I,11*(31-32);* II,36(64);
III,11*(61);* III,14*(86) (278)*
Tipasius, Passion of *(Passio Tipasii)*
AB, 9(1890), 116-123; Monceaux,
259-269
(136-137)
Victorinus of Pettau, St. (end of 3rd c.)
Commentary on the Apocalypse
Ed. J. Haussleiter, *CSEL,*
49(1916), 12-154
19*(59)*
Zosimus (2nd half of 5th c.)
Ecclesiastical History
Ed. L. Mendelssohn, *Zozimi
Comitis et Exadvocati Fisci His-
toria nova* (Leipzig, 1887);
trans. J. A. C. Buchon, *Ouv-
rages historiques de Polybe,
Hérodien et Zozime* (Paris,
1836)
2,2(205); 2,19,1(311); 2,28-
29(321); 2,29(313)

Secondary Sources

A. G. (initials). Review of *EL*. *Fraternité Evangélique*, May 1960.

Aland, Kurt. "Die religiöse Haltung Kaiser Konstantins." *SP*, 1 (Berlin, 1957), 549-600.

D'Alès, A. *Priscillien et l'Espagne chrétienne à la fin du IVe Siècle*. Paris, 1936.

———. *Théologie de Tertullien*. Paris, 1905.

Alföldi, A. *The Conversion of Constantine and Pagan Rome*. Oxford, 1948.

———. *A Festival of Isis in Rome Under the Christian Emperors of the IVth Century*. Dissertationes Pannonicae, 2nd ser., 7. Budapest, 1937.

Alföldi, M. R. *Die Constantinische Goldprägung: Untersuchung zu ihrer Bedeutung für Kaiserpolitik und Hofkunst*. Mainz, 1963.

Allard, P. *Histoire des Persécutions pendant la Première Moitié du IIIe Siècle*. Paris, 1886.

———. *La Persécution de Dioclétien*, I. 3rd ed. Paris, 1908.

Altheim, F. "Konstantins Triumph von 312." *Zeitschrift für Religion und Geistesgeschichte*, 9 (1957), 221-231.

Amélineau, E. *Les Actes des Martyrs de l'Eglise copte*. Paris, 1890.

Aron, R. *Introduction à une philosophie de l'histoire*. Paris, 1938.

Arpee, L. *A History of Armenian Christianity*. New York, 1946.

Aubé, B. *L'Eglise et l'Etat dans la Deuxieme Moitié du IIIe Siècle*. Paris, 1886.

Babut, H. C. *L'Adoration des Empereurs et les Origines de la*

Persécution de Dioclétien. Paris, 1916.

_____. *La plus ancienne décrétale.* Paris, 1904.

_____. *Priscillien et le Priscillianisme.* Paris, 1909.

_____. "Paulin de Nole et Priscillien." *RHL*, 1 (1910), 97-130, 252-275.

_____. *Saint Martin de Tours.* Paris, 1913.

Bainton, R. H. "The Early Church and War." *HThR*, 39 (1946), 189-212. Also in Rufus M. Jones, ed., *The Church, the Gospel, and War.* New York, 1948, pp. 75-92.

Banner, W. A. "Origen and the Tradition of Natural Law Concept." *Dumbarton Oaks Papers*, 8 (1954), 49-82.

Bardy, G. "Arles (conciles d')." *Catholicisme*, I (1948), cols. 837-839.

_____. *L'Eglise et les Derniers Romains.* 8th ed. Paris, 1948.

_____. *Paul de Samosate*, rev. ed. Louvain, 1929.

Baresta, Luc. "L'Objection de conscience." *France catholique*, no. 848 (March 1, 1963).

Batiffol, P. "Les Premiers Chrétiens et la Guerre." *Revue du Clergé français*, 67 (1911), 222-242.

Baudrillart, A. *Saint Paulin.* 4th ed. Paris, 1928.

Bavaud, G. "Pourquoi Saint Maurice et ses compagnons ont-ils été martyrisés?" *L'Echo*, October 21, 1961.

_____. "Les premiers Chrétiens étaient-ils objecteurs de conscience?" *L'Echo*, October 14, 1961.

Bayet, A. *Pacifisme et Christianisme aux Premiers Siècles.* Paris, 1934.

Baynes, N. H. "Eusebius and the Christian Empire." *Mélanges Bidez.* Brussels, 1934, pp. 13-18; repr. in his *Byzantine Studies and other Essays.* London, 1955, pp. 168-172.

Beckwith, I. T. *The Apocalypse of John.* New York, 1919.

Bennett, J. C. *Social Salvation.* New York, 1935.

Benoit, A. Review of *EL. RHPR*, 42 (1962), 341-342.

Berchem, D. van. *Le Martyre de la Légion thébaine.* Basel, 1956.

_____. "Le 'De Pallio' de Tertullien et le Conflit du Christianisme et de l'Empire." *Museum Helveticum*, 1 (1944), 100-144.

Berkhof, H. *Kirche und Kaiser: eine Untersuchung der Entstehung der byzantinischen und theokratischen Staatsauffassung im vierten Jahrhundert.* Zürich, 1947.

Besnier, M. *L'Empire romain de l'Avènement des Sévères au*

Concile de Nicée. Paris, 1937.

Besret, B. *Incarnation ou eschatologie.* Paris, 1964.

Bethune-Baker, J. F. *The Influence of Christianity on War.* Cambridge, 1888.

Biardeau, M. "Gandhi, histoire et légende." *Esprit,* 22 (1954), 176-214.

Bigelmair, A. *Die Beteiligung der Christen am öffentlichen Leben in vorkonstantinischer Zeit.* Munich, 1902.

Botte, B. "L'Authenticité de la Tradition apostolique de saint Hippolyte." *RTAM,* 16 (1949), 177-184.

———. Review of A. Salles, *Trois antiques rituels du baptême. BTAM,* 8 (1958), 174-176.

———. "Les plus anciennes collections canoniques." *Orient Syrien,* 5 (1960), 331-350.

———. "Le Texte de la Tradition Apostolique." *RTAM,* 22 (1955), 161-172.

Bouyer, L. *La Spiritualité du Nouveau Testament et des Pères.* Paris, 1960.

Brasseur, A. "Les deux visions de Constantin." *Latomus,* 5 (1946), 35-40.

Broglie, A. de. *Saint Ambroise.* Paris, 1891.

Brunet, A. M. "La Guerre dans la Bible." *LV,* 7, no. 38 (1958), 31-47.

Burgelin, P. "La Fin de l'Ere constantinienne." *Foi et Vie,* 58 (1959), 3-20.

Cadoux, C. J. *The Early Christian Attitude to War.* London, 1919.

———. *The Early Church and the World.* Edinburgh, 1925.

Calder, W. M. "The Epigraphy of the Anatolian Heresies." In W. H. Buckler and W. M. Calder, eds., *Anatolian Studies Presented to Sir William Mitchell Ramsay.* Manchester, 1923, pp. 59-91.

———. "Studies in Early Christian Epigraphy." *Journal of Roman Studies,* 10 (1920), 42-59.

Camelot, P.-T. "Bulletin d'histoire des doctrines chrétiennes." *RSPT,* 46 (1962), 735-773.

———. "Les conciles oecuméniques des IVe et Ve siècles." In *Le Concile et les conciles.* Paris-Chevetogne, 1960, pp. 45-73.

———. Review of *EL. RSPT,* 45 (1961), 530.

Campenhausen, H. von. "Christians and Military Service in the

Early Church." In his *Tradition and Life in the Early Church: Essays and Lectures in Church History.* Transl. A. V. Littledale. London, 1968, pp. 160-170.

Capmany, J. *"Miles Christi" en la Espiritualidad de San Cipriano.* Collectanea San Paciano, Serie Teológica, I. Barcelona, 1956.

Carson, R. A. G. "The Emperor Constantine and Christianity." *History Today,* 6 (1956), 12-20.

Casavola, F. "La Politiche dei Cristiani pregiustinianei." *Labeo,* 1 (1955), 55-73.

Case, S. *The Revelation of John.* Chicago, 1919.

Caspar, E. *Geschichte des Papsttums von den Anfängen bis zur Höhe der Weltherrschaft.* 2 vols. Tübingen, 1930-1933.

Cayré, F. *Patrologie et Histoire de la Théologie.* 2 vols. 3rd ed. Paris, Tournai, Rome, 1945.

Cerfaux, L., and J. Tondriau. *Un Concurrent du Christianisme, le Culte des Souverains.* Tournai, 1958.

Chadwick, N. K. *The Age of the Saints in the Early Celtic Church.* London, 1961.

Chavannes, H. *L'Objection de conscience.* Lausanne, 1961.

Chenu, M. D. "L'Evolution de la Théologie de la Guerre." *LV,* 7, no. 38 (1958), 76-97.

Christophe, J. *Saint Martin, le soldat pacifique.* Lyon, 1966.

Clarke, W. K. L., ed. *The Ascetic Works of St. Basil.* London, 1925.

Clercq, V. C. de. *Ossius of Cordova: a Contribution to the History of the Constantinian Period.* The Catholic University of America, Studies in Christian Antiquity, XIII. Washington, 1954.

Combès, G. *La Doctrine politique de Saint Augustin.* Paris, 1927.

Comblin, J. *Théologie de la Paix,* II, *Applications.* Paris, 1963.

Congar, Y. *After Nine Hundred Years: The Background of the Schism Between the Eastern and Western Churches.* New York, 1959.

Courcelle, P. *Histoire littéraire des Grandes Invasions germaniques.* Paris, 1948.

Cranz, F. E. "Kingdom and Polity in Eusebius of Caesarea." *HThR,* 45 (1952), 47-66.

Cullmann, O. *Christ and Time: The Primitive Christian Conception of Time and History.* rev. ed. Transl. F. V. Filson. London, 1962.

———. "Le Caractère eschatologique du Devoir missionaire et de la Conscience apostolique de Saint Paul." *RHPR*, 16 (1936), 210-245.

———. *The State in the New Testament*. rev. ed. London, 1963.

Cunningham, W. *Christianity and Politics*. London, 1916.

Dale, A. W. W. *The Synod of Elvira and Christian Life in the Fourth Century*. London, 1882.

Daniélou, J. *Les Anges et leur Mission d'après les Pères de l'Eglise*. 2nd ed. Collection Irénikon, new ser., V. Paris-Chevetogne, 1953.

———. *Essai sur le Mystère de l'Histoire*. Paris, 1953.

———. *Le Mystère du Salut des Nations*. Paris, 1946.

———. "La Non-Violence selon l'Ecriture et la Tradition." *Action Chrétienne et Non-Violence*. Compte rendu du Congrès national Pax Christi, Paris, March 19-20, 1955. Paris, 1955.

———. Prayer as a Political Problem. Ed. and. and transl. J. R. Kirwan. Compass Books, XVI. London, 1967.

———, and H. I. Marrou. *Nouvelle Histoire de l'Eglise*, I, *Des origines à Grégoire le Grand*. Paris, 1963.

Davids, J. A. *De Orosio et Sancto Augustino Priscillianistarum Adversarii*. Nijmegen, 1930.

Davis, H. F. "The Early Christian Attitude to War." *Blackfriars*, 30 (1949), 477-482.

Delaruelle, E. "La Conversion de Constantin." *BLE*, 54 (1953), 37-54, 84-100.

———. A. Latreille, and J.-R. Palanque. *Histoire du Catholicisme en France*, I, *Des origines à la Chrétienté médiévale*. Paris, 1957.

Delehaye, H. *Etude sur le Légendier romain, les Saints de Novembre et de Décembre*. Brussels, 1936.

———. "Le Culte des Quatre Couronnés à Rome." *AB*, 32 (1913), 64-71.

———. *Les Légendes grecques des Saints militaires*. Paris, 1909.

———. *Les Passions des Martyrs et les Genres littéraires*. Paris, 1921.

———. "Saint Martin et Sulpice Sévère." *AB*, 38 (1920), 5-136.

———. "Saints de Thrace et de Mésie." *AB*, 31 (1912), 161-300.

Demougeot, E. "Remarques sur l'Emploi de 'Paganus.' " *Studi in*

Onore di H. Calderini e H. Paribeni. 2 vols. Milan, 1956-1957, I, pp. 337-350.

———. *La Théorie du Pouvoir impérial au Début du Ve Siècle.* Mélanges de la Société toulousaine d'Etudes classiques, I. Toulouse, 1946.

Dibelius, M. "Rom und die Christen im ersten Jahrhundert." In his *Botschaft und Geschichte: Gesammelte Aufsätze,* ed. Günther Bornkamm. 2 vols. Tübingen, 1953-1956, II, 177-228.

Diehl, E. *Inscriptiones latinae christianae veteres.* Revised edition by J. Moreau and H. I. Marrou. 4 vols. Dublin-Zürich, 1967-1970.

Dölger, F. J. "Sacramentum Militiae." In his *Antike und Christentum: Kultur- und religionsgeschichtliche Studien,* II. Münster, 1930, pp. 268-280.

Dörries, H. *Constantine the Great.* Transl. R. H. Bainton. New York, 1972.

Domenach, J.-M. "Les pacifismes et la guerre." *Esprit,* 22 (1954), 161-175.

Downey, G. "Education in the Christian Roman Empire: Christian and Pagan Theories Under Constantine and His Successors." *Speculum,* 32 (1957), 48-61.

Dubois, J. "Dasius." *Catholicisme,* III (1952), cols. 470-471.

Duchesne, L. *Early History of the Christian Church.* London, 1922.

———. *Liber pontificalis,* I. Paris, 1886.

Dumas, A. "L'Eglise d'avant Constantin et la violence." *Esprit,* 39 (1961), 308-319.

Dupraz, L. *Les Passions de S. Maurice d'Augaune: Essai sur l'historicité de la tradition et contribution à l'étude de l'armée prédioclétienne (260-286) et des canonisations tardives de la fin du IVe siècle.* Studia Friburgensia, n.s., XXVII. Fribourg, 1961.

Durry, M. *Les Cohortes prétoriennes.* Paris, 1938.

Dvornik, F. "The Authority of the State in the Oecumenical Council." *The Christian East,* 14 (1934), 95-107.

———. *Byzance et la Primauté romaine.* Paris, 1964.

Edmonds, H. "Geistlicher Kriegsdienst: Der Topos der militia spiritualis in der antiken Philosophie." In O. Casel, ed., *Heilige Überlieferung,* suppl. vol. to *Beiträge zur Geschichte des alten Mönchtums und des Benediktinerordens.* Münster, 1938. Reprinted in A. von Harnack, *Militia Christi*. Darmstadt, 1963, pp. 133-162.

Eger, H. "Kaiser und Kirche in der Geschichtstheologie Eusebs von Cäsarea." *ZNW*, 38 (1938), 97-115.

Ehrhardt, H. "Some Aspects of Constantine's Legislation." *SP*, 2 (Berlin, 1957), 114-121.

Fabre, P. *Saint Paulin de Nole et l'Amitié chrétienne*. Paris, 1949.

Fast, H. A. *Jesus and Human Conflict*. Scottdale, Pa., 1959.

Flon, O. "Le principe de la non-résistance au mal par la force, étude historique." Unpublished thesis, Protestant School of Theology, Montauban, 1906.

Florès, A. *La Conversion de Constantin le Grand*. Mémoire de diplôme de l'Ecole pratique des Hautes Etudes. Paris, 1949 (mimeo. ed.).

Florovsky, G. "Eschatology in the Patristic Age." *SP*, 2 (Berlin, 1957), 235-250.

Foakes-Jackson, F. J. *Eusebius Pamphili*. Cambridge, 1933.

Fontaine, J. "Christians and Military Service in the Early Church." *Concilium*, 7 (1965), 58-64.

_____. "Une clé littéraire de la Vita Martini de Sulpice Sévère: la typologie prophétique." In *Mélanges Mohrmann*. Utrecht-Antwerp, 1963, pp. 84-95.

_____. "Sulpice Sévère a-t-il travesti S. Martin de Tours en martyr militaire?" *AB*, 71 (1963), 31-58.

_____. "Verité et Fiction dans la chronologie de la Vita Martini." *Studia Anselmiana*, 46 (1961), 189-236.

Frend, W. H. C. "The Persecutions: Some Links Between Judaism and the Early Church." *JEH*, 9 (1958), 141-158.

Fritz, G. "Service militaire." *DTC*, XIV (1941), cols. 1972-1981.

Gagé, J. "Le 'Signum' astrologique de Constantin et le Millénarisme de 'Roma aeterna.'" *RHPR*, 31 (1951), 181-223.

_____. "Stauros nikopoios, La Victoire impériale dans l'Empire chrétien," *RHPR*, 13 (1933), 370-400.

Gagnier, P. Review of *EL*. *Bulletin du CPED* (Centre protestant d'Etudes et de documentation), n.s., 53-54 (Aug. - Oct., 1960), 5-6.

Gaiffier, B. de. "Saint Marcel de Tanger ou de Léon." *AB*, 61 (1943), 116-139.

————. "Sub Juliano Apostata dans le martyrologe romain." *AB*, 74 (1956), 5-49.

Galletier, E., ed. *Panégyriques latins*, II, *Les Panégyriques constantiniens*. Paris, 1959.

Ganshof, F.-L. "Saint Martin et le Comte Avitianus." *AB*, 67 (1949), 203-223.

Gaubert, H. *Les Saints sur les Champs de Bataille*. Paris, 1941.

Gaudemet, J. *L'Eglise dans l'Empire romain (IV ^{e} - V ^{e} siècles)*. In *Histoire du Droit et des Institutions de l'Eglise d'Occident*, ed. G. Lebras, III. Paris, 1958.

————. "Elvire." *DHGE*, XV (1963), cols. 317-348.

Gavillet, M. "Un Problème à revoir." *Le Lien de l'Eglise évangélique du Canton de Vaud*, November 24, 1960.

Génier, R. *Vie de Saint Euthyme le Grand (377-473)*. Paris, 1909.

Gerest, R.-C. "Les premiers chrétiens face à leur monde." *LV*, 12, no. 73 (1963), 3-24.

Giannelli, G. "La Primitiva Chiesa cristiana di Fronte alle Persecuzioni e el Martirio." *Nuovo Didaskaleion*, 3 (1949), 5-22.

Giet, S. *Les Idées et l'Action de Saint Basile*. Paris, 1941.

Giocarinis, K. "An Unpublished Late Thirteenth-Century Commentary of the Nicomedian Ethics of Aristotle." *Traditio*, 15 (1959), 299-317.

Goguel, M. *The Birth of Christianity*. Transl. H.C.Snape (London, 1953).

————. *Les Chrétiens et l'Empire romain à l'époque du Nouveau Testament*. Paris, 1905.

————. *Jésus*. 2nd ed. Paris, 1950.

————. *The Life of Jesus*. Transl. O. Wyon. London, 1933.

————. "Juifs et Romains dans l'Histoire de la Passion." *RHR*, 62 (1910), 165-182, 295-322.

Greenslade, S. L. *Church and State from Constantine to Theodosius*. London, 1954.

Gregg, R. B. *The Power of Nonviolence*. 2nd ed. London, 1960.

Grégoire, H. "L'Authenticité et l'historicité de la 'Vita Constantini' attribuée à Eusèbe de Césarée." *BARB*, 39 (1953), 462-478.

————. "La 'conversion' de Constantin." *Revue de l'Université de Bruxelles*, 36 (1930-1931), 231-272.

————. "Les inscriptions hérétiques d'Asie Mineure." *Byz*, 1 (1924), 695-710.

————. "Notes bibliographiques." *BARB*, 34 (1947), 224-235.

————. "Notes epigraphiques, IV." *Byz*, 8 (1933), 65-69.

————. "Nouvelles Observations sur le Nombre des Martyrs." *BARB*, 38 (1952), 37-60.

————. "Nouvelles Recherches constantiniennes." *Byz*, 13 (1938), 551-588.

————. P. Orgels, J. Moreau, and A. Maricq. *Les Persécutions dans l'Empire romain*. Brussels, 1951.

————. "Travaux récent sur Constantin le Grand." *Byz*, 7 (1932), 645-652.

Griffe, E. "*La Chronologie des années de jeunesse de Saint Martin.*" *BLE*, 63 (1961), 114-118.

————. *La Gaule chrétienne à l'époque romaine*. Paris-Toulouse, 1947. 2nd ed., Paris, 1964.

————. "Saint Martin et le monachisme gaulois." *Studia Anselmiana*, 46 (1961), 3-24.

Guérin, D. *Jeunesse du socialisme libertaire*. Paris, 1959.

————. *La Lutte des classes sous la Première République*. 7th ed. 2 vols. Paris, 1946.

Guey, J. "La Date de la Pluie miraculeuse (172 après J.-C.) et la Colonne aurélienne." *MAH*, 60 (1948), 105-127; 61 (1949), 93-118.

————. "Encore la Pluie miraculeuse." *RPh*, 23 (1948), 16-62.

Guignebert, C. *Tertullien*. Paris, 1901.

Halkin, F. "Faux martyrs et inscriptions hagiographiques." *AB*, 67 (1949), 88-96.

————. "Une Nouvelle vie de Constantin dans un Légendaire de Patmos." *AB*, 77 (1959), 63-107, 370-372.

Hall, D. E. "La Conversión del Emperador Constantino." *Pensiamento Cristiano*, 6 (1958), 149-169.

Halphen, L. *Les Barbares*. 3rd ed. Paris, 1936.

Hamman, A., ed. *La Geste du Sang*. Paris, 1953.

Hanke, L. U. *The Spanish Struggle for Justice in the Conquest of America*. Philadelphia, 1959.

Hanssens, J. M. *La Liturgie d'Hippolyte, ses documents, son titulaire, ses origines et son charactère*. Orientalia Christiana Analecta, 155. Rome, 1959.

————. "La Liturgie d'Hippolyte, assentiments et dissentiments." *Gregorianum*, 42 (1961), 290-302.

352   It Is Not Lawful for Me to Fight

Harnack, A. von. *Militia Christi: Die christliche Religion und der Soldatenstand in den ersten drei Jahrhunderten.* Tübingen, 1905; repr., Darmstadt, 1963.

———. *The Mission and Expansion of Christianity in the First Three Centuries.* 2 vols. London, 1908.

Hartke, W. *Römische Kinderkaiser.* Berlin, 1951.

Heering, G. J. *The Fall of Christianity: A Study of Christianity, the State and War.* Transl. J. W. Thompson. New York, 1943.

Hefelé, C. J. von. *Beiträge zur Kirchengeschichte, Archäologie und Liturgik.* 2 vols. Tübingen, 1874.

———. *Conciliengeschichte.* 9 vols. Freiburg/Breisgau, 1855-1890.

———. *Histoire des Conciles d'après les documents originaux.* 2nd Fr. ed. 11 vols. (vol. 1-10, transl. H. Leclercq). Paris, 1907-1952.

Heggelbacher, O. *Vom Römischen zum Christlichen Recht: Juristische Elemente in den Schriften des sog. Ambrosiaster.* Freiburg/Breisgau, 1959.

Hegnauer, R. *Le Combattant non-violent.* Lausanne, 1960.

Heiland, F. *Die astronomische Deutung der Vision Konstantins.* Lecture, Zeiss Planetarium, Jena, October 1948.

Hershberger, G. F. *The Way of the Cross in Human Relationships.* Scottdale, Pa., 1958.

Herval, R. "La Province ecclésiastique de Rouen aux IV ᵉ et V ᵉ siècles." *MSR,* 16 (1959), 47-70.

Hildesheimer, E. "Les Clercs et l'exemption du service militaire à l'èpoque franque." *RHEF,* 29 (1943), 5-18.

Hobhouse, W. *The Church and the World in Idea and in History.* London, 1910.

Homo, L. *Les Empereurs romains et le Christianisme.* Paris, 1931.

Honigmann, E. *Patristic Studies.* Vatican City, 1953.

Horner, G. *The Statutes of the Apostles or Canones Ecclesiastici.* London, 1904.

Hornus, J.-M. "Christianisme et désordre établi." *CS,* 74 (1966), 662-673.

———. "Du côté des Mennonites." *CS,* 69 (1961), 698-701.

———. "Dieu et la Guerre dans la Théologie de Karl Barth." *CS,* 63 (1955), 580-590.

———. "Etude sur la pensée politique de Tertullien." *RHPR,* 38 (1958), 1-38.

────. "L'Excommunication des Militaires dans la Discipline chrétienne." *Communio Viatorum*, 3 (1960), 41-60.

────. "L'Imposture des Croisades." *Communio Viatorum*, 6 (1963), 143-166.

────. "Les Pères de l'Eglise et la non-violence." *Cahiers de la Réconciliation*, March 1962, 1-17; repr. in *Paix et Coexistence*, 3 (1962), 6-12.

────. Review of L. Dupraz, *Les Passions. RHPR*, 48 (1968), 285-288.

────. Review of Sulpicius Severus, *Vita Martini*, ed. J. Fontaine, *SCH. RHPR*, 50 (1970), 77-79.

Hünermann, G. *L'Apôtre des Gaules*. Transl. E. Saillard. Paris, 1964.

Isaac, J. *La Dispersion d'Israël, Fait historique ou Mythe théologique?* Algiers, 1954.

Jaffé, P. *Regesta Pontificum Romanorum ab condita ecclesia ad annum post Christum natum 1198*. 2 vols. Leipzig, 1885-1888.

Jardel, M. *Le Soldat du Christ, Saint Martin de Tours*. Paris, 1967.

Jaubert, A. *La Date de la Cène*. Paris, 1957.

Jolif. J.-Y. "Pourquoi la Guerre?" *LV*, 7, no. 38 (1958), 5-30.

Jones, A. H. M. *The Later Roman Empire, 284-602*. 3 vols. Oxford, 1964.

────. "Notes on the Genuineness of the Constantinian Documents in Eusebius' 'Life of Constantine.'" *JEH*, 5 (1954), 196-200.

Jong, K. H. de. *Dienstweigering bij de oude Christenen*. Leiden, 1905.

Journet, C. "Les Trois Cités (de Dieu, de l'Homme et du Diable)." *Nova vetera*, 33 (1958), 25-48.

Juster, J. *Les Juifs dans l'Empire romain*. 2 vols. Paris, 1914.

Kaufmann, C. M. *Handbuch der altchristlichen Epigraphie*. Freiburg/Breisgau, 1917.

Knopf, D. R., ed. *Ausgewählte Martyrerakten*. 3rd ed. Tübingen, 1929.

Kraft, H. "Kaiser Konstantin und das Bischofsamt." *Saeculum*, 8 (1957), 32-42.

────. "Zur Taufe Kaiser Konstantins." *SP*, 1 (Berlin, 1957), 642-648.

_____. "ὁμοούσιος." *ZKG*, 66 (1955), 1-24.

Kyriakides, S. P. "Kōnstantinos ho Megas kai hē autokratikē latreia", *Hellēnika*, XVII, 17, pp. 220-270.

Labhardt, A. "Tertullien et la Philosophie ou la Recherche d'une Position pure." *Museum Helveticum*, 7 (1950), 159-180.

Laboulaye, E. *Journal des débats*, October 2, 1860.

Labriolle, P. *Histoire de la Littérature Latine Chrétienne*. 3rd ed., rev. G. Bardy. 2 vols. Paris, 1947.

_____. "Paroecia." *ALMA*, 3 (1927), 196-205.

_____. " Παροικια, Paroecia." *RSR*, 18 (1928), 60-72.

_____. *Saint Ambroise*. Paris, 1908.

Lacombrade, C. *Synésios de Cyrène, Hellène et chrétien*. Paris, 1951.

Lanversin, P. de. "Une belle dispute: Hippolyte est-il d'Occident ou d'Orient?" *Proche-Orient chrétien*, 6 (1956), 118-122.

Laquer,   R. *Eusebius als Historiker seiner Zeit*. Berlin-Leipzig, 1929.

Lasserre, J. *War and the Gospel*. Transl. O. Coburn. Scottdale, Pa., 1962.

Latourette, K. S. *A History of the Expansion of Christianity*, I, *The First Five Centuries*. New York, 1937.

Laufer, F. "O Triunfo da Cruz no tempo de Constantino." *Estudios* (Brazil), 19, no. 73 (1959), 81-95.

Le Blant, E. *Inscriptions chrétiennes de la Gaule*, I. Paris, 1856.

_____. *Manuel d'Epigraphie Chrétienne d'après les marbres de la Gaule, accompagné d'une bibliographie spéciale*. Paris, 1869.

Lebreton, J., and J. Zeiller. *De la Fin du II e Siècle à la Paix constantinienne*. In Fliche et Martin, *Histoire de l'Eglise*, II. Paris, 1935.

_____. *The History of the Primitive Church*. Transl. E. C. Messenger of vols. I-II of Fliche et Martin, *Histoire de l'Eglise*. 4 vols. London, 1942-1948.

Leclercq, H. "Accusations contre les Chrétiens." *DAL*, I (1907), cols. 265-307.

_____. *Les Martyrs*, I. Paris, 1902.

_____. "Militarisme." *DAL*, XI (1933), cols. 1108-1181.

Leclercq, J. "Un document sur les débuts des Templiers." *RHE*, 52 (1957), 81-91.

Lecoy de la Marche. *Saint Martin.* 3rd ed. Tours, 1890.

Leenhardt, F. *Le Chrétien doit-il servir l'Etat?* Geneva, Switzerland, 1939

———. "Le Christianisme primitif et la Guerre." *CS*, 43 (1930), 331-337.

Lietzmann, H. "Der Glaube Konstantins des Grossen." *SAB* 29 (1937), 263-275.

———. *A History of the Early Church.* Transl. B. L. Woolf. 4 vols. London, 1961.

———. "Der Prozess Jesu." *SAB*, 23 (1931), 313-322.

Lightfoot, J. B. "Eusebius of Caesarea." *DCB*, II, cols. 308-348.

Lods, M. "L'Eglise du IIIe Siècle devant le Service de l'Etat." *Bulletin de la Faculté libre de Théologie protestante de Paris,* 13, no. 35 (1950), 13-26.

Lopuszanski, G. "Les Chrétiens dans l'armée romaine." Unpublished PhD thesis, Faculté de Philosophie et Lettres, Brussels University, 1949.

Lorson, P. *Défense de tuer.* Paris, 1953.

Lortz, J. *Tertullian als Apologet.* 2 vols. Münster, 1928.

Lot, F. *Nouvelles Recherches sur l'Impôt foncier et la Capitation personnelle sous le Bas-Empire.* Paris, 1955.

Lovsky, F. *Antisémitisme et Mystère d'Israël.* Paris, 1955.

MacMullen, Ramsay. *Soldier and Civilian in the Later Roman Empire.* Harvard Historical Monographs, 52. Cambridge, Mass., 1963.

Malone, E. E. "Martyrdom and Monastic Profession as a Second Baptism." In A. Mayer, J. Quasten, and B. Neunheuser, eds., *Vom Christlichen Mysterium* (Festschrift O. Casel). Düsseldorf, 1951, pp. 115-135.

Mansi, J. D. *Sacrorum Conciliorum Nova et Amplissima Collectio.* 35 vols. Florence, 1759 (facsimile reproduction, Paris-Leipzig, 1901-1902).

Marrou, H. I. "Civitas Dei, Civitas terrena: num tertium quid?" *SP*, 2 (Berlin, 1957), 342-350.

———. "La Fin du Monde n'est pas pour Demain." *LV*, 2, no. 11 (1953), 77-99.

———. Review of D. van Berchem, *Le Martyre. RHR*, 152 (1957), 236-240.

Martimort, A. G. "La Tradition Apostolique d'Hippolyte et le rituel baptismal antique." *BLE*, 60 (1959), 57-62.

Martin, C. Review of *EL*. *Nouvelle Revue Théologique*, 84 (1962), 1000-1001.

Marucchi, O. "Lavori nelle catacombe romane." *Nuova Bullettino di Archeologia Cristiana*, 6 (1900), 337-344.

Mascaux, A. "Les Martyrs militaires en Afrique à la Fin du III ^{e} siècle." Thesis, Faculty of Protestant Theology, Paris, 1925.

Mattingly, H. "The Later Paganism." *HThR*, 35 (1942), 171-179.

Maurice, J. *Constantin le Grand, L'Origine de la civilisation chrétienne*. Paris, 1924.

──────. *Numismatique constantinienne*. 3 vols. Paris, 1908-1912.

Mehl, R. "Le Christianisme primitif et le problème de la guerre." *Le Monde*, December 26, 1961.

Ménard, P. "Profil de Saint Martin." *Revue de l'Université de Laval*, 8 (1953), 3-19, 115-138.

Menoud, P. H. *L'Evangile de Jean*. 2nd ed. Neuchâtel-Paris, 1947.

Mercurelli, C. "Il sarcofago di un centurione pretoriano cristiano e la diffusione del cristianesimo nelle coorti pretorie." *Riviste di Archeologia Cristiana*, 16 (1939), 73-99.

Meslin, M. Review of *EL*. *Archives de Sociologie des Religions*, 10 (1960), 184-185.

Meyendorff, J. *Introduction à l'étude de Grégoire Palamas*. Paris, 1959.

Mihailov, G. *Inscriptiones Graecae in Bulgaria repertae*. Academia Litterarum Bulgarica, Institutum Archaeologicum, Series Epigraphica, IX. Sofia, 1966.

Milburn, R. L. P. *Early Christian Interpretations of History*. New York, 1954.

Misset, E. *Pourquoi Saint Martin refusa-t-il de combattre: Pugnare mihi non licet et le 74 ^{e} Canon d'Hippolyte*. Paris, 1907.

Moffat, J. "War." In J. Hastings, ed., *Dictionary of the Apostolic Church*. Edinburgh, 1915-1918, II, pp. 644-673.

Mohrmann, C. "Encore une Fois 'Paganus.'" *VC*, 7 (1952), 109-122; repr. in her *Etudes sur le Latin des Chrétiens*, III. Rome, 1965, pp. 277-289.

──────. "Epiphania." *RSPT*, 37 (1953), 644-670; repr. in her *Etudes sur le Latin des Chrétiens*, I. 2nd ed. Rome, 1961, pp. 245-275.

──────. "Sacramentum dans les plus anciens textes chrétiens." *HThR*, 47 (1954), 141-152; repr. in her *Etudes sur le Latin des Chrétiens*, I. 2nd ed. Rome, 1961, pp. 233-244.

──────. "Statio." *VC*, 7 (1953), 221-245; repr. in her *Etudes sur le Latin des Chrétiens*, III. Rome, 1965, pp. 307-330.

Molnár, A. "L'Eschatologie contre l'Impérialisme romain." Unpublished lecture given at the pastoral meeting of the Union of Czech Brethren, January 30-February 3, 1955. Reported in *Protestant Churches in Czechoslovakia*, 2, no. 2 (1956), p. 13.

Monceaux, P. "Etude critique sur la Passio Tipasii." *Revue archéologique*, 4, no. 4 (1904), 267-274.

──────. *Histoire littéraire de l'Afrique chrétienne*. 2 vols. Paris, 1901-1902.

──────. "La Question du Priscillianisme." *JS*, n.s., 9 (1911), 70-75, 104-113.

──────. "Saint Augustin et la Guerre." In P. Batiffol, *et al.*, *L'Eglise et la Guerre*. Paris, 1913.

──────. *Saint Cyprien*. Paris, 1914.

──────. *La Vraie Légende dorée*. Paris, 1928.

Monod, G. "L'Histoire." In F. Thomas, ed., *De la méthode dans les Sciences*. Paris, 1909.

Moreau, E. de. "Le Nombre des Martyrs des Persécutions romaines." *NRTh*, 73 (1951), 812-832.

──────. "Nouvelles Observations sur le Nombre des Martyrs." *BARB*, 38 (1952), 62-70.

Moreau, J. "Eusèbe de Césarée." *DHGE*, XV (1963), cols. 1437-1460.

──────. "Les Litterae Licinii." *AUS*, 2 (1953), 100-105.

──────. "Notes d'Histoire romaine." *AUS*, 2 (1953), 89-99.

──────. *La Persécution du Christianisme dans l'Empire romain*. Paris, 1956.

──────. "Vérité historique et Propagande politique chez Lactance et dans la Vita Constantini." *AUS*, 4 (1955), 89-97.

──────. "Zur Religionspolitik Konstantins des Grossen." *AUS*, 1 (1952), 160-168.

Mulders, J. "Vitricius van Rouan, Leven en leer." *Bijdragen*, 17 (1956), 1-25; 18 (1957), 270-289.

Musurillo, H., ed. *The Acts of the Christian Martyrs*. Oxford, 1972.

Nautin, P. *Hippolyte et Josipe. Contribution à l'histoire de la littérature chrétienne du 3ᵉ siècle.* Paris, 1947.

Neill, S. *A History of Christian Missions.* London, 1964.

Nève, F. "Constantin et Théodose devant les Églises orientales." In his *L'Arménie chrétienne et sa littérature.* Paris, 1886.

Newman, J. "Modern War and Pacifism." *Irish Theological Quarterly,* n.s., 28 (1961), 181-206.

Nielsen, E. "La guerre considérée comme une religion et la religion comme une guerre." *Studia Theologica,* 15 (Aarhus, 1961), 93-112.

Opitz, H.-G., ed. *Athanasius Werke,* III, i, *Urkunden zur Geschichte des Arianischen Streites.* Berlin-Leipzig, 1934.

Orgels, P. "A propos des erreurs historiques de la *Vita Constantini.*" In *Mélanges H. Grégoire, Revue Internationale de Philosophie.* Brussels, 1963, pp. 575-611.

Ortroy, F. van. "Saint Ambroise et l'Empereur Théodose." *AB,* 23 (1904), 417-426.

Ostrogorsky, G. *History of the Byzantine State.* Transl. J. Hussey. Oxford, 1956.

P. M. (initials). Review of *EL. Feuille d'Avis de Lausanne.* Nov. 15, 1960.

Palanque, J.-R. "Un anniversaire." *Le Monde,* March 30, 1966.

———. *Le Christianisme et l'Occident barbare.* Paris, 1945.

———. "Constantin, Empereur chrétien, d'après ses Récents Historiens." In *Etudes médiévales offertes à M. le Doyen Fliche.* Paris, 1952, pp. 133-142.

———. "Constantin Iᵉʳ le Grand." *DHGE,* XIII (1956), cols. 593-608.

———. "A propos du Prétendu Edit de Milan." *Byz,* 10 (1935), 607-616.

———, G. Bardy, P. de Labriolle, G. de Plinval, L. Brehier. *The Church in the Christian Roman Empire.* Transl. E. C. Messenger. 2 vols. London, 1949-1952.

Paredi, A. *S. Ambroglio e la sua Eta.* 2nd ed. Milan, 1960.

Parker, T. M. *Christianity and the State in the Light of History.* London, 1955.

Pasquali, G. *Storia della Tradizione e Critica del Testo.* Florence, 1934.

Peterson, E. *Le Mystère des Juifs et des Gentils dans l'Eglise*. Paris, n.d.

———. *Der Monotheismus als politisches Problem*. Leipzig, 1935.

———. "Das Problem des Nationalismus im alten Christentum." *ThZ*, 7 (1951), 81-91.

Petit, P. "Libanius et la 'Vita Constantini.' " *Historia*, 1 (1950), 562-582.

Peyer, E. de. "Chronique théologique: L'Eglise en son chemin vers la fidélité." *Journal de Genève, June 28, 1960*.

Pflaum, H. G. Review of D. van Berchem, *Le Martyre. RELA*, 34 (1956), 410-413.

Philip, A. *Le Christianisme et la Paix*. Paris, 1933.

Piganiol, A. "Bulletin historique, Histoire romaine, 5." *RH*, 219 (1959), 129-139.

———. *L'Empereur Constantin*. Paris, 1932.

———. *L'Empire chrétien, 325-395*. Paris, 1947.

———. "L'Etat actuel de la Question constantinienne, 1930-1949." *Historia*, 1 (1950), 82-96.

Pichon, R. *Lactance, Etude sur le Mouvement philosophique et religieux sous le Règne de Constantin*. Paris, 1901.

Plinval, G. de. "Tertullien et le Scandale de la Couronne." In *Mélanges de Ghellinck*. Gembloux, 1951.

Preuschen, E. *Analekta*, I, *Staat und Christentum bis auf Konstantin*. 2nd ed. Tübingen, 1909.

———. "Problemi di nonviolenza." *Protestantismo*, 1967, pp. 186-187.

Profillet, C. *Les Saints militaires, Martyrologe, Vies et Notices*. 6 vols. Paris, 1891.

Puech, A. "Les Origines du Priscillianisme et l'Orthodoxie de Priscillien." *BALAC*, 2 (1912), 81-95, 161-213.

———. *Saint Jean Chrysostome et les Moeurs de son temps*. Paris, 1891.

Pury, R. de. *La Maison de Dieu*. Cahiers théologiques, 14. Neuchâtel, 1946.

Quasten, J. *Patrology*. 3 vols. Utrecht-Brussels, 1950-1960.

Rahner, H. *L'Eglise et l'Etat dans le Christianisme primitif*. Transl. G. Zinck. Paris, 1964.

———. "Pompa Diaboli." *ZkTh*, 55 (1931), 239-273.

Ramsay, W. M. "The Cities and Bishoprics of Phrygia." *Journal of*

Hellenic Studies, 4 (1883), 370-436.

_____. *The Cities and Bishoprics of Phrygia.* 2 vols. Oxford, 189ι.

Regamey, P. R. "La conscience chrétienne et la guerre." *Cahiers St. Jacques*, no. 27 (1962).

Régnier, A. *Saint Martin.* 6th ed. Paris, 1925.

Régout, R. *La Doctrine de la Guerre juste de Saint Augustin à nos jours.* Paris, 1935.

Richard, M. "Bibliographie de la Controverse: Hippolyte-Josipe." *PO*, 27, ii (1954), 271-272.

_____. "Bulletin de Patrologie." *MSR*, 5 (1948), 273-308.

_____. "Comput et chronographie chez S. Hippolyte." *MSR*, 7 (1950), 237-268; 8 (1951), 19-50.

Richardson, C. C. "The Date and Setting of the Apostolic Tradition of Hippolytus." *Anglican Theological Review*, 30 (1948), 38-44.

Richard-Molard, G. Review of *EL. Réforme*, October 15, 1960.

Ricoeur, P. *Etat et Violence.* Geneva, 1957.

_____. "L'homme non-violent et sa présence à l'histoire." *Esprit*, 18 (1949), 224-234.

_____. "La merveille, l'errance, l'énigme." *Esprit*, 28 (1960), 1665-1676.

Riedel, W. *Die Kirchenrechtsquellen des Patriarchats Alexandrien.* Leipzig, 1900.

Robert, J., and Louis Robert. "Bulletin épigraphique." *Revue des Etudes Grecques*, 75 (1962), 130-226.

Robert, L. *Noms indigènes dans l'Asie-Mineure gréco-romaine.* Bibliothèque archéologique et historique de l'Institut Français d'Archéologie d'Istanbul, 13. Paris, 1963.

_____. "Séance du 4 Mai 1962." *Comptes-rendus de l'Académie des Inscriptions et Belles-Lettres pour 1962.* Paris, 1963, p. 115.

Roques, R. Review of *EL RHR*, 164 (1963), 239-242.

Rordorf, W. "Tertullians Beurteilung des Soldatenstandes." *VC*, 23 (1969), 105-141.

Rossi, G. B. de., ed. *Inscriptiones Christianae Urbis Romae septimo saeculo antiquiores.* 2 vols. Rome, 1861, 1888.

Roth, C. Review of D. van Berchem, *Le Martyre. Revue Suisse d'Histoire*, 1957, pp. 511-514.

Rouget, J. Review of *EL. Vie Protestante*, December 2, 1960.

Rouquette, R. Review of *EL. Etudes*, 308, i (1961), 424.

Runciman, J. C. S. *A History of the Crusades.* 3 vols. Cambridge, 1952-1954.

Ryan, E. A. "The Rejection of Military Service by Early Christians." *TS*, 13 (1952), 1-32.

_____. Review of *EL. Erasmus*, 15 (1963), cols. 453-454.

Sabatier, P. *Vie de S. François d'Assise.* Paris, n.d.

Salles, R. "La Tradition apostolique est-elle un témoin de la liturgie romaine?" *RHR*, 148 (1955), 181-213.

_____. *Trois antiques rituels du baptême. SCH*, LIX. Paris, 1958.

Schatz, W. "Studien zur Geschichte und Vorstellungswelt des frühen abendländischen Mönchtums." Unpubl. thesis, University of Freiburg/Breisgau, 1957.

Schilling, R. *La religion romaine de Vénus depuis les origines jusqu'au temps d'Auguste.* Paris, 1954.

Scott, E. F. *Man and Society in the New Testament.* New York, 1946.

Secrétan, H. F. "Le Christianisme des Premiers Siècles et le Service militaire." *RTP*, 2 (1914), 345-365.

Seston, W. *Dioclétien et la Tétrarchie*, I. Paris, 1946.

_____. "L'Opinion païenne et la Conversion de Constantin." *RHPR*, 16 (1936), 250-264.

_____. "A Propos de la Passio Marcelli Centurionis." In P. Benoit, *et al., Aux Sources de la Tradition chrétienne, Mélanges offerts à M. Goguel.* Neuchâtel, 1950.

Setton, K. M. *Christian Attitude Towards the Emperor in the Fourth Century.* New York, 1941.

Simon, M. *Verus Israël.* Paris, 1948.

Sirinelli, J. *Les Vues Historiques d'Eusèbe de Césarée durant la Période Prénicéenne.* Université de Dakar, Faculté des Lettres et Sciences Humaines, Publications de la Section des Langues et Littératures, 10. Dakar, 1961.

Soras, A. de. "Le Problème de l'Objection de Conscience." *Revue de l'Action populaire*, 36 (1950), 241-254.

Spanneut, M. "Eusèbe de Nicomedie." *DHGE,* 15 (1963), cols. 1466-1472.

Stauffer, E. *Christ and the Caesars: Historical Sketches.* Transl. K. and R. Gregor Smith. London, 1955.

Straub, J. "Kaiser Konstantin als episkopos tōn ektos." *SP*, 1 (Berlin, 1957), 678-695.

Sturzo, L. *Church and State.* Transl. B. B. Carter. Notre Dame, Indiana, 1962.

Tanquerey, A. "Synthèse de la doctrine théologique sur le droit de guerre." In P. Batiffol, *et al., L'Eglise et la guerre.* Paris, 1913.

Thamin, R. *Saint Ambroise et la Morale chrétienne au IV*ᵉ *Siècle.* Paris, 1895.

Treu, K. *Synesios von Kyrene, Ein Kommentar zu seinem "Dion."* *TU*, LXXI. Berlin, 1958.

Treu, U. "Etymologie und Allegorie bei Klemens von Alexandrien." *SP*, IV (*TU*, 79 [Berlin, 1961]), 191-211.

Turmel, J. "L'Eschatalogie à la fin du IV ᵉ siècle." *RHL*, 3 (1900), 97-127, 200-232, 289-321.

————. *Histoire des Dogmes.* 6 vols. Paris, 1931-1936.

Vacandard, E. "La Question du Service militaire chez les Chrétiens des Premiers Siècles." *Etudes de Critique et d'Histoire religieuse*, 2nd ser., Paris, 1910, pp. 127-168.

————. *Saint Victrice, Evêque de Rouen.* Paris, 1903.

Vanderpol, A. *La Doctrine scolastique du Droit de Guerre.* Paris, 1925.

————. "Le 'Droit de Guerre' de François de Victoria." In P. Batiffol, *et al., L'Eglise et la Guerre.* Paris, 1913.

————. "Le traité 'De Indis' de F. de Victoria." In P. Batiffol., *et al., L'Eglise et la Guerre.* Paris, 1913.

Verseils, P. Review of *EL. Etudes évangéliques*, 20 (1960), 120.

Vicaire, M. H. Review of *EL. RHE*, 56 (1961), 391-392.

Villemain, A. F. *Tableau de l'éloquence chrétienne au IV*ᵉ *siècle.* Paris, 1849.

Villey, M. Review of *EL. RHDF*, 40 (1962), 267-268.

Viollet, L. "L'Objection de Conscience." *L'Ami du Clergé*, 60 (1950), 369-376.

Vischer, L. Review of *EL. ThZ*, 17 (1961), 66-68.

Visser, A. J. "Christianus sum, non possum militare, Soldaten-martyria uit de derde eeuw." *Nederlandsch archief voor kerkelijke geschiedenis*, 48 (1967), 5-19.

Vittinghoff, F. "Eusebius als Verfasser der *Vita Constantini.*" *RhM*, 96 (1953), 330-373.

Vogt, J. "Die Vita Constantini des Eusebius über den Konflikt zwischen Constantin und Licinius." *Historia*, 2 (1953-1954), 463-471.

_____, and H. Last. "Christenverfolgung." *RACh*, II (1954), cols. 1159-1228.

Vogüé, A. de. *La Communauté et l'abbé dans la Règle de St. Basile.* Paris, 1961.

Waszink, J. H. "Pompa Diaboli." *VC*, 1 (1947), 15-41.

Weinel, H. *Die Stellung des Urchristentums zum Staat.* Tübingen, 1908.

Wilhelm, A. "Griechische Grabinschriften aus Kleinasien." *Sitzungsberichte der Preussischen Akademie der Wissenschaften*, Phil.-Hist. Klasse, 27 (1932), 792-865.

Willamowitz-Moellendorff, U. von. "Die Hymnen des Proklos und Synesios." *SAB*, 14 (1907), 272-295.

Wilmart, A. "Le texte latin de la Paradosis de Saint Hippolyte." *RSR*, 9 (1919), 62-71.

Windass, S. *Christianity Versus Violence: A Social and Historical Study of War and Christianity.* London, 1964.

_____, with a rejoinder by J. Newman. "The Early Christian Attitude to War." *Irish Theological Quarterly*, 29 (1962), 235-248.

_____. "Saint Augustine and the Just War." *Blackfriars*, 43 (November, 1962), 460-468.

Wurm, H. *Studien und Texte zur Dekretalensammlung des Dionysius Exiguus.* Bonn, 1939.

Zahn, T. *Der Hirte des Hermas.* Gotha, 1868.

Zeiller, J. *Origines chrétiennes dans les provinces danubiennes.* Paris, 1918.

Secondary Sources (Supplement)*

Aland, Kurt. "The Relation Between Church and State in Early Times: A Reinterpretation." *Journal of Theological Studies*, 19 (1968), 115-127.

Auer, Joan. "Militia Christi." *DS*, X (1979), cols. 1210-1223.

Barclay, W. "Church and State in the Apologists." *Expository Times*, 1 (1937-1938), 360-362.

Baynes, N. H. "Constantine the Great and the Christian Church." *Proceedings of the British Academy*, 15(1929), 341-442.

Beskow, P. *Rex Gloriae: The Kingship of Christ in the Early Church*. Stockholm, 1962.

Bienert, W. *Krieg, Kriegsdienst und Kriegsdienstverweigerung nach der Botschaft des Neuen Testaments*. Stuttgart, 1952.

Brock, P. *Pacifism in Europe to 1914*. Princeton, 1972.

Cadbury, H. J. "The Basis of Early Christian Antimilitarism." *Journal of Biblical Literature*, 37 (1918), 66-94.

Chadwick, H. *Priscillian of Avila*. Oxford, 1976.

Crescenti, G. *Obiettori di coscienza e martiri militari dei primi cinque secoli del Cristianesimo*. Palermo, 1966.

Delehaye, H. *Mélanges d'hagiographie grecque et latine*. Subsidia Hagiographica, 42. Brussels, 1966.

Dignath-Düren, W. *Kirche, Krieg, Kriegsdienst*. Hamburg, 1955.

Dolbeau, F. "A propos du texte de la 'Passio Marcelli Centurionis.' " *AB*, 90 (1972), 329-335.

---

*Materials which Dr. Hornus did not use in this study, either because he was unaware of them, or because they have appeared since 1970. They have been collected by Alan Kreider, who has edited this volume.

Dubois, D. *Annuaire de l'Ecole pratique des hautes Etudes, 1971-1972*. Paris, 1972.

Eppstein, John. *The Catholic Tradition of the Law of Nations*. London, 1935.

Fears, J. R. *Princeps a Diis Electus:* The Divine Election of the Emperor as a Political Concept at Rome. Papers and Monographs of the American Academy in Rome, 26. Rome, 1977.

Ferguson, J. "The Nature of Early Christian Pacifism." *Hibbert Journal*, 55 (1957), 340-349.

_____. "The Pacifism of the Early Church." In his *The Politics of Love: The New Testament and Non-Violent Revolution*. Cambridge, 1974, pp. 55-67.

Fontaine, J. "Chrétiens et barbares: un aspect éclairant du débat entre Tertullien et la cité romaine." *Romano-barbarica*, 2 (Rome, 1977), 27-57.

_____. "Romanité et hispanité dans la littérature hispano-romaine des IV ^{e} et V ^{e} siècles." *Assimilation et résistance à la culture greco-romaine dans le Monde ancien*, VI ^{e} Congrès international d'Etudes Classiques, Madrid, September 1974. Paris, 1977, pp. 301-322.

Gábriš, K. "The Question of Militarism at the Time of the Apostolic Fathers." *Communio Viatorum*, 20 (1977), 227-232.

Gaudemet, J., ed. *Conciles Gaulois du IV ^{e} Siècle. SCH*, CCXLI. Paris, 1977.

Gero, Stephen. "Miles Gloriosus: The Christians and the Military Service." *Church History*, 39 (1970), 285-298.

Gollwitzer, H. "Krieg und Christentum." In K. Galling, ed., *Die Religion in Geschichte und Gegenwart*. 3rd ed. Tübingen, 1960, IV, 66-74.

Grant, R. M. *Early Christianity and Society*. San Francisco, 1977.

_____. "Sacrifices and Oaths as Required of Early Christians." In P. Granfield and J. Jungmann, eds., *Kyriakon: Festschrift Johannes Quasten*, 2 vols. Münster, 1970, pp. 12-17.

Helgeland, J. "Christians and Military Service, A.D. 173-337." Unpublished PhD thesis, Divinity School, University of Chicago, 1973.

_____. "Christians and the Roman Army, A.D. 173-337." *Church History*, 43 (1974), 149-163, 200.

Hoppenbrouwers, H. A. M. *Recherches sur la terminologie du martyre de Tertullien à Lactance.* Latinitas Christianorum Primaeva, 15. Nijmegen, 1961.

Hornus, J.-M. "Les Inscriptions funéraires militaires chrétiennes anciennes." *Archiv für Papyrusforschung,* 22/23 (1974), 223-228.

Isichei, E. *Political Thinking and Social Experience: Some Christian Interpretations of the Roman Empire from Tertullian to Salvian.* Christchurch, 1964.

Jones, A.H.M. *Constantine and the Conversion of Europe.* London, 1948.

Karpp, H. "Die Stellung der alten Kirche zu Kriegsdienst und Krieg." *Evangelische Theologie,* 17 (1957), 496-515.

Klein, R. *Tertullian und das römische Reich.* Heidelberg, 1968.

Kretschmar, G. "Der Weg zur Reichskirche." In *Verkündigung und Forschung, Theologischer Jahresbericht,* 13 (Munich, 1968), 3-44.

Lopuszanski, G. "La Police romaine et les Chrétiens." *L'Antiquité Classique,* 20 (1951), 5-46.

MacMullen, Ramsay. *Constantine.* London, 1970.

Messineo, A. "L'Objection de Conscience devant la Morale." *Civilta cattolica,* February 18, 1950. Also in *Documentation catholique,* 45 (1950), cols. 525-532.

Minn, H. R. "Tertullian and War: Voices from the Early Church." *Evangelical Quarterly,* 13 (1941), 202-213.

Molland, Einar. "De kristne og militaerjenesten i gen gamle kirke." *Norsk Teologisk Tidsskrift,* 60(1959), 87-104

Molnár, A. *A Challenge to Constantinianism: The Waldensian Theology in the Middle Ages.* Geneva, 1976.

Nock, A. D. "The Roman Army and Roman Religious Year." *HThR,* 45 (1952), 187-252.

O'Reilly, D. F. "The Theban Legion of St. Maurice." *VC,* 32 (1978), 195-207.

Pietri, C. *Roma Christiana: Recherches sur l'Eglise de Rome, son organisation, sa politique, son idéologie, de Miltiade à Sixte III (311-440).* 2 vols. Rome, 1976.

Pietri, L., ed. *Saint-Martin, textes de Sulpice Sévère. Lettre de Ligugé,* nos. 172-173 (July-October, 1975), Supplement.

Regibus, Luca de. "Milizia e Cristianesimo nell' Impero romano." *Didaskaleion,* n.s., 2 (1924), 41-69.

Schöpf, B. *Das Tötungsrecht bei den frühchristlichen Schriftstellern bis zur Zeit Konstantins.* Regensburg, 1958.

Siniscalco, P. *Massimiliano: un obiettore de coscienza del tardo impero.* Historica, Politica, Philosophica, 8. Turin, 1974.

Spanneut, M. "Geduld." *RACh*, IX (Stuttgart, 1976), cols. 243-294.

―――. "La non-violence chez les Pères africaines avant Constantin." In P. Granfield and J. Jungmann, eds., *Kyriakon: Festschrift Johannes Quasten*, 2 vols. Münster, 1970, I, pp. 36-39.

―――. *Tertullien et les premiers moralistes africains.* Paris, 1969.

Venditti, R. *I reati contro il servizio militare e contro la disciplina militare.* Milan, 1968.

Watson, G. R. "Christianity in the Roman Army in Britain." In M. W. Barley and R. P. C. Hanson, eds., *Christianity in Britain, 300-700.* Leicester, 1968, pp. 51-54.

Winowski, L. *Stosunek chrześcijaństwa pierwszych wieków do wojny.* Lublin, 1947.

Yoder, John H. *The Original Revolution: Essays on Christian Pacifism.* Scottdale, Pa., 1971.

Zampaglione, G. *The Idea of Peace in Antiquity.* Transl. R. Dunn. London and Notre Dame, Indiana, 1973.

The Christian Peace Shelf

The Christian Peace Shelf is a selection of Herald Press books and pamphlets devoted to the promotion of Christian peace principles and their applications. The editor (appointed by the Mennonite Central Committee Peace Section) and an editorial board from the Brethren in Christ Church, the General Conference Mennonite Church, the Mennonite Brethren Church, and the Mennonite Church, represent the historic concern for peace within these constituencies.

For Serious Study

Christ and Violence by Ronald J. Sider (1979). A sweeping reappraisal of the church's teaching on violence.

The Christian and Warfare by Jacob J. Enz (1972).The roots of pacifism in the Old Testament.

It Is Not Lawful for Me to Fight by Jean-Michael Hornus (1980). Early Christian attitudes toward war, violence, and the state.

Jesus and the Nonviolent Revolution by André Trocmé (1973). The social and political relevance of Jesus.

Mission and the Peace Witness edited by Robert L. Ramseyer (1979). Implications of the biblical peace testimony for the evangelizing mission of the church.

Nevertheless by John H. Yoder (1971). The varieties and shortcomings of Christian pacifism.

No King but Caesar? by William R. Durland (1975). A Catholic lawyer looks at Christian violence.

The Original Revolution by John H. Yoder (1972). Essays on Christian pacifism.

Preachers Present Arms by Ray H. Abrams (1969). The involvement of the church in three modern wars.

War and the Gospel by Jean Lasserre (1962). An analysis of Scriptures related to the ethical problem of war.

War, Peace, and Nonresistance by Guy F. Hershberger (Third Edition, 1969). A classic comprehensive work on nonresistance in faith and history.

What Belongs to Caesar? by Donald D. Kaufman (1969). Basic arguments against voluntary payment of war taxes.

Yahweh Is a Man of War by Millard C. Lind (1980). The theology of warfare in ancient Israel.

For Easy Reading

The Christian Way by John W. Miller (1969). A guide to the Christian life based on the Sermon on the Mount.

The Tax Dilemma: Praying for Peace, Paying for War, by Donald D. Kaufman (1978). Biblical, historical, and practical considerations on the war tax issue.

The Upside-Down Kingdom by Donald B. Kraybill (1978). A study of the synoptic gospels on affluence, war-making, status-seeking, and religious exclusivism.

The Way of Peace by J. C. Wenger (1977). A brief treatment on Christ's teachings and the way of peace through the centuries.

For Children

Coals of Fire by Elizabeth Hershberger Bauman (1954). Stories of people who returned good for evil.

Henry's Red Sea by Barbara Claassen Smucker (1955). The dramatic escape of 1,000 Russian Mennonites from Berlin following World War II.

Peace Treaty by Ruth Nulton Moore (1977). A historical novel involving the efforts of Moravian missionary Christian Frederick Post to bring peace to the Ohio Valley in 1758.

Jean-Michel Hornus was born in Montauban, Tarn-et-Garonne, France, on October 10, 1926. He has earned degrees in philosophy, Syriac, and theology from universities and theological colleges in Toulouse, Lyon, Paris, and Montpellier, and from Union Theological Seminary in New York.

In 1952 Hornus was ordained as a minister in the French Reformed Church. Since then he was held several pastorates, including one (from 1953 to 1958) in the French-speaking evangelical church in Beirut, Lebanon. The contacts which he established at that time led to his being recalled to that region in the late 1960s by the Association for Theological Education in the Middle East. Between 1967 and 1970 he served as its first Executive Secretary.

From 1957 to 1961 Hornus was a fellow of the Centre National de la Recherche Scientifique, Paris, which supported his researches into the history of early Christian thought. Subsequent academic assignments have included lecturing in philosophy at the Free Protestant "Collège Cévenol" at Le Chambon-sur-Lignon and serving as associate professor of church history and missiology at the Faculté réformée de théologie, Aix-en-Provence. For three years he was also university chaplain at the University of Strasbourg.

Hornus has been a member of the French Fellowship of

Reconciliation since its reorganization in 1945. From 1974 to 1976 he edited its periodical *Cahiers de la Réconciliation*. He was one of the founding members of the Parti Socialiste unifié (PSU), for which he was a candidate in the 1973 national elections.

In the autumn of 1979 Hornus began his present assignment as Lecturer in the Theology of Mission and Ecumenism at the Selly Oak Colleges, Birmingham, England, in succession to Bishop Lesslie Newbigin.